John Calvin

John Calvin

The Strasbourg Years

(1538–1541)

EDITED BY

Matthieu Arnold

TRANSLATED BY

Felicity McNab

WIPF & STOCK · Eugene, Oregon

JOHN CALVIN
The Strasbourg Years (1538–1541)

Copyright © 2016 Presses Universitaires de Strasbourg. All rights reserved. Except for brief quotations in critical publications or reviews, no part of this book may be reproduced in any manner without prior written permission from the publisher. Write: Permissions, Wipf and Stock Publishers, 199 W. 8th Ave., Suite 3, Eugene, OR 97401.

Wipf & Stock
An Imprint of Wipf and Stock Publishers
199 W. 8th Ave., Suite 3
Eugene, OR 97401

www.wipfandstock.com

PAPERBACK ISBN: 978-1-4982-3962-2
HARDCOVER ISBN: 978-1-4982-3964-6
EBOOK ISBN: 978-1-4982-3963-9

Manufactured in the U.S.A.

Contents

Foreword | vii
—*Matthieu Arnold*

Introduction | xi
—*Matthieu Arnold*

Abbreviations | xvii

1. **Strasbourg** | 1
   Strasbourg in Calvin's Time
   —*Marc Lienhard*

2. **Correspondence** | 23
   Calvin's Correspondence during His Stay in Strasbourg
   —*Christoph Burger*

3. **Calvin the Poet** | 39
   The Strasbourg Psalter of 1539
   —*Philippe François*

4. **Church Music** | 50
   Calvin and the Church Music in Strasbourg
   —*Robert Weeda*

5. **School of Jean Sturm** | 61
   Jean Calvin and the School of Jean Sturm
   —*Anton Schindling*

6. **Calvin's Commentary** | 75
   Calvin's Commentary on the Epistle to the Romans
   —*Christian Grappe*

7. **The Institutio** | 96
   Possible Influences of Martin Bucer on the *Institutio* of 1539
   —*Stephen Buckwalter*

8. **Warnings to the Reader** | 107
The "Warnings to the Reader" of the 1539 Institutio and the 1541 French Edition
—*James Hirstein*

9. **Patristics** | 130
The Patristic Sources in the 1543 Edition of the Institutio Christianae Religionis
John Calvin and the Enarrationes in Psalms of Augustine
—*Frederic Chapot*

10. **Images of Calvin** | 143
Books by the Reformer Printed or Read in Strasbourg
A Franco-German Story
—*Olivier Millet*

11. **Sadolet** | 158
Jacques Sadolet (1477 to 1547) the Enemy of the Strasbourg Years
—*Annie Noblesse-Rocher*

12. **Christ Our King** | 169
Calvin and the Religious Colloquia of 1539–1541
—*Volkmar Ortmann*

13. **Consensus and Disagreement** | 183
Consensus and Disagreement in the *Little Treatise on Holy Communion* (1541)
—*Marianne Carbonnier-Burkard*

14. **Conclusions** | 211
The Objectivization of History, between Linguistics and Socio-Psychology
—*Gilbert Vincent*

Index of the Works of Jean Calvin | 231

Biblical Index | 236

Annex: Table of Quotations from Enarrationes | 237

Index of Modern Authors | 241

Subject Index | 245

Foreword

Matthieu Arnold

ON 9 OCTOBER 2009, on the initiative of GRENEP (Research group on the non-conformist religious persons of the sixteenth and seventeenth centuries and the history of protestantisms), the Faculty of Protestant Theology of the University of Strasbourg organized, at the University Palace, an international symposium intended to commemorate the 500th anniversary of the birth of Jean Calvin. The organising committee consisted of Marc Lienhard, honorary head of the Faculty of Protestant Theology and founder of GRENEP, Christian Grappe, head of the Faculty, and Matthieu Arnold, director of GRENEP.

This symposium, "When Strasbourg Welcomed Calvin, 1538–1541," organized in association with an eponymous exhibition in the National and University Library of Strasbourg, took care to bring a historically, literarily, and theologically lasting contribution to the study of the Reformer. That is why, during the year 2009, which was rich in events celebrating Calvin's memory, this scientific event chose to give special attention to a restricted theme, which deserved to be studied in a new way: Calvin's stay in Strasbourg (1538–1541) and its influence on the development of the thought and action of the reformer. In fact, for more than a century, biographies of Calvin continue, for the years 1538–1541, to be based almost exclusively on the great work of Emile Doumergue.[1] However, the publication of sources

---

1. See Matthieu Arnold, *When Strasbourg Welcomed Calvin 1538–1541*, catalogue of the exhibition at the National and University Library of Strasbourg, 22 October–12 December 2009 (Strasbourg University Press, 2009), 216 pages (pp. 33–41 are credited to Christian Wolff and Raphael Laurand).

2. Emile Doumergue, *Jean Calvin: The Men and Things of His Time*, vol. 2, *The First Essays* (Lausanne, 1902), third book, "In Strasbourg" (291–524), and fourth book, "In Germany" (525–649); see Matthieu Arnold, "Calvin's Stay in Strasbourg (1538–1541): A Simple Gap or a Capital Stage in the Biography of the Reformer? Historiographical Enquiry," in Bernard Cottret and Olivier Millet (eds.), *Jean Calvin and France* (Paris/ Geneva: Droz, 2009), *Bulletin of the Society of the History of French Protestantism* 155

has progressed notably, even if a scientific edition responding to the present constraints continues to lack Calvin's correspondence from September 1538.[2] Similarly, for a hundred years, there has been no lack of studies on the Reformation in Strasbourg, on the thinking of Martin Bucer and the other Strasbourg Reformers, on the politico-religious symposia of the years 1540–1541 or more on the birth and rise of the Haute Ecole, were Calvin taught. The 500th anniversary of Calvin's birth was very suitable for Calvinian studies, taking advantage of these inputs, so that it is no longer held, in the life and work of Calvin, that the years 1538–1541 were a simple "gap" between his two stays in Geneva—the failure of the years 1536–1538 then the success of the Calvinian project, between 1541 and 1564.

This symposium has mainly gathered Strasbourg-based teacher-researchers, while opening up to some well-known specialists on Calvin's work[3] and/or on the Reformation in Strasbourg[4] coming from other French or foreign universities. In these two days, there were fourteen historians, theologians, literary and musical experts who contributed to deepen and enhance our knowledge of Calvin during the years 1538–1541.

The present volume consists of the fruit of this symposium,[5] which could not have taken place without the support of the University of Strasbourg, the Town and the Urban Community of Strasbourg, the General Council of the Lower Rhine and the Alsace Region. We hope these institutions will find the expression of our deep gratitude here.

We are happy to publish these studies in the collection "Writing and society" that we have established last year in the University Press of Strasbourg. These editions, managed with competence and devotion by President Lucien Braun, had welcomed, in 2009, the catalogue of the Calvin exhibition; it was natural that, at the time when they are celebrating their 90th

---

(2009) 321–33; we have extended this enquiry into biographies which appeared at the end of 2008 and in 2009 in the work "When Strasbourg welcomed Calvin...," (see n1).

2. See below, 37–52, the article by Christoph Burger.

3. We have appreciated for its true worth the participation in our colloquium of Christoph Burger and Olivier Millet, while both of them have lived a particularly busy "Calvin year."

4. That is how Stephen Buckwalter, Volkmar Ortmann and Anton Schindling have witnessed their faith in the works of GRENEP.

5. We are very grateful to Marianne Carbonnier-Burkard (Protestant Institute of Theology, Free Faculty of Protestant Theology in Paris) for having completed the work of the symposium through an in-depth study of The Little Treatise on Holy Communion, a text which is extremely important for the work of Calvin between 1538 and 1541. (Initially planned as part of the the symposium, the presentation of this document could not take place). We have translated from the German the contributions of Christopher Burger, Anton Schindling, Stephen Buckwalter and Volkmar Ortmann.

anniversary, they should bring one more stone[6] to the building that consists of the history of the Reformation.

Patricia Carbiener (Faculty of Protestant Theology at the University of Strasbourg) has handled the printing of this work, with the assistance of Ariane Eichhorn (University Press of Strasbourg). To both of them, we wish to express our deep gratitude.

Strasbourg, 9 July 2010.

---

6. See the work published on the occasion of the 500th anniversary of the birth of Jean Sturm (1507–1589): Jean Sturm, *On the Good Way to Open Schools of Letters*, ed. Georges Ladrigue and Matthieu Arnold (University Press of Strasbourg, 2007).

Introduction

Matthieu Arnold

"In freedom and resting from his Genevan vocation," John Calvin was not however inactive between 1538 and 1541, far from it. Once Martin Bucer succeeded in convincing him, threatening him with "the example of Jonas," that his place was in Strasbourg, Calvin expended a great deal of energy in the city of the Rhine. The pastor of the small community of French-speaking refugees, he was also a teacher in the Haute Ecole; it is also from this teaching that he obtained his income, at a very modest rate, it is true to say. More than in Geneva, he had the leisure to dedicate himself to his literary work, notable particularly for writings of controversy and agreement. Finally, throughout long months, he took part in politico-religious negotiations with those in favor of the traditional faith. The symposium "When Strasbourg Welcomed Calvin" attempted to embrace these various fields of activity, without however aiming at an exhaustive presentation.

The author of various syntheses on Strasbourg at the time of the Reformation, editor of texts by Martin Bucer and Strasbourgian dissidents,[7] Marc Lienhard was particularly well placed to give an outline of the political, social, cultural and religious context of the free town of the empire on the eve of the year 1540, and to present the main Strasbourgian players. While emphasising the powers of Strasbourg, rooted in Protestantism more deeply than Geneva which had just sent Calvin away, Marc Lienhard does not hide the tensions between the magistrate and the pastors, particularly on putting discipline into effect; dealing with the supervision of the faithful (through worship, catechism, adoption of a confession of faith . . .), he recalls how much the pastors complained of the disaffection of the faithful in relation to new doctrines and practices.

---

7. Without exception, we do not give, in this introduction, the precise references of the publications to which we allude: the reader will refer to the different contributions, in which they are expressly quoted.

Christopher Burger has edited Calvin's correspondence up to September 1538, before budgetary constraints forced him to interrupt—we hope, momentarily—this reference edition. That is why in basing ourselves on the more ancient sources published by Aime-Louis Herminjard that he is interested, in the letters from 1538–1541, in the way in which Calvin adapted to Strasbourg and from which he has brought to life the religious symposia, as well as the laudatory judgments, over some months, Calvin's views remained turned toward Geneva, however much the wound which had been inflicted on him had remained alive, and how much the separation of the impetuous Farel and the proximity of Martin Bucer, who was more level-headed, had a more positive influence on his development.

Two contributions deal with the poetical and liturgical work of Calvin, together with his role as a pastor of the French-speaking community.

As an expert on French Protestant poetry, of which he edited an anthology, Philippe François applies himself to the circumstances of drawing up the first Huguenot psalter, *Aulcuns pseaulmes et cantiques mys en chant*, that Calvin brought out in 1539, for the requirements of his community of French refugees; he deals also the Calvin's relationship with poetry. For Philippe Francois, the presence, from this first collection, of poems by Clement Marot is explained by the meeting between the two men in Ferrara, in 1536. If Calvin were a "poet by complement," constrained to reply by his versified psalms by a "liturgical urgency," the comparisons laid down by Philippe Francois show that his compositions of 1539 are not all inferior to those of Marot, which progressively replaced them.

As a musicologist, the author of several works on "Calvin's psalter," and on the "Church of the French people" in Strasbourg, it is from the angle of melodies that Robert Weeda studied the collection of 1539. He examined the influences that the German canticles of Strasbourg (the compositions of Wolfgang Dachstein and Matthieu Greiter) exerted on him, then the—rare—testimonies of the practice of singing in the French-speaking community of Strasbourg, and finally the development of the reformed psalter until its full version in 1562.

There are two studies dealing to Calvin, as a teacher at the Haute Ecole.

The rare data dealing with Calvin's teaching at the Haute Ecole, which Jean Sturm had just founded in 1538, are well known. Anton Schindling had already worked on them in his 1977 work on the Gymnasium from 1538 to 1621. Rather than squeezing these sources, which no new document has completed since then, Anton Schindling presents the original institution of the illustrious gymnasium, marked as much by humanism as by the Reformation, and at the heart of which Calvin gave his lectures. Rather than compare the programmes at the Haute Ecole and those of the Academy of

INTRODUCTION

Geneva, founded in 1559, Anton Schindling shows, in a broader way, the "at least indirect" contribution of the academic teaching of Strasbourg to Calvinism and to the educative reformed tradition, in Europe and in North America.

As exegete of the New Testament, Christian Grappe studies Calvin's commentary on the Epistle to the Romans (1540), the fruit of the lectures that he gave in the Haute Ecole; for him, Calvin's originality—in which the Reformer is aware, as witnessed in the preface in which he positions his work in relation to the commentaries of Melanchthon and Bucer—manifests itself in his quest for the instance of the author (mens or consilium scriptoris), and especially in the importance that he gives to the "rhetoric gesture" of Paul, Calvin made his readers pay attention to the apostle's intentions, to the arguments that he used and to the figures that he placed at the service of his demonstration. This study confirms, for the commentary on the Romans, Olivier Millet's[8] conclusions in relation to most of the Calvinian corpus.

The editor of Martin Bucer's German works, Stephen Buckwalter examines the influence that Martin Bucer has probably had on the second edition of the Institutio (1539). This influence, which our author refrains from restricting to the years 1538–1541, does not mainly manifest itself in borrowing turns of phrase and words, but in accents and in theological motifs. That is how Stephen Buckwalter associates with Bucer and the Strasbourgian stay the growth of passages relating to the Anabaptists, the deepening of the doctrine of Holy Communion, and—what is even newer—Calvin's opening to aesthetics—with the celebration of the joys of life and the beauty of creation, in chapter 17 of the Institutio, "De vita hominis christiani."

The editor of the correspondence of Beatus Rhenanus, James Hirstein is familiar with humanist literary usages, which enables him to compare, in a nuanced way, the "advice to the reader" in the Institutio of 1539 and its French version of 1541. While one generally underlines the differences between the two types of readers, James Hirstein emphasises the similarities beween the two advises; he establishes that, even in the Latin advice, the studying public (the "sacrae Theologiae candidati") is in the minority: they are pious readers, which characterises their enthusiasm more than their degree of erudition, which Calvin mentions most and toward whom his thoughts are turning.

Knowing the Fathers, and especially Augustine's works, Frederic Chapot noticed the importance of references to the Enarrationes in Psalmos

---

8. Olivier Millet, *Calvin and the Dynamics of the Word: Study of Reformed Rhetoric* (Paris: Champion, 1992).

(twenty-six occurrences) in the 1543 edition of the *Institutio christianae religionis*, which makes important alterations in relation to the 1539 edition. These quotations, which Frederic Chapot refuses, for lack of a convincing argument, to attribute to Bucer's influence, show clearly the manner in which Calvin refers to the Fathers: he faithfully quotes Augustine—sometimes basing himself on a compendium or on a personal repertory—while making the *Enarrationes* a very personal read, together with, especially, his preoccupations in relation to church singing.

At the beginning of the Calvin year, Olivier Millet published the *Institution of the Christian Religion (1541)* in an edition which, at present, marks an epoch. From copies of the *Institution* which were consulted in Strasbourgian libraries, and including readers' notes, it presents some stages in the reception of Calvin's great work, from the sixteenth century up to the end of the nineteenth century. Examination of a copy which had belonged to Edouard Cunitz, one of the Strasbourgian editors of the *Calvini Opera* in the series of the *Corpus Reformatorum*, enables him to give an outline of the critical edition of the *Institution de la religion chrétienne*.

The last section of this volume is dedicated to the part played by Calvin in the concord and the religious controversies, with the evangelicals as the supporters of the traditional faith.

For several years, Annie Noblesse-Rocher has been interested in Jacques Sadolet, Calvin's "adversary" during his stay in Strasbourg. When the critic considers Calvin's *Reply* rather from the Genevan context, Annie Noblesse-Rocher throws light on the Strasbourgian environment which surrounded the Reform at the time that he wrote this *Reply*; she suggests, in fact, a synoptic reading of the exchanges not only between Calvin and Sadolet, but also between Jean Sturm and the Cardinal, which had caused the publication, in 1537, of *Concilium de emendanda ecclesia*. She does not forget either to present the theology—ambivalent—of the Roman prelate, as she opens out from 1535 in his *In Pauli epistolam ad Romanos commentariorum libri tres*.

Volkmar Ortmann studied Martin Bucer's participation in the politico-religious symposia of 1539–1541, before taking part in the edition of the proceedings of these symposia. Therefore he can study afresh Calvin's role at the time of the meeting in Frankfurt then of the religious symposia of Haguenau, Worms and Ratisbon. Throughout his three years in Strasbourg, Calvin gave no less than ten months to these meetings! He is shown there as a zealous advocate of the cause of the "evangelicals" who were persecuted in France, and is shown as an attentive observer and critic of the religious debates; in the same way as Luther, he considered the attempts at compromise with skepticism, placing his hopes in divine intervention. In addition,

INTRODUCTION

Volkmar Ortman confirms the importance that these meetings had for Calvin himself: he acquired a good reputation as a theologian, and enjoyed the consideration and growing friendship of Melanchthon.

The *Little Treatize on Holy Communion* (1541), published in Geneva after Calvin had left Strasbourg, is not always placed in relation to his stay in the free town of the empire. Most biographies of the Reformer present it succinctly, while they do not simply leave it out. However, in an very careful study in the context of the writing of this essay, Marianne Carbonnier-Burkard states that, beyond the French "evangelicals" and the Genevans, the *Petit Traité* was addressed also to the French-speaking refugees in Strasbourg: this pastorally-aimed opuscule, intended to pacify "infirm consciences," begins by laying down the foundations (finality, usefulness and practice of Holy Communion); it then fixes the basic "difference" with the "papists"; continuing Bucer's efforts, at last he seeks, more briefly, to resolve the "bone of contention" between the Reformers, proposing the terms of an agreement which could include the Swiss, who had not subscribed to the *Concorde of Wittenberg* (1536). This last outlook had not at all met an echo and brings nothing to the quality of the *Little Treatize*; by comparisons with the writings of Farel, Marcourt or Roussel on Holy Communion, Marianne Carbonnier-Burkard established the superiority of Calvin's essay, which is at the same time accessible, clear and well-reasoned.

Gilbert Vincent's conclusions, from whom one knows the master work on Calvin's hermeneutic, *Ethical Exigence and Interpretation in Calvin's work* (1984) take some distance in relation to the works of this symposium: he questions himself on the procedures used by the historians, and shows how much new approaches (with attention to the linguistic or pragmatic conditions of Calvin's statements . . .) have produced research on the Reformation, by deconstructing the traditional images which "celebrated his merits"; he takes up the question, raised several times during the symposium, of Calvin's originality and his "borrowings," by showing how much, in order to remain intelligible, innovation is impossible independently of all tradition; finally, he places the contributions of the present symposium in relation to those of a previous commemoration, the 400th anniversary of Calvin's death (1964), by connecting—the interrogatory method—Calvin's theological positions to his pastoral engagements and his identity as an exile in Strasbourg.

On many points, the fourteen contributions of this volume complement, refine and even renew, by correcting received opinions, our knowledge of Jean Calvin, throughout the three years that he spent in Strasbourg (September 1538–1541). While awaiting the continuation of the scientific edition of the Reformer's correspondence, and in the hope—illusory?—that new sources on his preaching in Strasbourg may appear, we hope that this collective work can contribute to stimulate Calvinian historiography, in the tradition of the Jubilee of 2009.

Abbreviations

BC: Peter Rodolphe, Gilmont Jean-François, Bibliotheca Calviniana. Les oeuvres de Calvin publiées au XVIe siècle. I. Ecrits Theologiques, littéraires et juridiques 1532–1554, Geneva, 1991 (Travaux d'Humanisme et Renaissance 255); Ecrits théologiques, littéraires et juridiques 1555–1564, Geneva, 1994 (Travaux d'Humanisme et Renaissance 281); III. [with the collaboration of Christian Krieger] Ecrits théologiques, littéraires et juridiques 1565–1600, Geneva, 2000 (Travaux d'Humanisme et Renaissance 339).

Calvin, *Institution*, Millet: Calvin, Jean. *Institution de la religion chrétienne*. 1541. Critical ed. Edited by Olivier Millet. 2 vols. Geneva, 2008.

Calvin, *Works*: Calvin, Jean. *Works*. Edition devised by Francis Higman and Bernard Roussel. Pleiade library 552. Paris, 2009.

CO: Calvin, Jean. *Opera quae supersunt omnia*. Edited by Guillaume Baum et al. 59 vols. Brunswick (then Berlin), Schwetschke, 1863–1900 (*Corpus Reformatorum* [= CR]).

Herminjard: Herminjard Aime-Louis (ed.), Correspondance des Réformateurs dans les pays de langue française. 9 vols. Geneva: Georg, 1866–1897.

OS: Joannis Calvini Opera selecta, ed. Barth, and W. Niesel. 4 vols. Munich, Kaiser, 1926–1962.

1. Strasbourg

Strasbourg in Calvin's Time

Marc Lienhard[1]

VARIOUS EDITIONS OF THE published sources during the last decades, such as the Anabaptist *Deeds*[2] or even the *Works*[3] and the *Correspondence*[4] of Bucer, but also several synthetic works on worship[5] printing[6] or political staff[7] on Bucer[8] or daily life in Strasbourg[9] have made it possible to refine our knowledge on all these aspects of the town toward 1540.

1. Grenep: Faculty of Protestant Theology in the University of Strasbourg.

2. See Matthieu Arnold, *Quand Strasbourg accueillait Calvin 1538-1541*, catalogue of the exhibition in the National and University Library of Strasbourg, 22 October–12 December 2009 (Strasbourg University Press, 2009), 216 pages (pp. 33–41 are due to Christian Wolff and Raphael Laurand).

3. *Martini Buceri Opera Omnia*, series 1, *Deutsche Schriften*, Robert Stupperich et al. (eds.) (Gutesloher Verlagshaus, 1960s), 18 vols. (abridged: *BDS*).

4. Martin Bucer, *Correspondance*, ed. Jean Rott, Reinhold Stupperich et al., Christian Krieger et al., 7 vols. brought out (Leiden: Brill, 1979–2008); see also Jacques Vincent Pollet, *Martin Bucer, Etudes sur la Correspondance*, 2 vols. (Paris: P.U.F., 1958 and 1962).

5. Rene Bornert, *La Réforme Protestante du Culte à Strasbourg au XVIe siècle (1523-1598)* (Leiden: Brill, 1981).

6. Miriam Usher Chrisman, *Bibliography of Strasbourg Imprints 1480–1599* (New Haven and London, 1982); idem., *Lay Culture, Learned Culture: Books and Social Change in Strasbourg 1480–1599* (New Haven and London, 1982).

7. Thomas A. Brady Jr., *Ruling Class, Regime and Reformation at Strasbourg* (Leiden: Brill, 1978); idem., *Protestant Politics: Jacob Sturm (1489-1553) and the German Reformation* (New Jersey: Humanities, 1995); Lorna Jane Abray, *The People Reformation, Magistrates, Clergy and Commons in Strasbourg, 1500–1598* (Ithaca: Cornell University Press, 1985).

8. Martin Greschat, *Martin Bucer (1491-1551) Un Rèformateur et son temps*, trans. Matthieu Arnold (Paris: P.U.F., 2002; 1st German ed., 1990). See also Christian Krieger and Marc Lienhard (eds.), *Martin Bucer and Sixteenth Century Europe*, 2 vols. (Leiden: Brill, 1993).

9. Roland Oberle, *La vie quotidienne en Alsace au temps de la Renaissance* (Strasbourg: Oberlin, 1983).

Society and Culture

It is thought that Strasbourg at that time had between 20,000 and 25,000 inhabitants[10] to which one must add those of the twenty-five villages which depended on the town; it is impossible to give a more precise figure, seeing the fluctuations caused by the arrival of refugees, who stayed more or less permanently, or to loss of life such as that caused by the plague of 1541, a year when 3,208 people died as against 800 or 900 in a normal year. Strasbourg was a large city of the Empire. By comparison, Wittenberg, this "hole in the world," as Luther said, had 3,000. Geneva, which Calvin had just left, had 9,000 inhabitants, a number which later rose to 16,000.

The inhabitants of Strasbourg were divided into three categories:[11] the so-called middle class, the *Schultheissenburger* (admitted by the listener, a bishop's official) and the other inhabitants. The first ones, either rich or poor, nobility or commoners, had the right to vote in corporations and could fulfill civil offices within the town. They were middle class by birth, by marriage or, as in Calvin's case, by purchase, which also meant integration into one of the twenty corporations (for Calvin, the tailors' one). Woman could avail of the same law, but they were excluded from public life.

As regards the second category, the *Schultheissenburger*, they were in a modest position, admitted, under the control of an Episcopal administrator, to live and work in the town, on payment of a small fee, on condition of taking the oath of obedience to the established authorities and not to be at the expense of the town. They had no civic right in itself.

Finally, the last category included, for a temporary residence in the town, as many rich representatives of the nobility as deprived refugees, or even domestic servants who came from the surrounding countryside. To these one must add the monks, contemplatives or even canons who had survived and resisted the Protestant Reformation and whom the magistrate of the town tolerated, even protected, without however granting them civic rights.

Let us take a look at the refugees.[12] A great many of them poured in during the first half of the sixteenth century. The religious reasons for this

---

10. Philippe Dollinger, "*La population de Strasbourg et sa répartition aux XVe et XVI siècles*," in Werner Busch, Klaus Fein et al. (eds.), *Die Stadt in der europaischen Geschichte*, Festschrift Edith Ennen (Bonn: Ludwig Rohrscheid, 1972), 521–38.

11. Joseph Fuchs, "*Droit de bourgeoisie a Strasbourg*," *Revue d'Alsace* 101 (1962) 19–50.

12. On this matter see the studies of Rodolphe Peter, Leon F. Halkin, Roger Zuber and Christian Wolff, in Georges Livet and Francis Rapp (eds.), *Strasbourg au Coeur religieux du XVIe siècle* (Strasbourg: Istra, 1977), 269–330.

refuge have often been favored, and also the welcome granted to the refugees by the authorities of the city and their housing by individuals such as Catherine Zell, Capiton and Bucer. Some of the nobility, such as Hartmut von Kronberg, reached Strasbourg after the failure of the knights' uprising. From the years 1524–1525 evangelical refugees from the Kingdom of France arrived, especially members of the Group of Meaux, of whom the best known, such as Lefèvre d'Etaples, went back later. Between 1525 and 1533 dissidents from all spheres of influence arrived: there were Anabaptists, illuminist disciples of Melchior Hofman or even spiritualists. A maximum of 2,000 dissidents seems to have been reached in 1530, a figure which is doubtless exaggerated as it relied on simple hearsay.[13] During the 1530s a great many more refugees from the Kingdom of France arrived, such as Nicolas Cop, just coming through, or for a longer stay for some of the nobility. The Netherlands also provided their share, one of which was Calvin's wife, Idelette de Bure.

Beside the religious reasons for immigration, socio-economic factors played a role: after the Peasants' War, one or other middle-class person, who was compromised in the rising, settled in Strasbourg; that is the case of Wolfgang Schutterlin, who set up his wood business there. Between 1528 and 1534, several famines due to bad harvests push a great many country people to settle in Strasbourg, a town which was prepared for periods of food shortage.

As to the French-speaking parish created in 1538, of which several of the faithful were also of German-speaking origin, it had about four hundred members, that is thirty-five family heads of which two hundred were middle-class people of the town.

The introduction of the Protestant Reformation had not changed the civil institutions of the town which were settled by the Constitution of 1482.[14] Let us content ourselves to recall them briefly. The middle-class people of the town were gathered into twenty corporations to which the *constofler* were added, of which the town's nobility were a part, country nobility and members of rich business families. For a year the town was governed by an *Ammeister* who came from the corporations and by a noble

---

13. *TAE* I, no. 224, 277, 5–6 (see n1); see also Jean Rott, "L'Eglise des réfugiés de langue française a Strasbourg au XVIe siècle: aperçu de son histoire, en particulier de ses crises à partir de 1541," *BSHPF* 122 (1976) 525–50, reed. in Jean Rott, *Investigations Historicae: Eglises et Société au XVIe siècle* (Strasbourg: Oberlin, 1986), 2:17–42.

14. On this matter see Ulrich Cramer, *Die Verfassung und Verwalztung Strasburgs von der Reformationszeit cum Fall des Reichsstadt* (Frankfurt, 1931); see also the studies of Philippe Dollinger and Thomas A. Brady Jr., in *Strasbourg au Coeur religieux du XVIe siècle* (see n11).

Stettmeister who changed every three months, and whose role was especially representative. The collective instance was the Senate, made up of ten noble members and of representatives of the twenty corporations. Elected for two years, half-renewed every year, the Senate sat most often with the XV and the XIII, two commissions whose members were co-opted for life. In charge of the internal politics for the XV and the external politics for the XIII, these two commissions operated most of the power. In exceptional circumstances, as when it was a question of abolishing the mass in 1529 or not, or to introduce the Interim in 1549, all of the magistrates were consulted.

In fact, it was an oligarchy which governed the town. In fact it had at the same time, the time and means in order to manage its affairs, full time for some people like Jacques Sturm. For the most part, it was people of independent means and the richest business people who managed the power. According to Thomas Brady, only 13.30 percent of the craftsmen were members.[15]

The power in place had without too much difficulty crossed to the Reformation. Certainly, connected with the religious orders, also affected by phenomena of iconoclasm, a part of the aristocracy had tried to resist. But, in front of the thrust from the base, that is to say craftsmen and the average middle class, power had yielded to the movement. Some people wanted to keep the peace in society, others acted by conviction. Some people had moreover gained from the secularization of church property in order to increase their capital. The change had brought an increase in power to the governors, as it was from henceforth the civil authorities who appointed pastors, who had become middle class people of the town, and the three elders who, in each parish, supervised the pastors. The authorities controlled matrimonial matters through the Matrimonial Court created in 1529, settled the doctrinal line and managed doctrinal or personal conflicts as well as disagreements created by the emergence of dissident movements.

If, toward 1540, the great majority of the ruling classes had taken on Protestantism, their zeal for the new order was unequally spread, and also their competence to judge religious matters. Thomas Brady[16] thinks he can distinguish between zealous people such as Claus Kniebs, followed by men such as Martin Herlin and Mathis Pfarrer, and politicians like Jacques Sturm. However, this distinction had to be qualified, for Sturm had certainly evangelical convictions, by having an official doctrine adopted in Strasbourg, he was according to Brady's own terms, "the architect of the

---

15. Brady, *Ruling Class* (see n6), 51.
16. Ibid.

fall of the Anabaptists."[17] The competence of the town's councilors to judge religious affairs had its limits: few of them had attended a university, and only Jacques Sturm had studied theology; three other councilors who were always in charge in 1540, Pierre Sturm, Claus Kriebs and Karl Mieg the Young, had had a legal training. When it was a question in 1534 of adopting doctrinal standards for the town, there was wavering among most of the councilors, as sources can show.[18]

Thanks to the works of Jacques Hart,[19] Thomas Brady,[20] and Lorna Jane Abray,[21] we know who sat in the councils and in the commissions, who held the roles of *Ammeister* or *Stettmeister*, and who were the men who were particularly involved in religious matters. There remained as supporters of the evangelical movement of the years 1523-1524, men such as Hans Bock, Batt von Duntzenheim, Martin Herlin, Claus Kriebs, Jacob Meyer, Daniel Mieg, Mathis Pfarrer, Egenolph Roder von Dierspurg and Jacques Sturm, dominant figures of the town's government up to the middle of the fifteenth century and even beyond. They were joined around the thirties and forties by men such as Ulmann Boecklin, Jorg Christman, Jacob von Duntzenheim, Mathis Geiger or Stephan Sturm, all operating in the Senate or in one of the commissions in 1540. Even others must be mentioned, who rallied to Protestantism later, such as Martin Betscholt. Some, such as Conrad Johann von Mundolsheim or Wolf Sigismund von Wurmser remained close to Catholicism. It seems it was also the case, of Jacob Werzel von Marsilien who was opposed to Bucer and to the Concord of Wittenberg. Particularly in the organs of power there emerges Jacques Sturm,[22] who almost single-handedly took on the diplomatic service from 1529 until his death in 1553. Ninety times he represented the town in various meetings of the Empire. He was also one of the three scholars who were responsible for managing the schools. His weight was considerable for the whole history of Strasbourg in the sixteenth century.

17. Thomas A. Brady Jr., "Architect of Persecution: Jacob Sturm and the Fall of the Sects at Strasbourg," *ARG 79* (1988) 262-81.

18. *TAE* II, 294, no. 323.

19. Jacques Hatt, *Liste des membres du grand Sénat de Strasbourg, des stettmeister, des ammeistres, des Conseils des XXI, XIII et des XV du ZIIIe siècle à Strasbourg* (Strasbourg: Mairie, 1963).

20. Brady (see n6).

21. See n6.

22. On this subject see the works of Thomas Brady quoted in n6, and Marc Lienhard, "Jakob Sturm," in Martin Greschat (ed.), *Gestalten der Kirchengeschichte*, vol. 5, *Die Reformationszeit* II (Stuttgart: Kohlhammer-Verlag, 1981), 289-306, picked up in Marc Lienhard, *Un temps, une ville, une Réforme* (Aldershot: Variorum, 1990).

At the time Strasbourg was a free town of the Empire. It could freely welcome whoever it wanted (privilege of the *freezer Zug*, in other words the freedom of access to the town), it was excused from the oath of allegiance to the emperor, and held completely to give its support for certain wars. It took part in diets, the meetings of the states of the Empire. It benefitted from the privilege of *non appellando*, that is to say from the right that any lawsuit where a middle-class person from Strasbourg was implicit would be judged by local judges. But the town's situation was fragile. Its territorial foundation—twenty-five villages—was weak, and its merchants were tributaries of the peace between Protestants and Catholics. And already, toward the middle of the sixteenth century, French armies appeared in Alsace. Up to 1529–1530, the external politics of the town were directed particularly toward the Swiss towns, which was cemented by adhesion on 9 January 1530, to the *Christliches Burgrecht*, a treaty of alliance with Basel, Bern and Zurich. But in front of the emperor and his vague attempts to submit the Protestant towns and territories, that was no longer enough. That is why, under the impulse of Jacques Sturm particularly, the town turned toward the territorial powers of Germany and in 1532 subscribed to the League of Smalkalde, while also accepting the Confession of Augsburg.[23] In 1532 the League obtained the Truce of Nuremberg, which, while awaiting a council, allowed Protestants the right to keep religious acquisitions. At the end of the thirties, relations with Charles the Fifth again opened up. The League of Smalkalde then signed a treaty of alliance with Denmark, and made contact again with France and England. During Calvin's time in Strasbourg, the Truce of Frankfurt was granted (1539), which took up the Truce of Nuremberg by applying to all the subscribers of the Confession of Augsburg, by putting an end to all the lawsuits of the Imperial Chamber and by proposing a colloquium in order to overcome the confessional disagreement. Let us remember also that during Calvin's time in Strasbourg, precisely between 1538 and 1533, a truce had been established between the King of France and Charles the Fifth.

In the cultural and pedagogic field, one must remember the creation in 1538 of the Haute Ecole.[24] It gathered together secondary teaching and

---

23. Hans Virck et al., *Politische Correspondenz der Stadt Strassburg im Zeitalter der Reformation*, vol. 1 (Strasbourg: Trubner, 1887), no. 135.

24. The base work of Anton Schindling, *Humanistische Hochschule und freie Reichsstadt, Gymnasium und Akademie in Strasburg 1538–1621* (Wiesbaden: Franz Steiner, 1977), version abridged in French in Pierre Schang and Georges Livet (ed.), *Histoire du Gymnase Jean Sturm, Berceau de l'Université de Strasbourg 1538–1988* (Strasbourg: Oberlin, 1988), 19–158; see also his contribution in the present volume, 79–92. On Jean Sturm see:

superior teaching which were provided until then. Lectures in theology, classical philology, mathematics, geology and rhetoric, as well as introductory lectures in law were provided for several years (from 1524 for theology), and two colleges or seminaries had been founded in 1534 and in 1535. Two, then three Latin schools existed. In January 1538, by agreement with Martin Bucer and the two school inspectors Gaspard Hedion and Jacques Bedrot, the scholars suggested creating a central school for the whole town in the old convent of the Dominicans. Jean Sturm, who had come to Strasbourg a year earlier, was going to provide the program and the pedagogic structure of the new school, the aim of studies being "piety, based on knowledge and on eloquence." Our plan is not to describe here at length the birth and rise of this Haute Ecole, nor Jean Sturm's personality, dealt with at the time of the colloquium held in Strasbourg in 2007 and by Anton Schindling in the present work. Sturm was a member and he remained in correspondence with Calvin after the latter left.

As regards public lectures, the first stage of university teaching, Calvin brought together men such as the Frenchman Claude Feray and Jacques Bedrot, who both taught Greek, Jean Sturm, Professor of Greek and Latin literature, Michel Delius, Professor of Hebrew, Christian Herlin, who gave lectures in mathematics, and Wendelin Bittelbronn, offered an elementary course in law. For theology, Bucer and Capiton commented on the Old Testament, Hedion and Calvin on the New. The latter was going to comment on the Gospel of John, then the Epistle to the Romans and other Pauline epistles. Outside these lectures, Bucer organized, as an exercise, some types of discussions on themes taken from his lectures. We do not know what Calvin did in this field, even if, according to Jean Sturm, he attended these discussions, even presided over them.[25]

We do not know either if he had attended, within the framework of the opening of the Haute Ecole, at the production of Sapidus's dramatic piece, *Lazarus redivivis* (1538), the first in a series of twenty-eight productions given at the Haute Ecole up to 1621,[26] with the uncertainties of biblical

---

1. Charles Schmidt, *La vie et les travaux de Jean Sturm, premier recteur du Gymnase et de l'Académie de Strasbourg* (Paris and Leipzig, 1855; repr. Nieukoop, De Graff).

2. Matthieu Arnold and Julien Collonges (eds.), *Jean Sturm: quand l'humanisme fait école* (Strasbourg: Bibliotheque Nationale et Universitaire, 2007).

3. Matthieu Arnold (ed.), *Johannes Sturm (1507–1589): Rhetor, Padagoge und Diplomat* (Tubingen: Mohr-Siebeck, 2009).

25. Jean Sturm, *Quarti antipappi*, 20, 21, quoted in Emile Doumergue, *Jean Calvin*, vol. 2, *Les premiers essais*, 434, n8.

26. August Jundt, *Die dramatischen Aufführungen im Gymnasium zu Strassburg.*

pieces that Calvin will find also in Geneva. Let us remember again that for the period from 1538 to 1531, six biblical plays in German will come out of the Strasbourg presses.[27]

The creation of the Haute Ecole and the activity of the teachers, partly top-level men who had come from outside, were going to restart publications and the activity of the Strasbourg printers. Humanist production had known a strong drop between 1534 and 1536. About ten books from this movement appeared in 1540. The number of Protestant works, dropped in relation to the twenties, also went up again also and again went above the number of ten. But it is particularly the production of scientific works which almost reaches its peak from 1530, that is to say an annual production of twenty to thirty works.

As regards theology, some major works by Bucer appeared between 1535 and 1538, especially his *Commentaire sur l'Epître aux Romains* and his *Traité sur la cure d'âme*. For his part, Capiton in 1537 brought out a treatize on the Church and its reforms (*Responsio de missa*) and, in 1539, his *Hexemeron Dei Opus*, which deals especially with the pope story of creation.

In the field of letters, Jean Sturm published the *De Literarum ludis*, the written program of 1538[28] and, in the same year, his book *De Amissa dicendi ratione*, then a set of sources, among which were lectures and philosophical treatises of Cicero. Ninety-five scholarly texts and classical editions were published by the teachers of the Haute Ecole between 1538 and 1550. After 1529, a great many scientific editions on botany and medicine had seen the light, including the *Kreuterbuch* of Jerome Bock (1539) which ran to about ten editions throughout the century.

Thus, Calvin arrived in a town with multiple centers of interest, religious on the one hand, but also cultural, a town which, thanks to its printers, to its Haute Ecole, to its teachers, thanks also to its authors, had a certain influence in sixteenth-century Europe.

We now need, for a second time to consider the religious and ecclesiastical in Strasbourg toward 1540.

Ein Beitrag zur Geschichte des Schuldramas im XVI. U. XVII, Jahrhundert," in *Programm auf das Schuljar 1881–1882* (Prot. Gymnasium zu Strassburg, Heitz, 1581).

27. Mirim Usher Chrisman, *Bibliography of Strasbourg imprints 1480–1599* (see n5) 197.

28. Jean Sturm, *De la bonne manière d'ouvrir des écoles de Lettres*, ed. Georges Lagarrigue and Matthieu Arnold (Strasbourg: Presses Universitaires de Strasbourg, 2007).

Religion and the Church

Before turning toward the Christian churches, especially toward the evangelical church established in Strasbourg, one must remember the existence of Jews in sixteenth-century Alsace. After the massacre of 1349 in Strasbourg, the survivors had been expelled from the town in 1388, and were restricted to living in the surrounding villages. It was still the case in the sixteenth century.[29] During the day, the merchants and doctors could carry on their profession in the town, on payment of a fee. When evening came, the playing of a horn forced them to go outside the gates. Among them there appears the great figure of Yossel von Rosheim. According to his own testimony, he attended Capiton's lectures, attracted by the great erudition, however withdrawing when Capiton dealt with questions of faith.

Different from other towns like Obernai and Colmar, the magistrate of Strasbourg was relatively tolerant in relation to the Jews in the sixteenth century. He had welcomed and protected a certain number of them during the Peasants' War. But, in 1530, he had forbidden middle-class people in Strasbourg to borrow money from the Jews. A problem lay on the relations between the magistrate and the Jews; it was the practice of some Jews to quote the middle-class people of the town before a foreign court, which contravened the privilege of *non appellando*, the right of the town to judge its nationals itself.[30] Yossel had issued a decree forbidding this practice for all Jews wishing to obtain a safe-conduct from the town of Strasbourg. They had to attend the local courts which were competent in the matter. But, even in 1536, the council of Strasbourg complains about this with Rosheim's town. In 1537, he sent a letter to the prince elector of Saxony in order to have a safe-conduct granted to Yossel and in order to ask the prince to listen to him kindly.

The correspondence with the Landgrave of Hesse shows that Jacques Sturm was opposed to the plan, which appeared in Hesse, to expel the Jews. Even in 1543, the magistrate refused the publication in Strasbourg of Luther's treatize *Des juifs et de leurs mensonges*.

As regards the Strasbourgian Reformers, two attitudes had appeared. On the one hand there was that of Capiton, which was exceptional in its

---

29. On this matter see Georges Weill, "L'Alsace," in Bernard Rosenberg (ed.), *Histoire des Juifs de France* (Toulouse, 1972); Freddy Raphael and Robert Weyl, *Les Juifs en Alsace* (Toulouse, 1977); similarly: "Les Juifs d'Alsace 7," in *Encyclopedie d'Alsace 7* (1984) 4358–85.

30. See Selma Stern, *L'Avocat des Juifs: Les tribulations de Yossel de Rosheim dans l'Europe de Charles Quint*, Strasbourg, *La nuée Bleue*, (translated from the German and introduced by Freddy Raphael and Monique Ebstein).

time. If, from 1532, he had become less tolerant toward dissidents,[31] he continued to remain open to the Jews. In 1537, he had sent a letter to Luther in order to support Yossel's efforts in order to have the anti-Jewish order of the prince elector of Saxony annulled.

> I have pity on this people who were blinded for long centuries, and, except for harming Christ, we must treat them with respect, for they came out of the blessed root and were men with the promise of alliance. But now they are branches cut from the true olive-tree in which we are implanted. They deserve mercy all the more that they little knew the one who is the accomplishment of the Law of Moses. That is why we, who follow him on the way of the Gospel, have not accepted hard measures against them.[32]

Bucer's orientations were different: they are expressed in his *Commentaire sur l'Epitre aux Romains* and in his *Avis sur la question de savoir s'il convient qu'une autorité chrétienne peut tolérer que les juifs puissant habiter parmi les chrétiens et sous quelle forme il faut les tolérer*.[33] The warning was sent to the civil authorities of Hesse, incited by the pastors and officials to expel the Jews after the expiry, in 1538, of an edict which granted them the right to stay. According to Bucer, a Christian magistrate had the duty to promote true religion and to punish everyone who was against it. That also concerned the Jews, and could justify their expulsion. However, according to canon law and according to the Code of Justinian, the Jews were most often tolerated. If it tolerated them, the Christian state however had to protect Christians in the face of the Jews. The Jews of Hesse had proposed, in order to be able to stay, to attend sermons which were intended to evangelize them and to renounce all propaganda. Bucer wanted to compel them to engage by oath not to blaspheme against Christ. He also strongly recommends forbidding the building of new synagogues. Economically, he suggests banning them from usury even from any business. The Jews must earn their living honorably, but in humble professions: sewage workers, coalmining or quarrymen. These steps, which Bucer certainly had not invented, but which revealed a hardening in his relationship with the Jews, must, according to him and within the framework of a Christian society, repress the wicked ones (the Jews!) and bring them to improve, that is to say to become Christian.

Bucer's advice was not fully followed by the Landgrave of Hesse, who was more sensitive to the biblical promises about Israel and more inclined

---

31. Selma Stern does not take into account this inflexibility (on this matter see Van'T Spijker, n47) and idealizes Capiton's tolerance, ibid., 144.

32. WA Br, vol. 8, no. 3152.

33. BDS, vol. 7, 1964, 321–76.

1. STRASBOURG

to insist on the need for Christians to love the Jews. On the other hand, one must note that the Jewish question was brought up several times in the Frankfurt meeting (1539) and in the religious colloquia of Hagenau, Worms and Ratisbon[34] in which Calvin took part. It is possible that he may have met Yossel de Rosheim there and discussed with him, but the silence of the sources does not permit affirmation with certainty.

Let us next deal with the confessional orientations and organization of the evangelical Church in Strasbourg.

At the start, one must remember the close ties which existed between the Strasbourgian Reformers and others such as, especially, Luther, Melanchthon and Zwingli. These ties appear clearly in the correspondence from one and the other.[35] Luther's influence on the Strasbourgians is manifest, even if some divergences about Holy Communion stretched relations with Wittenberg for several years. Close links appear with Basel,[36] Zurich and Bern, with the towns of South Germany such as Ulm, Augsburg and Constance, or even with Hesse. For the period from 1538 to 1541, seventy-seven letters sent by Bucer to the Landgrave of Hesse, twenty to Ambroise Blaurer (Constance) and fifteen to his sister Marguerite Blaurer were kept. For the same period, Jean Rott listed a dozen of Bucer's journeys. Relations bypassed Switzerland and South Germany, toward the Kingdom of France, England and Eastern Europe. They are also conveyed by the welcome of foreign delegates such as the Czech Brothers in 1540. Bucer's horizon was truly Europe.[37] His many contacts had the purpose of mutual aid to clarify questions of doctrine or organization of the Church. We also know with what passion Bucer was engaged in the service of unity, that of the evangelical camp first of all, then, in 1540–1541, in the company of Calvin and Jean

---

34. Wilhelm H. Neuser, "*Calvins Beitrag zu den Relgionsgesprachen von Hagenau, Worms und Regensburg* (1540/41)," in L. Abramowski et al. (eds.), *Studien zur Geschichte und Theologie der Reformation* (Melanges Ernst Bizer, Neukirchen-Vluyn, 1969), 213–37; Johannes Maarten, *Johannes Calvin en de godsdienstgesprekken tussen roomskatholicken en protestanten in Hagenau, Worms en Regensburg (1540-1541)* (Kampen: Uigeverij-Kok, 2004). See also the article by Volkmar Ortmann in the present volume, 205–22.

35. For Bucer, see n3 and Jean Rott, *Correspondance de Martin Bucer: Liste alphabétique des correspondants* (Strasbourg: Association of publications of the Faculty of Protestant Theology, 1977); for Capiton: Olivier Millet, *Correspondance de Wolfgang Capiton (1478-1541): Analyse et index* (Strasbourg: Biblioth Nationale et Universitaire, 1982).

36. See Hans R. Guggisberg, "*Strasburg et Basle dans la Réforme*," in *Strasbourg au coeur religieux* (see n110, 333–40).

37. Marc Lienhard, "*Martin Bucer, le réformateur européen*," BSHPF 138 (1882) 161–80.

Sturm, unity with the tenants of the Roman Church, not without stirring up reserves with friends such as Marguerite and ... Calvin.

Let us see more closely how things happened in Strasbourg and what the Church's situation was toward 1540.[38] The town had passed into the field of the Reformation during the twenties. The evangelical movement had led in 1529 to the suppression of the last masses which were still celebrated in the town. The same year, the representatives of Strasbourg were associated with Spire's presentation, and the next year they presented the Tetrapolitan, a confession of faith which was close but distinct from the Confession of Augsburg. Catholicism had not so far disappeared in the town. Of the four canonical chapters, only that of Saint-Thomas had become Protestant. Toward 1540, out of fourteen convents, three women's convents still resisted the Protestant wave: the Dominicans of Saint-Nicholas of the Waves and Sainte-Marguerite, and the Penitents of Saint Magdalen. A convent of men, that of Chartreux, resisted up to 1592. To these one must add the two commanderies, that of Saint John and the Teutonic Commandery. Contacts with Bishop Guillaume de Honstein were tied in 1538, and in 1541 with his successor Erasmus of Limburg, but they remain undeveloped.[39] Some inhabitants of the town seem to be still close to Catholicism. Thus one learns in 1540 that the members of the magistrate are going to spend Easter in Eschau, a village near Strasbourg.

Within the framework of the 1533 synod,[40] a confession of faith in sixteen articles, particularly aimed against the Anabaptists, had been presented. On 4 March 1534, the Tetrapolitan[41] as well as the sixteen articles[42] were adopted by the civil authorities as a standard of the Church's doctrine.

Little by little, Strasbourg was going close to Lutheranism. If the signing of the Confession of Augsburg in 1532 particularly responded to political needs, Bucer's efforts to find communion with the theologians of Wittenberg had a greater range. They especially led to the 1536 Concord of Wittenberg, according to which the true body and the true blood of

---

38. For an overall view, see Marc Lienhard, "*La Réforme a Strasbourg*," in Georges Livet and Francis Rapp (eds.), *Histoire de Strasbourg des origines a nos jours*, vol. 2 (Strasbourg: Dernieres Nouvelles, 1981), 365–540.

39. Brady, *Protestant Politics* (n6) O, 115.

40. Fundamental for this Synod: Francois Wendel, *L'Eglise de Strasbourg: Sa constitution et son organisation 1532-1535* (Paris: P.U.F., 1942).

41. Text in *BDS* 3 (see n34), 13–185; Marc Lienhard, "Bucer and the Tetrapolitan," *BSGPF* 126 (1980) 270-85; idem., "*Evangelische Alternativen zur Augustana? Tetrapoitana und Fidei Ratio*," in Wolfgang Reinhard (ed.), *Bekenntnis und Geschichte* (Munich: Ernst Vogel, 1981), 81–100. The two studies have been reedited in Lienhard, *Un temps, une ville, une Réforme* (see n22).

42. Text with Wendel (see n41), 343–52.

Christ are given and received in Holy Communion, and received also by the unworthy. This agreement, to which the Swiss could not bring themselves to participate in through fear of a connection which was too well affirmed between the elements and the body and blood of Christ, strengthened the theological closeness between Strasbourg and Wittenberg. In the sixteenth century, the historians of liberal obedience considered that this closeness was the work of the "wicked" Marbach in the second half of the century. The historians of the twentieth century generally state that it began with Bucer.[43] This closeness moreover does not only express itself doctrinally, but also in hymnology, canticles coming from South Germany. On the other hand, the Luther's *Petit Catéchisme* will gradually supplant the other catechisms.

As regards the confession of faith of the Strasbourg Church, the town council will henceforth hold onto the Confession of Augsburg at the same time as the Tetrapolitan, whose authority was recalled at the time of the 1539 synod. It will only be abandoned in 1563. But the fact that in 1540 there were two versions of the Confession of Augsburg had introduced some ambiguity: some, especially the Lutheran theologians, held on to the 1530 *Invariata*; the others such as Jean Sturm called for the *Variata*, which was closer to the Swiss ideas. We should note that the Strasbourg Synod which met in 1539 was in practice content to go back in its twenty-two doctrinal articles to the positions of the Sixteen Articles of 1533.

Insofar as Strasbourg had adopted an official confession of faith[44] and set out a standard doctrinal orientation exactly, the repression of dissidents, who were very numerous in Strasbourg toward 1540, was going to be strengthened.[45] The 1527 order, renewed in 1529, had not had a great effect. On their side, the preachers, who again were joined by Capiton,[46] who had been sensitive for several years to certain dissident ideas, did not cease to pester the magistrate to ask him to intervene. The latter had no intention of restraining consciences, a position repeated many times since 1527.[47] On the other hand he wished to reply to the criticisms addressed by the

---

43. Johann Adam, *Evangelische Kirchengeschichte der Stadt Strassburg bis zur französischen Revolution* (Strasbourg: Heitz, 1922), 315; Abray (see n), p. 77ss; Greschat (see n7), 104ss; Brady, *Protestant Politics* (see n6), 115–16, n85.

44. TAE II, 285–86, no. 518.

45. Deppermann (see n13), 267ss.

46. Willem Van't Spijker, "'*Capito totus noster nunc est*': Capito's Return to the Reformed Camp," in Elsie McKee and Brian Y. Armstrong (eds.), *Probing the Reformed Tradition: Historical Studies in Honor of Edward A. Dawey* (Louisville, 1989), 220–36.

47. Marc Lienhard, "*Les autorités temporelles et les anabaptistes: attitudes du Magistrat de Strasbourg (1526 to 1532)*," in Lienhard (ed.), *The Origins and Characteristics of anabaptism*: *Les débuts et les caractéristiques de l'anabaptisme* (The Hague: Nijhoff, 1977), 196–215.

dissidents to the official Church and the doctrine, and to fight the divisions. In June 1533, the representatives of the various dissidents were heard by the authorities. The ideas of Clement Ziegler, of Melchior Hofman and some Swiss Brothers were refuted by Bucer and his colleagues and rejected by the town council. The latter took on the defense of the preachers. According to an order of 13 April 1534, the Anabaptists who did not wish to be reconciled with the Church of Strasbourg must leave the town with their family within eight days. Those who wished to stay had to promise that they were prepared to take an oath, to abstain from organizing conventicles or to take part in them. Moreover, the children had to be baptized within six weeks of birth. The 1535 decrees of application however softened the range of these decisions. The dissidents had only to take a civic oath and not to engage on the Tetrapolitan and the Sixteen Articles. However, after the catastrophe of Munster-in-Westphalia, the Strasbourg authorities did not trust them and were more severe toward them.

First of all, the number of dissidents, whose chiefs such as Marpeck had been expelled, diminished. In 1537, there were no more than about two hundred of the faithful living in Strasbourg,[48] of which a part stayed in the surrounding countryside. But in fact, the numerous interrogations between 1536 and 1538, as well as various writings by Bucer, show that the problem was far from being resolved; also, the Anabaptists from the Netherlands, the Brabant and Flanders reached Strasbourg in 1538. The order of 23 March 1538 order slightly repeated things that were close to the provisions of 1535. According to the magistrate, even a great many Strasbourgians considered dissidents as good Christians, and deviants like the schwenckfeldians met sympathies in the controlling environments.

The outstanding fact was, in 1538, the progressive dissolution of the Melchiorite movement, whose chief, Melchior Hofman, was in a damp prison. The prophetic pretensions of David Joris, reaching Strasbourg in June, had not won adherence. The Strasbourg group was going to dissolve in the space of a year; some of its members went to join the Swiss Brothers who reached new heights in the surrounding countryside from 1539. Others, certainly a small number, allowed themselves to be convinced by Bucer, then by Calvin, to come back into the bosom of the official Church.

Let us recall the ecclesiastical institutions and the ministers who were in place in Strasbourg in Calvin's time. They always operated according to the orientations taken in the twenties and decisions made at the 1533

---

48. According to Lorna Jane Abray (see n6) 109, out of some eighty-six sectarians interrogated between 1536 and 1573, only nine would be converted and would have returned to the official Church.

synod.[49] The number of parishes had been reduced from nine to seven, to which in 1538 the French community had been added. The parishes were served by pastors who had obtained the right of middle-class people and who were married; they were excused from military service and excluded from civil functions. According to the ecclesiastical Decree of 1534, the candidate pastor in a vacant parish was chosen, after having preached there, by a commission made up of "three elders of the parish, twelve God-fearing men," as well as by examiners. The chosen candidate had to be confirmed by the magistrate of the town. The pastors met every eight days in Zell's house. Every fortnight, a Thursday, a larger meeting, the *Convocation*, which gathered all the pastors, vicars and twenty-one elders, had to take place. A Decree of 1531 had put in place for each parish three elders or curators who were appointed by the council, one having to be a member of the town council, the second was a magistrate, the third came from members of the parish. With the pastors, they had to deal with the current affairs of the Church. In fact, their role was to supervise the pastors, and, in the case of a problem, to refer it to the magistrate. They were more reticent in taking part in exercising ecclesiastical discipline which was so dear to Bucer. Only two synods met, one in 1533, the other in 1539, to become obsolete later. No personal direction of the Church was laid down in the ecclesiastical Decree of 1534, the magistrate considering himself as the supreme authority. In fact, Bucer was going to impose himself more and more by his capacity as a theologian and debater, and by his capacity to organize the Church. From 1534, Capiton, in a letter to Grynee of 13 September, describes him as "bishop of our Church." But it will be only in 1541 that the magistrate will recognize him as president of the Ecclesiastical General Assembly, and only in 1544 that he will describe him as superintendent.

The retributions of pastors, in nature or in kind, were fed by various sources, especially the incomes of the chapters, as was the case, for example, for the pastors of Saint-Peter-the-Young.

Who were the men in place when Calvin reached Strasbourg in 1538?[50] At the Cathedral, Mattieu Zell, who had preached in an evangelical way from 1521, was still in position, reinvigorated in 1538 by a journey that he made to Wittenberg with his wife Catherine. His assistants Jean Schmidt (1540) and Georges Biermann (1543) are little known. After 1523, Gaspard

---

49. On this matter see Wendel, *L'Eglise de Strasbourg* (see n41), and Bornert, *La Réforme Protestante du Culte* (see n4).

50. See Marie Joseph Bopp, *Die evangelischen Geistlichen und Theologen in Elsass und Lothringen von der Reformation bis zur Gegenwart* (Neustadt a.d. Aisch, Degener, 1959); idem., *Die evangelischen Gemeinden und Hohen Schulen in Elsss und Lothringen von der Reformation bis Gegenwart* (Aisch: Degener, 1963).

Hedion held the role of preacher at the cathedral. At Saint-Thomas, it was Martin Bucer from 1529, assisted from 1531 by Conrad Hubert. In 1540, another pastor deacon is attributed in the person of Conrad Schnell. At St. Pierre the Younger, Capiton is still in place. When the plague carried him away on 3 November 1541, Calvin had already left for Geneva, where he arrived on 13 September. From 1537, Capiton was assisted by Martin Schalling. At Saint-Guillaume, the pastor from 1534 was the Wurtemberger Caspar Steinbach, assisted from 1536 to 1541 by Jean Lenglin. At St. Pierre the elder, was still Theobald Schwarz, who had in 1524 celebrated the first German language mass. He was assisted from 1535 by the Wurtemberger Georges Morinweg. From 1531 Antoine Firn officiated at Saint Nicholas, and at Saint Aurelia it was, from 1531, Jean Steinlin. We should recall that only two or three (Schnell, Schwarz (?), Steinlin) on a total of fifteen were from Strasbourg.

If Calvin was warmly received by Capiton and Bucer, with whom he was going to live for several months, Zell seems to have remained more distant, according to Calvin's statements: in a letter of 14 December 1540, he describes less than fully, the character of "Matthew, who does not easily put up with being advised, with a stronger reason that he should be taken back."[51] But is the same true of Zell?

At this stage of our presentation, it would be right to expose the theological orientations of the Strasbourg pastors toward 1540. One should especially recall the most eminent publications among them, those of Bucer, Capiton and Hedion and their theology. Let us limit ourselves to some brief observations about Bucer. As adept as Capiton in what one has called the Rhine School of exegesis,[52] Bucer was, in the sixteenth century, one of the most fertile commentators of Holy Scripture. The latter, including the Old Testament, was for him the standard of all doctrine and all preaching.

> "I may be stoned" he could say, "if I preach something other that what is contained in Holy Scripture."[53]

---

51. *CO* XI, col. 132; Doumergue (see n25), 328n2.

52. For the Rhine school of exegesis, see Guy Bedouelle and Bernard Roussel (dir.) *Le temps des Réformes et la Bible* (Paris, 1981), 215–33; Bernard Roussel, "De Strasbourg a Bâle et Zurich: Une 'Ecole rhénane' d'exégèse (ca 1525 to 1540)," *RHPhR* 68 (1988) 19–35: ibid., "Bucer exégete," in Christian Krieger and Marc Lienhard (eds.), *Martin Bucer and Sixteenth Century Europe*, vol. 1 (Leiden: Brill, 1993), 39–54; Gerald Hobbs, "Martin Bucer and the Upper Rhine School," in Magne SAEBO, *Hebrew Bible/Old Testament: The History of Its Interpretation*, vol. 2, *From the Renaissance to the Enlightenment* (Gottingen: Vandenhoeck-Ruprecht, 2008), 452–511.

53. *BDS* 1, 175.

1. STRASBOURG

Countless biblical quotations fill his doctrinal writings. Different from Luther, Scripture in Bucer is not subjected to ambivalence between the Law and the Gospel, between the letter and the spirit.

> It is complete and without marked duality marked by divine perfection, thanks to the Holy Spirit which makes its whole work the Word of God.[54]

Second, the place of the Holy Spirit in Bucer's theology, this spirit which is "the main agent of the divine presence in the world and among humans."[55] "It is God's finger, even His power."

It is the action of the Holy Spirit which brings up the principles, so dear to Bucer, of progression, of growth and love, as well as its ecclesiology. The emphasis placed on the Holy Spirit underpins the constant attention granted to ethics, to love and sanctification, without all the same losing sight of justification by faith.[56]

> "All ministers," he writes, "especially those in civil authority, have an essential task to collaborate with improvement (*Besserung*)."[57]

One must finally point out that Bucer's theology is always attentive to the Church, a community outcome and anticipation of the reign of Christ, sensitive to the diversity and action of the ministers, always careful of the unity of the Church. According to Calvin, sometimes criticizing Bucer on this point, the latter literally burns with the zeal for unity, at the point of being ready, especially within the framework of the 1541 colloquia, to concessions refused by his friends such as, for example, the adoration of the Holy Sacrament.

How did the pastors supervise the faithful toward 1540? From 1526, they had introduced catechetical instruction for children. From 1523, a great many catechisms or instruction manuals was placed at their disposal by the Strasbourgian printers[58] Beyond the contribution from outside and printed or reprinted in the town, three texts written by Strasbourgian pastors, of unequal length and quality: Zell's questionnaire on faith (1525), the

---

54. Gottfried Hammamm, "*La démarche théologique de Bucer*," in *Martin Bucer und Sixteenth Century Europe* (see n53), 71–81, quotation at 74.

55. Ibid., 76.

56. Ibid., 77.

57. Gottfried Hammann, *Entre la secte et la cité: Le projet d'Eglise du Réformateur Martin Bucer* (Geneva: Labor et Fides, 1984), 74.

58. August Ernst and Johann Adam, *Katechetische Geschichte des Elsasses bis zur Revolution* (Strasbourg: Friedrich Bull, 1897); *BDS* (see n34) 6, 3, 19–22; Chrisman, *Bibliography of Strasbourg Imprints* (see n5), 293–94.

Kinderbericht und fragstuck de Capiton (1527 and 1529), or even Bucer's *Kurze schrifftliche erklarung* (1534). The latter, not very well suited to instruction of young people, had not been reedited. It was replaced in 1537 by a *Kurtzer Catechismus*, with wood engravings and written by Bucer, but published under the name of all the Strasbourgian preachers. It was more successful, but later it gave way to Luther's *Petit Catéchisme*. Used in the first place by teachers, the catechisms also contained answers that the children had to learn by heart. At the request of the preachers and in accordance with the ecclesiastical Decree of 1534, the parents were vigorously exhorted to send their children and their servants to the Sunday catechism, the latter being complemented by a three-monthly "common catechism" uniting all the children. The ecclesiastical decree even stipulated that the catechism must not only be taught on Sundays, but also on a special day during the week in schools. Religious instruction led to an examination, prior to admission to first communion. In 1538, Bucer introduced confirmation in Hesse[59] beyond the examination and the personal confession of faith, it included a blessing and a laying-on of hands. On 18 May 1540, Strasbourg Council rejected this practice. The existence of confirmation in Strasbourg was witnessed for the first time certainly by Bucer's *Catéchisme* in 1543.[60]

The impression of about ten collections of songs,[61] to which one must add that of the Moravian brothers prefaced by Catherine Zell, shows the importance of singing in Strasbourg in worship, but also in daily life. People sing not only psalms, in the popular tongue, but also other songs, related to popular songs, and which inculcate doctrinal truths, paraphrasing biblical stories and expressing the believer's response to the Gospel. It is Bucer's collection of canticles that is the first to be authorized officially for worship. Bucer thinks that one must absolutely teach beautiful songs to children, as "this age is itself inclined to sing and wants to be led to the good by pleasant means."

Worship[62] was celebrated in the language of the people. What is striking first of all, is its multiplicity. Every day, three services were the rhythm of the day: the morning prayers, in all the parishes at 4 o'clock and at 5 o'clock in winter, the 8 o'clock service in the cathedral, and the evening sermon, also in the cathedral. On Sundays, the faithful person could attend six different services, at the cathedral or in the other parishes. Preaching held a central

---

59. On this matter see Bornert, *La Réforme Protestante du Culte* (see n4), 360–69.

60. Ibid., 366.

61. Ibid., 179–82; Edith Weber, "*Musique et théâtre à Strasbourg*," in *Strasbourg au Coeur religieux* (see n11), 577–93, 584.

62. Bornwer, *La Réforme Protestante du Culte* (see n4).

place there. However toward 1530, some disaffection took place, vilified by the preachers. In vain they asked the town council to make attendance compulsory; the council was content to encourage members to attend at least one service on Sundays.

Holy Communion was celebrated every Sunday at the cathedral, in other churches every fortnight or once a month. The Holy Communion services were preceded by a preparatory service on Saturday afternoon, that the faithful could prolong by a personal soul healing with the pastor. Rene Bornert's work on worship has made the point on liturgy used in Strasbourg. In 1539, the second Synod made an effort to unite the liturgical practices.[63] In the first years, organ playing had been restricted by Bucer or reserved only for solemn Sunday services. But in 1531, the magistrate decided that it must be played during the daily services.

In the beginning, every Sunday was the same after the introduction of the Reformation: the liturgical year was no longer considered, except for Easter and maybe Pentecost. But the celebration of Christmas was first witnessed in 1537. Collections of canticles from 1537 and 1538 suggested songs for the nativity, the New Year or circumcision, Passiontide, Easter Day and the Feast of the Ascension.

In relation to the mediaeval tradition, the ritual of baptism had been simplified. As regards marriage, the public ceremony was definitively imposed in Strasbourg as elsewhere toward the middle of the sixteenth century. For funerals, greatly simplified in the first years of the Reformation, where people objected to masses for the dead, a conservative reaction was confirmed toward 1537. It was now arranged that, after the protests on behalf of the faithful toward 1533, the minister would intervene at the tomb, after the shroud had been carried directly from dead person's home to the cemetery. He read a passage from Scripture, addressed a brief exhortation to the believers and, after a moment's silence, ended the ceremony by a prayer.

In view of the civil, cultural and religious life, one could think that for the most part, everything was all right in Strasbourg toward 1540. It is true that, in relation to Geneva, the town had in some way found its cruising speed in its passage to Protestantism: the ecclesiastical institutions seemed to operate, the Haute Ecole had taken off, values which were suitable for the Reformation found the adherence of the great majority. Historians like to emphasize moreover how happy Calvin was in Strasbourg, a town that he only left regretfully in 1541. In a more general way, some historians, particularly with Protestant obedience, have shown, in a rather exaggerated triumphalism, progress brought in by the Reformation in Strasbourg.

---

63. On this matter see *BDS* (see n34) 6, 2.

> In all layers of the population a more ardent zeal was shown in the accomplishment of special duties, an intense desire life the dignity corresponding to the beliefs that one held.[64]

But, toward 1540, Bucer and his colleagues were far from sharing this optimism. From the beginning of the thirties, they were sensitive to some disaffection of a great many of the faithful in front of the new doctrines, and above all in respect of worship,[65] a disaffection which had replaced "the enthusiasm of the beginning of the evangelical movement with its strong ingredient of anticlericalism and infringement of liberty from 'human' religious prescriptions."[66] They thought, moreover, that the moral life of the Strasbourgians had not really improved, while in the beginning they were convinced that their sermons were going to improve the life of the faithful.[67] As a result, they turned even more determinedly than in the beginning toward the civil authorities to impose change and morals by law. It was Bucer who energetically became engaged for the sanctification of the city while awaiting the coming of Christ's kingdom on earth. The magistrate moreover did his best. As Jean Rott has shown,

> the general rules were taken over more quickly: there were about six during the previous fifty-three years, five were edited and nothing than in twelve years, and more spreading thanks to using a printed poster more often.[68]

On 7 August, Capiton, Hedion, Bucer and Zell met the town council[69] and described in very somber tones the disaffection with worship, including on the part of the magistrate and the young people, and the increase in vices among the Strasbourgians, especially adultery, drunkenness and gambling. A written position taken[70] followed this oral intervention and confirmed the criticisms. It suggested that some zealous men should be put in place to supervision the application of orders, that excess should be punished by harsher penalties and that the brothel which had just been built by the town should be closed. As Jean Rott points out, it was especially Bucer who stamped his feet impatiently. On the other hand, Capiton and Calvin knew

---

64. Henri Strohl, *Protestantisme in Alsace* (Strasbourg: Oberlin, 1950, 2000), 75-76.
65. Wendel, *L'Eglise* (see n41), 43ss.
66. Jean Rott, "*Le Magistrat face a l'épicurisme*," in Marc Lienhard (ed.). *Croyants et sceptiques au SXVIe siècle* (Strasbourg: Istra, 1981), 59 (5-71).
67. Abray (see n6).
68. Rott, "*Le Magistrat face à l'épicurisme*" (see n67), 59.
69. *TAE* II, 473.
70. Ibid., 474.

how to make allowances. Thus, the former writes at the end of June 1540 to a senator:

> We know very well that in a large community (*Gemeinde*) everyone cannot be punished, but one can at least suppress public scandals, for people sin without fear.[71]

As for the latter, he confided to Farel on 31 December 1539:

> I certainly see that one must tolerate some of the stupidity of men and that one must not stiffen rigor to the point that one is not allowed to lose one's head in anything.[72]

Since the council's orders about customs or taking part in religious services were in fact so little followed, were there not other means of putting the situation right? The idea came up that discipline must be exercised by the Church and lead, in extreme cases, to exclusion from Holy Communion. In 1527 Capiton had affirmed its principle,[73] "There can be no Christians without exclusion (*Bann*)." In his 1534 catechism, Bucer thought that the culpable, (*Lasterhafte*) had first of all to be exhorted in private, then in front of witnesses and finally in front of the elders. The impenitent people had to be set aside, but only if they broke points about the ecclesiastical community. In his treatise on pastoral care (1538), Bucer pleaded for a church discipline, which was required according to him in order to improve the life of Christians.

Who should operate the discipline? Was it the magistrate himself or his representatives, in other words the elders *Kirchenpfleger*, but the definitive text of the ecclesiastical excluded pastors of the disciplinary jurisdiction, which remained reserved only to the *Kirchenpleger*,[74] ready for the advice they wanted from the pastors. Bucer seemed to go along with this. On the other hand, from that time, Capiton wanted to grant the operation of discipline to the ecclesiastical General Assembly, to which only three elders would be added, a system which will only be put into action by the ecclesiastical General Assembly of 1598. From 1536, Bucer, called in on this matter by the Anabaptists, changed his mind in his turn in order to require a disciplinary exercise by an autonomous organ. The magistrate was not as Christian as Bucer had believed, and the elders installed by the magistrate were not zealous enough to censure their citizens.

71. Archives Municipales de Strasbourg, Archives de Saint-Thomas 84, no. 38, quoted by Rott, "*Le Magistrat face à l'épicurisme*," (see n67) 62, n11.
72. We have translated the German and Latin quotations.
73. Quoted by Adam, *Evanvelische Kirchengeschichte* (see n44), 191.
74. Wendel, *L'Eglise* (see n41), 186.

It is poignant to read in the implementation of decisions of the 1535 Synod that the town council rejected,[75] especially the supervision and the convocation (*beschicken*) of the flock by the pastor and exclusion from Holy Communion.

Not a great deal is known on the manner in which Calvin handled ecclesiastical discipline in the French community, except that it came to ask a member of the faithful flock to abstain from Holy Communion.[76]

---

75. *BDS* (see n34), 6, 2, 195ss.
76. Doumergue, *Jean Calvin* (see n25), 412–15.

2. Correspondence

Calvin's Correspondence during His Stay in Strasbourg

Christoph Burger[1]

Editions of Calvin's Correspondence

FROM 1872 TO 1879, or during an astonishingly short space of time, the Strasbourgian theologians Guillaume Baum, Edouard Reuss and Edouard Cunitz published an edition of Calvin's correspondence.[2] In the years 1866–1897, Aime-Louis Herminjard edited, in nine volumes, the correspondence of the French-speaking Reformers. He had to restrict himself to the years 1512–1544, but he achieved a performance which was no less remarkable. By his editing, which did not limit itself to the correspondence of an author, he showed how much, in the French-speaking space, the leaders of the Reformation consulted each other and kept the others informed about what was happening.[3] Moreover, Herminjard published a great many letters from the burgmasters and counselors of the towns where the main Reformers were operating. The fact that it may be limited to the French-speaking territories however constitutes a limit of its editing: thus, it has hardly dealt with the efforts of the Reformers in Basel in favor of Calvin.

But these two publications do not meet the present scientific requirements of a critical publication of an epistolatory correspondence.[4] On the

---

1. Amsterdam Free University.

2. Cf. Frans Pieter Van Stam, "General Introduction," in *Ioannis Calvini Epistolae*, vol. 1, ed. Cornelis Augustijn, Frans Pieter Van Stam (Geneva, 2005), 23–26. This volume has appeared in the new series Calvini opera omnia denuo recognita . . . series 6, and it is why we are abbreviating it from now on as follows: CORVI/i.

3. Cf. ibid., 22–23 and 24–26.

4. On the different aims that the publications of correspondence of the Reformers which are illustrated from Melanchthon, see Cornelis Augustijn, "Melanchthons

other hand, the high requirements are rarely accompanied by the availability of finance for such research, and we should note the treatment of scientific publishers. I have had personal experience of this: when, in 2005, the team of editors that I managed in Amsterdam finished editing volume 1 of the new critical edition of Calvin's correspondence, which stopped at the expulsion from Geneva in 1538,[5] the dean of my faculty appointed me to find in the future, for the continuation of our enterprise, funds from a place elsewhere than in our university. That proved to be very difficult. Also I have to base the present contribution on the old editions of the nineteenth century, while I would have much preferred to draw on the editorial work of the second volume of Calvin's correspondence, which must be devoted exactly to the letters in the years 1538–1541. To the extent that Aime-Louis Herminjard's edition is more careful than that of the Corpus Reformatorum, and the notes are richer, I shall adhere to this edition.[6]

In the Herminjard edition, the correspondence of the years 1538–1541 (Reformers and political authorities) constitutes almost sixteen hundred printed pages. I was able to study about 250 deeply. I therefore had to be limited. In the first place, I researched information on the manner in which Calvin adapted to Strasbourg or in which he lived through his participation in the religious colloquia, as well as witnesses of the respect in which he was held by the Strasbourgians, who had learned to appreciate him when he was recalled to Geneva. I shall end my article by showing how Farel's separation and Bucer's proximity had a positive influence on Calvin's development.

I am aware that reading letters can only communicate subjective impressions: it reveals to us what the letter-writers were feeling and what they were seeking to convey to their correspondents, and not by an objective image. Thus, in order to anticipate one of the results, totally unexpected, of my research, our letters give the impression that, during at least six months, from September 1538 to March 1539, internally Calvin does not seem to have absolutely arrived in Strasbourg! The explanation which comes to be is that, being wounded in his honor, he remained so fixed on the fact that he had been dismissed from his roles and sent away from Geneva that, throughout this period, he only managed to make a tour of the horizon of Strasbourg, his new field of activities. The same observation can be made about Farel, who, internally and on reading the letters that he wrote to Calvin, does not seem truly to have arrived in Neuchatel! Throughout these

---

Briefwechsel, Kritische und kommentierte Gesamtausgabe," *Nederlands Archief voor Kerkgeschiedenis / Dutch Review of Church History* 72 (1992) 195–212.

5. See n1.

6. I quote according to Herminjard, indicating the volume and the page.

months, Farel is, at a distance, the most important correspondent of Calvin. And he also had to overcome, during this period, his interrogations about the banishment which had struck Calvin and himself.

I do not think, in documents which are as personal as their correspondence, the two men have faked what was truly in their hearts: if, in these letters, Strasbourg and Neuchatel play a lesser role than Geneva, that means that, over some months, Farel and Calvin have not succeeded in digesting the terrible offense which was made to their self-esteem and the important break which affected their biography.

Throughout these six months, as we have said above, it is mainly with Farel that Calvin exchanged letters. No letter sent to Pierre Viret, the pastor of Lausanne, or coming from the latter is found in the Herminjard edition. This absence is surprising: throughout the year and a half that Calvin worked at Geneva in Farel's company, Viret was one of his favorite correspondents.

Farel and Calvin assure one another and assure their colleagues in Geneva that they are absolutely not guilty of the conflict which led to their banishment. They also refuse to listen to Bucer's statements, according to which they are found guilty of a fault. In the correspondence between Farel and Calvin, it is said that Bucer was too conciliatory. But things could be interpreted very differently. In fact, the one who remembers the young Calvin with such arrogance had dared to give, from Geneva, directives to Bucer, who was much older and more experienced that him, could only admire, even more, the sovereign character of Bucer: the Strasbourgian Reformer precisely invites Calvin, this haughty young man, to come to Strasbourg, after, in Geneva, the lively Farel and himself are placed in an untenable situation. Not everybody would have pardoned Calvin for the tone with which he had written his letter of 12 January 1538. I quote several extracts from this letter from Calvin, aged twenty-eight, to Martin Bucer, who was forty-six and who, among the Reformers, had then more weight than Calvin: "It seems to us (I speak on behalf of my colleagues and in my own name) that you must be asked immediately (and we dare to allow ourselves this liberty, confident and in your singular moderation) that, when you are dealing with the Word of God, and most particularly in questions which, today, are discussed, you apply yourself to measure your speech in such a way that you offend as few people as possible.[7] In reading these statements, I am asking

---

7. "Iam ipse quoque (meo et collegarum meorum nomine nunc loquor) adiurandus nobis videris—atque id licentiate suere nobis in te audemus, singulari tua moderation freti—quod in tractando verbo Domini ac prasertim in capitibus hodie controversis, tua orationem temperare studes, ut quam paucissimos offendas" (Calvin, letter of 12 January 1538; COR VI/1, p. 301, 1, 150–54, no. 56A).

myself a question, that I am composing in a fairly direct manner, intentionally: "But therefore what is this greenhorn allowed?"

Return on the Expulsion of Farel and Calvin

Under the influence of Farel, who was older than him, Calvin had not ceased to radicalize his positions, throughout the eighteen months of their common activity in Geneva, from 1536 to 1538. Under Farel's influence, he rejected the fact that Christians could have reforming convictions without to some extent distancing themselves radically from the mass celebrated by the Pope's Church.[8] And from that moment, Calvin stigmatized these Christians by treating them as "Nicodemites." The open letter that Farel sent in 1543 to the evangelical community in Metz shows very clearly that it was Farel who distinguished the "Nicodemites" so severely from other Christians. According to this open letter, Farel thinks he finds himself in an eschatological position, in which there could only be a "yes" to Christ and a "no" to the Church of the Pope. Also in Neuchatel, Farel was thrown up against a strong opposition, and it is not amazing that the Swiss Reformers did not want, after having been sent out of Geneva in 1538, Farel and Calvin to work together again in the same community.

Anyone who, basing himself on Calvin's correspondence during the eighteen months of his common activity with Farel in Geneva, tries to issue an objective judgment on the beginnings of the two pastors, will arrive, according to me, at the conclusion that the two men overestimated their independence in relation to the magistrate of Geneva. Moreover, they have not sufficiently taken into consideration the fact that, for his part, the magistrate of Geneva depended on the one in Bern. Geneva needed military support from Bern in order to resist the appetites of the Duke of Savoy. That is why the magistrate of Geneva could not allow himself to enable the pastors working under his protection to act against the interests of Rome.

It is only because Farel and Calvin were too aware of this position that they dared to interfere in the ecclesiastical affairs of the French-speaking communities of the Pays de Vaud. Bern had conquered the Pays de Vaud; that is why the magistrate of Bern felt himself entitled to determine the forms that the Reformation would take in this territory. Farel and Calvin had miscalculated their field of action when they thought they could impose, in the French-speaking parishes of Vaud, their own concepts of the organization of the Church. One must also add to that their conflict with

---

8. Cf. Christoph Burger, "Farels Frommigkeit," in *Actes du colloque Guillaume Farel*, 29 September–1 October 1980 (Geneva, Lausanne and Neuchâtel, 1983), 149–59.

Pierre Caroli, to which Bern had granted a controlling position in the community of Lausanne. Already before that, Caroli had had trouble with Farel, and pastor Viret, who was the ally of Farel and Calvin, did not recognize the position as head of the clerks of Lausanne, the main town of the Pays de Vaud.[9]

To sum up, it can be said that, for Calvin's development in the years 1536-1538, his collaboration with Farel was not favorable: this older colleague, who was not level-headed, pushed Calvin not only to defend his own convictions of faith without any compromise, but even to show himself as too intransigent in his relations with the magistrate.

Making Contact with Strasbourg

Having been sent away from Geneva, Farel and Calvin wrote from Basel, from 14 June 1538, to their friends in Lausanne, pastors Pierre Viret and Corauld, that they had set out their viewpoint in letters addressed to Strasbourg and Zurich.[10] It was important for them to win over the Strasbourgians to their own view of the Genevan conflict. On 10 July 1538, Calvin wrote from Strasbourg to his friend Louis de Tillet (Paris), from whom he felt more and more distant, that two Strasbourgians—we can, without any doubt, identify them as Bucer and Capiton—had pressed him without such insistence that he had had to go to Strasbourg.[11] He added that he wanted to live off the money that Tillet had offered to him, and follow his road to Basel: the Strasbourgians had enough worries, and he did not want to be a burden for them.[12] It is surprising that Calvin signed this letter by "Your humble servant and complete friend."[13] In fact, both friends had just developed ideas which were radically different on the idea that the vocation addressed by the magistrate of a town to a pastor was the same thing as a

9. On the conflicts between Carol on the one hand, Farel and Calvin on the other hand, see, e.g., Christoph Burger, "Werben um Bullingers Beistand: Calvins Briefe von 1537/1538," in *Die Zurcher Reformation: Ausstrahlungen und Ruckwirkungen*, ed. Alfred Schindle and Hans Stickelberger (Bern, 2001), 111-18 (101-20); Cornelis Augustijn, Christoph Burger and Frans Van Stam, "Calvin in the Light of the Early Letters," in Herman J. Selderhuis (ed.), *Calvinus praeceptor Ecclesiae* (Geneva, 2004), 139-57; Christoph Burger, "Calvins Beziehungen zu Weggefahrten in der Scweiz 1536-1538," in Peter Opitz (ed.), *Calvin im Kontext der Schweizer Reformation: Historische und theologische Beitrage zur Calvinforschung* (Zurich, 2003), 44-40 (41-55).

10. Farel and Calvin, letter to Viret and Corauld from 14 June 1538 (Herminjard 5, 30).

11. Calvin, letter to Louis de Tillet, 10.7.1538 (Herminjard 5, 43).

12. Ibid., 44.

13. Ibid., 45.

divine vocation: Calvin felt himself called legitimately; for his part, du Tillet contested this interpretation and he ended up going back into the bosom of the Roman church.

In a letter to Farel, in which he wished him the strength for his new ministry in Neuchatel, Capiton set out the problems that some parishioners were causing him which were considered emancipated and they said to their pastor: "I understand the Gospel well enough. I am capable of reading by myself. In view of which, do I need your efforts?"[14]

Toward 1 August 1538, Bucer wrote to Calvin, who was in Basel, that he had to come to Strasbourg: certainly, he was only called by a small flock, but the latter needed his care very deeply[15] they could only offer him a small pastoral ministry, a parvum ministeriolum.[16] But Bucer puts a great deal of pressure on Calvin, recalling the fact that the cause of Christ could be placed in danger by the serious error that he, Calvin, had committed in Geneva: also he had to atone for it, by becoming a pastor in Strasbourg.[17] Bucer adds that Calvin must not operate in the same place as Farel, in Neuchâtel.[18] This letter will set straight all those who reproach Bucer for not being hard enough.

Too Low a Salary

Jean Rott has brought attention on the precarious financial position of Calvin throughout his Strasbourg years.[19] In a letter to Farel of the first half of October 1538, Calvin wrote: "If I do not want to be an expense for the brothers, I have to live here on what I own."[20] No doubt Calvin is referring to the receipts for the sale of books, as a short while before he spoke of the Basel printer Oportin.[21] On 1 May 1539, the Scholars, responsible for teaching in Strasbourg, granted Calvin a salary of 52 Florins per year;

---

14. Capiton, letter to Farel, no doubt end of July—beginning of August 1538 (Herminjard 5, 64; COR VI/I, 420, I. 30/31).

15. Bucer, letter to Calvin, no doubt at the end of July–beginning of August 1538 (Herminjard 5, 64/ COR VI/I, 420, I, 30–31).

16. Ibid., 66; COR VI/I, 421, 56.

17. Ibid., 65: COR VI/I, 420, I, 37–41.

18. Ibid.: COR VI/I, 420, l. 42–44.

19. Bucer, letter to Calvin, doubtless end July–beginning of August 1538 (Herminjard 5, 64; COR VI/I, 420, 1. 30–31).

20. Calvin, letter to Farel, first half of October 1538 (Herminjard 5, 147).

21. Ibid., 146.

this sum corresponding to a deacon's salary.[22] In a letter of 27 July 1540 to Farel, Calvin himself informs his friend that he is the holder of a prebend of a chaplain at Strasbourg Cathedral, that the Reformation has turned away from its initial use.[23] It was a question of two prebends attached to the altar of the Apostles Peter and Paul.[24] It was Baron Erasmus of Limbourg who had the right to grant these prebendaries. During his studies in Paris, Erasmus had become acquainted with Jean Sturm, the future rector of the Strasbourg gymnasium; he was a canon of the Great Chapter and he approved for the revenues connected to these chaplaincies to be used to reward the teachers in the Gymnasium. No doubt this source of revenue was not a goldmine: the Scholars wanted to give Calvin—as he wrote in his letter—a prebend bringing in 100 Florins, that is nearly twice his own. But the grant of this other prebend depended on the emperor, who had assigned his right to his brother Ferdinand; also this exchange of prebends was a long shot. To the extent that, in September 1541, the Strasbourgians considered that Calvin's return to Geneva was only temporary, the Scholars waited four years to ask him to return his chaplaincy to them; it was only in 1546 that Calvin returned this prebend.[25]

In Strasbourg Also, Calvin Is Trapped by His Genevan Past

Calvin left Basel at the beginning of September 1538[26] to go to Strasbourg. He wrote to Farel that he had left Basel by moving at great haste.[27] In Strasbourg, Capiton and Bucer were well intentioned toward him; but both of them judged Farel and his activities in Strasbourg rather critically. In a letter to Farel of the first half of October 1538, Calvin wrote that he would prefer Bucer not to praise him so much. Farel and he, like good and wise men, if only he could stop pretending that they had sinned.[28] Capiton and Bucer had regular epistolary contacts with the Bern pastor Pierre Kunz, which was

22. See Herminjard 5, 231, n19.
23. Calvin, letter to Farel of 27.7.1540 (Herminjard 6, 254–55).
24. Cf. Rott (see n18), 322.
25. Calvin, letter to Conrad Hubert of 24.2.1546 (CO 12, Braunschweig 1874, col. 262, letter 755). According to Rott, a document of 21.1.1546 is attached to this letter.
26. Calvin, letter to Farel from Strasbourg to Neuchâtel, toward 11.9.1538 (Herminjard 5, 109).
27. Ibid. (Herminjard 5, 109); "tumultuarie," i.e., "in very great haste."
28. Calvin, letter to Farel from Strasbourg to Neuchâtel, first half of October 1538 (Herminjard 5, 143).

not simple for Calvin:[29] in fact, Calvin was totally hostile to Kunz. From the time that Calvin was in Geneva, the Basel pastor Simon Grynaeus had tried to show him the qualities of the Bernians: certainly, having grown up in the Alps, Kunz behaved like a peasant, but he was a faithful servant of Christ.[30] But not more in Geneva than at the beginning of his stay in Strasbourg, Calvin had not been marked by this judgment. The efforts of the Bernian Simon Sulzer to reconcile Calvin and the magistrat of Bern proved also to be in vain.[31] A reconciliation would have included the confession, by Calvin, that Farel and himself had made mistakes. No, wrote Calvin to Farel in mid-September 1539, I shall never admit that it was the fault of both of us that the Church of Geneva has fallen into the pitiful state that it is at present. We are not guilty of any mistake.[32] It is manifest that, more than a year after the events, Calvin continued to suffer a deep wound. He knew well that, contrary to Farel and himself, Bucer enjoyed the consideration of the Bernians.[33] Still in this letter, Calvin also recalls his activities in Strasbourg: the Sunday before that, that is at the beginning of September, he preached in Saint-Nicholas: and he also wished to celebrate Holy Communion.[34]

It is doubtless to the bearer of this letter that, on the same day, Bucer gave a letter for Farel. He wrote particularly that Calvin would become a jewel for the kingdom of Christ, even if his field of action in Strasbourg is modest.[35] He writes, no doubt thinking about the Anabaptists, that some inhabitants of Strasbourg, among the members of the French-speaking community, are always touched by the illness of heresy.[36]

On 1 October 1538, Calvin himself wrote to Geneva to please witness his sympathy with those who will read his letter. These ideas, which do not seem to be a problem, constitute, de facto, for the pastor who was sent away from Geneva, an attempt to remind him of his supporters' memory. Manifestly, some weeks after Calvin's arrival in Strasbourg, his heart and his thoughts remained in Geneva.[37] He assures his correspondents that it is

29. Calvin, letter to Farel from Strasbourg to Neuchâtel, toward 11.9. 1538 (Herminjard 5, 110 and n3).

30. Grynaeus, letter to Farel and Calvin of 4.3.1538 (COR VI/I, 336, l. 31–36).

31. Calvin, letter to Farel from Strasbourg to Neuchâtel, toward 11.9. 1538 (Herminjard 5, 111).

32. Ibid. (Herminjard 5, 111).

33. Calvin, letter to Farel from Strasbourg to Neuchâtel, toward 11.9.1538 (Herminjard 5, 111).

34. Ibid. (Herminjard 5, 112).

35. Bucer, letter to Farel, toward 11.9.1538 (Herminjard 5, 114).

36. Ibid. (Herminjard 5, 114).

37. Calvin, letter to Geneva, 1.10.1538 (Herminjard 5, 121).

the divine vocation which, throughout some time, he has allied this to the Genevan community.[38] This way of seeing things is all the more interesting than Louis du Tillet, the youthful friend of Calvin, contests precisely the fact that God could call a pastoral ministry by any manner other than by a bishop; for du Tillet, it is not God who had made Calvin a minister in Geneva.[39] More broadly, one should compare the claim of being allied with Geneva by God in person with the fact that, later, Calvin cried out vehemently when his supporters wanted to call him back to Geneva.

Farel and Calvin tried to win over to their cause the influential Bern official Watteville.[40] In a letter to Farel in the first half of October 1538, Calvin deplored the fact that the Strasbourg pastors were negligent in introducing ecclesiastical discipline.[41] He added that he had, meanwhile, for the first time celebrated Holy Communion with his Strasbourg community.[42]

From Neuchâtel and Strasbourg, Farel and Calvin continued to take the trouble to strengthen their supporters in Geneva, and they took great trouble to present, fighting back, their own role as an intervention in favor of the teaching of the pure Gospel. That is how, on 5 January 1539, Calvin could write to his old student friend from Orleans, Antoine Pignet, who had become a pastor in the Geneva neighborhood, that his supporters thought it was criminal to celebrate Holy Communion with people who were corrupted or to receive it from the hands of bad pastors.[43] Calvin had tried to exert some influence by a letter addressed to Geneva, and he confirmed now that he had had to overcome some scruples in order to do this.[44] The requirement according to which a pastor must not mingle affairs of his old parish does not therefore date from yesterday! In writing to parishioners who, in any way, did not accept new pastors, Calvin contributed naturally to intensify the tensions which existed in Geneva.

Upon reading Calvin, he considered it his duty to tell the members of the Geneva community what was the correct way of taking part in the sacraments.[45] In his letter, he reproached the Genevan pastors for not even worrying that the parishioners only took part in Holy Communion after

---

38. Ibid. (Herminjard 5, 122).

39. On this subject see supra, n12.

40. Calvin, letter to Farel from Strasbourg to Neuchâtel, first half of October 1538 (Herminjard 5, 142, n7, and 143, n9).

41. Ibid. (Herminjard 5, 144).

42. Ibid. (Herminjard 5, 145).

43. Calvin, letter to Antoine Pignet of 5.1.1539 (Herminjard 5, 212).

44. Ibid. (Herminjard 5, 212).

45. Ibid. (Herminjard 5, 213).

carefully examining whether they could do so with a clear conscience. Also they did not distinguish, according to Calvin's criticism, the requirements which applied for a pastor of those applying to a simple parishioner.[46] In this letter of 5 January 1539 to Antoine Pigner, Calvin is happy to evoke, in one sentence, the fact that his parish of Strasbourg was in good condition.[47]

The influence of Farel on Calvin endures, even if the two men are separated. In a letter of 18 September 1538, Farel qualifies Geneva as Sodom. Now the wrongdoings that he reports dealt only with misappropriation of the fund for supporting the poor[48] or to attempts to have extra-marital relations.[49] Certainly, all these things can be condemned, but is it sufficient reason to speak of Geneva as a Sodom? Further on, Farel states that Marcourt, a pastor in Geneva, would have said that people like Saunier, the rector of the Gymnasium, should be killed, as better people could be found.[50] Let us compare this statement with the facts: Herminjard has established that the Council of the Two-Patrons had decreed, at the end of December, that Saunier and his family had to leave the town in three days. Saunier had a child aged one and a half; naturally, moving house in the depths of winter with such a young child held some dangers: the child could catch bronchitis and die.[51] But in no case can one state that the father of this young child must die! At least the research relating to a new edition of Calvin's correspondence do not bring to light new activities, it is Farel who, once more, gave a free run to his antipathy for the pastors established by the magistrate of Geneva, thus distorting the facts. Furthermore, Farel states that the pastor Morand publicly attacked the "Confession of Faith" formulated by Calvin, Corauld and himself.[52] He would have said that as much as this confession brought an obligation made to the bourgeoisie of Geneva to judge it, they had not been ordered by Christ and that they were deprived of a biblical foundation.[53] To Pastor Marcourt, Farel reproaches him for allowing the magistrate to rule on ecclesiastical affairs.[54] As for Morand, his submission to the magistrate would go so far that even if thirty parishioners

---

46. Ibid. (Herminjard 5, 213), "ministrum a private Ecclesiae membrum non distinguunt [. . .]."

47. Ibid. (Herminjard 5, 214), "Ecclesia notra utcumque se sustentat."

48. Farel, letter to Calvin of 18.9.1538 (Herminjard 5, 116).

49. Ibid. (Herminjard 5, 116).

50. Ibid. (Herminjard 5, 116).

51. See Herminjard 5, 216 and n4 of 215.

52. Cf. Herminjard 5, 216–17, n6.

53. Farel, letter to Calvin of 15.1.1539 (Herminjard 5, 216).

54. Ibid. (Herminjard 5, 217); he would not even be allowed to visit his own family without the permission of the magistrate.

accused him of fornication, he would not dare to admonish them without beforehand having asked permission from the magistrate! Pastor Henri de la Mare, himself, did not want the Bible to be in the vernacular language: without that, even the women could criticize the pastors.[55] And that saying that the fact that people qualify the mass as holy?! In short, the newly nominated pastors destroy everything that Farel and Calvin have built up, and they tolerate scorning of the Word of God. Also Farel concluded that the pastors of Geneva are more furious than the magistrate.

According to the research carried out by Herminjard, at Christmas of the year 1538 some parishioners refused to receive Holy Communion from the hands of the pastors that the magistrate had recently nominated. Among these people, those who were not from the Genevan bourgeoisie had to leave the town in ten days. As in the case of the rector Saunier, one can judge that sending people into exile at the end of the month of December was extremely harsh. But, on the other hand, one understands that the government of Geneva had not wanted to tolerate the fact that, from Neuchatel and Strasbourg, Farel and Calvin, the pastors whom he had expelled, tried to depict their successors as people from whom one did not have the right to receive Holy Communion.

In the second half of the month of August 1539, Calvin wrote to Farel that Capiton had pressed him, against his will, to operate a public position in Strasbourg: every day, he taught or preached. This statement can surprise one: in fact, if Calvin was receiving a deacon's salary, as we have described it above, the Strasbourgians could expect, in return, his accomplishing a certain public position, even if, according to the contemporary criteria, it was asking a great deal of him to demand a lesson or a sermon every day.

On 5 February 1539, in a letter to Calvin, Farel describes as "pious (pii)" the people who are favorable to both of them. In doing so, he denies the supporters of the Genevan pastors the fact of their also being pious. Farel expresses the wish that Calvin and himself should join a synod of Swiss churches, which would relieve them from reproaches formulated upon meeting them.[56] In Geneva, he continued to have people who wanted Calvin again as their pastor, even more than Farel at the same time.[57]

On 12 March 1539, they came at last to sign an agreement between Calvin and Farel on the one hand and the new pastors of Geneva on the other hand.[58] The merit of this agreement goes back to the pastors of Stras-

---

55. Ibid. (Herminjard 5, 217).
56. Farel, letter to Calvin of 5.2.1539 (Herminjard 5, 234).
57. Calvin, letter to Farel of 16.3.1639 (Herminjard 5, 252).
58. Reconciliation of the Genevan pastors with Farel, Calvin and their supporters,

bourg and Basel. They had asked Pierre Kunz, the main pastor of Bern, to bring about the reconciliation: it was a question of Kunz, with whom Calvin thought that he could never get along![59] The pastors of the Pays de Vaud wanted, also, to be reconciled with the new pastors of Geneva.[60]

On 16 March 1539, Calvin went to Frankfurt: he wanted to meet Philippe Melanchthon at the religious colloquium which was taking place, and to intervene on behalf of the Protestants in France, who were persecuted. This attitude was natural and understandable, anyone who dreamt of the needs of his little community of French-speaking refugees in Strasbourg would wonder who, in Calvin's absence, preached, baptized, buried and celebrated Holy Communion in French.

On 18 March 1539, the letter from Cardinal Jacques Sadolet invited the Genevans to come back into the bosom of the Roman Catholic Church. Originally from Modena, Sadolet was sixty-one years old at the time, and that meant that he had been the Bishop of Carpentras for twenty-two years. He was a top-class humanist and a respected theologian. Four years earlier, an edition of his works had appeared in Lyon. Sadolet was also in a position to combat the Protestants by a commentary on the Epistle to the Romans. In the letter which accompanies his epistle, he declares already that he wishes to lead the Genevans back toward "the one and only sense that the Catholic Church keeps."[61] According to Sadolet, his envoy Jean Durandus had to complement, in his own words, what the Cardinal had to say to the Genevans. In his letter, he wrote particularly that faith alone is not enough: one must add, as a Christian, the will to do what is pleasing to God.[62]

On 23 May, the magistrate of Bern wrote to the one in Geneva that he had received the letter from Sadolet and ordered some of the pastors to draft a detailed reply. In the deeds of the city of Bern, it is noted, on 24 May, that Pierre Kunz asked the magistrate to appoint Calvin to write this reply.[63] In doing so, Kunz strongly emphasized Calvin's theological capabilities: not only the pastors of Geneva, but even those of Bern considered themselves incapable of replying to Sadolet on the required theological level. Thus therefore, the light of Calvin, the exile, shone again with all its sparkle.

Morges, 12.3. 1539 (Herminjard 5, 243–46).

59. I am basing myself here on the annotation in the Herminjard edition.
60. Calvin, letter to Farel of 16.3.1539 (Herminjard 5, 252).
61. Sadolet, accompanying letter (Herminjard 5, 261).
62. Sadolet, letter to Farel of 16.3.1539 (Herminjard 5, 261).
63. F. Herminjard 5, 322, n3.

2. Correspondence

Calvin, the Lawyer for the Huguenots at the Time of the Empire Colloquia

In Strasbourg, Calvin remained closely connected to France, his country, as he remained throughout his life, in Geneva. He intervened with all his weight in favor of supporters of the evangelical doctrine in France. For some years, a critical edition appeared of the deeds of the religious colloquia of the Empire. In 2004, one of my pupils, Maarten Stolk, maintained a thesis on Calvin's role at the time of these colloquia.[64]

From Strasbourg, Calvin took part in the Frankfurt negotiations (1539), at the religious colloquium of Haguenau (1540), at the religious colloquium of Worms (1540–1541) and at the Diet of Ratisbon (1541). Naturally, the fact that he did not master German considerably restricted his capacity to take part in the debates. Certainly, he conversed in Latin with the other theologians and the scholars; but all the politicians present had no Latin.

He went from Frankfurt to Hagenau on his own initiative: he wanted to meet Melanchthon and talk about the position of the persecuted Huguenots On the other hand, the town of Strasbourg sent him officially to Worms and to Ratisbon.[65] He especially lambasted the papal legates, then the main Catholic theologians, Eck and Cocklaeus, and finally Prince Henry of Brunswick and the Dukes of Bavaria. He particularly waited for the Palatine Elector, the Elector Prince and Archbishop of Cologne and the Duke of Cleves.

In a letter to Farel, which he wrote on returning from Frankfurt, he brought back the wish, expressed by the emperor, to be able to count on support for the Protestant states against the Turks. It is for this reason that the Protestant and Catholic delegates had to have a discussion on a reformation of the Church of Germany.[66]

In Haguenau, Calvin and the other members of the Strasbourgian delegation took the trouble to, on behalf of the German Protestants, intervene with the King of France in favor of persecuted co-religionists.[67] On 19 May 1540, he wrote to Viret: "If the Lord does not offer us something new, it only remains to us to uphold our unfortunate brothers by our prayers and our encouragements."[68]

---

64. J. M. Solk, *Johannes Calvijn en de godsdienstgesprekken* (Kampen, 2004).

65. Cf. ibid., 320.

66. Cf. ibid., 127, n62. Stock refers to Calvin's letter to Calvin of 16.3.1539 (Herminjard 5, 255).

67. Cf. Stikj (see n63), 176.

68. Calvin, letter to Viret of 19.5.1540 (Herminjard 6, 227). On this subject see

On 1 January 1541, Calvin wrote a poem in which he reproached the discussions in the religious colloquium of Worms for being fruitless. Melanchthon and Jean Sturm also wrote similar poems. In his poem, Calvin makes fun of Eck, with his face still red from the win that he had abused the night before, forced to run behind the triumphal wagon of Christ; as for Cochlaeus, he mocks his impotence.[69] But in reality, the Worms debates did not turn out to be so glorious for the evangelicals.

Calvin Accepts Being Recalled to Geneva

In my presentation of Calvin's correspondence throughout his stay in Strasbourg, I am now taking a great leap, which leads me to his return to Geneva. In a letter of 20 July 1541, Pierre Toussain pressed Calvin to return to Geneva.[70] On 20 August 1541, the magistrate of Geneva wrote to the one in Strasbourg that he hoped that Calvin would shortly return. In his letter, he said the gain that he expected from this return would be the same for the Genevan church as the gain for the whole Church![71] He asked Strasbourg to return Calvin to his old flock, promising compensation.

Farel upheld the request from the magistrate of Geneva. In a letter to Calvin of 25 August 1541, he posed a rhetorical question to his friend: was he waiting, to come back to Geneva, for the stones to cry out?[72] Even his adversaries were constrained to recognize that it was God in person who was calling him back to Geneva and that he had to obey this call if he did not want to resist God himself.[73] For Farel, Viret could not any longer bear the responsibility which weighed on him in Geneva: Calvin had to come to his aid; Calvin was outraging God if he did not hurry to come back to Geneva.[74]

Upon reading his letter of 1 September 1541, one sees that the magistrate of Strasbourg had not been particularly impressed by the recent letter from Geneva. Certainly, the Strasbourgians had understood well the argument of their correspondents, according to which it was necessary, for

---

Stolk, 178.

69. On this subject see Stolk, 228, n173 and n174.

70. Pierre Toussain, letter to Calvin from Strasbourg to Montbeliard, 20.7.1541 (Herminjard 7, 192).

71. Magistrate of Geneva, letter to the magistrate of Strasbourg, 20.8.1541 (Herminjard 7, 222).

72. Farel, letter to Calvin of 25.8.1541 (Herminjard 7, 223).

73. Farel, ibid. (Herminjard 7, 223).

74. Farel, ibid. (Herminjard 7, 225).

2. CORRESPONDENCE

the good of the whole Church, for Calvin to return to Geneva.[75] But for the Strasbourgians, the good of the Church required more that he should stay in their town.[76] In fact, they continued, very few people are capable of grasping the interests of the whole Church and defending its doctrine in writing.[77] They concluded also that Calvin should stay in Strasbourg and that somebody else should be found who was ready to work in Geneva. But, since Calvin assured them that his conscience was pressing him to go back to Geneva in order to examiner there, where God wanted him to serve him, the Strasbourgians stated that they were ready to let him go. However the Genevans had to send him back as soon as possible, as he could give more services to the Strasbourg church than to that in Geneva.[78] In a letter of the same day to the magistrate of Geneva, the Strasbourg pastors emphasized that the Senators' wish was that, once the Reformer had finished his task, Geneva could send Calvin back to Strasbourg.[79]

On the same date as these two letters, 1 September 1541, Calvin went on his way to Geneva. No doubt he went first of all to Neuchatel, where, once more, Farel was undergoing the worst difficulties. In a letter of 7 September 1541, Calvin tried to explain to the magistrate of Geneva why he had felt obliged to intervene in Neuchatel in Farel's favor, which had prevented him from taking the shortest route.[80] However, Geneva sent a rider to look for him: what a contrast with his expulsion, three years before! He sent to Bern letters from Strasbourg and Basel, which warmly recommended him.[81] But the Bernians had enough experience of his extremely restive attitude; that is why the magistrate of Bern refrained from giving him such positive recommendations as Strasbourg and Basel expected. On 16 September 1541, Calvin reported to Farel that he had given the magistrate of Geneva his wish to be able to introduce an ecclesiastical decree.[82] He continued, asking for Farel to adapt as much as possible to his parishioners, without at the same time offending the duties of his work.[83]

---

75. Magistrate of Strasbourg, letter to the magistrate of Geneva of 1.9.1541 (Herminjard 7, 227–28).

76. Ibid. (Herminjard 7, 228).

77. Ibid. (Herminjard 7, 229).

78. Ibid. (Herminjard 7, 230).

79. Pastors of Strasbourg, letter to the magistrate of Geneva of 1.9.1541 (Herminjard 7, 231).

80. Calvin, letter to the magistrate of Geneva of 7.9. 1541 (Herminjard 7, 239–40).

81. Calvin, letter to Farel of 10.9.1541 (Herminjard 7, 242, with n4 of 242–43).

82. Calvin, letter to Farel of 16.9.1541 (Herminjard 7, 249).

83. Ibid. (Herminjard 7, 250).

Calvin's Strasbourgian Years: A Time of Development

Anyone who considers Calvin from a great distance will no doubt be mainly tempted to see in him the masterly Instiutio of 1559, the organizer of the Genevan church, the preacher, the untiring letter-writer, counselor, debater and consoler. He would underestimate the path that Calvin had to follow in order to reach this place. On the other hand, whoever approaches the future Reformer by reading his first letters one after the other, attentively, in order to prepare an edition for other researchers, would be rather surprised by the process of development which he had to undergo in order to become the mature personality which is familiar to most of his admirers. While recognizing the genial talents of Calvin, which are expressed in his mastery of thought and language, one may state that, humanly, in his youth, Calvin did not come from a simple beginning.

Also the fact that Calvin could live and work in Strasbourg between 1538 and 1541 was a blessing for him: it is during these years that, in particular under the influence of Martin Bucer, he became the Reformer who, afterwards and at the time of his second stay in Geneva, he was able to achieve the success that we know.

(Translated from German by Matthieu Arnold)

3. Calvin the Poet

The Strasbourg Psalter of 1539

Philippe François[1]

WHEN IN SEPTEMBER 1538, John Calvin arrived in Strasbourg from Geneva to take responsibility for, upon the appeal of the Reformer Martin Bucer, the community of French refugees, he was, as pastor of the parish, confronted straightaway with the problem of establishing a liturgy for the services in the French language. Thus there was put into production the edition of a psalter, entitled *Aulcuns psaulmes et cantiques mys en chant*. It comprises nineteen versified paraphrases of psalms called "of David," as well as Simeon's song, the Ten Commandments and the Creed. No author's name is indicated: the work, published in Strasbourg in 1539, really by the publisher Johannes Knobloch the Young, is anonymous.[2] Thirteen of these psalms are from the hand of Clement Marot;[3] the six others are attributed to Calvin.[4]

Long considered as lost, the only copy at present known of the collection is found in the *Bayerische Staatsbibliothek* in Munich. This volume was the subject of at least four reissues: David Deletra[5] (1919), Richard Runciman Terry[6] (1932), Hendrik Hasper[7] and Gert-Jan Buitink[8] (2003).

1. Doctor in theology, member of GRENEP.
2. Pierre Pidoux, *The Huguenot Psalter of the XVIth Century*, vol. 2 (Basel, 1962), 3.
3. Psalms 1, 2, 3, 15, 19, 32, 51, 103, 114, 115, 140, 137 and 143.
4. Psalms 25, 36, 46, 91, 113 and 138.
5. David Deletra, *Aulcuns psaulmes et cantiques mys en chant, a Strasbourg 1539*, photographic reprint, Geneva, 1919.
6. Richard Runciman Terry, *Calvin's First Psalter (1539)*, London, 1932.
7. Hendrick Hasper, *Calvijn beginsel voor den zang in den Eredienst I* (The Hague, 1955).
8. *Aulcuns psaulmes et cantiques mys en chant* (Brasschaat: Boekmakerij Gert-Jan Buitink, 2003). This edition is presented in the form of a facsimile, accompanied by an introduction volume written by Jan R. Luth, presented in three languages, English, German and French (French translation: Edith Weber, 65-94, who is especially interested in the relationship between this first psalter and the liturgy of the French parish of Strasbourg). I wish to express my gratitude to M. Robert Weeda, who has allowed me

Among recent works on the 1539 Psalter, it is suitable to quote the study entitled "Marot and Calvin: singing psalms," given by Olivier Millet at the colloquium organized in Cahors in 1996, on the occasion of the five hundredth anniversary of Clement Marot's[9] birth. The first paragraphs of this important contribution to the study of Protestant poetry are dedicated to the Strasbourg psalter; they comprise for our eyes a reference synthesis, on which we are greatly dependent for this essay. Finally, we would like to testify to our debt to Gerard Defaux, a specialist in Marot's work, and especially to his work *Cinquante psaumes de David mis en francois selon la vérité hébraique*. His portrait[10] of the evangelical theologian contrasts singularly with the accusation of "elegant banter" thrown at him in 1674 by Nicolas Boileaux-Despreaux in his *Art Poétique*. Gerard Defaux shows how, during the last fifteen years of his existence, Marot is transformed, passing from the official status of king's poet to that, self-proclaimed, of poet "chosen by God."

Our interest went toward the genesis of the *Aulcuns psaulmes et cantiques mys en chant*, of which Jan Luth remarks, rightly, that the historical details are "obscure."[11] But the meeting in a single work of a theologian and a poet, both exceptional, surely deserves the attention of lovers of French Protestant poetry, of which the 1539 Strasbourg psalter is, chronologically, the first great work.

Why Was Marot Interested in the Psalms?

The first hypothesis, very general, is formulated synthetically by Jan Luth, for whom Marot was "truly" allowed to be guided by the general interest of the Humanists of his time for the translations of the Psalms.[12] This hypothesis is hardly questionable. There is in fact an extremely favorable context with, between 1500 and 1535, a great many publications in Latin or in French relating to the psalms, would it not be that the works of Jacques

---

to obtain a copy of this facsimile.

9. Olivier Millet "Marot and Calvin: Singing Psalms," in *Clement Marot "Prince of the French Poets" 1496-1996*, deeds of the international colloquium of Cahors in Quercy, 1996 (Paris: Honore Champion, 1997), 463-76.

10. Gerard Defaux, "Clement Marot et la traduction des psaumes: du poète de roi au poète de Dieu," in Clement Marot, *Cinquante psaumes de David en françoy selon la vérité hébraique*, introduction, variantes et notes par Gerard Defaux (Paris: Honore Champion, 1995), 5-69.

11. Jan Luth, *op. cit.* (see n70) 69.

12. Ibid., 69.

3. CALVIN THE POET

Lefèvre of Etaples or of Martin Bucer who will be such working instruments for the future translator poets.

But this single explanation is not sufficient. Olivier Millet crossed an extra bridge by very opportunely recalling the influence of the king's sister, Marguerite de Navarre: How did Marot obtain the idea of composing a French paraphrase of the psalms? The answer from Plattard (1912) is that doubtless the idea came from Marguerite de Navarre and from her circle. A more exact context about the essential size of these paraphrases, their strophic form which makes them into song, is indicated by Lenselink (1969); it is a question of Marguerite's association with Strasbourg, where for the first time liturgical singing appeared, by the assembly in unison, of psalms versified into German with a melody which was original if possible in each case, singing which is characteristic of the Strasbourg reformation, to which the French evangelist refugees in Strasbourg, the friends of Marguerite of Navarre, were very sensitive. Two Strasbourgian letters from Gerard Roussel, dated December 1525, bear witness of this enthusiastic discovery of community singing of versified psalms in the vernacular language.[13] It is a question therefore of a sort of requirement, even an order, on behalf of the king's sister. This same hypothesis is developed at length by Gerard Defaux, for whom one may "formulate, totally safely, the hypothesis that it was Marguerite who herself very quickly took the initiative to suggest to Marot the idea to put this into action."[14]

Analyzing one portion of the Augereau edition of the *Miroir de l'ame pécheresse*, a work of Marguerite de Navarre of 1533, in which an edition of Psalm 6 translated by Marot appears, on the other hand Marot's letter sent from Venice *a la reyne de Navarre* in 1536, Defaux comes to the fairly radical conclusion that it is from 1527, therefore well before Calvin, that "Briconnet, Marguerite and Marot were determined to contribute to the evangelization of the kingdom, that they have already defined their strategy and their means of action, and that among these there already appears quite certainly, parallel to the works of Lefèvre and Erasmus, the publication of the French translation of the Psalter into verse."[15]

There we would have had a sort of plot theory which would have failed at the time of the affair of the Warnings.

A third element must be quoted: it is about the personal circle that would have taken certain translations of Marot. Still according to Gerard Defaux: "However one notices very quickly, in this corpus of the 'Thirty first

---

13. Olivier Millet, *op. cit.* (see n8), 463–64.
14. Gerard Defaux, *op. cit.* (see n9), 18.
15. Ibid., 19.

psalms,' which in didactism at first sight seems irreproachable, psalms which are a great deal less innocent, psalms that Marot has perhaps translated less for the consolation of other people than for his own."[16] And Defaux cites as an example Psalms 5, 6, 10, 11 and 14. And he continues: "All these translations have unquestionably a strong personal colouring. They have not any evidence been placed in a building to instruct or edify the faithful, in order to make them discover and make them admire the power of God, but rather to allow Marot to express his own feelings and to publicly settle his accounts which all the wicked people who are persecuting him."[17]

One is somewhat amazed by this opposition between instruction/ edification, on the one hand, and personal/autobiographical considerations on the other hand. A contemporary understanding of the idea of an author suggests that the one who deserves the title of author is the one who undertakes personal work in a system of constraint or control.[18] The opposition, led in Defaux's presentation, is not going well. Besides, the psalm considered as the first one which was composed by Marot in Psalm 6, with strong personal coloring: the hypothesis which is generally accepted is that Marot would have composed it after a serious illness.[19]

Why Was Calvin Interested in the Psalms?

Just like Marot, it is likely that Calvin, who had an intellectual training of the humanist kind, bathed in this intellectual climate of research around the psalms. But there is nothing but books: in his wanderings in the years 1535 to 1536, Calvin was really in direct touch with the singing of psalms in one or other German-speaking town or another, for example Basel in 1535, or Strasbourg in 1536. And, like Rousssel in 1525, he must have been favorably impressed by it to the point when in January 1537, in Geneva, he planned to introduce psalm-singing in the liturgy: "On 16 January 1537,

---

16. Ibid., 61

17. Ibid., 62.

18. Coming out of cinematographic criticism, this famous formula describes the author within the framework of the "authors' policy" initiated by the filmmaker François Truffaut at the end of the fifties. See Serge Daney, *Le Salaire du zappeur* (Paris: Ramsey, 1988), 251.

19. This hypothesis is based on the date of the illness (plague) contracted by Marot in 1531, the probable date of the text (around 1530) and the psalm's argument: "David who is ill in extremity, is afraid of death: he wishes, before he dies, to glorify the Name of God: then suddenly he rejoices in his convalescence, and from the shame of those who were waiting for his death" (Clement Marot, *Cinquante psaumes de David* [see n9], 109).

3. Calvin the Poet

in the Articles concerning the organization of the Church and worship in Geneva, proposed to the ministers, Calvin with Guillaume Farel stated his wish to sing Psalms in worship. Calvin based his wish on the argument that Psalms encouraged the building of the Church and were public prayers. By singing them, men pray to God and sing his praises, so their hearts can be touched. By singing Psalms, the faithful are encouraged to prayer, to praise and to gratitude. The model which was followed in this case, was that of the old Church and the witness of the Apostle Paul who, in his Epistle to the Colossians (3, 16) invites them to "sing with the heart and the mouth." Calvin finds the prayers of the believers, in his time, were shamefully cold. On the other hand, the Psalms lift the hearts toward God and place men in a position to announce the glory of his name.[20] But Calvin and Farel's wish will remain a dead letter because it is from the first stay in Geneva.

In 1538, Calvin arrived in Alsace at the time of the publication of the complete psalter in German in Strasbourg.[21] He often visits Martin Bucer, who is one of the great specialists in the Old Testament psalms. Two months after the beginning of his public ministry, people sang psalms in the French community. There are few details on the way in which things are put together if it is not that, in December 1538, Calvin wrote that he rhymed Psalms 25 and 46 and that the others followed.[22] There is a chronological summary of the facts which clearly indicates that the idea of the psalms in French at the time of worship does not come up from the time of Calvin's Strasbourgian period, but it goes back at least to the 1525 years, when friends of Marguerite de Navarre bore witness to the interest in singing psalms in the vernacular language: there is therefore no reason to be surprised at the speed with which the psalms were introduced into the French liturgy in Strasbourg.

Let us come then to an important point which is the Calvinian idea of the way to use the psalms of the Old Testament. In his *Preface to the commentary on the Psaulmes* (1557), Calvin wrote: "I have been used to calling this book an anatomy of all the parts of the soul, because there is no affection of man which is not represented here as in a mirror. Even, to express it better, the Holy Spirit is there as a living portrait of all the pains, sadnesses, fears, doubts, hopes, worries, perplexities, even up to confused emotions by which the minds of men are used to be moved."[23]

---

20. Jan Luth, *op. cit.* (n7), 74-75.

21. *Psalter mit aller Kirchenubung die man bey der christlichen Gemein zu Strasburg und anderswa pflagt zu singen* (Kopfel, 1539).

22. "*Ita Psalmi duo, 46, et 25, prima sunt mea tyrocinia; alios postea attexui*" (letter of 29 December 1538, published by Herminjard, vol. 5, 446, no. 762a; quoted by Pierre Pdoux, *op. cit.*, n1, vol. 2, 2).

23. Quoted by Véronique, "La lyre protestante: Calvin et la réforme poétique en

This passage bears witness to the influence that the psalms had on the spirituality of the French Reformer. Upon reading these lines, as well as the following ones, one understands better the reasons which drove Calvin to undertake, then accompany, up to the end of it, this gigantic task of rhyming paraphrase for the faithful.

"[. . .] it has been a great consolation to conform to the example of such an excellent person [David]. And even this recognition and experience have served me a great deal in understanding the Psalms, so that I may find something too new as if I were in a strange land. And in fact, the readers (as I think) acknowledge that in declaring the internal affections both of David as well as others, I am talking about this as if they were things with which I am familiar.[24] One can see very well here, that the opposition, suggested by Defaux about Marot, between didacticism and autobiography does not correspond with the Calvinian use of reading the psalms, at least as he expresses it in 1557. Otherwise, the natural autobiographical inclination of Marot seems to agree with the manner of approaching the psalms which is the Reformer's own way.

Calvin the Poet?

At the beginning of the twentieth century, the historian of Yale University Williston Walker wrote, about Calvin's translations:

> If these compositions were not from a high poetic inspiration, they were at least worthy, clear and not commonplace. He himself believed he was to some extent gifted in poetry and in his youth, like many others, wrote some poems. But when other versions of the psalter appeared, Calvin's critical sense led him to substitute, more and more, compositions which were more inspired by Marot than his own[25]

That is an opinion which one can take up, practically as a whole, a century later. On his interest in poetry, the Reformer has expressed in a letter to Conrad Hubert of 19 May 1557:

> By nature, I was rather drawn to poetry but I said good-bye to it, and for twenty-five years I have written nothing, if it were not that, in Worms [in 1541], upon the example of Philippe

---

France," *Revue de l'histoire des religions* 226 (2009), 64.
   24. Veronique Ferrer, ibid., 65.
   25. Williston Walker, *Jean Calvin: The Man and the Work* (Geneva, 1909), 249.

3. CALVIN THE POET

[Melanchthon] and Jean Sturm, I was led to write this poem that you read, as an amusement.[26]

For twenty-five years means the year 1532, that is just before the theoretical date of his conversion. From this quotation, one can draw two conclusions: the first is that Calvin was interested in poetry in his youth, which in the sixteenth century must have been common among intellectuals; the second is that it was not a deep vocation, at least as an author. One can even go so far as to say that his reputation as a poet must have been nonexistent, as in witness, indirectly, the violent argument between Ronsard and the Protestant poets, in the 1560s,[27] where the designated enemy was well and truly Theodore de Beze, the only enemy that Ronsard considered as an equal.

But the main point about Calvin and poetry, is what Walker calls "the critical sense" of the Reformer. One does not manage such a monumental work as the Psalter without a well-developed critical sense. One must here say a word on a particular episode in the life of the Reformer, that is his stay in Ferrara in April–July 1536, just after the appearance of the first Latin edition of the *Institution*. Not a great deal is known about what happened during these few weeks with the Duchess Renee of France, the daughter of Louis XII, cousin of Francis I and Marguerite de Navarre, if it is not that Clement Marot had found refuge in Ferrara and was staying there at the same time. From which the question arises about the meeting of the two men, the young theologian who was the author of a first work under Lutheran influence and the great poet in flight, accused of "Lutherism" by his Parisian enemies. I know that historians are disinclined to become engaged when the material indexes are missing, but it would all the same be surprising if the meeting had not taken place, that Marot and Calvin missed each other, in such a small place. If the meeting did happen, one must imagine that an exchange must have taken place, between the forty-year-old poet whose theological consistency was proved by Defaux, and the young theologian of twenty-seven years of whom it is known, if he did not like putting himself forward, he would not hesitate, given the opportunity, to advise even to pick up authors who were more experienced than himself, in front of Bucer. If one accepts that the author of the *Institution* and the translator of the Psalms talked to each other face to face, it is unimaginable that the discussion did not include the current situation of one another's research. The question

---

26. "*Ad poeticen natura satis eram propensus: sed ea valere iussa, ab annis vinginti quinque nihil composui, nisi quod Wormaciae exemplo Philippi et Sturmii adductus sum, ut Carmen illud quod legisti per lusum scriberem.*" (CO XVI, no. 2632, col. 488).

27. See Matthieu Arnold, "Your theology . . . is all rancid, stinking, and musty: Ronsard's complaints against Luther and the Reformation," *Positions Lutheriennes* 56 (2008) 95–113.

that Olivier Millet puts, is to discover how Marot's psalms were found in the Strasbourg psalter and even anyone wanting to find out if Calvin knew who was the author of these thirteen psalms would discover a clear answer: Calvin would have left Ferrara with a copy of Marot's psalms.

Finally, one last question: why did Calvin withdraw these translations from the later editions of the Psalter? Walker's hypothesis about the critical sense, which was self-critical, of the Reformer is doubtless the true one. One can be convinced by taking for example Psalm 25, translated by Calvin for the Strasbourg Psalter of 1539, and by Marot, in Geneva, in 1541. One can therefore consider that Marot's translation is a correction of Calvin's version. These two texts are profoundly different. It is not a question of what, in German, would be called a "cosmetic correction." Another text was proposed by Marot: his version is shorter, more concise, nineteen quatrains instead of twenty-three; Marot's verses are seven feet, Calvin's eight.

It goes without saying that the poetical technique of the experienced Marot was very superior to that of Calvin the beginner, as the first verses show:

> Calvin (Ps 25, stanza 1 and 2)
>
> To you Lord I shall lift
> My soul to receive help:
> Do not allow, as a lost one that.
> I should be confused from my hope.
> Do not allow my enemies
> To make fun of me.
> Seeing me in great distress
> Put into a long oppression.
>
> Marot
>
> To you, my God, my heart goes up,
> In you I place my hope,
> Prevent me from falling into shame,
> In the hands of my enemies

But some of Calvin's enemies, by example 5 and 10, by their clarity and their theological correctness do not appear inferior to the equivalent quatrains in Marot:

Calvin (Ps 25, stanza 5)

Guide me in the light
Of your holiest instruction.
My heart is stayed in thee,
Oh god of my salvation.

Marot

May I walk in the path
Of your open truth,
As God of mine aid
Where I wait every day.

Calvin (Ps 25, stanza 10)

Our God totally holds
Compassion and truth,
For all those who loyally
Keep His law and Testament.

Marot

Goodness, safety, remembrance,
These are the paths of God,
To those who keep
His covenants faithfully.

Generally, if these translations had to be qualified, we would be tempted to see the theological precision in Calvin the teacher at the price of an obvious stiffness in expression while, for the poet Marot, the fluidity and warmth of his style allow the reader not so much to be taught as, literally to give him the word of God.

Conclusion

Aucuns psaulmes et cantiques mys en chant announces, from 1539, the Huguenot Psalter which, as regards translation, will be finished in 1562, at the dawn of the wars of religion. The final work, versified paraphrases of the one hundred and fifty psalms of the Old Testament, bears the signatures of Clement Marot, for forty-nine psalms, and of Théodore de Bèze, required by Calvin after Marot's death in 1544, for the remaining hundred and one psalms. Calvin, sole mastermind of the project, did not visibly consider it was useful to keep his own translations.

One could say of Calvin as a translator that he was a sort of complementary poet. As for the Reformer, the author who was best placed to undertake this work is Clement Marot. If he had to face this difficult exercise, it is after what could be called a liturgical emergency. It is our hypothesis that the various psalms of Marot (for "worldly" use) that he had, perhaps from Ferrara, would not cover all the liturgical requirements of the first Protestant assemblies.

But as Marot's works advanced, Calvin naturally effaced himself before Marot, as he was one of the rare people, in the field of the Reformation, who as a theologian,[28] in spite of his flamboyant lifestyle, was the opposite of his own. One can see there a further manifestation of the literary genius of Calvin, the great prose-writer, great critic, and great editor.

Annex

Psalm 25 versified by Calvin and by Marot

Calvin, Psalm XXV (1539)

To you Lord I shall lift

My soul to receive help:

Do not allow, as a lost one

I should be confused from my hope.

Do not allow my enemies

To make fun of me.

Seeing me in great distress

Put into a long oppression.

Thus in safety I shall never

Be refused by you,

---

28. In the opposite of Théodore de Bèze, who while underlining Marot's poetic genius, states that the latter did not know any languages, or sciences (*Les vrais portraits des homes illustres* [1581 ed.], 162). In his "Elements de bibliographie chronologique et critique" relating to paraphrases of the psalms by Marot, Gerard Defaux shows that, apart from an exception (e.g., Pierre Bayle), the Protestants had an ambivalent opinion as to the quality of the poet's work.

3. Calvin the Poet

Whoever holds your truth:

But the sinful one will be confused.

Marot, Psalm XXV (1541)

To you, my God, my heart goes up,

In you I have put my trust.

Let me not fall into shame,

In the hands of my enemies.

They shall even have no shame

Who rely upon you,

But those who provoke them

Severely without cause.

4. Church Music

Calvin and the Church Music in Strasbourg

Robert Weeda[1]

The Senate of Strasbourg having opened a church in the year M.D.XXXVIII for the French-speaking faithful poor, fugitives on account of the true Religion [. . .], John Calvin was responsible for preaching there from the beginning.[2]

CALVIN'S DEAREST WISH WAS to join the parishioners there by liturgical singing, which is why he began his project for a collection of Psalms.

Sent on 9 November from Constance, a letter from Jean Zwick to Heinrich Bullinger in Zurich tells is that the matter is in hand:

> Gallis Argentorati ecclesia data est, in qua a Calvino quarter in septimana canciones audiunt, sed et coenam agunt et psalmos sua lingua canunt.[3]

Hardly two months after Calvin's arrival, singing has therefore already found its place in the "French church," long before the publication of the *Aucuns psaulmes et cantiques mys en chant!*[4]

On 29 December 1538, Calvin sent a letter to Guillaume Farel in Neuchatel: he reminds him that he

---

1. Choirmaster, musicologist.

2. Jean Crespin, *Histoire des Martyrs persecutez et mis a mort pour la vérité de l'Evangile, depuis le temps des apôtres jusques à présent* (Geneva: Pierre Aubert, 1619), vol. 1, book 3, 12.

3. "A French church was created in Strasbourg where Calvin preached four times a week, where Holy Communion is celebrated and where psalms are sung" (Herminjard 5, no. 751, n20).

4. A facsimile edition was published by Boekmakerij Gert-Jan Buitink, Brasschat (Belgium), 2003; we have taken out the two psalms illustrating our text.

has sent psalms so that they may be sung in your church.⁵ We have decided to publish them shortly. As I very much liked the German melody [of the psalms], I was obliged to try what I valued in poetic art.⁶ Thus, the two psalms 46 and 25 are my first attempt; the others will follow.⁷

The Melodica Germanica

In the opposite of the Gregorian chant, the first German melodies of the Reformation are printed in gothic notes (closed), but with a special shape: derived from ornamentations, the signs are based on the diamond-shaped note (GRAPHIC) and are distinguished by fairly large features. During the fourteenth century, these signs were thickened by taking the shape described by the name of "notes in iron horse nails (*Hufnagel-Rossnegelschrift*)."

From the fifteenth century, it is stated that a development toward a measured notation, which today allows the melodies noted in this way to be transcribed with a fairly precise time. It is exactly this notation that is found in the Strasbourg collections, as also in a large part of Germany.

Here is a view of the shapes of notes used in these collections and their values in modern notation:⁸

The first German collections in Strasbourg already contain ten psalms composed by the cantor of the cathedral Matthias Greiter (v. 1490 to 1550) and by Wolfgang Dachstein (v. 1487 to 1553), the organist in the Saint-Thomas Church first of all and later at the cathedral: Dachstein wrote his three melodic versions toward 1525, while Greiter published his seven melodies between 1524 and 1527.

Martin Bucer exerted a great influence on Calvin: it is described on his writings,⁹ on the design of a liturgy for "the French Church," as on the

---

5. This wish of Calvin's was only carried out with great difficulty; see Robert Weeda, "Tensions between Music and Church in Neuchâtel in Farel's Time," in Jean-Daniel Morerod et al. (eds.), *Cinque siècles d'histoire religieuse neuchâteloise: Approches d'une tradition protestante* (Neuchatel, 2009), 181–213.

6. See article by Philippe François, 58–65 (53–65).

7. Hermlnjard 5, no. 762, 451–52.

8. According to Théodore Gerold, *The oldest melodies of the Strasbourg protestant Church and their authors* (Paris, 1928), 43–45.

9. This influence is also verified in the 1539 version of the *Institutio*. See Stephen Buckwalter's article, 123–34. In his catalogue of the exhibition *When Strasbourg Welcomed Calvin 1538 to 1541* (Strasbourg: National and University Library / Strasbourg University Press), Matthieu Arnold refers to the pages which are dedicated to this aspect of authors Willem van't Spijker, Jean Cadier and Herman J. Selderhuis. See esp. his

importance of singing psalms. Doubtless it is also Bucer who led Calvin to the cathedral in order to discover these German psalms[10] whose influence will be felt in the design of the music of the six psalms from his pen in his 1539 collection, and very specially his Psalms 25 and 46 (Report on the melodies in *Aulcuns Psaulmes et cantiques mys en chant*).

Calvin chose the melody of Psalm 125 "*Nun welche hye ir hoffnung gar*" by Matthias Greiter (Strasbourg 1526) for his "Psalm XXV" the original of which is shown opposite.

As for "Psalm XLVI," his melody comes from Psalm 15, *O herr wurt wonunge han*, by Wolfgang Dachstein (Strasbourg 1525). As shown by the two examples given below, the transcription of the German melody[11] toward that of the 1539 Psalter underwent a slight alteration: at the beginning—on the text "Our God to us"—"Psalm XLVI" is in fact transposed by a third toward the top.

It is probably a mistake, since the increased edition of this Psalter created by Jean Garnier in 1545 prints the notes at the same height as in Dachstein.

With its high notes, the German melody used for this psalm rather recalls that of Luther in 1529 for the same Psalm 46 with its text *Ein Feste Burg ist unser Gott* "(Our God is a safe stronghold)": Calvin was perhaps sensitive to the symbolism of a text which expresses God's movement (the high notes) toward man.[12] Then is this choice of Calvin for the melody of Dachstein's psalm a curious coincidence or a deliberate choice?

---

study "*Le séjour de Jean Calvin en Strasbourg (1538 a 1541)* in the Biographies of the Reformer," 23, n26 and n29.

10. See Robert Weeda, "The Beneficial Influence of Strasbourg on Calvin's Personality," *Annuaire de la Société des Amis du Vieux Strasbourg* 28 (2001) 18–20.

11. According to the transcription made by Christian Meyer, *Les mélodies des Eglises protestantes de langue allemande. Catalogue descriptif des sources et édition critique des melodies*, vol. 1, *Les mélodies publiées à Strasbourg (1524 to 1547)* (Baden-Baden & Bouxwiller: Valentin Koerner, 1987), 181. See also *Das deutsche Kirchenliled: Verzeichnis der Drucke von de Anfangen bis 1800* (Kassel: Rism, B/VIII/1, 1975).

12. We have developed this theme in Robert Weeda, "Hymns Sung in the Protestant Churches," in Yves Lehmann (ed.), *The Old Hymn and Its Public* (Turnhout: Brepols, 2007), esp. 661–62. No doubt the relationship with the *musica mundane*; see Christopher Richard Joby, *Calvinism and the Arts: A Re-assessment* (Louvain and Paris: Peters, 2007), 66–67: During the Middle Ages vocal music, like other music was considered to have close association with the music of the spheres or Boethius' musica mundansa, and so with heaven. Now it was considered by man to be ontologicaly separate from this and to be more a product of human design than one of divine origin. This is certainly how Calvin understood vocal music, and it is clear that he was not alone in this regard. "*L'utilisation pédagogique des théories de Boece est traitée par Jean Sturm dans sa lettre de mars 1565 au Professeur de Musique du Gymnase Matthias Stiffelreuter*; see Robert Weeda, "A Pedagogy of the Art of Singing," in Matthieu Arnold (ed.), *Johannes Sturm*

4. Church Music

For these two psalms—as also for the whole collection—the printer Jean Knobloch the Young adopted the notes which were left out—therefore—"blanked," a notation which has its origin in solo songs. Who took the initiative in this choice: Calvin himself? We do not know . . .

On the other hand, the modes are kept from the German models,[13] as also the writing on a five-line section as well as the key of C third or fourth line; the marker (*custos*) is also kept at the end of each section, which indicates the first note of the next section. Finally, we also find the vertical bars marking the structure of the musical phrases.[14]

The melody of these two psalms however undergoes an essential alteration which is found in the notation: this only adopts two values of notes, the *breve* and the *semibreve*. This simplification of the notation certainly makes it easier for a composite people who are not well used too singing from a printed sheet. Who decided on this alteration: a musician? Greiter? Dachstein? Calvin himself?

In order to create this Psalter, the printer has applied the technique as a block that he has already used for other German collections: instead of using mobile types (like Gutenberg) he has made it in one printing, as a deep study of the facsimile will prove.[15]

Pastoral Initiative

By only keeping these two values of notes, Calvin has rather hidden the original melodies: in so doing, he announces the fundamental binary aspect of the music of the French psalms. By the syllabic treatment of the text—his "metre"[16]—Calvin narrowly associates poetry and music, and does so in favor of the intelligibility of the words;[17] thus, his work is perfectly situated within the space of his time.[18]

(1507 to 1589): *Rhetor, Padagoge und Diplomat* (Tubingen: Mohr Siebeck, 2009), 219.

13. The ecclesiastical modes which are still used in the psalms tend however toward the major and minor tonalities (with some sensitive notes increased, as well as the final major agreement).

14. See n7.

15. We owe this information from our colleague Beat Follmi (Faculty of Protestant Theology in the University of Strasbourg).

16. The English term *metrical* is, it seems to us, more suitable.

17. On this point, Calvin does not at all mark down from the Gregorian psalmody, where the text is the first item, and the music its "servant."

18. Collected around Ronsard in the "*Pléiade*," at the same time the poets defend imitating Greco-Latin authors of the cultural value of the French language while also imposing the alexandrine and the sonnet as major poetic forms.

As well as attaching itself to popular songs and allowing the faithful to sing in unison and without accompaniment (*a capella*), this new notation certainly had another reason. In fact Calvin found himself in front of a vital requirement: in Strasbourg he is the pastor,[19] and therefore he must bring a human project to the "French Church"; being made up at the same time of people of French stock and foreigners, this church required a liturgical tool for unification.

Going from one church to another,[20] this community suffered from the absence of a permanent home, lacking a house of God.[21] Facing the German culture of Strasbourg,[22] Calvin also had the worry of a "gallicization" of his church and its services: now, this necessarily passed by word of mouth[23] and through the music, that of "community" singing—which is even expressed in a text as "I."[24] Thus, all the psalms begin by a "whole note" (as also in popular music) allowing the "tone" to be taken up and to ensure the unification of the meeting.[25]

Coming from songs—and already fashionable in France—the unity of notation in the melodies brought to Calvin a long-sought solution. But this unity did not bring a uniformity of musical execution and will not at all bring in slow singing, in fact it was the opposite.

---

19. Matthieu Arnold, "John Calvin's Stay" (see n8), 22, n20, quotes Thomas H. L. Parker, who quite rightly states that Calvin "cultivated [. . .] a pastoral ministry with individuals" and recalls (28n91) the articles of W. Van't Spuker on Bucer's influence as to this pastoral activity.

20. First of all based in St Nicholas, it was moved into the chapel of the Repentants, on the present site of the Church of Saint-Madeleine. Later, it will move again to settle in the town center, in the Dominican choir.

21. Christopher Richard Joby, *Calvinism and the Arts* (see n11), 89s.

22. In his *Calvin: A Man, a Work, an Author* (Gollion: Infolio, 2004), 66, Olivier Millet rightly recalls that, like his French-speaking parishioners, "Calvin would not have been able to insert himself deeply into the social, political and cultural life of this German-speaking city, where people spoke in dialect and in a language which were totally foreign."

23. Should one be reminded that these psalms are a poetic paraphrase of the biblical text?

24. Christopher Richard Joby (see n11), remarks on this (58) "[. . .] in hymnody, and, by analogy, the singer becomes part of a group process, [. . .] This is to some extent due to the words themselves and that the vocalized 'I' or 'we' of the [psalm] becom[es] part of the involvement with the public worship. When singing the psalms of David, the 'I' of David becomes the 'I' of each singer [. . .] the character of metrical psalms is both expressive and congregational. They provide us with the means to express spiritual problems, hopes, fears, and individual emotions."

25. Today, the length of the notes is divided by two and they are transcribed in minims and crotchets.

4. Church Music

As for the "other [psalms] to follow" which were announced in his letter to Farel, his Psalter will effectively offer four more paraphrases as well as three "canticles," the "Song of Simeon," "The Ten Commandments" and the Creed,[26] all from Calvin's pen.[27]

Among the latter, "The Ten Commandments" are distinguished by a beautiful pedagogic design: by announcing them first of all in his first stanza ("Let us hear the law"), Calvin makes them follow by ten stanzas for so many commandments and ends them by a twelfth and last stanza.

Teaching

The changes which are described are in some way the impact of the Psalter. But, for whatever reason, the latter needs its apprenticeship in the Gymnasium: it was in fact essential for Calvin that the singing of psalms is learned in school; thus trained to this new repertoire, the children would lead the singing in the assembly, under the direction of a cantor.

In 1537, Calvin had in fact suggested to the council of the town of Geneva that it would be "a very expedient thing for building the church, to sing some psalms in the form of public prayer [. . .] [and that] the manner of doing so seemed very sensible to us, if some children who had previously recorded a modest and ecclesiastical song, were to sing aloud clearly, the people would listen attentively, and following by heart what is sung by mouth, until little by little each person will become used to singing in a communal manner.[28] This pedagogic principle must from that time be practiced in Strasbourg, at the Haute Ecole founded by Jean Sturm.[29] In 1538 exactly, Sturm will then talk about music: "On the last day of the week, during the hours of the afternoon, all the pupils must take part in music. In fact, the knowledge and practice of this art are worthy of a free man, and if we do not learn it deeply in childhood, it is too late, at a more advanced age, for us to get to know it."[30]

We do not have any information on the work of a cantor in the French parish; singing by the assembly is however remarkable, as is witnessed by

---

26. The collection also offers thirteen paraphrases of Clement Marot.

27. See Robert Weeda, *Eglise des français*, 146–51.

28. See Robert Weeda, *Le Psautier de Calvin, Histoire d'un livre populaire au XVIe siècle (1551-1598)* (Turnhout: Brepols, 2002), 93–127.

29. See Robert Weeda, "Une pédagogie de l'art du chant" (see n11), 215s.

30. *De literarum ludis recte aperiendis liber. De la bonnière manière d'ouvrir des écoles de Lettres*, ed. Georges Lacarrigue et Matthieu Arnold (Presses Universitaires de Strasbourg, 2007), 102.

a student coming from Lille on the occasion of the time that he spent in Strasbourg between 1545 and 1547 in order to study at the Haute Ecole. Attending the French church, which was at the time under the control of Jean Garnier,[31] he wrote in a letter:

> There is a French church [...] in the morning [...] they sing a psalm of David or another prayer taken from the new testament, which psalm or prayer they all sing together, both men and women in such harmony, that thing is beautiful to see.

And later:

> On Sundays, instead of one mass they sing two psalms or a prayer and after that there is a sermon. They only sing one psalm before the sermon and the other one later, the first one that they sing, is the ten commandments.[32]

As our student very rightly says, community singing in unison "everyone together"—also included women which, during the century, will be scandalized by the Catholics.

Another letter sent to Jehan du Bois in Tournai[33] also says that

> everyone has a book of music in his hands, both man and woman, everyone praises the Lord.[34]

Calvin's Liturgy in Strasbourg

Until the time when the *Aulcuns psaulmes et cantiques mys en chant* appeared, it is possible that the parish used the order of service for the German parishes in Strasbourg, and that it will do so until the publication in 1540 of its Liturgy (sadly lost); a second edition appearing in 1542 under the responsibility of Pierre Brully, Calvin's successor, gives us some details.[35]

---

31. Responsible for publishing *La Forme des prières et chantz ecclesiaastiques*, which came out in Strasbourg in 1545; this one offers forty-seven psalms.

32. In this letter, the author uses the pseudonym Martin Du Mont, as "that is how I am called here, as I have changed my name on the advice of a good man, there is no need for anyone to know." Quoted according to Philippe Denis, "The Correspondence of Hubert de Bapasme, Refugee from Lille in Strasbourg (1545 to 1547)," *Bulletin de la Société de l'Histoire du Protestantisme Français* 124 (1978) 96.

33. This is exactly the town where, after his ministry in the "French church" of Strasbourg, Pierre Brully led the young parish until his death at the stake in February 1545.

34. Philippe Denis "*La correspondance ...*" (see n32), 84s.

35. *The method of making prayers in the French churches*: announced as a new

4. CHURCH MUSIC

By saying that "on Sundays, instead of one mass two psalms or a form of praise and later a sermon, only one psalm is sung before the sermon and the other one afterwards, the first one that is sung, is the ten commandments,"[36] the letter from the Walloon student is even more explicit.

The *"Liturgical Sacra"* of Valerand Poullain appearing in London in 1551[37] developed even more the aspects taken since 1541; however it only forms a skeleton, since a number of the psalms are only indicated at the "discretion of the Minister," or "according to what is in order."

Evolution of the Psalter, from Strasbourg to Geneva (1562)

On his return to Geneva, Calvin wrote a preface for the edition of the 1542 Psalter which he completed on 10 June 1543 for the new edition of the Psalter of this same year:[38]

> The whole work clearly shows his principles as to the "public prayers" [where] there are two kinds of them. Some are made by a plain word; the others with the song [...] Now in speaking about the Music, I understand two parts: that is, the letters, or the subject and matter: secondly, the song, or the melody, [...] Therefore what is to be done? It is to have songs[39] which are not only honest, but also holy: which are to us like arrows to encourage us to pray and to praise God, to meditate on his works, in order to love him, fear him, honour and glorify him[.] We will not find better songs which are more suitable for doing so, than the Psalms of David: which the Holy Spirit has spoken to him and carried out. And however, when we sing them, we are certain that God puts the words in our mouth, as if he himself were singing inside us, to exalt his glory [...] As far as melody

---

edition ("wiederumbin druck" writes Brully in his appeal to the council of Strasbourg) of Calvin's Liturgy of 1540, this collection is called *Pseudoromana*, because the bottom of p. 159 stated that it was "printed in Rome by the commandment of the German Pope Theodore Brusz, his ordinary printer," in order to avoid any suspicion of heresy!

36. See also n33.

37. After Pierre Brully's departure for Tournai and until the election of Jean Garnier as the pastor of the "French church" in 1545, Valerand Poullain had ensured in the interim, work of which he kept a very grateful memory; see Robert Weeda, *French church* (see n27), 85–86 and 96–102.

38. This *Form of prayers and ecclesiastical songs* is without doubt his most pastoral text; it also shows how Calvin could deepen his idea of the service and the singing of psalms from Strasbourg; see the full text in annex 2 of Robert Weeda, *Calvin's Psalter* (see n28), 157–60.

39. In the sixteenth century, the term "song" is generally used to mean sung psalms.

is concerned, it seemed best that it should be moderate,[40] so that we[41] have put it in in order to bring weight [i.e., the sense "first," the spirit of the text] and majesty [i.e., what relates to God] which is suitable for the subject, and even in order to be suitable for singing in Church, according to what has been said.[42]

As Joby said, "Calvin may have already seen the value of singing during the time in Basel, before the publication of the Institutes.[43] But, what does seem beyond doubt, is that Calvin did shift his position in respect to singing over time, a fact reflected both in his writing on the subject and the contents of the various Psalters whose compilation he oversaw."[44]

In his preface to the Psalter published in Geneva in 1542, Calvin wrote:

> We know from experience [i.e., that of Strasbourg] that singing has a great power and vigour to move and inflame the heart of men in order to invoke and praise God with a more vehement and ardent zeal.

1. Thus, we see that in Strasbourg, the melodies were chosen for the first stanza, while in Geneva they will be designed by the three musicians from the text of this 1st stanza; their setting of the text to music will therefore only apply to the text, which could sometimes create surprises for the following stanzas, and even perhaps musical aberrations with the text!

    One should moreover acknowledge that in Geneva, these melodies often develop an independence of writing, while being composed in a "spiritual manner," they expressed an independent search for the inner life of the Psalter;[45] that is why Beze could use pre-existing melodies for the twenty-five psalms written in Germany.

---

40. Essential for Calvin, moderation is treated by Yves Krumenacher, *Calvin—Au dela des légendes* (Paris: Bayard, 2009), 497; also see n45.

41. This plural of "we" is surprising: in the first place, Calvin had entrusted the writing of melodies to the cantor Guillaume Franc; which could have been, in the end, his influence on their design? Olivier Millet, *Calvin* (see n2) 165, writes however that Calvin and Franc "have doubtless collaborated, [. . .] in researching the coherence of the melody with the text of the corresponding psalm." This collaboration will no longer be similar with the two other musicians who succeeded Franc.

42. In speaking of "weight and majesty," Calvin also refers to Saint Augustine, saying, "that no-one can sing things that are worthy of God, unless he has received it from Him." See the article of Frederic Chapot, 159–73.

43. See book 3, xx, 31, in Robert Weeda, *Le Psautier de Calvin* (see n28), annex 1, 155.

44. Christopher Richard Joby, *Calvinism and the Arts* (see n11), 54, n18.

45. This point of view is placed in an epigraph by Christopher Richard Joby.

4. Church Music

2. They almost never went past an octave; thus they make it easy to sing the songs which are intended, as we know, for mere amateurs.[46]

3. In Strasbourg, the pauses measured between the musical phrases will still not have been put in place; they will be adopted by the musicians in Geneva, thus allowing the assembly to get its breath back without causing a break in the unfolding of the music and its text.[47]

4. In Geneva, the teaching of singing will be developed by the cantors as well as in the College created in 1559.[48]

5. As for the liturgy, some of those acquired in Strasbourg will disappear quickly in Geneva: the socio-ecclesial influence of Strasbourg will develop in Geneva toward a doctrinal attitude which is frankly French-speaking, thereby confirming the break with the Catholic Church. Besides, the integral Psalter of 1562[49] will not retain more than two out of the three "Canticles" of 1539, the "Commandments" and the "Song of Simeon."

From 1549, the order of the service in Geneva will be fixed according to a model which will remain in force until in 1560; due to a distribution of psalms over several weeks (first of all 17 from 1546, then 28 from 1553), the tables published at the end of the Psalter will indicate which should be sung in the two services of Sunday and those of Wednesday.

Calvinism and the Arts (see n11), 67:

> Calvin seemed to view melody as a vehicle with which to funnel text into memory. Clearly, for him, the means by which man could be improved was by imbibing and reflecting upon the words of the Psalms. But, I wonder if this meant that the melody had no independent voice of its own.

Jerome Cottin will say of this "independent voice of its own":

> Art [. . .] consists of another language, often fuller, more complete, in order to state in an analogue manner the mystery of the presence of God among men.

(*The Mystique of Art* [Paris: Cerf, 2009], 14.)

46. Christopher Richard Joby, *Calvinism and the Arts* (see n11): "This of course made it easier for untrained singers to sing them, whilst also conforming to Calvin's call for moderation" (68); see also n24.

47. One may here think with Olivier Millet, *Calvin* (see n22), that Marot's texts would be carried "by airs of well known songs" (p. 1640).

48. For further details on the teaching of singing in Geneva, see Robert Weeda, *Le Psautier de Calvin* (see n28), 105–8.

49. For further details on the teaching of singing in Geneva, see Robert Weeda, *Le Psautier de Calvin* (see n28), 105–8.

The School of God

Preaching in 1553 in Geneva Cathedral, Calvin will say:

> Being here, I am not talking only so that people will listen to me: but it is necessary from my side I am a pupil of God, and that the Word coming from my mouth should be good for me: otherwise misfortune may fall upon me.[50]

Throughout his life, Calvin welcomed "the Word" in "the school of God,"[51] the latter itself must also, according to him, guide the singing, for otherwise "there shall be no melody."[52] This intimate conviction is in fact understood in his "First sermon on justification," where he proclaims that

> one can easily sing in one voice; but we shall not have a perfect melody, unless there are several voices and good correspondence. It is so with faith: for if the word of God does not go before, and faith goes with it, there shall be no melody.[53]

---

50. CO col. 492. See also the commentaries in n46.

51. Thus, in his "Notice to the French Reader" of the *Institution of the Christian Religion* of 1541 (see the article by James Herstein, 135–57) where he says: "I am not here for myself alone: it us true that we must all do well in common, it is not only for teaching others, I am not keeping myself apart for I must be a scholar, and the word which comes from my mouth must serve me as well as you."

52. See also n44.

53. CO 23, col. 689.

5. School of Jean Sturm

Jean Calvin and the School of Jean Sturm

Anton Schindling[1]

ON 1 FEBRUARY 1539, the scholars of the free empire town of Strasbourg engaged Calvin, as a "Frenchman, who is an educated and pious man (*ein Frantzos, so ein gelahrter frommer gesell sein soll.*"[2] In fact, such is the inscription which appears in the register of the scholars, these members of the magistrate who were responsible for completely reorganizing the schools in the town, on an evangelical basis. In fact, the reform of teaching was closely linked to the Reformation of the Church; one of the main creators of it was the Stettmeister Jacques Sturm, who was, among the three scholars, the dominant personality. This son of the nobility quickly became, in internal affairs as in the external politics of the town, the main political figure of the Reformation in Strasbourg.[3]

The previous year, in 1538, the three scholars had founded, in the long building of the Dominican convent, which had been dissolved, an important school: a Gymnasium, which crowned university teaching, in particular *lectiones publicae* on the theology and on philosophical matters. The management of the new establishment was given to Jean Sturm (1507 to 1589), who was hardly thirty years old.[4] This humanist was originally from Schleiden

---

1. University of Tubingen.

2. Anton Schindling, *Humanistische Hochshue und freie Reichstadt: Gymnasium und Akademie in Strasburg 1538 to 1621* (Wiesbaden; Steiner, 1977), 350.

3. On the Reformation in Strasbourg, see Miriam Usher Chrisman, *Strasbourg and the Reform: A Study in the Process of Change* (New Haven: Yale University Press, 1967); Marc Lienhard and Jakob Willer, *Strasburg und die Reformation: Die hohe Zeit der Freien Reichsstadt*, 2nd ed. (Kehl: Morstadt, 1982); Bernd Moeller, *Reichsstadt und Reformation* (Berlin: Evangelische Verlagsanstalt, 1987); Francis Rapp, "Strassburg: Hochstift und Freie Reichsstadt," in Anton Schindling and Walter Ziegler, *Die Territorien des Reichs im Zeitalter der Reformation und Konfessionalisierung: Land und Konfession 1500 to 1660*, vol. 5, *Der Sudwesten* (Munster: Aschendorff, 1993), 72–95.

4. See Matthieu Arnold (ed.), *Johannes Sturm (1507 to 1589) Rhetor, padagoge und*

in the Eifel, in the county of Manderscheid. He had been trained in Liege, Louvain and Paris. A son of the middle class, he was not related to the noble Jacques Sturm. He was appointed, for an unlimited time, to be the rector of the new teaching establishment. In connection with the foundation of this school and its nomination, Sturm wrote, in 1538, a programmatical educational text, *De literarum ludis recte aperiendis (De la bonne manière d'ouvrir des écoles de Lettres)*.[5] In this text, he described his idea of humanist education, in Latin and in letters as in scientific matters. This program had to be achieved, in a decisive manner, on the ground of the Reformation, and to contribute to establishing evangelical faith and customs.[6]

In this framework, the public lectures in theology were partly integrated, from the beginning, into the new scholarly creation. The three theologians of the Reformation in Strasbourg, Martin Bucer, Wolfgang Capiton and Gaspard Hedion, gave lectures on the Bible.[7] Unfortunately, we do not know how the three Strasbourgians shared the time and content of these lessons with Calvin, the new arrival. In any case, from 1538 to 1539 Calvin commented on the Gospel of John, then the Epistle of Paul to the Romans, and no doubt other Pauline epistles. He had his commentary on the Romans printed in Strasbourg. It was there also that in 1539, he published a second edition, greatly increased, of his *Institutio religionis christianae*. But it is not known if this manual of systematic theology was also based on one of his lectures.[8]

Throughout the three years when he taught at the Haute Ecole in Strasbourg, Calvin became acquainted with the Sturms' establishment, which was in the course of being built, as well as its pedagogic principles. A great many historians have supposed that, when Calvin in 1559 founded the Academy of Geneva, he was leaning on his Strasbourgian impressions.[9]

Diplomat (Tubingen: Mohr Siebeck, 2009).

5. Jean Sturm, *De literarum ludis recte aperiendis liber: De la bonne manière d'ouvrir les écoles de Lettres*, ed. Georges Lagarrique and Matthieu Arnold (Presses Universitaires de Strasbourg, 2007).

6. Matthieu Arnold and Julien Collonges, *Jean Sturm: Quand l'humanisme fait école* (Strasbourg: Bibliotheque Nationale et Universitaire, 2007).

7. Beate Steible, *Capito al Humanist* (Gutersloh: Mohn, 1974); James M. Kittelson, *Wolfgang Capito, from humanist to reformer* (Leiden: Brill, 1975); Hartwig Keute, *Reformation and Geschichte: Kaspar Hedio als Historiograph* (Gottingen: Vandenhoeck & Ruprecht, 1980); Martin Greschat, *Martin Bucer. Un Réformateur et son temps (1491–1551)* (Paris: P.U.F., 2002); Thomas Kaufmann, *Die Abendmahlstheologie der Strassburger Reformatoren bis 1528* (Tubingen: Mohr Siebeck, 1992).

8. Matthieu Arnold, *Quand Strasbourg accueillait Calvin 1538 to 1541* (Presses Universitaires de Strasbourg, 2009).

9. Ulrich Im Hof, "Die reformierten Hohen Schulen und ihre schweizerischen

Even if the Haute Ecole did not influence this creation as far as detail, doubtless its founding principles acted as a model for Geneva, beginning by its educational ideal of a *"sapiens atque eloquens pietas."* In fact, this idea broadly covered the ideas of the French Reformer, and one can recognize the influence which brought the Christian and humanist spirit of reform from the University of Paris to both men. Thus, the narrow link which Calvinism established later between education and Reformation found a model in the Strasbourg of both Sturms—the *Stettmeister* and the rector of the Haute Ecole.

How, in 1538, did the school founded in Strasbourg and which Calvin knew very well, first of all as a teacher for several years, then from Geneva, as an attentive observer, appear?

As shown by the act of employing Calvin, it was a municipal institution: the temporal authority of the magistrate had a decisive importance for the creation and scientific bases for the new learned establishment. In the Protestant towns and territories, the assets of the dissolved convents were used according to Luther and in the original aim of these foundations: *ad pias causas*.[10] Education and charity were held to be the most important of these pious aims. This was also the case in Strasbourg, where, during the Reformation, a whole series of convents were dissolved by the magistrate. The Dominican convent—or convent of the preachers—was one of the largest and richest of them.

The learned model of the *gymnasium illustre* on one hand corresponded to the educational idea of humanism and on the other hand to the educational needs of a state at the beginning of the modern era, particularly on the scale of a free town of the Empire. The *gymnasium illustre* held several Latin classes, which, united by a similar didactic concept, backed one another, with a first-year program of scientific lectures.[11] In the Middle

---

Stadtstaaten," in Erich Masche et Jurgen Sudow (ed.), *Stadt und Universitat in Mittelalter und in der fruheren Neuzeit* (Sigmaringen: Thorbecke, 1977), 53–70; idem., "Die Entstchung der reformierten Huhen Schule: Zurich (1525)—Bern (1528)—Lausanne (1537)—Genf (1559)," in Peter Baumgart and Notker Hammerstein (eds.), *Beitrage zu Problemen deutscher Universitats-grundungen der fruhen Neuzeit* (Nendeln, Liechtenstein: KTO/Pr, 1978), 243–62.

10. Anton Schlindling, "Die Reformation in den Reichsstadten und die Kirchenguter—Strasburg, Nurnberg und Frankfurt im Vergleich," in Jurgen Sydow (ed.), *Burgerschaft und Kirche* (Sigmaringen: Thorbecke, 1980), 67–88; idem., "Der Passauer Vertrag und die Kirchengutfrage," in Winfried Becker (ed.), *Der Passauer Vertrag vib 1552, Oikutuscge/ebtstehung, reichsrechtliche Bedeutung und konfessiongeschichtliche Bewertung* (Neustadt an der Aisch: Degener, 2003), 105–23.

11. Anton Schindling, "Institutionen gelehrter Bildung im Zeitalter des Spathumanismus. Bildungsexpansion, Laienbildung, Konfessionalsierung und Antike-Rezeption nach der Reformation," in Sabine Holtz and Dieter Mertens (eds.), *Nicodemus Frischlin*

Ages, teaching which preceded the university had not received any systematic organization. Now, it is exactly on the turn between the fifteenth and the sixteenth century that the humanists demanded, strongly, that general teaching should be reorganized in order to make it a preparation for university studies and, and this according to the didactic and pedagogic homogenous principles. This emphasis corresponded to the manner in which the humanists understood Antiquity; for them it manifested itself in the Latin language and literary witnesses. The future lay Christians like the future carers of souls had to receive the same foundation—general teaching in the ancient languages, emphasizing form—in order to master the art of public debate as well as preaching, trained by reading classical models. A Protestant school such as the establishment founded by Jean Sturm reproduced, in its aims and in its structures, the ideal type of the *gymnasium illustre*.

Situated in the old Gothic cloister, the Strasbourg Gymnasium quickly brought ten classes together. From the beginning, its teaching also included scientific lectures, that is, on philological and philosophical subjects, and also later on law and medicine. Very soon, this school looked like a higher learning establishment. This type of establishment is generally described as a *gymnasium illustre* or a *gymnasium academicum*. The *gymnasium illustre* combined the Latin school and a series of university lectures. The most authentic type of the humanist reform of education, it also expressed a certain acceptance of Antiquity. A school of this type responded to two aims: to improve Latin and to cultivate the *artes dicendi* as the foundations of all disciplines. It is thus that the Strasbourg Gymnasium, the "School of Jean Sturm" became a model humanist establishment.[12]

In its Latin classes, the *gymnasium illustre* gave general teaching which prepared pupils for superior disciplines given out in the form of public lectures, theology, law and medicine, which were traditionally taught in the university. For Jean Sturm's pedagogy, the methods of teaching and apprentice-ship of these disciplines were less important than those of the classes which prepared for them; this first year teaching—that we could today describe as primary and secondary—were above all addressed toward the future management classes, in the temporal world as among the clergy. For the humanists, the reform of the Latin language constituted the way for a general reform, that of morals and piety; in other words, the quality of the

---

(1547 to 1590) *Poetische nd prosaische Praxis unter den Bedingungen des konfessionellen Zeitalters* (Tubingen: Vortrage, 1999), 81–104.

12. Notker Hammerstein, *Res publica litteraria, Ausgewahlte Aufsatze sur fruhneuzeilichen Bilsungs-, Wissenschafs-, Universitatgeschichte*, published by Ulrich Muhlack and Gerrit Walther (Berlin: Duncker & Humblot, 2000); idem., *Bildung und Wissenschaft vom 15, bis zum 17, Jahrhundert* (Munich: Oldenbourg, 2003).

Latin school, of the Gymnasium, decided the future of society, of the state and the Church. These ideas at the same time marked a break with the past and a new impetus. The new learned institutions acted to spread a general humanist knowledge, rooted in an educational canon which linked the classical Antiquity of the Greeks and Romans to Christianity.

These humanist aims also corresponded to the thought of the Reformation, which came from Scripture on its own, likewise with the Word of God. The ineluctable condition for this return to the written source for faith and morals—*sola scriptura*—was a well-informed reading of the biblical text, and therefore a reading within the three original languages, Hebrew, Greek and Latin. Just as the translation of the Bible into the vernacular language was a requirement and a consequence of the Reformation, the scholars, in their research and their debates, had to cultivate these languages of the biblical text—especially Latin and Greek- as well as interpreting this text by the Fathers of the Church.

The importance of the training which preceded the university teaching was emphasized also by the fact that several Protestant universities, such as Tubingen or Marbourg, created first year establishments, called "*pedagogium*."[13] As a general rule, they were seminaries. In the Strasbourg school, such a seminary was also founded in the old Dominican convent. Placed under the control of the scholars, this seminary bore the name of *Collegium praedicatorum*, entitled "Preachers' College," which referred back at the same time to its Dominican past and to the new aims set by the Reformers.

Didactically, the humanists granted an importance which was central to the idea of *methodus*, which at the same time described the method of teaching and that of apprenticeship. There is found at the heart of this teaching, the requirement of good Latin and a knowledge which is as much classical as biblical. What is the method by which this knowledge can be transmitted and is it appropriated? It was recommended to collect, classify and learn by heart the *loci communes*. These *loci communes* determined the didactic method which Sturm advocated at the same time for the Latin classes and for the public lectures.[14]

---

13. Matthias Asche and Anton Schindling, "Von der Reformation bis zur Französischen Revolution," in Ulrich Kopf et al. (ed.), "Brunnen des Lebens" *Orte der Wissenschaft, Ein Rundgag durch 525 Jahre Universitat Tubingen*, 3rd ed. (Tubingen: Tagblatt, 2003), 37–39.

14. Paul Joachimsen, *Gesammelte Aufsatze. Beitrage zu Renaissance, Humanismus und Reformation, zur Historiographie und zum deutschen Staatsgedanken*, selected and introduced by Notker Hammerstein, 2 vols. (Aalen Scientia, 1970 and 1983).

In the sixteenth century, printing enabled the considerable development in producing manuals. For academic purposes, a large number of catechisms, Latin grammars, works offering stylistic models, collections of proverbs, fables, academic editions of classical texts or even anthologies of poems or letters were written, put together and printed. In Strasbourg and Basel, as at the great fairs of Frankfurt-on-Main and Leipzig, there was a book market reserved for academic works. These works had to convey knowledge in languages, in ancient education and in the Christian faith.

The discussion on teaching and on the methods put forward by the manuals did not weaken in the century of the Reformation. On the Protestant side, the names of Philippe Melanchthon, Jean Sturm and their pupils can be picked out, not to mention other teachers up to Jan Amos Comenius. The programmatic writings of Sturm make good examples of this humanist teaching carried out in the Hautes Ecoles: after the *De literarum ludis recte aperiendis* (1538), the article written at the foundation of the Gymnasium quoted above, Sturm wrote two treatises in the next year after Calvin's death—*Scholae Lauinganae et Epistolae Classicae* (1565), to which the *Epistolae Academicae* (1569) are added.[15] In these writings of the 1560s, Sturm went deeper and developed his ideas, on the basis of the experience that he had gathered in Strasbourg. Even beyond the Protestant states of the German Holy Roman Empire, his school was known as a model establishment for humanist teaching and acceptance of Antiquity, and in this direction it influenced a great many academic establishments.[16]

The expansion and success of the new Strasbourg school took place after Calvin left Strasbourg in 1541, even after his death in 1564. However, it seems to us that it is justified, within the framework of this school connected with Calvin, to be interested in the Strasbourg Gymnasium up to the end of the confessional era. On the one hand, from Calvin's time in Strasbourg, the programmatic aims of the new school were firmly established, and, on the other hand, Strasbourg was a model not only for the Geneva Academy, established in 1559, but even for the reformed schools which were created

---

15. Jean Sturm, *Classicae epistolae sive Scholae Argentinenses restitutae*, Strasburg 1565 edition, commented and translated by Jean Rott (Strasbourg: Fides, 1938).

16. Zdislaw Pietrzyk, *W Kregu Strasburga. Z peregrynacji mlodziezy z rzczypospolitej plskoolitewsk w latach 1538 to 1621* [*In the Strasbourg circle, the Peregrinatio academica of the young people from the Kingdom of Poland and Lithuania in the years 1538 to 1621*] (Krakow: Biblioteca lagellonica, 1997); ibid, "Die Ausstrahlung Strassburgs im Zeitalter des Humanismus. Pereginatio academica auz der polnisch-litauischen Republik und die Hohe Schule Johannes Sturms im 15, und 17, Jahrhundert," translated from Polish by Robert Bartczak, *Zeitschrift fur die Geschichte des Oberrheins* 158 (2010) [to appear].

5. School of Jean Sturm

in its wake. Thus, the Strasbourgian school of Jean Sturm was, for Calvinist schools and education, a prototype and precursory establishment.[17]

In 1566, a privilege of the emperor Maximilian II raised the Gymnasium to the rank of Academy, which from that time allowed this "semi university" to confer degrees of Bachelor and Master. One had to wait until 1621 for the Haute Ecole to become a true university (a privilege granted by Ferdinand II), which granted, in all the Faculties, but all the titles including that of doctor. It is true that the limited privilege of 1566 responded to the wishes of the magistrate of the town: this model school of a free town of the Empire was copied by the free town of Nuremberg, with its Altdortf school and, in 1578, it received a corresponding privilege from the emperor.[18]

At the end of the sixteenth century, the Strasbourg school proposed an offer of teaching covering all the subjects of the time. There were nine or ten chairs for philological or philosophical disciplines: one, even two, for rhetoric; one for dialectics and Aristotelian logic; one for Aristotelian ethics and politics; one for Aristotelian physics; one respectively for mathematics, Hebrew, Greek, poetry and history. In the "Upper Faculties," four lawyers taught the *Corpus Juris Civilis,* one of the *Institutions* of Justinian, two *Pandectes* and one feudal law; moreover there were two doctors and four professors of theology—of which two were professors of the Old Testament and two were professors of the New Testament. That therefore amounted to nineteen to twenty professors, who thus could make a very rich offer of lectures and a high level university training, even if, before 1621 and the elevation of the Academy to the rank of University, students could not receive a doctor's degree.

17. Gerhard Menk, *Die Hohe Schule Herborn in ihrer Fruhzeit (1584 to 1660), Ein Beitrag Zum Hochschulwesen des deutschen Kalvinismus im Zeitalter der Gegenreformation* (Wiesbaden: Historische Kommission fur Nassau, 1981); idem., "Die kalvinistischen Hochschulen und ihre Stadte im konfessionellen Zeitalter," in Heinz Duchhardt (ed.), *Stadt und Universitat* (Cologne: Boldau, 1993), 83–106; *Vierhundert Jahre Arnoldinum 1588 to 1988,* Festschrift (published by the Kreisheimatbund Steinfurt in association with the town of Steinfurt: Greven, 1988); Heinz Holzhauer and Richard Toellner (eds.) *400 Jahre Hohe Schule Steinfurt, symposion 1988* (Steinfurt: Stadtarchiv, 1991); Thomas Elsmann, "Humanismus, Schule, Buchdruck und Antikenrezeption, Anmerkungen zur Bremer Entwicklung biz 1648," in Klaus Garrer et al. (eds.), *Stadt und Literatur im deutschen Sprachraum der Fruhen Neuzeit,* vol. 1 (Tubingen: Niemeyer, 1998), 203–38; Joachim Castan, *Hochschulwesen und reformierte Konfessionalisierung: Das Gymnasiu Illustre des Furstentums Anhalt in Zerbst 1582 to1652* (Halle/Saale: Mitteldeutscher Verlag, 1999).

18. Wolfgang Mahrle, *Academia Norica. Wissenschaft und Bildung an der Nurnberger Hohen Schule in Altdorf (1575 to 1623)* (Stuttgart: Steiner, 2000); idem., "Wissenschaft nach Strassburger, Wittenberger oder Paduaner Art? Die Entwicklung des Lehrangebots an der Nurnberger Hohen schule in Altdorf 91575 to 1623)," *Historisches Hajrbuch* 120 (2000) 80–96.

The Strasbourg Haute Ecole owed its fame to the fact humanists held it as a model establishment. In the first place, it was there that the work and merit of Jean Sturm who led this institution from 1538 to 1581, as *rector perpetuus*. The masters and teachers in the school both boasted of their school as a model: they strongly insisted on the specific nature of its method of teaching and the organization of its classes and particularly on the unity of the academic course. Full of pride, they explained that the *methodus*—the method of teaching and apprenticeship—of the Strasbourg Gymnasium was so perfect that, "without boasting, there was doubtless that at the time, there was nothing better in any other school" [es besser, ohn ruhm zu melden, gewisslich dieser zeit in keener anderen partikularschul nicht].[19]

This method, the rector Jean Sturm had recommended it in his programmatical writings for the Gymnasium. The 1568 statues and those of 1564 laid down that in Strasbourg Sturm's *docendi discendive methodus* had to be followed. The rector's writings offered a pedagogic and didactic theory for the model and the educative aims of the *gymnasium illustre*. As the writings were printed in 1538, they made the Strasbourg school known in the whole of cultivated and humanist Europe. Jean Sturm, his method and his school were celebrities, and the Gymnasium, with the academic Latin shows performed within the framework of his theatre, a true Strasbourgian attraction.

The *methodus Sturmiana* was aimed to embrace all disciplines and their teaching from rhetoric. For Sturm, what one could not express clearly and according to the rules of rhetoric was also false from the angle of logic, or at least useless. That is why one must reject "academic" logic and, with it, the traditional understanding of the disciplines and the whole educational "academic" system. Only rhetoric—the language and the style—could, according to Sturm, lead to a methodical renewal of teaching.

Among the humanists, these ideas were broadly spread around. But no humanist tried, with the methodical reflection of a Sturm, to put them into practice in courses and in academic manuals. Sturm wrote nearly all of these study programs and these manuals for the Strasbourg Haute Ecole. As rector, he took care to see that both the masters and the professors applied his pedagogic principles. Beyond Strasbourg, several schools adopted this model: Jean Sturm personally organized the gymnasia of the Palatine principalities of Deux-Ponts and Neuburg, Hornbach in the Western Palatinate and Lauingen-sur-le-Danube.[20] For the Lauingen school, he even wrote a

---

19. Marcel Fournier and Charles Engel, *Les Statuts et Privilèges de l'Université françaises depuis leur fondation jusqu'en 1789*, vol. 4/1, *Gymnase, Académie, Universite de Strasbourg* (Paris, 1894).

20. Anton Schindling, "Scholae Lauinganae, Johannes Sturm, das Gymnasium in

programmatical composition aimed at promoting the studies, the *Scholae Lauinganae* (1565).[21]

The Jesuits must have known Jean Sturm's pedagogic ideas when they renewed the teaching in the Tricoronatum Gymnasium in Cologne. These ideas also presided at the foundation, in 1588, of the reformed Haute Ecle of Burgsteinfurt by Count Arnold IV of Bentheim.[22] Therefore, in a parallel manner, both the Lutherans—the Palatine Wolfgang of Deux-Ponts and Neuburg—and the Calvinists—Count Arnold IV of Bentheim—or the Jesuits adopted the pedagogic and didactic principles of Jean Sturm.[23] Indications are also found of the Strasbourgian influence on the creation of schools in central Europe and in Eastern Europe: Bohemia, the Lithuanian-Polish Rzeczpospolita and the Baltic countries.[24] Coming mostly from the nobility, a great many students from these territories, but also from Hungary and Siebenburgen, went to Strasbourg.[25]

Sturm's Strasbourgian study plan stipulated that the pupils of the ten classes would learn, step by step, Latin then Greek, as well as the elements of grammar, rhetoric and teaching. Sturm proceeded according to the following principles: division into classes, each class having a competent master; organization of the subject in terms of its degree of difficulty; its division into teaching given in each class, in which one stayed for a year; annual exams; a reading plan, rules on interpretation and style exercises which aimed

---

Lauingen und die Jesuiten in Dillingen," in Matthieu Arnold (ed.), *Johannes Sturm (1507-1589), Rhetor, Padagoge und Diplomat* (Tubingen: Mohr Siebeck, 2009), 261-92.

21. Jean Sturm, "Lauingens Schulordnung (Scholae Lauinganae) Introduction et traduction par Kurt Schondorg and Ernst Wenzell," in *Albertus, Jahresbericht 2006/2007 des Albertus-Gymnasiums* (Lauingen/Donau Albertus-Gymnasium 2007), lii–cxxvii.

22. Thomas Rohm and Anton Schindling, "Tecklenburg, Bentheim, Steinfurt, Lingen," in Anton Schindling and Walter Zeigler (eds.), *Die Territorien des Reichs im Zeitalter der Reformation und Konfessionalisierung: Land und Konfession 1500 to 1650*, vol. 3, *Der Nordwesten* (Munster: Aschendorff, 1991), 182-98.

23. Matthias Asche, "Humanistiische Bildungskonzeptionen im Konfessionellen Zeitalter: Ein Problemaufrifs in zhen Thesen," in Julius Oswald and Rita Haur (eds.), *Jesuitica: Forschungen zur fruhen Geschichte des Jesuitenordens in Bayern zur Aufhebung 1773* (Munich: Beck, 2001), 373-404.

24. Martin Kloke, *Literarisches Leben in Reval in der ersten Halfte des 17, Jahrhunderts (1600 to 1657), Institutionem der Gelehrsamkeit und Dichten bei Gelegenheit* (Tubingen: Niemeyer, 2005).

25. Wilhelm Kuhlmann and Anton Schindling, *Deutschland und Ungarn in ihren Bildungsund Wissenschaftsbeziehungen wahrend der Renaissance* (Stuttgart: Steiner, 2004); Marta Fata, Gyula Kurucz and Anton Schindling, *Peregrinatio Hungarica: Studenten aus Ungarn an deutschen und osterreichischen Hochschulen vom 16, bis zum 20. Jahrhundert* (Stuttgart: Steiner, 2006); Marta Fata and Anton Schindling, *Calvin und Reformiertentum in Ungaro und Siebenburgen. Helvetisches Bekenntnis, Ethnie und Politik vom 16. Jahrhundert bis 1918* (Munster: Aschendorff, 2010).

to imitate the model authors of antiquity. In the public lectures for higher education on rhetoric and teaching, the students had to be familiarized with the whole of rhetorical theory. The academic theatre was intended for the schoolchildren and the students the opportunity to put into practice the rules and rhetorical models that they had learned.

Jean Sturm gave a special value to the reading of ancient rhetorical manuals: Aristotle, Cicero and Hermogenis. He edited several of these manuals for academic requirements, as well as the speeches of Demosthenes and Cicero, which acted as examples of practical eloquence. For Sturm, Cicero was the absolute standard, a standard to which the schoolchildren and students had to measure their manner of thinking and speaking. The Roman orator acted as a model for the *imitation oratoria* to which the pupils had to aspire. As a consequence, in teaching, the ancient sources were almost exclusively interpreted as regards form and style.

As regards the technique of teaching and apprenticeship, its framework lay in the Sturmian idea of the *loci communes*. Sturm recommended sorting out each text according to its *loci* and to analyze them, then put them in order in terms of their meaning and their theme. The topic—the teaching of *loci communes*—acted for him as formulating reasoning in order to discover, try out and correctly apply each point of view, each argument, each comparison and each conclusion. The ancient literary tradition provided a reserve of topical models, like a treasure-house of themes and quotations. It was not a question of a simple rhetorical technique: Sturm held the *loci communes* as the central instrument in any cognitive thought, and as a result he classified them in logic. Sturm thought that the *loci*, when they were well known and classified within the connections of universal meanings, produced a logical system for explaining the world. Thanks to the method of the *loci*, according to Sturm, rhetoric could become the pilot science in schools and universities. This doctrine of topical rhetorical knowledge, constitutes a completely original contribution of Sturm to the rhetorical understanding of the sciences by humanism and to the debate on the teaching methods which led the humanists.

However, contrary to his pretentions, Sturm's concept did not succeed in completely influencing other mattes in the Haute Ecole in Strasbourg. However, Sturm's influence remained decisive for a long time, to the extent that either he or his pupils trained almost all the Strasbourgian schoolchildren and students. It can be said that Sturm's study programs and methods were considered as a guiding thread and were followed at least up to the first decade of the seventeenth century, until the death of Melchior Junius, Sturm's pupil and successor, in 1604.

5. School of Jean Sturm

Jean Sturm's educational concept was inserted into a fundamentally Protestant and humanist vision: *Propositum a nobis est, sapientem atque eloquentem pietatem finem esse studiorum*, such is the document that, in 1538, Sturm had formulated in a programmatic manner in his essay aimed at promoting the studies for the new school.[26] The eloquent and familiar humanist of the ancient sources presented, according to Sturm, the best provisions for also proving oneself a good Christian. The daily exercises, throughout the school lessons as well as for higher learning lectures, had to train the mind and character of the schoolchildren and students according to the standard of a *sapiens atque eloquens pietas*. For Sturm, this was the way, promising success, which led to true piety, the one which had renounced all superstition. Here, the concept of the man of Antiquity and that of Christianity melted together. In the Strasbourg Haute Ecole, the model and values of this Christian humanism stayed lively as an educational aim.

However, toward 1600, at the time of late humanism, the model of the "Haute Ecole in a free town of the Empire" came nearer more and more, in Strasbourg, to that of a whole traditional separate university.[27] Its result was that the "semi university" which the Haute Ecole had needed and wished for, obtained finally, in 1621, from the Emperor Ferdinand II the privilege of a whole separate university, with its four Faculties. And gaining from a favorable political situation, the free town of the Empire led the development of its teaching on its own terms. This time again, Nuremberg the free town of the Empire attached itself to the Strasbourgian model for its Haute Ecole of Altdorf.[28] Meanwhile, it had been proved, convincingly, that the Reformation, the humanist reform and the structure of the medieval university,

---

26. See n4.

27. On the role of a model played by the universities in the middle of Germany, see Manfred Rudersdorf and Thomas Topper, "Furstenhof, Universitat und Territorialstaat. Der Wittenberger Humanismus, seine Wukungsraume und Funktionsfelder im Zeicher der Reformation," in Thomas Maissen and Gerrit Walter (ed.), *Funkionem des Humanismus: Studien zum Nutzen des Neuen in der humanistchen Kultur* (Gottingen: Wallstein, 2006), 214–61; Manfred Rudersdorf, "Weichenstellng fur die Neuzeit: Die Universitat Leipzig zwischen Reformation und Dreifsigjahrigem Krieg 1539 to 1660," in Enno Bunz et al. (eds.), *Geschichte der Universitat Leipzig 1409 to 2009*, vol. 1, *Spates Mittelalter und Fruhe Neuzeit 1409 to 1830/31* (Leipzig: Universitatsverlag, 2009), 327–515.

28. Anton Schindling, "Strasburg und Altdorf: Zwei humanistische Hochschulgrundungen von evantelischen freien Reichsstadten," in Peter Baumgart and Nocker Hammerstein (eds.), *Beitrage zu Problemen deutscher Universitatsgrundungen der fruhen Neuzeit* (Nendeln, Liechstenstein: KTO-Pr, 1978), 149–89; idem., "Die humanistische Bildungsreform in den Reichsstadten Strassburg, Nurnberg und Augsburg" in Wolfgang Reinhard (ed.), *Humanismus im Bildungswesen des 15, und 16, Jahrhunderts* (Weinheim: Acta Humaniora, 1983), 107–20.

with its four Faculties, were compatible: this is what the Protestant leaders such as Marbourg, Konigsberg and Helmstedt stated, as well as the noting reform of universities before the evangelical movement, such as Wittenberg, Tubingen and Rostock.[29]

What did the Strasbourg experience of a humanist *gymnasium illustre* mean for John Calvin the Genevan Reformer and for his supporters, the Reformed or Calvinist people? It belongs to the theologians and philologists to judge up to what point Calvin can be considered as a humanist and find in his thought and in his writings elements of the scientific humanist method. This remark also applies to the importance—and, perhaps, the limits—of his knowledge of the authors of classical Antiquity. Are the veneration of Cicero by Jean Sturm and his method of the *loci communes* reflected in Calvin's work, or is it more opportune to speak about an absence of reception? Do the rhetoric and didactic representations of the academic theatre play a role in the schools marked by Calvin's mind? No doubt it is still premature to wish to answer these questions.

However, the narrow link between Reformation and education of the scientific level constitutes, without any discussion, a strong parallel between Strasbourg and Geneva.[30] In Strasbourg, the future Reformer of Geneva had the experience of creating a new humanist teaching establishment, in the service of the Reformation; it was a question of winning over the young generations to the new religious ideas. This experience made it possible to strengthen Calvin in the influence that Christian humanism had on him, in the University of Paris. Founded in Geneva in 1539, the Academy must have been the mistress part of the Calvinian Reformation, and its schools contributed strongly in spreading reformed Protestantism in the whole of Europe.

---

29. Matthias Asche, "Frequenzeinbruche und Reformen. Die deutschen Universitaten in den 1520s to 1560 Jahren zwischen Reformation und humanistischem Neuanfang," in Walther Lud (ed.), *Die Musen im Reformationszeitalier* (Leipzig: Evangelische Verlagsanstalt, 2001), 53–96; idem., "Humanistische Distanz gegenuber dem "Konfessionalisierungs-paradigma: Kritische Bemerhkungen aus der Sicht der deutschen Bildungs—und Univerisitatgeschichte," *Jahrbuch fur Historische Bildungsforschung7* (2001) 261–82; idem., "Bildungslandschaften im reich der Fruhen Neuzeit: Uberlegungen zum landsmannschaftlichen Prinzip an deutschen Universitaten in der Vormoderne," in Daniela Siebel (ed.), "*Orte der Gelahrtheit,*" *Personen, Prozesse und Reformen an protestantischen Universitaten des Alten Reiches* (Stuttgart: Steiner, 2008), 1–44; idem. *Von der reichen hansischen Burgeruniversitat zur armen mecklenburgischen Landeshochschule: Das regionale und soziale Besucherprofil der Universitaten Rostock und Butzow in der Fruhen Neuzeit (1500 to 1800)*, 2nd ed., rev. (Stuttgart, 2010).

30. Peter Baumgart, *Universitaten im konfessionellen Zeitalter. Gesammelte Betrage* (Munster: Aschendorff, 2006).

5. School of Jean Sturm

The reformed Hautes Ecoles bear witness in a very special manner to this link between Reformation and top-level teaching: in the Swiss towns of Zurich, Bern and Lausanne; in Herborn-sur-le-Westerwald, in the county of Nassau-Dillenburg; in Hanau-sur-Main in the county of Hanu; in Burgseinfurt, in Westphalia, in the county of Bentheim; in Zerbst, in the principality of Anhalt, just as in the free town of Breme; in France, in Saumur and Sedan; in Hungary and in the Sieburgen, to Debreczen, in Sarospatak and to Alba Julia; in the Puritan colonies of New England, in Harvard and Yale.[31] All these reformed Hautes Ecoles had the *gymnasium illustre* as an institutional model. They followed—at least with variations—the model of Jean Sturm in Strasbourg, which sometimes was translated by using Strasbourgian manuals.

Also in Calvinist circles, as indicated by the acceptance of Pierre de la Ramee's philosophy, it seems also that care was taken in scientific teaching and apprenticeship, as well as rational logic;[32] it is precisely in the reformed Hautes Ecoles that Ramism played a role as a method of thinking for the sciences; Pierre de la Ramée prolonged, while modifying it, the Sturmian idea of a reform of logic marked by rhetoric. It is true that this movement appeared after Calvin's death and Jean Sturm's deposition.

Therefore, the educational reform led by Sturm in Strasbourg influenced the reformed confessional culture. This influence agrees with the fact that throughout the intra-Protestant confessional arguments, the Strasbourgian rector felt he was more and more attracted by the reformed world and in particular by Calvinists. For this reason, at the end of his career, he came into open conflict with the Strasbourgian Lutheran theologians as well as with the magistrate, who became more and more involved with the latter.[33] In 1581, Jean Sturm was dismissed from his duties as rector. However, some Calvinist students, coming mainly from the nobility, continued to go

31. Anton Schindling, "Universtaten und Hohe Schulen im Heiligen Romischen Reich deutscher Nation im Spannungsfeld von Spathumanismus und konfessioneller Orthodoxie um 1600," in Horst Carl and Freidrich Lenger (eds.), *Universalitat in der Provinz. Die vormoderne Landesuniversitat Giessen zwischen korporativer Autonomie, staatlicher Abhangigkeit und gelehrten Lebenswelten* (Darmstadt: Hessische Historische Kommission, 2009), 3–61.

32. Joseph S. Freedman, *European Academic Philosophy in the Late Sixteenth and Early Seventeenth Centuries, the Life, Significance, and Philosophy of Clement Timper (1563/4 to 1624)*, 2 vols. (Hildeshem: Olms, 1988); Howard Hotson, *Commonplace Learning, Ramism and Its German Ramifications, 1543 to 1630* (Oxford University Press, 2007).

33. Anton Schindling, "Humanismus oder Konfessionsfundamentalismus in Strassbourg Furstbistum und freie Reichsstadt," in Heinz Schindling (ed.), *Konfessioneller Fundamentalismus: Religion als politischer Faktor in Europaischen Machtesystem um 1600* (Munich: Oldenbourg, 2007), 149–65.

to Strasbourg, from the Lithuanian-Polish Rzeczzpospolita or Hungary and Siebenburgen.

Thus, on account of the humanist studies which were offered in Strasbourg in the rhetorical tradition of Jean Sturm, the Haute Ecole, which was from that time officially Lutheran, kept a special place on the teaching map of reformed Europe. By their influence, Calvin's time in Strasbourg and his academic teaching in Strasbourg were not of a minor nature: on the contrary, they acted as a guide to reformed educational tradition, in Europe and North America. From this fact, one may consider the proximity of Calvinism and rational education, of science and higher education as at least an indirect contribution of Strasbourg to the Genevan Reformation.

6. Calvin's Commentary

Calvin's Commentary on the Epistle to the Romans

Christian Grappe[1]

Editions of the Commentary

FOR A CONTEMPORARY EXEGETIST of the New Testament, Calvin's commentary on the Epistle to the Romans appears like an original work, full of authority and independence, remarkable for the same method of commentary and presenting a totally modern appearance on a great many points. In summary, one is dealing with a harmonious monument, of which one perceives very quickly that it was broadly innovative for its time, even if, because the approach methods have developed and the textual and historic criticisms have progressed significantly.

What we would like to do first of all to give evidence during our presentation,[2] are the innovative and original aspects of the work, which, from our point of view, are its strength, even if we shall also show certain limits of which it seems possible moreover that Calvin himself may have been aware.

---

1. Group of Inter-testamentaries, Faculty of Protestant Theology in Strasbourg University.

2. Our thanks are addressed most particularly to Frédéric Chapot, Olivier Millet and Annie Noblesse-Rocher who, by their assistance and their precious remarks, have enabled us to refine our research and to take up again, on several points, our contribution. We must also be precise in the whole work that, each time Calvin's commentary on the Romans is quoted in this study, including in the annexes, the references that appear between square brackets indicate on what page and on what line they can be found, in the edition of T. H. L. and D. C. Parker, quoted in n2, the relevant passage. The cross-references are normally carried out in the 1540 edition, which here is of the foremost interest to us. Those which were made in a later edition, whether it is a question of the 1551 one, that of 1556 or even both of them at the same time, are duly pointed out by mentioning this edition or these editions between square brackets.

It is known that Calvin suggested several successive editions of his commentary, which knew three editions in Latin, the first in 1540, developed to this sole work, the second in 1551, where it is revised and integrated into a commentary of the whole of the Pauline corpus and of Hebrews, the third in 1556 where, newly revised, the text appears inside a commentary on all the New Testament epistles. In parallel, two French translations were published, respectively in 1550 and 1556, but they were preceded in 1542 and 1543, with an *Exposition sur l'Epistle de Sainct Paul aux Romains, Extraicte des Commentaires de M.I. Calvin*. Differences in translation appear from one volume to the other, as T. H. L. and D. C. Parker have shown very well in their edition of the Latin commentary.[3]

The 1556 translation, taken up by the editor Meyruels in the edition that he offered, in 1854 to 1855, of all the commentaries that Calvin wrote on the New Testament[4] is from that time in line on the site of the Faculty of Theology in Geneva.[5] It enables precious probing to be made in a certain number of fields, especially where it is about marking the appearance of certain terms which proved useful for the enquiry we have carried out. We have also greatly relied on it in order to undertake such probing, in particular where we had to mark rhetorical terms or the usage of certain verbs. However we were always carried back to Parker's edition to return to the Latin text of the first Strasbourgian edition of 1540. When we quote Calvin's French commentary, it will therefore most often be in the French translation that he offers in 1556 of passages that were already found in the Latin edition of 1540.

We shall devote the main part of our attention to the relative originality and method of the commentary, which is characterized, according to us, by the more particular search for the author's intention and by the importance granted to the "rhetorical gesture of Paul."[6] We shall also recall the interest, for Calvinist hermeneutics, of the recording of a particular figure, the *anticipation*. Finally we shall touch on one of the limits (possibly conscious) of Calvin's commentary.

Relative originality and method of the commentary: the search for the author's intention and the importance granted to "Paul's rhetorical gesture."

---

3. Jean Calvin, *Ioannis Calvini Opera exegetic*, vol. 13, *Commentarius in Epistolam Pauli ad Romanos*, ed. T. H. L. Parker and D. C. Parker, Ioannis Calvini Opera omnia, series 2, Opera exegica Veteris et Novi Testamenti (Geneva: Droz, 1999), xxv–xxviii.

4. Jean Calvin, *Commentaires de Jehan Calvin sur le Nouveau Testament: le tout revue diligemment et comme traduit de nouveau, tant le texte que le glose* (Paris: Ch. Meyrueis, 1854–1855).

5. The electronic address where one can find the text thus numbered is: http:/www.unige.ch/theologie/numerisation/Calvin_NT/volume3.pdf.

6. The expression is used by Benoît Girardin, *Rhétorique et théologique: Calvin et le Commentaire de l'Epître aux Romains* (Paris: Beauchesne, 1979), 299.

6. Calvin's Commentary

When Calvin, then teaching at the Haute Ecole, finished, in 1539 (the preface is dated 18 October), his commentary on the Epistle to the Romans, let us remember that he was just thirty years old, and it cannot be said that he chose an easy path. In fact, he went tranquilly assured, straight to the essence.

> The epistle then in the first place stirs up the interest of those who are going to be shown as the main Reformers. From the years 1515 and 1516, Martin Luther had started his lectures on the *Epistle to the Romans* which was going to hold a very important place in his personal itinerary. However he did not make particular use of the rhetorical method, which will interest more particularly here, so that we shall *only quote it. In 1519, Philippe Melanchthon, who was going to play at Luther's side the role that is* known as the initiator of the Reform in the German Holy Roman Empire and Tutor of Germany,[7] had proceeded, in an essay which was preparatory to the publication of his *Loci communes*,[8] to a methodical analysis of the plan of *Romans* while relying on the classical layout of the ancient *dispositio*.[9] He returned several times to the epistle[10] until he offered a commentary, in 1532.[11]

---

7. As emphasized and shown by Kees Meerhoff, "Logic and Creation according to Melanchthon: In Search of the Common Place," in idem., *Entre logique et littérature: Autour de Philippe Melanchthon* (Orleans: Paradigme, 2001), 81 (63–82), he "was also, and more than has been said, the tutor of France."

8. Philippe Melanchthon, *Loci communes rerum theologicarum seu hypotyposes theologicae* (Wittenberg, 1521).

9. Philippe Melanchthon, *Theologica Institutio in epistulam Pauli ad Romanos* (1519). This brief essay is reproduced in the collection edited by Ernst Bizer, *Texte aus Anfngszeit Melanchthons* (Neukirchen-Vluyn: Neukirchener Verlag, 1966), 89–99. Let us recall that the classical layout of the *disposition*, particularly formalized by Aristotle, was followed: preface (entry to the subject); *narratio* (description of the facts); *confirmation* (description of the arguments frequently included in a thesis or *proposito*), in all cases an *argumentatio* or *probatio*, and, when that is found useful, a *refutatio* or *altercatio); peroration* (epilogue). To these four parts another can be added, a *regression* or *digression*, liable to find its place at any time. Later, Quintillien put forward a layout in five parts by distinguishing *confirmation* and *refutation* in order to make two distinct sections of it.

10. Philippe Melanchthon, *Artificium epistulae Pauli ad Romanos a Philippo Melanchthone*, 1520 [?], a treatize appearing also in Ernst Bizer (ed.), *Texte aus der Anfangszeit Melanchthons* (see n8), 9–30; *Rapsodoai en Paulou ad Romanos*, 1521, in ibid., 39–85; *Annotationes Phil. Melanchthonis in Epistolas Paul ad Romanos et ad Corinthios*, Norimbergae (Nuremberg: Joh. Stuchs, 1522); *Dispositio orationis in epistula Pauli ad Romano* (Wittenberg: Joseph Clug, 1529; the edition that we were able to consult and which is quoted here is this one, brought out in 1530, by the same publisher).

11. Philippe Melanchthon, *Commentarii in Epistulam Paul ad Romanos, recens scripti a Philippe Melanchthon*, 1532. (One can easily consult the work in Melanchthons Werke, vol. 5, *Romerbrief-Kommentar 1532*, ed. Rolf Schafer (Gutersloh: Ged Mohn, 1965).

All along his path in the company of *Romans*, Melanchthon had persisted in his rhetorical approach, moreover correcting his first intuitions during his journey to the point of denying, at the time when his commentary appeared, his previous writings with the exception of the work that he had dedicated, in 1529, to the *disposition* of the epistle.

We shall be content here[12] to emphasize that Melanchthon has been shown to be flexible and innovative in his approach. That led him to consider that Romains did not solely come from the judicial field, to which he had initially assigned the epistle[13] but from a mixed field, which he added to the three great fields, judicial, epidictic and deliberative, which distinguished ancient rhetoric, the didactic field (*genos didaktikon*, in Greek,[14] *genus didacticum* in Latin[15] or didascalic *genus didascalikon*);[16] adapted to preaching, this field made it possible to have, within the speech, some sections which would raise the judicial field, which he emphasized was equally suitable for teaching and others, the deliberative field,[17] and the others, from the deliberative

---

12. A very fine analysis wil be found of the method used by Melanchthon with Carl Joachim Classen, *Rhetorical Criticism and the New Testament* (Tubingen: Mohr Siebeck, 2000), 99–177. See also, for the rhetorical approach that Melanchthon proposes on *Romains*, Christian Grappe, "Justice et grace dans l'epître aux Romains: Eclairages rhétoriques de Melanchthon a l'exégèse récente," in Annie Noblesse-Rocher (ed.), *Justice et grace dans l'épître aux Romains* (Strasbourg: Association des Publications de la Faculté de Théologie Protestante, 2008), 16–30 (15–44). As for the importance which is associated with Calvin and Melanchthon's work, it is emphasized in Olivier Millet, *Calvin et la dynamique de la Parole. Etude de la rhétorique réformée* (Paris: Honoré Champion, 1992), more particularly in 122–51.

13. Philippe Melanchthon, *Theologica Institutio in Epistulam Paul ad Romanos*, 37, 1. 22, in the 1519 edition of Bucer mentioned in n7.

14. Philippe Melanchthon, *Artificium Epistulae Pauli ad Romanos*, 1st 2. (See also *Texte aus der Aufangszeit Melanchthons*, 20.)

15. Philippe Melanchthon, *Disposito orationis in epistula Pauli ad Romanos*, 1st av.1.11–12 (Clug edition, 1530 [the edition pubished in 1529 at Hagenau with Iohannes Secetius does not contain the passage in question]. (See also CR 15, col. 445, 1.30–313.)

16. Philippe Melanchthon, *Commentarii in Epistulam Pauli ad Romanos*, 1 vii, 1.6 (see also Melanchthons Werke, vol. 5, *Romerbrief Kommentar* 1532, 32, 1.140: *Genus causae est daskalikon*. On the emergence of this didascalic field, its importance in Melanchthon's reflection and the posterity he knew, see particularly Olivier Millet, *Calvin et la dynamique de la parole*, 137–51.

17. Philippe Melanchthon, *Dispositio orationis in Epistula Pauli ad Romanos*, 1st Av. 1, 1.11–14. *Propie pertinet haec Epistula ad genus didacticum, quia finis eius est, ut ducat nos quid sit justicia coram Deo. Potest tamen ad judicable genus referri, quia hoc quoque ad docendum accommodatum est.* (See also CR 15, col. 445, 1.30–34.) In the presentation that he offers of the *Artificium Epistolae Pauli ad Romanos* in the work *Texte aus der Anfangszeit Melanchthons*, 11–12, Ernst BizerI shows that, from his work *De rhetorica libri tres* (Basel: Froben, 1519), Melanchthon has also taken the demonstrative

6. CALVIN'S COMMENTARY

field.[18] Thus distinguishing the parts of the epistle, Melanchthon was able to apply flexibly the layout of the classic *disposition*, which certainly represents another strength in his approach. Following the path of Paul's line of argument, at the same time paying attention in the *disposition* of the different parts of the discourse,[19] to the processes and figures used by Paul,[20] and certainly also the *loci*,[21] he also took into account the three main motheroperations of the *techne rhetorike*, *l'inventio*, the *disposition* and the *elocutio*, in order to structure and support his own commentary which moreover has as its particularity to dwell on some passages while leaving others aside.[22]

After him, Bullinger commented on the epistle in his turn.[23] Fixing himself globally on the same rules as Melanchthon, he attributes the mistakes in reading and understanding of the epistle to the neglect of the idioms and figures (*ex idiomatum et schematum neglectu*) to the absence of taking the context into account (*non obsergato orationis contextu*), and he insists

---

or epidictic field in the direction of teaching by assigning it as a function before even mentioning the praise and the criticism. Melanchthon also makes the *genus demonstrativum* a means of teaching (*artificium docendi*), while considering in a parallel manner that the judiciary field may also serve the same purpose.

18. In his *disposition orationis in Epistula Paula ad Romanos* (1st E 5r, 1.5–9, in the Wittenberg edition of 1530), Melanchthon, about 12.1, either at the junction between what is usually called the doctrinal part and the parenetic, exhortative part, of the work: "We have classified the early part of the epistle in the judicial field; in fact, it discharges itself from teaching. The following chapters, which are like an appendix to this debate, take some persuasion [or advice] from the field, since they contain moral precepts" [*Superiorem Epistulae partem collocauimus in genere iudiciali, uersatur enim in docendo. Sequentia capita, quae sunt uelut appendix illius disputationis, pertinent ad genum suasorium, quia continent praecepta de moribus*]. (See also CR 15, col. 483, 1. 37–41.)

19. The importance that he gives it in the *Argumentum* is, uniquely, revealing (Melanchthons Werke, vol. 5: *Romerbrief-Kommentar* 1532m 1, 10–34). One will find in p. 373–78 of the quoted volume, a synthetic presentation of the *disposition* of the epistle that Schafer proposes from Melanchthon's indications in his commentary.

20. The index offered by Rolf Schafer, in Melanchthons Werke, vol. 5, *Romerbrief-Kommentar* 1532, 370–92, enables a certain number of them to be checked.

21. There again, Rolf Schafer's index is found to be previous and synthetic in the presentation that it offers for the use that Melanchthon makes of the *loci*, whether it is a question of the *loci dialectici*, of the *loci* associated classically with the various parts of the discourse and finally of the *loci communes* (386–87).

22. The fact that, in Rolf Schafer's edition, the commentary on ch. 12, keeps, after a general introduction of four pages, ten pages on v. 1, two pages on v. 2, one page on v. 3, two lines on vv. 4–6, two pages on vv. 7 and 8, three lines on vv. 9–18, and finally one page and a half on v. 19 can make up an illustration of this phenomenon.

23. Heinrich Bullinger, *In sanctissimum Pauli ad Romanos epistulam . . . commentaries* (Zurich, 1533). On Bullinger's commentary and its importance, one could particularly consult Peter Opitz, "Bullinger on Romans," in Kathy Ehrensperger and R. Ward Holder (eds.), *Reformation Readings of Romans* (London: T. & T. Clark, 2008), 148–65.

on the fact that there is no other way to reaching this understanding than to hold onto the thread of the discourse (*si non teneatur orationis filum*).[24] He is also convinced that Romans as a whole cannot be assigned to a single kind of text, and considers that within it various kinds of text alternate between demonstrative (epidictic), judiciary and deliberative.[25] He goes away from the evidencing of the articulations or of the figures of the discourse in order to interpret it, thus at the same time taking into account the *disposition et de l'elocutio*.[26]

Martin Bucer did not rest and in his turn he made a start on a commentary on Romans.[27] He also lays an emphasis on the *invention*, the *disposition* and the *elocutio*,[28] and offers an exegesis of the Epistle which is very much marked by taking the context[29] into account, implicitly attaching Romans to the judiciary kind of text,[30] he applies, according to him, the layout of the *disposition* to the scale of the whole of the Epistle, quite naturally finds the *status disputationis* in 1:16-17, and acknowledges a great syllogism on the scale of 1:18—3:31. His highly developed commentary however tends to run out of steam beyond this great syllogism, therefore from chapter 4, the main point having been made earlier, before being brought back to what was already written, from that time onwards.[31]

---

24. Heinrich Bullinger, *In sanctissimam Pauli ad Romanos* (see n22), first asterisk of the preface to Berchtold.

25. Heinrich Bullinger, *In sanctissimam Pauli ad Romanos* (see n22) second-last part of *l'argumentum: Porro orationis genus si illam spectes demonstrationem qua docet fidem esse institutiam, non legem, si inquam institutum Pauli summarium generatim spectes,* Demonstrativum *fuerit. At si expendas accusationem qua inter initia et Iudeos et Gentes peccati courguit, vel pensites quod in 6. et 8. Hortatur et consolatur, illud sane* Iudicale *fuerit, hoc* Deliberativum*. Sed ita fiery sole tut praecippuum aliquod dicendi genus reliqua in se contineat, imo sine reliquis absolui nequeat.*

26. It is enough, in order to be convinced, to refer back to the exegesis that he offers of the *exposition* (1.8-15) or, successively, about vv. 8-12, that he explains in the same block, and about v. 1.3, on which he comments in isolation, he departs from the assessment on which one deals respectively with the *exposition* itself and with a *preoccupation*.

27. Martin Bucer, *Metaphrases et Ennarationes Perpetuae Epistolarum D. Pauli Apostoli* [. . .] *Tomus Primus continens Metapphrasim et ennarationem in Epistolam ad Romanos, Argentorati* (Strasbourg: Rihel, 1536).

28. Bernard Roussel, *Martin Bucer lecture de l'Epitre aux Romains*, vol. 1 (University of Strasbourg, Faculty of Protestant Theology, unpublished thesis), 129, emphasizes it.

29. Bernard Roussel, *Martin Bucer* (see n27), 128-29, in particular puts it into an epigraph.

30. On this point, Bernard Roussel, *Martin Bucer* (see n27), 133.

31. Bernard Roussel, *Martin Bucer* (see n27), 139-40, clearly marks this limit.

6. Calvin's Commentary

In the preface to his commentary, dedicated to Simon Grynee, Calvin pays homage to each of these three precursors:

Monsieur Philippe Melanchthon, according to the excellent doctrine, industry and dexterity that he has in all sciences, has made the matters treated in those much clearer, above the others, which before him had placed something in the light. But because his aim was (as it appears) to deal only with the most notable points: however he ceased to do all of that, deliberately he let a great many things slip, which could not in any way trouble those who are not among those with great minds.

Later on there came Bullinger, who also has a good right to be greatly praised: for he also had a facility with doctrine, which has made it very pleasant.

Finally Bucer, throwing light on his work, (as a manner of speaking) finished the work. For this person (as you know) beyond the deep wisdom and the great knowledge that he has of several things, beyond the subtlety of his mind, his wide reading, and many other diverse virtues, which are seen today, when there are few people to be compared with him, on the contrary he is greater than many people: has received praise which is proper and special to him, which nobody else in our time has been engaged in interpreting Scripture with the greatest diligence.[32]

In writing that, Calvin is recognized incontestably indebted to his precursors, which should be taken into account, even if his commentary, being informed by the work of those precursors, is no less a personal work.[33] He

---

32. Here we refer to the translation that Calvin offered in the preface, dated 18 October 1539, from the first Latin edition (4,12–26).

33. A study of David Steinmetz can be found useful, "Calvin the Natural Knowledge of God," in Heiko A. Oberman, Frank A. J. L. James (eds.), *Via Augustini, Augustine in the Later Middle Ages, Renaissance and Reformation* (Leiden: Brill, 1991), 142–56, referenced in David Steinmetz, *Calvin in Context* (Oxford: Oxford University Press, 1995), 23–39. He shows what is indebted in Calvin, in the exegesis that he proposes on Romans 1:18–32, on the works of Melanchthon, Bullinger and Bucer, with whom he agrees in emphasising that creation displays the existence of God and is a mirror of divine glory, and in which he also manifests his originality when it is a question of validating that human beings have become almost blind through sin so that their view of God is very seriously altered. He arrives, in another contribution, "Calvin and Abraham: The Interpretation of Romans 4 in the Sixteenth Century," *Church History* 57 (1988), 443–45 (= *Calvin in Context*, 64–78), at the same conclusions about Romans 4 (see particularly 73–74). On the connections which can be established with Melanchthon, see particularly Alexandre Ganoczy, *Le jeune Calvin, Genèse et évolution de sa pensée réformatrice* (1966), 150–56, which compares essentially *L'institution de la religion chrétienne matrice* (1966), 150–56, and the *Loci communes* of Melanchthon, and comes to a conclusion very similar to that of Steinmetz. On the connections which can be made with Bullinger's commentary, see particularly Fritz Busser, "Bullinger as Calvin's Model in Biblical Interpretation: An Examination of the Preface to the Epistle to the Romans,"

is therefore placed in an exegetic tradition. That is why he does not hesitate to refer to the Fathers of the Church,[34] of whom he had an excellent knowledge[35] and whose translations he discusses regularly[36] and the interpretative choices[37] of Erasmus. Strengthened by a humanist education which in particular drew him to contact Guillaume Bude,[38] he enrolled himself in a vast movement which was careful to put back in honor the ancient pedagogic rhetoric, in a pedagogic intention. It was in this movement that the Reformers enrolled, who freed themselves from the scholastic exegesis by precisely claiming the rhetoric, which provided a new paradigm under the yardstick of which it became possible to interrogate and understand the texts. And, within their bosom, the pioneering works of Melanchthon certainly represented a decisive drive as far as it makes of rhetoric not simply a method of production of the discourse but also, and particularly, a method of exegesis of the text.[39] It is in this movement that one can from that time describe as

---

in E. J. Furcha (ed.), *In honour of Jean Calvin 1509–1564* (Montreal: McGill University Press, 1987), 64–95; J. E. Kok, "Heinrich Bullinger's Exegetical Method: The Model for Calvin?," in Richard A. Muller and John L. Thompson (eds.), *Biblical Interpretation in the Era of Reformation* (Grand Rapids: Eerdmans, 1996), 241–54. On those that may be carried out with Bucer's commentary, see Willem Van't Spuker, "The Influence of Bucer on Calvin as Becomes Evident from the Institutes," in B. J. Van Der Walt (ed.), *John Calvin's Influences, His Opus Magna*, in Christian Krieter and Marc Lienhard (eds.), *Martin Bucer and Sixteenth Century Europe*, 2 vols. (Leiden: Brill, 1993), 1:461–70; in "Bucer's Influence on Calvin: Church and Community," in David F. Weight (ed.), *Martin Bucer: Reforming Church and Community* (Cambridge University Press, 1994), 32–44.

34. If one is restricted to the first Latin edition of 1540, the following are quoted: Augustine (10 times, about 1.1 [13,22]; 1.23 [34, 1]; 1,28[38,8]; 4,19 [94,30]; Origen (4 times, about 1.1 [13,24]; 3,20 [66,15]; 5,14 [111,3]; 7,14 [143,29], in the last two cases, wrongly; Chrystostom (3 times, about 3,20 [66,14]; 6,5 [120,25]; 16,16 [312,34]; Lactance (twice, about 1,23[34,1] and 10,2 [215,2]; Eusebia (once, about 1,23 [34,1] and Jerome (once, about 3,20 (66,15]. For the presentation which is made, here and everywhere else—including in the annexes—of references to Calvin's commentary, one should refer to n1 of the present study.

35. On this point, see Olivier Millet, *Calvin et la dynamique de la Parole* (see n11), 168.

36. Thus about *Rm* 1.14,23; 6,17; 8,3 [153,35]; 12,3 [258,30]; 15, 16 [301,9]; 15,30 [308,11] (we restrict ourselves also to the 1540 edition).

37. It is thus in the case of *Rm* 8,3 . The 1556 edition becomes particularly severe for the interpretation which defends Erasmus of 5, 14 (111.7).

38. On this humanist education, see again Francois Wendel, *Calvin et l'humanisme* (Paris: P.U.F., 1975), and also Olivier Millet, *Calvin et la dynamique de la Parole* (see n11), 28–111.

39. We are grateful to Olivier Millet for having drawn our attention in this respect to the works of Kees Meerhoff which one will find gathered in *Entre logique et littérature, Autour de Philippe Melanchthon*, a work quoted in n6. See also idem., "Melanchthon aux Pays-Bas et en France: quelques sondages," in Gunther Frank and Kees Meerhoff (eds.), *Melanchthon und Europa*, vol. 2, *Westeuropa* (Stuttgart: Thorbecke, 2002), 163–93; idem., "Philippe Melanchthon et les débuts du College de France," in N.

6. Calvin's Commentary

Melanchthonian those who move and are already famous, before Calvin, Bullinger, Erasmus, Bucer and Sturm.[40] That is why we only speak here of a "relative" originality of Calvin, for, however impressive his mastery, his precocity, his authority and his confidence may be, one finds similar features in Melanchthon (1797–1560), who was just twenty-two years old when he published the first of his radically innovative approaches on the Epistle to the Romans, or in a Bullinger (1504–1575) who, like Calvin, was thirty-one years old when his first commentary on the Epistle appeared.[41]

That being said, it is right to acknowledge that Calvin's commentary also presents distinctive features which enable one to speak about his originality.

If he praises his predecessors, he is moreover as capable of emphasizing which are, from his point of view, their limits:

> M. Philippe Melanchthon has reached what he was claiming, that is to clarify the [3] most necessary points. And having stopped at these main points, he has left aside a great many other things which are not to be scorned, he did not wish to prevent others from amusing themselves in going through them with a fine-tooth comb them also.

C. Soares et al. (eds.), *Latineuropa: latim e cultura neolatina no proceso de construcao de identidade europeia* (Instituto de Estudios Clasicos da Universidade de Coimbra, 2008), 201–24; idem., "Melanchthon," in *Centuria latina (1): Cent une figures humanistes de la Renaissance* (Geneva: Droz, 1997), 537–49 (= Melanchthon [1497–1560], "Entre rhétorique et théologie," in *Entre logique et littérature*, 9–24, a short study which provides, in a synthetic manner, the essence of the author's theses).

40. The importance of this movement was already emphasized by Olivier Millet, *Calvin et la dynamique de la Parole* (see n11), 113–35. As Kees Meerhoff, *Entre logique et littérature* (see n38), 25–38, it is suitable also to establish a filiation between Georges de Trébizond (1395–1472 or 1473), Rodolphe Agricola (1444–1485), Erasmus (1466 or 1469–1536) and Melanchthon, it is, for Agricola, "the methodical reading of a text is [...] the indispensable preliminary to the production of the text" (32), a reading which goes beyond the discovery of the author's intention, his *concilium* and the evidencing of the logical organization of the text (ibid.). Speaking of the manner in which Melanchthon has leaned on Agricola, he notes: "Melanchthon, is the man who fashions, the man who knows how to reduce a message which is at the same time complex and dispersed to simple, elegant and clear proportions" (34). Melanchthon is also the man who is going to systematize a "circular movement" between analysis and text production (14). Meerhoff insists on the role that Basel and Strasbourg have respectively played in the receipt and spread of the Melanchthonian thought, the first across the importance of the one who had already been Erasmus's printer and showed himself to be a zealous distributor of Melanchthon, Jan Froben (38), the second, due to the arrival, in 1537, of Sturm, which encouraged him to have Melanchthon's *Dialectique* with a publisher, Crato Lylius (Kraft Muller) who again was going to publish, in 1541, his *Discours choisis*.

41. Raymond A. Blacketer, *The School of God: Pedagogy and Rhetoric in Calvin's Interpretation of Deuteronomy* (Dordrecht: Springer, 2006), 3–9, is a warning against approaches which, ending up considering Calvin's work for itself, tend to increase its originality.

> Bucer is too long, to be read quickly by those who are distracted by other occupations: and too highbrow to be easily understood by children, and by those who do not consider things closely. However incontinently he decides to deal with any subject, the unbelievable fertility of spirit that he has, puts so many things into his hand, that he cannot quench them in order to come to an end.[42]

Melanchthon's selective approach does not go so far as to fully satisfy Calvin, and that of Bucer, which was rather prolific, does not manage to convince him. He is going to choose a median way, a way which he claims from the beginning of his preface to Simon Grynee, by recalling their meeting, three years earlier, at the time of what doubtless was Calvin's first stay in Basel (1535 to spring 1536):

> I remember that three years ago, as we were privately conversing between us what would be the best way of interpreting Scripture, that the means of doing so which you most approved of, was also the one which I liked more than all the others. For we were both of the same opinion, that the main virtue of a demonstrator consists in easy brevity, and has no obscurity. And in fact, as it is that almost all his duty is contained in this sole point, that is to properly declare and reveal the author's intention (*mentem scriptoris*) which he has undertaken to demonstrate.[43]

Thus, this way is that of the *perspicua brevitas*, of precision and clarity, with, in a constant background, the search for the author's intention. This intention of the author, whether it is a question of *mens*,[44] of *sensus*,[45] of *propositum*[46] or of *consilium*[47] or that the term *in animo habuit*[48] is often explic-

---

42. He would take up again the translation that Calvin offered of the preface, dated 18 October 1539, of the first Latin edition [4,37–5,6].

43. We recall once again the translation that Calvin proposed of the preface, dated 18 October 1539, of the first Latin edition [3, 5–12].

44. Thus in Gryn [3,10] and about 5,5 [104,35]; 6,22 [132,18]; 9,11 [196,9]; 9,22 [206,10]; 10,14 [225,6]; 14,6 [284,3]. It must be clear that we do not claim, here as well as later, to being exhaustive from the time that such a term, such a figure is mentioned ... in the 1540 Latin edition. That being said, the work, which moreover is remarkable, of Benoit Girardin, *Rhétorique et théologique* (see n5) is found to be incomplete and sometimes inaccurate in the reference to figures (n54 and n55, 217 and 218). That is why we think it is useful to provide here the results of our own probing.

45. Similarly, about 6,19 [130,33].

46. Similarly about 1,28 [37,11]; 5,8 [106,14]; 5,17 [113,13]; 10,6–7 [219, 5–6]; 15,18 [302,22–23].

47. Similarly about 1,28[276.16]. Agricola already granted a more particular importance to discovering the "persuasive intention of the author, his concilium" (Kees Meerhoff, *Entre logique et littérature*, see n35, 32).

48. Similarly, about 2,26 [54,10].

6. CALVIN'S COMMENTARY

itly present at the heart of the Calvinian commentary—and one may add, if that does not take us away from the 1540 edition, that the phenomenon only increases throughout the editions of the work,[49] and into the French translation.[50] But this search for the *mens* or for the *consilium scriptoris* is, even more, implicitly omnipresent, if one takes into account the passages where Calvin places in evidence what Paul wants, wanted or has not wanted, or even what he wants to do: to confirm, link, console, detract, say, express, make understood, establish, win a point with the readers, show, oppose, prove, send packing, mean or finally touch.[51] And when one adds to the file the passages where Calvin gives evidence of what Paul states, hones and incites, alleges, leads, begins to show, confirms, demonstrates, makes understood, teaches, exhorts, incites, indicates, infers, shows, proves, wakens up, means or touches.[52] One realizes how involved he is in tracking down, into the greatest nuances, Paul's argumentative gesture.

The search for the author's intention is thus found to be very privileged by Calvin. It arises from a methodological choice, and we have seen that Calvin makes this choice to back to conversations that he had in Basel with Simon Grynee, an eminent philologist and theologian.

Relying on a suggestion on Gerald Hobbs, who in the field of searching for the hypothesis of the existence of an exegetic Strasbourg-Basel school.[53] Benoit Girardin suggested going close to the Calvinian method of the program detailing the method of theological teaching in this second town, a

---

49. Thus, for *mens*, about 8,19 [168,34] [1556]; 8.30 [178, note v–w]; 15,26 [306,7] [1556]; for *sensus*, about 3,27 [76,22] [1556]; 8,4 [156,13] [1556]; for *propositum*, about 3,21 [70,2] [1556]; 9,30 [212,1][1556]; for *concilium*, about 1,18 [30,2] [1556]; 2,2 [39,24] [1556]; 4,25 [99,17] [1556]; 8,5 [157,10] [1556]; 8,9 [160,30] [1556]; 8,17 [167,15] [1556]; 8,28 [175,27] [1556]; 8,31 [180,4] [1551 and 1556]; 9,1 [187,14; 11,22 [244.26] [1556].

50. It is in this way that, in 7,2 *nolebat* [135,23] as rendered as "it was not his intention here"; in 7,3, the intention does not correspond with the Latin text; in 8,31, *iam re bene comprobata* is rendered as "having definitely proved its aim"; in 14,17, *argument accommodavit* is reconstructed by "his intention was to apply."

51. The occurrences of these verbs or verbal expressions are listed in annex 1.

52. The occurrences of these verbs are listed, after the verbs expressing Paul's wishes, in annex 1.

53. R. Gerald Hobbs, *An Introduction to the Psalms Commentary of Martin Bucer*, 2 vols. (University of Human Sciences in Strasbourg, Faculty of Protestant Theology, 1971), 1:231–37. Bernard Roussel, "De Strasbourg à Basle et Zurich: une 'école rhenane' of exegesis (CA 1525 to CA 15400," *Revue d'Histoire et de Philosophie Religieuses* 68 (1988) 19–30, proposed that it should be constituted "from Strasbourg to Basle and Zurich" (20), that "the vetero-testamentary works should be revealing" and that it is characterized by: the exegetic work; its aim, which would be the legitimation of the clerks; the required abilities (to Hebrewise as far as possible) on behalf of people who are true linguists; the reference to the Jewish tradition; the choice of the typological exegesis; full acknowledgement of the authority of Scripture (25–34).

model described in 1536 by Carlstadt upon the express request of Simon Grynee.[54]

This program can be summed up as follows:

1. One considers a type of sentence to explain the obscure or difficult terms and in order to clear the argument: it is the *quid*.

2. One shows its form, which must be simple and manifest (*tropus*) or enveloping (*schema*): it is the *quomodo*.

3. The aim of the word is declared, what is its trend, what advice does the prophet give: that is the *propter quod*.

4. The sentence is compared to other parallel passages: that is the *collation*.

5. The passages which appear to contradict each other by resorting to analogy of the faith are reconciled: that is the *conciliation*.

6. One proceeds to the ethical application in the present day: it is the *accommodatio*.[55]

It does not seem dubious to us that, by privileging the search for the author's intention, Calvin grants a more particular importance to the *propter quod*, to this "aim of the word" which he tracks down in every way, while being particularly attentive to the *quid* and the *quomodo*. At the same time, as Girardin[56] points out elsewhere, one cannot say that Calvin follows in a servile manner the framework built as a model in Basel and suggests an exegetic itinerary signalized by each of the detailed stages by Carlstadt. "The Calvinian exegesis appears at the more integral beginning of the work: these procedures often recur, but taken in a single flow"[57] Even more, as we shall have occasion to revert to, Calvin moves most often from "Paul's rhetorical gesture"[58] that he gives as evidence of the elements relating to the *inventio*, the *elocutio* or of the *dispositio*.

Beforehand, one could wonder if the more particular accent that Calvin places on the author's intention could not also be explained partially due to the fact of his training as a lawyer.[59] There was in fact, in law, a custom of being interested not only in the *verba*, that is the letter, but more to the objective meaning of the law, its logic (*ratio legis*), and, in a more subjective

---

54. Benoit Girardin, *Rhétorique et théologique* (see n5), 195.

55. Ibid.

56. Ibid., 299.

57. Ibid.

58. Once again, Benoit Girardin, *Rhétorique et théologique* (see n5), 299, resumes, across this beautiful formula, a characteristic aspect of Calvin's exegesis.

59. This suggestion was made to us, at the time of the colloquium, by Frederic Chapot.

way, to the *mens legislatoris*, the legislator's intention.[60] That enabled the light that Calvin placed on Romans to be sharpened, to the extent that he also regularly uses, in order to describe his adversaries' opinions, and stigmatize the interpretation of passages of the Epistle that they offer,[61] of the verb *caviller*—or of the noun *cavillation*; certainly used in rhetoric in order to denounce a sophism,[62] this verb was also used in the juridical field in order to describe a wrong interpretation.[63] In such a similar perspective, and although, in the humanist climate where Calvin bathed, the rhetoric would have left the courtrooms in order to go to the schools, it has been proposed that there is, especially in his study on the first chapters of Romans, marked by the atmosphere of the court and the case, a picture presented "Paul, or rather his Evangel, which is the Word of God, as a lawyer.[64] Whatever it may be, there again, Calvin, by taking up a concept which goes back very far into the history of ancient exegesis[65] and is also present in mediaeval exegesis[66]

---

60. On this point see particularly Ian Maclean, *Interpretation and Meaning in the Renaissance, the Case of Law* (Cambridge University Press, 1992), 142–57.

61. As regards the term *cavillare*, see in particular about 2,11 [45,4]; 8,7 [159,1]; 15,8 [297, note g–h]. As regards the nouns *cavillum* and *cavillatio*, see respectively about 2,13 [45,35]; 3,21 [69,28]; 13,8 [276,32] (passages to which 9.16 [201,7] is added in the 1556 edition); 4,6 [82,33] and 3,8 [61,7]; 3,21 [69,9]; 9,16 [230,6].

62. Quintillen thus, *De institutione oratoria* 10,7,14.

63. On this matter, one could again refer to Ian Maclean, *Interpretation and Meaning in the Renaissance* (see n59), 135–38.

64. T. H. L. Parker, *Commentaries on the Epistle to the Romans 1532 to 1542* (Edinburgh: T. & T. Clark, 1986), 117.

65. The concept of the author's intention is already present in Chrysostom, especially in his homily XIX,2 on the *Eie aux Romans*: "*It is not enough for us to hear these words; we must know the intention and the aim of the one who pronounces them, to know towards what aim is his trend*: what I always ask of your charity. If, in fact, we are studying this text in this spirit, we shall see that it does not include any difficulty. Now, *the aim that Paul is now proposing*, is to destroy the pride which his words could have inspired in the Gentiles; by learning to be modest, they had to be more solid in their faith, and the Jews, saved from despair, could come to grace with more confidence. Therefore having this *intention* present in mind, let us now listen to what this passage includes. Therefore what does the apostle say? *How does he prove* that the fall is not irreparable, that they are not forever rejected? He proves it by the Gentiles themselves, by saying: By their sin, salvation came to the Gentiles, who also had to give them emulation." (Latin translation under the direction of M. Jeannin, in *Saint Jean Chrysostome, Oeuvres complètes*, r. X [Bar-le-Duc: L. Guerin & Cie, 1864], 347). It is possible that Calvin, who held Chrysostom's homilies in high esteem since he had planned to offer a French translation to act as a reading guide to his own commentaries before replace this project by the translation of his own *Institution de la religion chrétienne*, could have found a model in it. See again what will be said, in the following note, on Augustine.

66. The search for the author's intention has in fact its importance in the bosom of mediaeval exegesis. Ceslas Spicq, *Esquisse d'une histoire de l'exégèse latine au moyen age* (Paris: Vrin, 1944), emphasizes thus that it "appears with Anselme de Laon [1050 to 1117] until Prevostin [+1150 to +1210]. The three things that must be made clear in the

and is also present in mediaeval exegesis,[67] grants it a particular importance and gives it a proper emphasis.

Let us return now to the manner in which Calvin emphasizes Paul's rhetorical gesture by placing an epigraph on points which come from the first three operations of the *techne rhetorike*.

In the chapter on the *inventio*, one could find Calvin's interest for the arguments and for the causes and reasons that Paul puts forward.[68]

In the register of the *elocution*, there are numerous figures that he gives in evidence and from which he works most often in order to develop his commentary. Here the allusion, amplification, *anapodoton*, anastrophe, anthropopathy, anthypophora, anticipation, antithesis, communication, comparison, concession, correction, emphasis, epanorthosis, epiphonemon, exception, exclamation, excuse, expolition, *geminatio*, gradation, hyperbole, hyporyposis, hyppalagis, illation, interrogation, irony, metaphor, metonomy, objection, parenthesis, protestation, rejection, repetition, reprehension or *obiurcatio*, reticence, similitude, synecdocis and tautology can be noted.[69]

Finally, as regards the *disposito*, Calvin only applies the classical plan with relative prudence and is found to be more careful to reveal the progression of the discourse, to follow the thread of the theme (*filum disputationis*)[70]

---

exegesis of a book, is the intention, the end and the method, in order words the group of "parts" which are allowed to lead to a main theme; or the author's intention, the subject dealt with, and especially St. Thomas, were careful, endlessly expressed, to determine the "intention" of the author that they are studying. In the different explanations of which a text is capable, it wil always be the writer's intention which will decide the exegesis to adopt. The role of the commentator is nothing else than to find and express what the inspired author had in mind and wanted to translate into his text. Witness, this constant formula of St. Thomas: "*Hoc magis facit ad intentionem Apostoli*" [*In Tim.* Cap ii, lect.1, 193] [. . .] The thirteenth century thus found the hermeneutic principle of St. Augustine [*Super Genesim ad Litteram*, liber 1, cap. 21; PL XXXIV, col. 262; *scilicet quod in diversate sensuum, "qui ex paucis verbis oriuntur et fidei consonant, id potissimm diligamus, quod certum apparuerit auctorem sensisse"*], expressly recalled by Ulrich de Strasbourg and who asked to look for the meaning that the author wanted, with the control of faith, and *ex circumstantial litterae*." With the chain Georges de Trebizonde, Rodolphe Agricola, Erasmus, Melanchthon of whom it is a question in note 39, one has also to deal with writers who in their own way sensitized to the author's intention. However that does not prevent Calvin from making an original use of the idea.

67. One could also make a comparison with the original and creative manner in which he is situated in relation to the previous exegetic tradition.

68. In annex 2 one will find a summary of the passages in which Calvin points out the arguments, causes and reasons that Paul puts forward.

69. One can find in annex 3 a cumulative schedule of the occurrences of these different figures that we were able to mark over his commentary.

70. About 3,20 [67,15].

by studying and regularly naming the processes used by Paul.[71] Rather than mark the plan as classical rhetoric, he therefore prefers to show the profound coherence of the Epistle.

Melanchthon distinguished, after the epigraph (1, 1–7) and the Exorde (1,8–17), a first part (1,18–5,11), the *disputatio*, articulated around two *propositiones* (1,18; 3, 21–31).[72] He presented the second part as a type of new book, which is at the same time *analysis* and *methodus* and, thus, analytical revision of the first one around concepts of sin, grace and law.[73] According to him, the work would have been able to end there, and would not have needed to satisfy the Jews one a very serious question,[74] the one with which the debate in chapters 9–11 is charged. Then chapters 12–15 propose, according to him, a methodical presentation of the precepts (*methodus praeceptorum*)[75] arranged successively around the private life, of political life and religious life,[76] but whose relatively minor or annex nature is underlined by him, for "Christ did not come first of all in order to lay down moral precepts [. . .] but in order to reconcile us with God."[77] Finally the greetings in ch. 16 follow.

Bullinger, who also likes to research Paul's rhetorical gesture, discerned according to him made out the end of the first book at the end of chapter 8 and considered that this group could be brought close to John 15:8–11.[78] He considered that the second part was not in any way disconnected from the first (*a superior non prorsus divulsa*), while holding it nevertheless for a "new treaty (*nova tractatio*)."[79] On the other hand, he speaks about "various precepts about various matters (*varia quaedam de variis rebus praecepta*)" (96) about the third part, which according to him leads to chapters 12 to 16.

---

71. The appendix which Benoit Girardin, *Rhétorique et théologique* (see n5), 369–87, to the *dispositio* of the epistle according to Calvin, enables the progression that Calvin finds in the argumentation of *Romains* to be followed.

72. See more particularly Melanchthons Werke, vol. 5, 68, 1, 23, p. 69, 1,2 (beginning of the commentary of 1,18 and therefore of the *disputatio*).

73. Beginning of the commentary of 5,12, at the bridge between *disputatio* and *analysis* (Melanchthons Werke, vol. 5, 169, 1. 13–29 (esp. 1.15–18).

74. Introduction to ch. 9 (Melanchthons Werke, vol. 5, 249, 1.2–4: "*Absolvit totam disputationem et methodum de iustificatione; ac poterat iam desinere, nisi Iudaeis saisfacerre cogeretur de queastione gravissima*").

75. That is the title that he gives them (Melanchthons Werke, vol. 5, 284, 1.17)

76. Melanchthons Werke, vol. 5, 282, 1. 1–2–4–6: "*Quare non ob hanc causam praecipue venit Christus, ut traderet praecepta de moribus [. . .] sed [. . .] reconciliari Deum.*"

77. Melanchthons Werke, vol. 5, 284, 1.34 = 285, 1.4.

78. Heinrich Bullinger, *In omnes apostolicas epistolas, divi videlict Pauli XIII, et VII, canonicas, commentarii* (Tiguri: Christophorum Fro., 1549), esp. 2 and 76.

79. Heinrich Bullinger, *In omnes apostolicas epistolas . . .* (see n77), esp. 77.

Bucer, on his own behalf, by granting the place that acknowledges him in the great syllogism of 1:18—3:31, tends to reduce chs. 4-9 to an explanatory role and chapters 9-11 to a supplement in the bosom of a group which could have ended with them (*hic finem imponere epistolae poterat, nisi . . .*).[80]

Calvin operates one more cut than his predecessors. Certainly, he distinguishes, like Melanchthon, four great parts of which the first two have contours which are slightly different from those that the Preceptor of Germany recognized; they go respectively from 1:18 to 5:21, from 5:22 to 8:31, from 9 to 11 and from 12 to 14. But without naming them as such, he expressly says the opposite of Melanchthon from that time that it is a question of determining which is the first—and, for him, the main—*proposito* of the epistle and to situate it not in 1:18, but from 1:16b-17.[81] Finally, different from his predecessors, Calvin finds a deep coherence in the whole. Thus he begins the commentary that he proposed in 12:1:

> After Saint Paul dealt with the matters through which were necessary to begin in order to build reign of God, that is to say that in God alone men must look for justice, and in his sole mercy wait for salvation: that in Christ lies the perfection of all good things, and in him day by day is offered to us: *now following a very good order, he comes to create our customs*. And in fact, by this knowledge of God and of Christ, in which salvation is found, the soul is, in a manner of speaking, regenerated into a heavenly life: but by holy exhortations and teachings this life comes as if being ruled and ordered. For in vain one will work to show to men the care that they must take in leading their life, unless beforehand they have been shown that the source of all justice is in God and in Christ: which is to raise them from the dead.

Chapters 12 to 14 have nothing to do here with some appendix containing various provisions in a given arrangement: they appear as the logical and necessary continuation of what is above as the condition of possibility of the formation of customs and of a controlled and ordered life resides in the salvation and justice granted by God in Christ and in regeneration in a heavenly life. The third stage of the Law is here implicitly and no doubt enables Calvin to offer this global understanding of the epistle which goes straight to the parenetic section of chs. 12-14.

---

80. Martin Bucer, *Métaphases et Ennarationes* [. . .] *Tomus Primus*, 7b. This point is well analyzed by Benoit Girardin, *Rhétorique et théologique* (see n5), 168-270, which we follow here.

81. About 1,18 [29,35–30,2]: "Nobody thinks that the first proposal *prima propositon* [29,36], such that Saint Paul begins to deduct from his material by the proposal of repentance. But *as for me*, I think that the battle and the dispute begin here; and that the point for which he wants to debate, has been placed in the previous proposal (*in propositione superiori* [30,-2])."

6. Calvin's Commentary

In addition, the way in which he develops his exegesis may appear modern even if, on a number of points, it is also dated. Calvin, when he does not leave Paul's rhetorical gesture, each time it seems necessary, takes his point of departure from questions of translation or, more rarely, of establishing the text. The preoccupation for the text, in its realization, its dynamic and its coherence thus appears in him first of all and marks a real sensitivity for what from now on we can the exegesis in a synchronic perspective. Such an approach may appear, even today, to be coherent and strong, even if the way in which Calvin conceives the philological choices is no longer our own and if the material available to him to establish the text may seem rather poor.

Nonetheless, the fact remains that the primacy granted to the Word—which here is confused with Scripture—a saving word in which the condition of possibility of an adequate effect in an existence which is "regenerated into a heavenly life,"[82] leaves little room for an exegesis of a strictly historic and critical nature. The proposed commentary of 3:23 enables this relative defiance for history to the benefit of the dynamic and even more to the primacy of the Word-Scripture:

> The pagans told the truth. That history is the mistress for teaching us to live: but as they wrote it, nobody can gather an assured gain from it: it is Holy Scripture alone which can rightly give it such mastery. For in the first place, it offers us general rules, to which a separate history should be brought, so that we have some gain for ourselves. Then afterwards it discerns really well the deeds that we must follow, together with those that we must avoid.[83]

Interest in the Location of a Particular Figure, Anticipation

If priority thus comes to the Word-Scripture, that does not for all that make the subject of a linear reading which would led to granting the same importance and the same value to each element of the discourse.

A previous path in the company of Melanchthon's commentary had led us to put into an epigraph the fact it comes, in one place or another, to put into perspective Paul's statement in the name of the logic of development. Such is the case about 2:14, a verse in which it is shown that by

---

82. On the importance granted to the Word, at the same time written and preached, within the bosom of the Reformation, see the beautiful pages of Olivier Millet, "La Réforme protestante et la rhétorique (circa 1520–1550)," in Marc Fumaroli (ed.), *Histoire de la rhétorique dans l'Europe moderne, 1450 à 1950* (Paris: P.U.F., 1999), 259–312 (esp. 263–65).

83. This passage corresponds to lines 7–12 on page 98 in the edition of T. H. L. Parker and D. C. Parker (see n2).

nature, pagans do what the Law requires. Melanchthon states here that, "as the meaning of Scripture must be sought rather from the discussion as a whole than from any verse, those who claim that this verse pleads in favor of the justice of human powers, are exploiting Paul. For, in this case also, one must consider order and the logic of the sermon."[84] The dynamic and coherence of the epistle lead to register wrongly to those whose consideration of the canon led naturally to granting an intangible value to each verse. Melanchthon states in the event, in the name of his rhetorical reading, that a scriptural statement must be put into perspective, is even refuted by continuing the line of argument.

Calvin, without being so direct, relativizes also some passages in the epistle by bringing into evidence a very particular figure: anticipation. It may be symptomatic that it is about the verse which immediately precedes 2:14 that he uses this figure, not in order to revive a verse in terms of the logic of the subject but in order to warn one against an interpretation that he considers mistaken, implicitly in the name, of the intention of the apostle since those who are lost according to him are mistaken in failing to acknowledge the point on which Paul insists:

> *For those who hear the Law.* It is an anticipation by which he warns of the defence that the Jews could have alleged for them. For because they heard it said that the Law is the rule of justice, they glorify themselves with the only knowledge of that. Now in order to show their dream, and to take them away from this vain confidence, the Apostle says that from hearing the Law, or to have knowledge of it, is nothing, to say that through that a man may allege his justice before God: but one must bring ones work, according to what is said elsewhere, who has done things, will live in them, Deut., IV,1. Therefore this sentence does not mean anything else, except that if one seeks justice through the Law, one must fulfil the Law: because the justice of the Law consists in perfect accomplishment of works.
>
> Those who exploit this passage in order to establish the justification of works, deserve that small children themselves should laugh at them, and point at them. However it is madness and something outside the question, to pile up here long

---

84. Philippe Melanchthon, *Annotations Phil. Melanchthonis in Epistolas Pauli ad Romnos* . . . (see n9), 1522, F. b 4R, 19–23, on the Strasbourgian manuscript of 1523: "[. . .] *cum sentential scriptorium potius petenda sit ex tota disputatione quam ex uno aliquot uersu. Abutuntur Paulo, qui hung unum uersiculum pro institititia uirium humanarum probanda iactant. Iam et hic spectandus est ordo et ratio sermonis*" (= f.B IVr-v, on the *princeps* edition according to Classen, *Rhetorical Criticism and the New Testament* [see n11], 156).

6. Calvin's Commentary

questions on justification in order to untangle such a frivolous cavil. For the Apostle speaking to the Jews, insists only on this judgment of the Law, which he had mentioned, that is that nobody can be justified by the Law, except those who fulfil the Law: and if they break it, they will be heavily cast out by a curse. Now as for us, we do not deny that the Law does not contain perfect justice: but insofar as all men are found, and convinced against its transgressors, we say that one must seek another justice. And even contrary to what our enemies say, one may conclude from this passage, that nobody is justified by their works. For if nobody is justified by the Law, except those who fulfil the Law, it follows that nobody is justified, insofar as one will not find that he can boast about having fulfilled the Law.[85]

One of the limits, possibly conscious, of Calvin's commentary

Let us come at last to one of the limits, possibly conscious, of reading Calvin.

It is known that Calvin saw his *Institution de la religion chrétienne* as the way of accessing in the best way the reading of his commentaries, and also as a framework and a guide for a suitable interpretation of Scripture. He wrote this, in the preface of the 1539 edition which appeared in Latin in Strasbourg:

> My aim was to so prepare and instruct those who are devoted to studying theology, that they may easily access the reading of Holy Scripture and may advance without stumbling. For I think I have so understood the complete Christian religion in all its parts and to have distributed it in such order, that if someone holds on to it, he will have no trouble in deciding what he must look for in Scripture and for what purpose he must take away its content. As a result, it is not necessary that in my commentaries on Scripture I should argue at length on dogmas and extend myself into common places, considering that the road will have been paved; I shall always place them in the form of the compendium.[86]

---

85. This passage corresponds to 45,24–46,3 of T. H. L. Parker and D. C. Parker's edition (see n2).

86. Translation borrowed from Benoît Girardin, *Rhétorique et théologique* (see n5), 205.

This is how he was able to authorize the *perspicua brevitas* which makes one of the strengths of his commentary. The intricacy between *Institution* and commentary is therefore strong, even if it is not very visible. Calvin also thus succeeds with the feat of only sending back his reader twice to the *Institution* during his commentary.[87] The network of theological reading is no less real and comes sometimes to lead the way on the logic of the discourse.

An obvious example seems to us to be represented by his reading— with, it is true, most of the Reformers of his time—of chs. 7 and 8 of the epistle, in the name of a principle which can be translated in the formula of the *simul Justus et simul pecator*.

At the beginning of chapter 7, he comments on v. 6 ("but now we are delivered from the Law, being dead to that in which we were held: so that we may serve in newness of spirit and not oldness of the letter") in these terms:

> He follows his argument based on the nature of contrary things: If it was so necessary for the link to the Law not to serve in any way for holding the flesh in restraint, that rather it was a goad for inciting to sin: it must be said when we are delivered from it, that it is so that we should stop sinning. *If it is for this purpose that we are delivered from the servitude of the Law, that is that we should serve God: those who from this take a licence to sin, are doing wrong. These persons also say the wrong thing, who teach that by this means the bridle is loosened to lechery. Let us therefore note that we are delivered from the Law, when God, having delivered us from the rigour and curse of it, arouses us by his Holy Spirit, so that we travel on his way.*[88]

Thus it seems to take into account the fact, broadly admitted in contemporary exegesis, that Paul foresees that those who are regenerated in the blessing of the Spirit, would be effectively dead to sin.

However, from 7:15, he applies the following statement to the regenerated: "I am not doing what I want: but I am doing what I have" and, in 8:4, he begins the verse ("so that the justification of the Law should be fulfilled in us who do not travel at all according to the flesh, but according to the Spirit") in these terms:

> Those who understand by this, that men renewed by the Spirit of Christ should fulfil the Law, dream of quite another sense which is not Saint Paul's intention. For the faithful, while they are travellers in this world, never gain from that, for the Law

---

87. About 3,21–22 [70,24–25] and from 3,28 [77,14]

88. The passage corresponds to 137,23–31 of T. H. L. Parker and D. C. Parker's edition (see n2).

to be full and whole in them. One must therefore bring this to pardon: because when obedience to Christ is imputed to us, the Law is satisfied, so that we are considered righteous.[89]

Calvin certainly refers to the apostle's intention but not to his rhetorical gesture. In fact he has recourse to a theological argument by invoking the principle of *simul Justus* and *simul peccator*, that he reformulates in his own way. By renouncing the rhetorical argument, from this passage one may draw the impression that he is avoiding turning away this discipline to supporters' aims.

It seems to us that a new sign of the great respect that he shows for rhetoric, a discipline of which he would have known, with some of his contemporaries, show all interest in, from reading Paul's epistles. On this point, with the Melanchthons, Bullinger and another Bucer, his approach shows an exemplary character. The contemporary exegetists who are rediscovering the interest in rhetoric in order to better evaluate the dynamic of the Word contained in the Paulinian letters would often be well inspired to go and look at Calvin's commentary and a their own, in order to find there models of erudition and also, often, of wisdom, particularly as regards the very flexible use that they make, most of the time, of the plan of the *dispositio*.

---

89. The passage corresponds to 156,12–24 of T. H. L. Parker and D. C. Parker's edition (see n2).

7. The Institutio

Possible Influences of Martin Bucer on the *Institutio* of 1539

Stephen Buckwalter[1]

IT IS LEGITIMATE TO ask the question of the possible influences of Martin Bucer on the 1539 edition of the *Institutio* of Jean Calvin. In fact, it is almost a commonplace, in the research on the Reformer, that to state that the time in Strasbourg of the young Frenchman, a law graduate and marked by humanism, had a decisive influence on his theology. Already in 1925, Jacques Pannier wrote about this: "But Calvin, when he left Strasbourg, was more himself, was more Calvinist."[2] Ten years later, Jacques Courvoisier expressed himself similarly: it was in Strasbourg that Calvin became Calvin "the Calvin that we know, the prototype of the Reformed man."[3] Also it is easily conceivable to look for traces of Bucer's influence in the basic revision of the *Institutio* which appeared in Strasbourg in August 1539.

But before following these possible influences, it is advisable to turn one's head to some mistaken hermeneutical presuppositions.

In the first place, Bucer's influence on Calvin is not restricted to the period which begins by Calvin's arrival in Strasbourg, in September 1538.[4] Calvin knew and appreciated the writings of Martin Luther and was influenced by the latter without ever having met the Wittenberg Reformer. That Bucer had a really great influence on Calvin well before 1538, it is that he had emphasized and shown in a convincing manner—from 1966,

---

1. Bucer-Forschungsstelle, Heidelberger @Akademie der Wissenschaften.

2. Jacques Pannier, *Calvin a Strasbourg* (Strasbourg, 1925), 55.

3. Jacques Courvoisier, "Les catéchismes de Genève et de Strasbourg, Etude sur le développement de la pensée de Calvin," *Bulletin de la Société de l'Histoire du Protestantisme francais* 84 (1935) 107 (105–21); see also Christophe Strohm, *Johannes Calvin, Leben und Werk des Reformators* (Munich: Beck, 2009), 48.

4. See Matthieu Arnold, "Strasbourg" and "Calvin in Strassburg," in Herman J. Selderhuis (ed.), *Calvin Handbuch* (Tubingen: Mohr-Siebeck, 2008), 37–43, 74–78.

7. The Institutio

Alexandre Ganoczy in his work which became a classic, *Le jeune Calvin*.[5] The 1536 *Institutio* already presents a rich material which enables Bucer's influence on Calvin to be seen.[6]

In second place, one must consider that Calvin's work on the second edition of his *Institutio* was already well advanced when he settled in Strasbourg. On 1 October 1538, that is shortly after his arrival in Alsace, he wrote to Antoine Pignet how frustrated he was that the printing of this second edition was taking so long; after the date of the Frankfurt Autumn Fair was missed, he hoped in any case for an appearance for the Frankfurt Spring Fair, in March 1539.[7] In Calvin's eyes, the work finally sent to printing in 1539 was subject to a considerable delay. Also, is it legitimate to wonder if the 1539 edition of the *Institutio* is the only source—and even if it is the main source—to estimate Bucer's influence on Calvin during the Strasbourg years of the latter. In fact, during these three years, the young Frenchman wrote other works and other writings, such as his reply in September 1539 to Cardinal Sadolet,[8] his commentary on the Epistle to the Romans of March 1540,[9] or even his French treatize on Holy Communion,[10] written toward the end of his time in Strasbourg, not to mention his numerous letters. It is also entirely possible that Bucer's influence on these works may also be tiny, even less than what can be found in the *Institutio*.

Finally, the fact that we should concentrate on Bucer's reception by Calvin during the years 1538–1541 must not make us forget that Calvin could be marked by Bucer's heritage also in the years which followed.

One may resume these three considerations as follows: one could not limit Bucer's influence on Calvin to his influence on the second edition of the *Institutio* (1539); and however, our initial interrogation remains legitimate, for this edition is the first revision of the *Institutio* undertaken in the immediate surroundings of the Strasbourgian Reformer.

---

5. Alexandre Ganoczy, *Le jeune Calvin, Genèse et évolution de sa vocation réformatrice* (Wiesbaden: Steiner, 1966), 166–78.

6. Beyond Ganoczy, Ford Lewis Battles gives many proofs of Bucer's influence on the 1536 *Institutio*. (See John Calvin, *Institutes of the Christian Religion*, 1536 edition, trans. Ford Lewis Battles (London: Collins, 1975), 240–47 *et passim*).

7. "*Catechismi nostri edition valde me anxium habet, praesertim cum iam instet dies*" CO col. 261 (edition DVD: *Calvini opera database*, prepared by Herman J. Selderhuis et al. [Appeldoorn, 2005]; letter also published by Herminjard, vol. 5, 134, see particularly nn17–19).

8. *CO* 5, col. 385–416.

9. *CO* 49, col. 1–574.

10. *Petit traicté de la saincte cène*, *CO* 5, xol. 429–60. On this matter, see Marianne Carbonnier-Burkard, 223–49, and Matthieu Arnold, "Strassburg" (see n3), 41.

But what traces of Bucer's influence can be discovered in this revision? Between the 1539 *Institutio* and that of 1536, the first change which jumps to the eyes consists in the passage of six chapters to seventeen, which is accompanied by the noteworthy increase of the volume of the work: the in-octavo of 514 pages became an in-folio of 436 pages, in other words a work containing nearly three times' more material. Which up to then was no more than a detailed catechism became a true dogma.[11]

In the rewriting of the *Institutio*, in 1539, chapter 1, *De lege*, becomes chapter 3;[12] it is preceded by two new chapters, chapter 1, *De cognition Dei*, and chapter 2, *De cognitionehominis et libero arbitrio*. The old chapter 2, *De fide*, is henceforth chapter 4, and four unpublished chapters are added to it: 5, *De poenitentia*; 6, *De justification fidei et meritis operum*; 7, *De similitudine et differentia veteris et novi testament*; 8, *De praedestinatione et providentia Dei*. Chapter 3 of the 1536 edition, *De oratione*, becomes chapter 9, and chapter 4, *De sacramentis*, is arranged henceforth in three chapters: 10, *De Sacramentis*; 11, *De baptism*; 12, *De coenia Domini*. Three entirely new chapters follow: 13, *De libertate Christiana*; 14, *De potestate ecclesiastica*; 15, *De politica administratione*. Calvin himself gave great importance to this change, as the modified title already indicates: while the work was called, simply, *Christianae religionis institution*, "Instruction in the Christian religion," the 1539 edition is entitled *Institutio christianae religionis vere demum suo titulo respondens*, "Instruction in the Christian religion which from now on truly corresponds to its title."

The deep change brought to the first lines of the *Institutio* deserves, itself, being granted a great deal of attention. In 1536, this passage stated soberly: "*Summa fere sacrae doctrinae duabus his partibus constat; cognition Dei ac nostri*"[13] [The sum of almost all holy doctrine consists in these two parts: the knowledge of God and of ourselves]. The 1539 edition states exactly: "*Tota fere sapientiae nostrae summa, quae demum ac solida sapientia censeri debeat, duabus partibus constat: cognition Dei et nostri*"[14] [Almost all our wisdom, insofar as it truly deserves the name of wisdom and is truthful and strong, consists of two parts: the knowledge of God and of ourselves].

---

11. See Willem Nijenhuis, "Calvin, Johannes," *Theologische Realenzyklopadie* 7 (1981) 571; Arnold, "Strassburg" (see n3), 400s.

12. CO 1, LI-LVIII offers a useful synoptic view on the developments of the *Institutio* in its editions of 1536, 1539, 1543/45, 1550/54 and 1559.

13. OS 1, 37.

14. *Institutio Christianae Religionis* (from now on: *Institutio* 1539), Strasbourg, Wendelin Rihel, 1539, p. 1. We quote below the copy which is found in the "Johannes a Lasco" Library at Emden (side: Theol. 20 0126H), which can be consulted online, http:/herdenberg.jalb.de/display-dokument.php?elementId=12103.

7. THE INSTITUTIO

"What is striking, is that the concept of *sapientia* has replaced that of *sacra doctrina*. In this Chrisoph Strohm sees that, under the influence of the humanist spirit, Calvin underlines the reference to life and the existential dimension as characteristic of true theology.[15] For his part, William Bouwsma, another Calvin expert, believes that in this he can find a relativization of theology, as a limited human enterprise: according to this author, what Calvin proposes in the *Institutio* would not have the claim to be an absolute divine *doctrina*, but would only expose a limited human *sapientia*.[16] How does this change of terms go back to Bucer's influence? One can only speculate on this question. In any case, this alteration appears for the first time in Strasbourg, and it will remain in all the later editions of the *Institutio*.

When one quickly examines the 1539 *Institutio*. paying attention to the passages that are new in relation to the 1536 edition, we will discover a throng of interesting finds. Within the framework of this study, it is impossible to develop all of them, under the angle of a possible influence of Bucer. That is why I shall content myself with a selection.

First of all, what is striking is that the 1539 *Institutio* has been increased by a great many passages with debate with Anabaptism. Calvin attacks the Anabaptists, by reproaching them for claiming the Holy Spirit in order to scorn Scripture, and for thinking they can completely renounce the written Word of God.[17] Although, naturally, Calvin knew Anabaptism before September 1538,[18] it is entirely possible that his arrival in Strasbourg would have particularly sensitized him to this phenomenon: from 1526, this movement was represented uninterruptedly in the Empire town: almost all the main Anabaptist leaders, from Hans Denck to Pilgrim Marpeck passing by Michael Sarder, had lived there for a fairly long time; there were even, in the town, several Anabaptist communities. In the person of Bucer, Calvin met a

---

15. Strohm, *Calvin* (see n2), 49.

16. William J. Bouwsma, *John Calvin: A Sixteenth-Century Portrait* (Oxford University Press, 1988), 160.

17. "Emerserunt enim nuper vertiginosi quidam, qui spiritus magisterium fastuosissime obtendentes, lectionum ipsi omnem et corum irridrnt simplicitqtem, qui emortuam et occidentem, ut ipsi voantm literam afdhuc consectantur" (*Institutio* 1539, 13s. [CO 1, COL. 300S]). In the best known edition of the *Institutio*, that is, that of 1559, this passage corresponds to paragraph 1, ix,1, which is published in CO 2, col. 69. In order to be able to more easily identify the passages quoted according to the 1539 *Institutio*, in which we also give references to the 1559 edition, in the following we give also the references to the 1559 edition, as it is on the 1559 edition that the present editions of the *Institutio* are based.

18. On this subject, see particularly: Willem Blake, *Calvin en de doperse radikalen* (Amsterdam, 1973; English translation: *Calvin and the Anabaptist Radicals* [Grand Rapids, 1981]; German translation: *Calvin und die Taufer* [Minden, 1985]), 15-36 (German translation: 10-28).

Reformer who was justifiably devoted to discussion with the Anabaptists.[19] Thus, shortly after Calvin's arrival Bucer went to Hesse, where the Landgrave Philippe had engaged him to negotiate at Marbourg with incarcerated Anabaptist leaders.[20]

The arguments that Calvin uses against the Anabaptists in the 1539 *Institutio* are very similar to those that Bucer uses at the same time in Hesse.[21] Both of them criticize the fact that the Anabaptists are seeking to attain perfection, and both of them insistently emphasize that it is impossible for the Church to claim to be a perfect community. Christian existence, Calvin writes in chapter 1, does not consist in restoring an original state which claims to be innocent, but in the imperfect man progressing, with perseverance, under God's guidance and in the daily fight against sin.[22] In chapter 4, *De Fide*, Calvin writes, in a new passage in 1539,[23] that the ethical failures and insufficiencies of the Church do not constitute a reason to be separated from it. Some pages further on, he states again that a Church in which the Word of God is preached and where the sacraments are administered does not cease to be the Church on account of its moral deficiencies.[24] After having warned, shortly before, that in applying discipline it was not necessary to omit mildness,[25] Calvin gives evidence of a certain pastoral pragmatism,

---

19. See John S. Oyer, "Bucer opposes the Anabaptists," *Mennonite Quarterly Review* 68 (1994) 24–50; idem., "Bucer and the Anabaptists," in Christian Krieger, Marc Lienhard (eds.), *Martin Bucer and Sixteenth Century Europe*, 2 vols. (Leiden: Brill, 1993), 2:603–13.

20. On this subject see Martin Greschat, *Martin Bucer (1491-1951)* (Paris: P.U.F., 2002), 166–68.

21. These arguments are published—in an unsatisfactory manner, it is true—by Gunther Franz in *Urkundliche Quellen zur hessischen Reformationsgeschichte*, vol. 4, *Wiedertauferakten 1527-1626* (Marbourg, 1951), 213–37 (from now on: *Tauferakten Hessen*), a new edition will appear soon in volume 14 of the *Bucers Deutsche Schriften* (BDS), published by the Bucer-Forschungsstelle of the Heidelberger akademie der Wissenschaften.

22. 1539 *Institutio*, 44s. (*CO* 1, col. 350s.) = 1539 *Institutio*, III, iii, 14 (*CO* 2, col. 443s.).

23. 1539 *Institutio*, 143s. (*CO* 1, col. 545–47 = 1539 *Institutio*, IV, I, 13 (*CO* 2, col. 756s.).

24. 1539 *Institutio*, 147 (*CO* 1, col. 553) = 1559 *Institutio*, IV, ii, 1 (*CO* 2, col. 767s).

25. "Quod autem adeo difficulter ignoscebant iis qui dignum aliquid animadversione ecclesiastica perpetrarant, non ideo fiebat quod difficiilem illus apud Dominum veniam putarent; sed hac severitate volebant alios deterrere, ne temere proruerent in flatigia, quorum merito ab ecclesiae communion alienarentur. Quamquam verbum Domini, quod hic pro unica regula nobis esse debet, maiorem certe moderationem praescribig. Siquidem eo usque intendendum docet [2 Co. 2,6] disciplinae rigorent, ne absorbeatur a tristitia is cui praecipue consultum oportet, ut fusius supra disseruimus" (1539 *Institutio*, 151 [*CO* 1, col. 677] = 1539 *Institutio*, IV, I, 29 [*CO* 2, col. 767).

7. THE INSTITUTIO

which strongly recalls that of Bucer. Just as Bucer, at the same time in his negotiations with the Anabaptists of Hesse,[26] Calvin claims the example of the Corinthian community to fight a misunderstood perfectionism:[27] although the Corinthian community had succumbed to sin and led anything but an exemplary community life,[28] Paul, Calvin remembers, did not look for the slightest pretext to separate himself from it, but even described it as the Church of Christ and communion of saints.[29] In chapter 3, *De Lege*, Calvin attacks it—just as Bucer, some years before, in his negotiation with Pilgram Marpeck[30]—on refusing to take the oath: in order to justify this attitude, the Anabaptists are based on a literal interpretation of the Sermon on the Mount, which Calvin considered wrong.[31] Finally, one is struck by the fact that, in the 1539 edition, Calvin emphasizes, more than before, the external Word of God, in conjunction with his discussions with the Anabaptists;[32] one notes a similar development in Bucer from 1527, also in connection with his conflict with the Anabaptists, as is shown in his work *Getrewe Warnung*, and even more his *Bericht aus der Heiligen Schrift* (1534).[33] I am not stating that there are irrefutable proofs that Bucer influenced Calvin; but, in any case, we are dealing with striking parallels.

As regards the probable influence of Bucer on the Calvinian idea of predestination, throughout Calvin's Strasbourgian years, it was analyzed deeply by the Dutch Willem van't Spijker.[34] That is why to take up this file, in basing itself on the *Institutio*, does not seem to me to be fruitful at all. I shall therefore content myself with pointing out that van't Spijker thinks he can establish Bucer's influence on the Calvinist idea of predestination as far as the terms used by Calvin. However, in the first place he establishes that

---

26. Tauferakten Hessen (see n20), 219.

27. *Institutio* 1539, 144 (*CO* 1, col. 546s.) = 1559 *Institutio*, IV, i, 14 (*CO* 2, col. 757).

28. See 1 Cor 5 and 6.

29. See 1 Cor 1:2.

30. See *Quellen zur Geschichte der Taufer*, 5.7: *Elsass, 1. Teil: Stadt Strassburg 1522–1532*, ed. Manfred Krebs and Jean Rott (Gutersloh, 1959), 521, 1.33s.

31. 1539 *Institutio*, 14s. (*CO* 1, col. 399s.) = 1559 *Institutio*, II, viii, 26 (*CO* 2, col. 285).

32. 1539 *Institutio*, 14s. (*CO* 1, col. 302s.) = 1559 *Institutio*, 1, ix, 3 (*CO* 2, col. 71s.).

33. See the unpublished thesis of W. Ian Hazlett, *The Development of Bucer's Thinking on the Sacrament of the Lord's Supper in Its Historical and Theological Context 1523–1534* (University of Munster, 1975), 198–201, 375–84.

34. See Willem Van't Spijker, "Predestination bei Bucer und Calvin," in Wilhelm Neuser (ed.), *Calvinus Theologus* (Neukirchen, 1976), 85–111.

in the commentary on the Epistle to the Romans (March 1540) and not in the *Institutio*.[35]

On the other hand, we must examine in more detail the way in which Calvin understands Holy Communion. Before dealing with the paragraph of the *Institutio* which is dedicated to it, I would briefly like to present the Bucerian understanding of Holy Communion, by comparing it in particular with those of Martin Luther and Huldrych Zwingli. It is true that Luther refused to see in John 6 a text relating to Holy Communion. In a drastic way, he states, in *Of the Babylonian captivity of the Church* (1520), that this text does not utter the slightest syllable about the sacrament.[36] Luther wanted to drive away the traditional use of John 6, which served to justify the *communio sub una specie* and, more broadly, the Roman Catholic understanding of the sacrament. Naturally, Zwingli shared the rejection, by Luther, of the Roman understanding of Holy Communion, and he even agreed with the Wittenbergen in order to acknowledge that John 6 did not deal with the institution of Holy Communion; however, he revealed himself to be more open to this biblical text, particularly granting importance to v. 63, "*caro non prodest*" (the flesh is no use). For Zwingli, this verse confirmed its metaphysical dualism, which radically opposed spirit and matter, making it impossible to receive corporally the beneficial deeds of Christ.[37]

On the contrary, Bucer held vv. 51–58 as more central, and he interpreted them from the context of the words of the institution.[38] Thus, Bucer understood v. 51, "this bread is my body, that I shall give for the life of the world," as an interpretation of "take, eat, this is my body, given for you." He found in John 6:55, "my body is the true food," the basis for spiritual eating, which for him had a decisive importance. This verse means, for Bucer, that when Christ acts on us with the visible signs of bread and wine, he is offering himself to our soul, by a parallel process, as *cibus animae*, a true food for the soul. There cannot be any corporal and external eating of this food for the soul. Thus, for Bucer, the decisive metaphorical element is not—contrary to Zwingli—the *is* in the sense of "*means*," in the expression "*hoc est corpus meum*," but rather the verb "to eat," as it is used in John 6:51–58. This is what he expressly emphasizes in a letter of February 1531 to Zwingli: "*Metaphoram agnosco in verbo manducandi*." In the verb "to eat," I see a

---

35. See Van't Spijker, "Pradestination" (see n33), 102–7.

36. WA 6, 502, 7s.

37. See Greschat, *Bucer* (see n19), 79.

38. This matter was the subject of a precise study by Ian Hazlett, "Zur Ausdegung von Johannes 6 wahrend der Abendmahlskontroverse," in Marijn de Kroon and Friedhelm Kruger (eds.), *Bucer und zeine Zeit* (Weisbaden: Steiner, 1976), 74–87.

metaphor[39]). Between the 1536 edition of the *Institutio* and that of 1539, the passage dedicated specifically to Holy Communion was considerably increased and reworked. In the first place, we find that what was only a relatively short passage in chapter 4, *De sacramentis*, in 1539 becomes an independent chapter, *De coena Domini* (ch. 12). What is striking, in the first edition of the *Institutio*, is that John 6 is only recalled in passing[40] and that it was never the basis of Calvin's argumentation. If we turn our eyes toward the 1539 edition, we find, at this precise lace, a short but decisive addition, in which Calvin explicitly claims John 6:51 (*panis, quem ego dabo, caro mea est, quam ego dabo pro mundi vita*—"The bread that I shall give you is my body, that I shall give for the life of the world"), and where he makes one notice that this body serves the spiritual life of the soul.[41] Moreover, in the 1539 *Institutio*, pp. 330 to 335,[42] almost totally, perfectly unpublished in relation to the 1536 edition. In this new passage, we find for example the following formulation: "What therefore is Holy Communion but the visible witness of the promise which is found in *John* 6, that is that Christ is the bread of life which comes down from heaven?"[43] Some lines later, Christ's body is described as "*spiritual alimentum*" [spiritual food]. One must wait through several pages to find this pithy explanation; "*Christum esse panem vitae, quo in salute aeternum nutriantur fideles, nemo est, nisi prorsus irreligiousus, qui non fateatur*" [Nulle personne qui confesse—si ce n'est quelqu'un totalement depourvu de religion—que le Christ est le pain de vie, par lequel les

---

39. Martin Bucer, *Correspondance/Briefwechsel*, vol. 5, Septembre 1530–Mai 1531, ed. Reinhold Friedrich et al. (Leiden: Brill, 2004), 276, 1.17, 277, l. 1.

40. Only in the following passage: "Non ergo praecipuae sunt sacramenti partes, corpus Christi simpliciter nobis exhibere, sed magis, promissionem illam, qua carnem suam vere cibum esse testator, et sanguine suum potum quibus in vitam aeternam pascamur; qua se panem vitae esse affirmat, de quo qui manducaverit, vivet in aeternum: illam, inquam, promissionem obsignare et confirmare (Ioan 6)." (*OS* 1, 138 = *CO* 1, col. 120).

41. "*Quae sentential verbis illusluculenter comprobatur: panis quem ego dabo caro mea est, quem ego dabo pro mundi vita. Quibus haud dubie Dominus innuit suum nobis corpus ideo pro pane futurum ad spiritualem animae vitam, quia in mortem pro salute nostr exponendum erat. Semel enim ipsum dedit quo panis fieret, quam in mundi redemptionem crucifigendum exposuit; quotidie dat, ubi participandum, quatenus crucifixum est, evangelii verbo nobis offert*" (*Institutio* 1539, 329 [*CO* 1, col. 994]; slightly altered in 1539 *Institutio*, IV, xvii, 5 [*CO* 2, col. 1005]).

42. This passage of the 1539 *Institutio* corresponds, *grosso modo*, to the text edited in *CO* 1, col. 995–1005. One finds there, but in a different order, elements in paragraphs IV, xvii, 5.8.14 and 20s. of the 1559 *Institutio* (*CO* 2, col. 1005–8, 1012s. and 1018–21).

43. "Quid enim est coena nisi visibilis et conspicua promissionis eius testificati quae Ioannis sexton habetur: nempe, Christum esse panem vitae qui e coelo descendit?" (1539 *Institutio*, 330 [*CO* 1, col. 995]. See *Instituio*, IV, xvii, 14 [*CO* 2, col. 1013]).

croyants sont nourris pour le salut eternel].[44] And finally, on the next page, Calvin again claims the Johannic metaphor of food: "*Quin et ipsam, in qua residet, carnem vivificam nobis reddit, ut eius participation ad immortalitatem pascamur*" [Yes, he also allows the body, in which he lives, to be alive for us, so that, by our participation in it, we may be fed for immortality].[45] Calvin continues, by quoting John 6:51; "I am, he said, the bread of life, coming down from the sky [. . .] and the bread that I shall give is my body, that I shall give for the life of the world."[46]

It is not possible to examine in detail all the other additions that Calvin brought, in 1539, to his chapter on Holy Communion. But the examples that we have quoted show clearly how much, in the 1539 edition, John 6—and particularly the verses of this chapter which held importance for Bucer—is found at the center of developed additions, while, in 1536, this biblical passage was still recalled briefly and in passing. When, in 1539, Calvin deals with the doctrine of Holy Communion, the spiritual food of believers becomes a central axis of his argumentation. It is difficult not to see a sign of Bucer's influence.[47]

I would like, in conclusion to enter a domain which is perhaps more customary in which it is probable that, throughout his Strasbourgian years, was under Bucer's influence. Shortly before the end of the *Institutio*,[48] in a new passage of chapter 17, *De vita hominis christiani*, Calvin finds, in a remarkable manner, words full of sensitivity in order to depict the joys of life, the beauty of creation, with its colors and perfumes. He writes thus:

---

44. 1539 *Institutio*, 332 (*CO* 1, col. 999) = 1559 *Institutio*, IV, XVII, 8 (*CO* 2, col. 1005).

45. 1539 *Institutio*, 333 (*CO* 1, col. 1001) = 1559 *Institutio* IV, xvii, 8 (*CO* 2, col. 1008).

46. "Ego sum, inquit, panis vitae qui de coelo descendi' et panis quem ego dabo, carom ea est, quem ego dabo pro mundi vita" (1539 *Institutio*, 333 [*CO* 1, col. 1001] = 1559 *Institutio*, IV, xvii, 8 [*CO* 2, col. 1008]).

47. Another very important theme, that I cannot deal with here, and in which Bucer influenced Calvin, is that of the alliance. On this matter see Marc Lienhard, "Human experiences, theological enthusiasm and church life: Calvin in Strasbourg (1538–1541)," *Revue d'Histoire et de Philosophie religieuses* 89 (2009) 456s. On the importance of the notion of alliance with Bucer, see Gottfried Hammann, *Entre le secte et la cité. Le projet d'Eglise du Reformateur Martin Bucer (1491–1551)* (Geneva: Labor et Fides, 1984), 89s., 129–31, 144s., 193–95, 106, 211, 312 and 346; Thomas Kaufmann, *Die Abendmahlstheologie der Strassburger Reformatoren bis 1528* (Tubingen: Mohr Siebeck, 1992), 157–59; Achim Detmers, *Reformation und Judentum. Israel-Lehren und Einstellungen zum Judentum von Luther bis zum fruhen Calvin* (Stuttgart: Kohlhammer, 2001), 186–98.

48. At the time of the 1559 revision, this passage, which until then ended the *Institutio*, became ch. 10 of book 3 (*CO* 2, col. 528–32), and received the new title of *Quomodo utendum praesenti vita eiusque adiumentis*.

7. The Institutio

"Beyond their various uses, herbs, trees and fruit are pleasant and charm us by their scent [...] The Lord has decorated flowers with such a beauty that it strikes our eyes [...] Beyond their necessary use, has he not given us innumerable commendable things?"[49] In other words, Calvin understands the joys of creation as an expression of the goodness of God. He considers as a plan of God the fact that his creatures are not only useful, but also beautiful, spreading joy for the senses. Thus, his theology opens up to a feature which, according to me, is still more marked in Bucer.

It is thus that, in his matrimonial notice for the town of Ulm (November 1533), the Strasbourgian Reformer writes:

> How many are the sweet and pleasant tastes, the perfumes, the shapes, the sounds and other joyful and charming things that God has created for us! Moreover, he gave us even the capacity and power to use everything conveniently. And all that, with the only aim being that human beings should live here with one another, in a manner which is full of joyful and pleasing love, without planning that could have a particular use. It was also in this aim that, in the Old Testament, God ordained human beings to organize, at regular intervals, common feasts, eating the best dishes there and drinking there and rejoicing. This was for no purpose other than to renew and increase their friendship in God and with Him. But this custom is so great that one can hardly express it. In fact, when true love and joy between men are lacking, it is all human life which is lacking.[50]

---

49. Here is the whole paragraph: *"Iam si reputemus quem in finem alimenta creaverit, reperiemus non necessitati modo, sed oblectamento quoque ac hilaritati voluisse consulere. Sic in vestibus, praetor necesitatem, finis ei fuit decorum et honestas. In herbis, arboribus et frgibus, praetor usus varios, aspectus grtia et iucunditas odoris. Nisi enim id verum esset, non recenseret propheta intr beneficia Dei, quod vinum laetificat cor hominis, quod oleum splendidam eius faciem reddit [Ps 104, 15]. Non commemorarent passim scripturae, ad commendandam eius benignitatem, ipsum eiusmodi omnia dedisse hominibus. Et epsie naturals rerum dotes satis demonstrant quorsum et quatenus frui liceat. An vero tantam floribus pulchritudinem indiderit Dominus, quae ultro in oculus incurreret, tantam odoris suavitatem, quae in olfactum influeret, et nefas erit vel illos pulchritudine, vel hunc odoris gratia affici? Quid? Anon colores sic distinxit ut alios aliis faceret gratiores? Quid? Anon auro et argento, ebori ac marmori gratiam attribuit, qua prae aliis aut metallis aut lapidibus pretiosa redderentur? Denique anon res multas, citra necessarium usum commendable nobis reddidit?"* (1539 *Institutio*, 433 [CO 1, col. 1149] = 1539 *Institutio*, III, x, 2 [CO 2, COL. 522 9S.1]).

50. "Wie fil hat vnns doch Gott suesser gutter geschmack, veruch, farben, gestalten, gegons vnd anderer lustlicher vnnd zierlicher dingen, erschaffen, da zu auch geschicklikeyt vnnd kunst, das selbig alles artlich zugeprauchen, verlauhen, Alles darumb, das die leut sich hi emit eymanderylieplich, lustlich vnndanmuertig machen, on sonderen nutz, der weiters darauss kome solicherley ist auch, das der Herr den alten verordnet,

Maybe he dared to find, in this aesthetic and pastoral pragmatism of Bucer, a model for the opening that Calvin suddenly shows, in the final pages of the 1539 *Institutio*, because, in creation, it is beautiful and pleasant. In any case, in that there are sentences which Bucer could have written.

Nevertheless, the conclusion of our brief incursion into the 1539 *Institutio* remains the following: the influence that Bucer probably had on the second edition of the *Institutio* is not marked first of all in the turns of phrase and in the words, but the accents, in the motifs and in theologically guiding ideas. As Pannier had it observed in 1930, in opposition to Bucer, Calvin was a writer of great talent, who could give a new literary shape to the ideas that he had borrowed from his elder colleague.[51] One does not know how to be content to establish Bucer's influence on Calvin's work from apparent linguistic borrowings; a careful in-depth reading is required. It is therefore clear that the work begun by August Lang,[52] Jacques Pannier,[53] Jacques Courvoisier,[54] Marijn de Kroon,[55] and Willem van't Spijker[56] consists in establishing Bucer's influence on Calvin, is only at the beginning, and it asks to be continued.

(Translated from the German by Matthieu Arnold).

---

zun zeiten vor im gemeine zech zu halten, das best zu essen vnnd trincken vnnd frolic susein, das dann anders nichs vff im hat, dann das es dazu dienet, da sie ire freintschafften inn vnnd mit got erfrischeten vnnd mehreten. Dis ist aber dan so ein grosser nutz, das er nit auss zusprechen ist. Dan woe s an dem fehlet, das die leut zu einander ware lieb vnnd lust haben, so fehlets am gantzen menschlichen leben." (*Bucers Deutsche Schriften*, vol. 10, *Schriften zu Ehe und eherecht*, ed. Stephen E. Buckwalter [Gutersloh, 2001], 346, 1, 1–11).

51. Jacques Pannier, "Recherches sur la formation intellectuelle de Calvin," *Revue d'Histoire et de Philosophie religieuses* 10 (1930) 422s. (145–76, 264–85 and 410–47). See also Courvoisier, "Catéchismes" (see n2), 119s; Arnold, "Calvin und Strassburg" (see n3) 75.

52. See August Lang, *Der Evangelienkommentar Martin Butzers und die Grundzuge seiner Theologie* (Leipzig, 1910), 9–11, 25s. et passim.

53. See *Supra*, n1 and n51.

54. See *Supra*, n2.

55. See Marijn de Kroon, *Martin Bucer and Johannes Calvin: Reformatorische Pwespektiven* (Gottingen: Vandenhoeck & Ruprecht, 1991).

56. See Willem Van't Spijker, "Bucer's influence on Calvin: Church and Community," in David F. Wright (ed.), *Martin Bucer, Reforming Church and Community* (Cambridge University Press, 1994), 32–44; idem., "Bucer and Calvin," in Christian Krieger, Marc Lienhard (eds.), *Martin Bucer and Sixteenth Century Europe* (see n18), 1:461–70, as well as the study quoted in n33.

8. Warnings to the Reader

The "Warnings to the Reader" of the 1539 Institutio and the 1541 French Edition

James Hirstein[1]

Introduction

IT IS OUR AIM to understand how John Calvin designed and conceived his readership in the *Epistola ad lectorem* of the *Institutio christianae religionis* published in Strasbourg in 1539, in the "Argument of the present book" of the French translation of the same text published in Geneva in 1541, and in the first lines of the chapter which closes these two publications, the "*De vita Christiana*."[2]

In order to restrict ourselves to the publications in the French language, the differences between the two warnings to the reader, and more precisely the differences between the two warnings to the reader, have been studied in a rich and interesting manner at the end of the last century.[3] We are allowing ourselves to offer this study because the point of view of the

---

1. Université de Strasbourg.

2. The *Epistola* and the "Argument" are quoted according to John Calvin, *Institution de la religion chrétienne* (1541). The critical edition by Olivier Millet, 2 vols. (Geneva: Droz, 20008), (continuous pagination) 171–78 (*Epistola*) and 107-11 ("Argument"); we have numbered the lines of these texts taking into account their titles in the count (= Calvin, *Institution*, Millet). We quote here the Latin text of the *De vita Christiana* according to *CO*.

3. Cf. Olivier Millet, *Calvin et la dynamique de la parole: étude de rhétorique reformee* (Paris, Honore: Champion, 1992), 763-86 (= Millet, *Calvin et la parole*) and Jean-Francois Gilmont, *Jean Calvin et le livre imprimé* (Geneva: Droz, 1997), 155-65 (= Gilmont, *Calvin et le livre*).

scientific editor of a humanist correspondence almost of the same era (Beatus Rhenanus, 1485–1547) may help to establish certain important terms in their context.[4]

At the beginning of his recent edition of the *Institution* of 1541, Olivier Millet showed to what point the French translation of the *Institutio* was an outstanding event.[5] If truly translations of the Bible in the vernacular language (Luther translated the New Testament into German in 1522, the whole Bible in 1534 and Olivetan the Bible into French in 1535) and also translations of works of pious, moral or political edification existed, the idea of putting into vernacular language a treatise of doctrine had a challenge. There were at least two obstacles. The first one was that it seemed inconvenient, even dangerous, to give to a doctrinal discussions which should only come to specialists, to a non-erudite public. It was, in a sense, to lower the material of the discussion itself, without being able to prejudge distressing consequences. It was the opinion of other specialists who had enjoyed the same humanist training as Calvin: one could name Erasmus by example. The second obstacle lay in the very nature of the public. Were the *plebs Christiana*, the "popular" readers, whose training had armed them only with a knowledge of French, interested in such a book?[6]

But we must recall that Calvin was not afraid of challenges. From the first Latin edition of the work of six chapters published in Basel in 1536 covers a public which was enlarged on account of its pressing and persuasive appeal to the king and to the people.[7] It was therefore a risky gamble, and we shall see the mistaken joy and the strong feeling of obligation toward his readers which Calvin will display after such a warm welcome reserved for his work.[8]

It is partly this success which pushes the Reformer to go further. But how? Millet emphasizes that Calvin, who was looking with all his heart to reach more people by using the vernacular language, did not manage to find the approach or context that was needed. A first translation project

---

4. See *Epistulae Beati Rhenani: La correspondence latine et grecque de Beatus Rhenanus de Selestat*, vol. 1 (1506–1517), critical edition raisonnée with translation and annotation, project managed by François Heim and by James Hirstein, volume ed. James Hirstein (Turnhout: Brepols, 2010) (= *EHR*, 1 [Hirstein]).

5. Calvin, *Institution*, Millet, 1:20–22.

6. Calvin himself referred to these two obstacles, see his *Praefatio in Chrysostomi Homilia*, CO 9, 831–33, and Millet's analysis, *Calvin et la parole*, 170–76 and 772. There, the Reformer uses the expression of *plebs Christiana*, see later.

7. It is possible that this wish for vulgarization better explains that a translation project had already conceived the literary and stylistic features of the 1536 *Institutio* which were picked up by Millet, in Calvin, *Institution*, 24.

8. For Calvin and the feeling of obligation, cf. Gilmont, *Calvin et le livre*, 121–22.

for the 1536 *Institutio* undertaken in Geneva failed. In 1537, in this same town, Calvin schematically published an *instruction de foy*. Sent away in April 1538, he was again in Basel, and it was no doubt in this town that the Reformer began to translate homilies by Saint John Chrysostom into French, without doing well in this work. There are therefore two attempts at vulgarization into the vernacular language that Calvin has behind him when he arrives in Strasbourg in September 1538.[9]

Without mentioning his other activities, the Reformer is going to devote himself until the month of August 1539 to the spectacular rewriting of the *Institution* into Latin, which enlarged the first edition by more than twice its original size.[10] Although the first French translation of 1541 appeared in Geneva, it can only reflect the time that Calvin spent in Strasbourg from 1538 to 1541.

The Idea of "Warning to the Reader"

One is inclined to call the main texts "prefaces" that we are going to study here. We prefer the term of "warning to the reader" to that. First of all, the Latin text essentially bears this title: *Epistola ad Lectorem*, which in 1553 will become *Ioannes Calvines lectori*, a small change which eventually prefigures the great revision that the Warning will undergo in 1559. In the sixteenth century, the warning to the reader effectively takes the form of a letter. In order to quote two examples produced in Basel in June 1518 in a publication of biographies and Roman historians, one reads

> *Ioannes Frobenius candido lectori S[alutem] D[icit]* and *Io[annes] Frobenius candidis lectoribus S[aluem] D[icit]*

with, in the same work, the passage of the address to a single reader in that to a group of readers.[11] In both cases, these warnings end by using the second person, by the expected *vale* and *valete* with, in the first example, the vocative of *candide lector*.[12] As is often the case, one finds the second

---

9. See Calvin, *Institution*, Millet, 22–26, and Millet, *Calvin et la parole*, 170–76 and 772.

10. See Gilmont, *Calvin et le livre*, 69.

11. See James Hirstein, "Beatus Rhenanus and the 'Warnings to the reader' signed 'Jean Froben' on the *Histoire* of Ammien Marcellin and on the *Histoire Auguste* in the Basel edition of June 1518," *Annuaire des Amis de la Bibliothèque Humaniste de Selestat* 39 (1939) 32 (candidis lectoribus) and 42 and 47 (candido lectori) 27–50.

12. For other cases of warnings to the reader, see *EBR*, 1, Hirstein, Ep. 12, 13, 21, 24, 31 ("to the Studious"), 36, 49 (= "to the Studious"), 50 ("to the Studious"), 74, 76, 79, 83 and 95.

person of the reader only at the beginning and at the end of the warning. What may strike us in Calvin's Latin warning of 1539 is that the name of the sender, so to speak, is absent and is replaced by the description of *Epistola*. This increases the anonymous nature of the document, in this sense that no personal author is named.

In fact, since the warning to the reader as a genre is addressed to an anonymous reader, more freedom is allowed within the field of literary paternity. For example, in the case of Basel, it is possible that the author of the warning is not Johann Froben, but his scientific advisor, Beatus Rhenanus. In any case, Calvin's Latin Warning bears anticipated generic marks, with a developed "farewell," as may be the case, at the end:

> *Vale amice Lector, et siquem ex meis laboribus fructum precipis, me precibus tuis apud Dominum adjuva* [Keep well, reader friend, and if you see any fruit of my labours, help me with your prayers to the Lord].

If we have no hesitation in describing the Latin text as a "warning," it is not the case for the French text. We find ourselves, according to the title itself, before an "Argument for the present book." One may well thus read the word "*argumentum*" in the sixteenth century before the texts that he describes. We go back for example to a study of editions of Tertullien obtained by Beatus Rhenanus. Frédéric Chapot notes that in the third edition of 1539, each treatise is preceded by an *argumentum* and then *annotationes*.[13] The *argumentum* briefly resumes the main ideas which animate Tertullius' demonstration and places them in relation with the other treatises."[14] Therefore the argument exposes in a few words the subject or the theme in the economy of the work. The sixteenth-century French word has the same meaning in such a context.[15]

But Calvin's French text, for us, does not conform to this; it is an explanation of what he is going to do more than being a summary of what he has done. It is the type of explanatory material that one finds in a warning to the reader. From this fact, we must ask ourselves about the reasons which

---

13. Frederic Chapot, "Dans l'oficine d'un philologue, Beatus Rhenanus éditeur de l'*Adu. Hermogenem* of Tertullien (Basel 1521, 1528, 1539)," in *Beatus Rhenanus (1485–1547), lecteur et éditeur des textes anciens*, ed. J. Hirstein (Turnhout: Brepols, 2000), 265 (263–83) (= *BRLE*).

14. Ibid., 268.

15. Cf. E. Huguet, *Dictionnaire de la langue française du XVIe siècle*, vol. 1. (Paris: Didier, 1925), 301–2: "subject of a literary work, of a discourse." Huguet also notes the meaning of "cause, occasion" and of "subject of an act," but neither the examples provided nor their contexts are appropriate to the entitled Calvinian work in question.

8. Warnings to the Reader

pushed Calvin to choose the title "Argument for the present book" for his warning to the reader.[16]

We can therefore also justify our appellation by recalling that, for the 1560 French translation published by Jean Crespin, our 1541 French text will not at all be resumed as such (although that was the case up to then for the preceding French editions). This time, it will be properly replaced by a translation of the 1559 revised Latin Warning. That is to say that our word "Argument" will finally be replaced by the title: "Jean Calvin to the reader" and by the other expected epistolographic forms.[17]

The use of the term of warning seems important for another reason. It explains better the function of the text in the economy of a sixteenth-century book. In fact, in the Basel book of Roman biographies and historians of 1518 that we recall, the warning to the reader is preceded by an important dedicatory letter from Erasmus to the Dukes Frederick and George of Saxony.[18] The Dutch humanist addresses the Dukes of Saxony and deals with the contemporary interest that the imperial biographies present and the collection that in our time we call the *Histoire Auguste*. The presence of a dedicatory letter which exposes the interest of the publication for the dedicatee and deals with the author and the nature of his work better fulfils the function

---

16. The editors of Calvin's *Opera selecta* bring up an argument of the differences between the two *Avis* in order to say that the French warning had been written before the Latin warning in order to appear in the French translation of 1536, whose existence they try to prove, see OS, vol. 3:

> *Institutio christianae religionis 1559 quibus accessionibus per singulas editions ab anno 1536 usque ad annum 1559 locupletata sit, apparatu critic oculis subicitur, loci theologorum et aliorum scriptorium a Calvino allai under hausti sint demonstrator. Huius operis libros I and Ii secondum editions principles ediderunt Petrus Barth Guilelus Niesel*

Munich, 1928, VII-XVII (= OS 3). Otherwise, they say (p. xvii), Calvin would simply have translated the 1539 Latin Warning into French for the 1541 translation (this was the case for the transition beteen the 1559 Latin edition and the 1560 French translation, see below and Millet, *Calvin et la parole*, 774–75).

17. See CO 3, 7–9 and Jean Calvin, *Institution de la religion chrestienne livre premier*, ed. Jean-Daniel Benoit (Paris: Vrin, 1957), 23–24 (= Calvin, *Institution*, Benoit). For the meaning of this change, cf. Millet, *Calvin et la Parole*, 773–75 and 786, pages to which we shall return. For example one reads at the end of the translation published in 1560: "Surquoy ie vous recomanderay à la garde de Dieu, desirant aussy n'estre point oublié en voc sainctes priers, selon le fruict que vous recevrez de mes labours. A Genève, ce premier jour d'Aoust, M.D. LIX" etc. (Calvin, *Institution*, Benoit, 24), cf. the formula of Latin "valediction" of 1539 reproduced above.

18. Title page (f. alpha 1] r" Ep. Ded. (ff. alpha 2 r - [alpha 4] r . . . Avis (f. beta 8 r), Herzog August Bibliothek, wolfenbuttel (Lh 4 229). See also *Opus Epistolarm Des. Erasmi Roterodami*, vol. 2, ed. Percy Stafford Allen (Oxford: Clarendon, 1910), 579–86, no. 586.

of a modern preface, in our eyes. Moreover, the dedicatory letter effectively frees, so to speak, the author of the warning to the reader from his exegetic responsibilities, so that the warning is rather technical, often "ecdotic." For example, the first warning from Basel which was mentioned above has as its subject the discovery of a new manuscript and the arrival of a new printed edition of the *Histoire Auguste* and acts to introduce the textual variations. The second explains first of all the corrupt state of the manuscripts in general in order to provide thereafter precisions on the origin of a text by another author (Ammien Marcellin) among those which are published. It finishes by observations on the etymology of the name of *Alleman*. These documents are therefore technical, explanatory and secondary; they do not come back at all on message or messages of the publication itself.

One may think in the present case that the Epistle to the King of the *Institutio* very broadly satisfied the requirements of a dedicatory preface. Nevertheless, one must note that, in the editions with which we are concerned, the Warnings to the reader begin on the back of the title page in order to precede the royal letter.[19] But this move of the warning toward the beginning of the book is not the case in Tertullien's 1521 edition (which does not include the warning to the reader at the beginning of the work), it is for those of 1528 and 1539.[20]

Finally it seems useful to us to call both documents "warnings to the reader" in order to emphasize that in our minds the Latin Warning is the model of the French Warning, that is to say that we take as a hypothesis of work that Calvin would have translated the Latin text into French in proving a certain liberty according to the modern idea of "translation" and by adapting it, up to a certain point, to his readership.[21] If it is true that we must prove that for a large part of the text in what follows, we think that

19. See *BC* 1, 58–64 (39/4) and 98–00 (41/3).

20. For the 1521 edition (Bibliothèque Humaniste de Selestat K 944), there is the title page (f. [aI] r), then on the back of the title page the table of contents: *Catalogus* (f. [a1] v), then the dedicatory letter from Rhenanus to Stanslas Turzo, bishop of Olmtz 9ff. a2 r = [a5] r) etc. the 1528 edition (BHS K 1040): title page [AA1 r), *Catalogus [AA1] V*), Beatus Rhenanus Lectori S[alutem dicit] (ff.AA2 R-V) ..., Ep. Ded. (ff. BB1 r-BB4] r) etc. The 1539 edition (BHS K 1039): title page (a*1]r), *Catalogus* ([a1] v), *Beatus Rhenanus Theologiis et Piis Omnibus S[alutem] D[icit] (a*2r)* ... Ep. Ded. (ff.a*4 r"-b1r), etc. These data come from an unpublished conference at the time of the stud days at the House of Erasmus in Anderlecht, Brussels, on 17 and 18 December 1999.

21. For the very rich question of translation in the sixteenth century, and more precisely in the manner in which translated himself, see Millet, *Calvin et la parole*, 753–870. The time and place to deal with it in detail are lacking. We can only say here that the practice for the translation of the treatize *Des Scandales* in 1550 (787–808) and for the "more radical form of adaptation" (809) which offers the revision of the 1536 *Epistola* to Duchemin which produces the 1543 *Petit traité* (809–28).

our readers will agree to say as a whole that the passage by Calvin on the usefulness of the *Institutio* as a *compendium* (abridged) for the readers of his commentaries to appear (Latin warning, l. 25-33) has been well translated by him for the French Warning (l. 40-46).

Latin Warning

The Latin warning to the reader bears the place of Strasbourg and the date of 1 August 1539. The French Warning does not include them, but a reference enables one to date it with a certain precision. In fact, as we are coming to recall it, in lines 40-46 Calvin notes that, thanks to his *Institution*, if the Lord gives him the opportunity to make some comments, he can use the greatest brevity, given that he as written in detail in the *Institution* "all the articles which belong to Christianity." Calvin essentially says the same thing (lines 25-33) in the Latin warning and names the text which will prove his statements, the *Commentaire sur l'Epitre aux Romains*. This commentary (*BC* 1 40/3) will be finished two months later, in October 1539. We can conclude, with the other commentators,[22] that Calvin was preparing the French translation of the *Institution* and writing the French Warning before this commentary appeared, that is to say before the month of October 1539.

This similarity between the Warnings has made a great deal of ink to flow. The publishers of the *Opera Selecta* have used it as one of the main arguments to say that Calvin had written the *Institutio* in French first of all.[23] Now, according to the more recent bibliographical works,[24] this thesis does not stand up to analyses, a judgment that we share.

The Latin Warning is divided into two parts. The first, lines 2 to 18, leans on the almost divine unexpected success of the much shorter first edition of 1536. We must think that Calvin places the word *successum*, announced by *eum*, after the subject of the relative pronoun *Dominus* to emphasize this success. Then, to believe the author (l. 4-5), in 1536 it was an unimportant work that he had carried out without thinking, for the most part. Afterwards, on ten lines (5 to 14) Calvin again emphasizes his reaction, a reaction which is almost of embarrassment, before the success of his effort at popularization. The success given by God is now described as the "favour of almost all the pious reader (*eo piorum fere omnium favore*, l. 5-6)." Thus we have a reference to "almost" all the pious readers of the first

---

22. Cf. Calvin, *Institution*, Millet, 110, n7.
23. *OS* 3, vii-ix, xvii and especially 8.
24. Cf. *BC* 1, 98.

edition of 1536.[25] Their favor is something that Calvin would never have dared for nor called for in his wishes nor, for a better reason, hoped for *quem nunquamuoto expetere, nedum sperare, ausus fuissem* (l. 6–7).

This favor inspires two thoughts in him, which are explained by a comparative proposal of equality *ut . . . ita . . .* (l. 7–8): on the one hand, he sincerely thinks that he was honored a great deal more than he deserved to be: on the other hand, this excessive honor makes him very indebted. If he does not want to be seen as ungrateful, he is obliged to reply, insofar as his smallness allows, to the zealous ones who back him so strongly (adeo propensis in me studitis, l. 9) and who themselves appeal (ac [. . .] *sponte invitantibus*) to his industry. One must note that these *studia* must be able to be pious readers. It is no doubt this antecedent which leads Calvin to use a metonymy. He cannot help it, the *studia* are going to call for a more limited, more precise description of a reader.

Calvin now recalls the 1539 edition, the new work. The favor of readers (eo [. . .] then becomes their "favourable reception" (*gratia*, l. 11) of the work. The description of readers also changes. They become "*studiosi*" (1.11). One might think that Calvin is simply seeking to vary his discourse and that by *studiosi* he again understands the *pii fere omnes*.[26] It must be said that his manner of expressing himself shows what he thinks both of the readers of the 1536 edition and those of the new edition of 1539. He actually asks the "studiosi" for the same favorable reception that they have already given to him in the past (*Non igiru aliam a studiosis gratiam noui opera postulo quam qua me adhuc immerentem iam ante prosecti sunt*). However, nothing in the text prevents us from understanding that it is a question of a "subdivision" of the *pii fere omnes*. In fact, the metonymy of *studia* (*adeo propensis in me studiis*) allows Calvin the use of an upgrade.

The "studious people" are normally students or other individuals who are very keen to learn; they are often opposed to the lecturers, the specialists who are already trained. A warning to the reader written by Beatus Rhenanus and Bruno Amerbach for volume 9 of the *Works* of s. Jerome and printed in Basel by Johann Froben in June 1516 illustrates this meaning. The volume in question contains a certain number of comments transmitted by the tradition but of which Jerome is not the author:

---

25. One may wonder if the addition of *fere* is an oratory precaution or a real one.

26. Millet, *Calvin et la parole*, 773, understands *studiosi* in this way: "The preface of the 1539 *Institutio* marks a considerable turn. This time the pubic which has so warmly welcomed the 1536 edition is described in the following terms: *piorum fere omnium*, which describes the community of the cultivated Evangelical Europeans. Further on, the author addresses these *studiosi*.

8. Warnings to the Reader 115

'But by admitting even that in the middle of a great deal of straw, it is given to us to find one grain or anther, due to the fact that so many writings of Jerome have come down to us, we mark these commentaries with a "black stone" and judge that they do not deserve for the studious people to mis-use their time by giving good hours of reading to them. But the scholars and those who have a "flair" (we are sure of that) will do the same as us; as to incompetent and thick people, we are not waiting for their judgment.[27]

After the condemnation of false texts, the authors of the warning no doubt thought about the "honest reader" (lector candibus) to whom they are addressed at the beginning of their letter. They do not want their students to waste their precious time in reading texts which are not by Jerome. They are convinced that the scholars and those who have flair will do the same as them. Other texts offer this contrast between the *studiosi* and the *lecturers*.[28] The existence of a "technical meaning," so to say, of studios leads us to give it this meaning here.

To the studious therefore, the Reformer only asks for the new work to have another favorable reception as the old one knew. It is at least the construction which was expected, an opposition between the new work and the old one, but that is not what happened. Calvin only asks (l. 10–12) for a reception like that with which the studious people had honored it already in the past, without his deserving it. That is to say how, as an author and a man, he was amazed by the good welcome given to the work. And Calvin said again that he was linked by the benevolence of the studious people to such a point that it would be enough if he succeeds in paying fairly in return for this reception for which he is indebted to them. Calvin would have done so

---

27. "Caeterum ut detur etiam multas paleas aliquod granulum reperirie, cum tantum supersit Hieronymi scriptorium, istos commentaries nigro calculo notamus, et indignos cenemus in quibus legendis studiosi bonas horas male collecent. Docti quique sunt naris enunciate (certo scimus) nobiscum facient, imperitorum and crassorum uidicium nihil *moramur*." (See EBR, 1, Hirstein, Ep. 76, divs. 16–17. One notes the memoirs of Erasmus, Martial and Horace.)

28. A passage in the dedicatory epistle that Beatus Rhenanus wrote for Bishop Bernard de Trente at the end of 1532 for his 1533 edition of Tacitus provides another example. He describes his difficulties and his aims as a scientific editor: "*Taedium ego laboris, nec est ulla res in orbe fastidiosior, facile contempsi subinde cogitans quantum utilitatis hinc peruenturum esset ad studiosos. Quos ut amplius demererer, adieci thesaurum locuionum constructionumque et uerborum, quibus Tacitus frequenter utitur. In quo fateor esse multa vulgo protrita, sed tamen insent quaedam non indigna studiosorum adulescentium cognitione.*" See James Hirstein, "The philological method of Beatus Rhenanus, his 'Treasure of the Tacitian style' (1533) and the first book of the *Annals* of Tacitus," in BRLE, 385–86 (377–95). The last sentence makes us understand that the students may be young or, in opposing these *studiosi adulescentes*, of a riper age. Note that one may also translate *studiosi* by the "supporters of fine letters" but that obscures the distinction which may exist between the *docti* and the *studiosi*.

sooner, if the Lord had not tested him in an astonishing manner throughout the last two years[29]

Calvin closes this consideration by a proverb: it is done quickly enough, if it is done well enough (l. 16). And now, he leaves aside the studious people and himself in order to say that he will judge the work to have been well received if he feels that he brought some fruit to the Church of the Lord.

It is thus that this first part is dedicated to the reception given to the first Latin edition which had already appeared and to the reception desired for that of 1539. The Reformer is also strongly indebted to God and to his readers, this debt from which he wished to be released in at least an adequate manner. One notes several shifts of vocabulary which may not relate only to a wish for *variation*. In the field of reception, there is first of all, *successus*, then *favour*, finally *gratia*. Then, in the field of the receivers, so to speak, of the readers, there are the *pii fere omnes*, then the *studia* and finally the *studiosi*.

In the second part of the Latin Warning, Calvin exposes the aim that he proposes by revising and increasing the first edition. Here there is an even more exact description of the potential readers of the new 1539 edition; it is a question of *sacrae Theologiae candidate* (l. 19) that Calvin wants to prepare and learn to read God's words.

The word *candidates* may seem unremarkable to us due to its present universal usage, but in the sixteenth century, writers were conscious of the diverting it and of its Roman electoral meaning,[30] in order to make a figured use of it, following Quintilien. In fact, the author of the *Institution oratoire* (6, Pref. 13) uses it in the meaning of "aspiring to eloquence (*eloquentiae candidatus*)." The humanists follow the usage of Quintilien,[31] in order, very often, to assimilate the *candidate* to the *studiosi*. For example, in a very well-developed warning to the "students of theology and of a purer literature (*Beatus Rhenanus . . . Theologiae et sincaerioris Literaturae ~Studiosis S[alutem] P[lurimam] D[icit]*) = 13 August 113, Beatus Rhenanus turns toward them again at the end, saying "*Vos itaque melioris eruditionis candidate, quod summe precamur, eloquentiam cum sacrorum scientia copulate* [. . .]" [It is thus that you, the candidates for better erudition, join together—what we request at the highest point in our prayers—eloquence to sacred science (. . .)] in order to recommend to them the radical rewriting

---

29. Calvin must refer to his working conditions and to his exile from Geneva (April 1538). For another interpretation, see *BC* 1, 62.

30. It is well known under the meaning of "candidate" (wearing the white toga) which is a magistrature. (For knowledge of the era on Roman committees, cf. *EBR*, 1, Hirstein, Ep. 80.)

31. Cf. *EBR* 1, Hirstein, *Ep. 48, div. 2a*.

8. Warnings to the Reader

of the *Libri sententiarum* of Pierre Lombard carried out by Paolo Cortesi in his *In sententias*. One sentence further, Rhenanus begins to end the warning, by asking for the support of the *candidati*:

> *Et Beatum vestrum amate, qui studiosis omnibus simper gratificari cupit. Bene Valete* [...] [And love your Beatus who always seeks to gratify all studious people. Keep well (...)].[32]

Except for a mistake on our part, our linguistic researches show that *candidatus* in Latin was not expanded as a mediaeval university term.[33]

Calvin applies this word to theology. But one must ask the question in order to find out who these "aspirants" to "sacred theology" were. The Strasbourg gymnasium was not, in 1539, capable of issuing masterships or doctorates in theology.[34] It was a preparatory school, a *ludus trivialis* which taught the *trivium* to those who were intended for university studies, even if the university level was in sight, particularly through the *lectiones publicae* in theology and lectures in law and medicine. It is known that Calvin proposed theology conferences in 1539.[35] But, from the university point of view, the *candidate* could not aspire to diplomas, which takes nothing away from their desire to learn and to progress. Nonetheless, in the economy of the Latin Warning, we can understand it as representing a "subdivision" of the largest group made up of the *studiosi* described by Calvin above.

The lines 18–21 (*hoc mihi* [...] *propositum fuit*) seem to describe an effort made in favor of the *candidate* only. In order to describe what he hopes will be the consequence of their preparation and instruction, Calvin uses the very broad metaphor of the way or the easy road (*facile* [...] aditum, l. 20) with a light step (*inoffenso*)[...] *gradu*, l. 20–21) toward reading the divine word (*divini verbi lectionem*, l. 19) that the *candidate* will obtain.[36] In fact he uses a consecutive proposition: *ita praepare et instuere, ut*.

---

32. See *EBR* 1, Hirstein *Ep*.49, divs. 19 and 21 and cf. *Ep*. 53, div. 5 (*eloquentiae studiosis*).

33. We have checked Niermeyer, Du Cange, *Lexicon latinitatis Nederlandicae Medii Aevi*, etc. According to the *Tresor de la langue française*, the word, used in the sense of "aspiring to an academic degree," would have come into French in 1580 by taking up the German term of "*Kandidat*."

34. The Gymnasium will become an Academy—or a semi university, granting degrees of Bachelor and Master—in 1566, and a university in 1621. See the article of Anton Schindling, "Jean Calvin et l'école de Jean Sturm," 79–92*.

35. See Anton Schindling, *Humanistiche hochschule und freie Reichsstadt: Gymnasium und akademie in Strassburg1538-1621* (Wiesbaden: Franz Steiner, 1977), 341–77 ("Die theologischen Vorlesungen") and, for Calvin himself, 350–60.

36. Cf. *EBR*, vol. 1, *Ep*. 49, div. 8 (Beatus Rhenanus about the advantages of the *In Sententias* of Paolo Cortesi, see above).

The strong punctuation (full stop-comma) placed by the publishers after *queant* is in our view correct. The linking word *siquidem* ("in fact," "in truth," translated by "for" at the head of a sentence in the 1560) confirms what was said, but also announces another development which may not only concern the *sacrae Theologiae candidati*. In fact, Calvin thinks he has embraced the essence of religion in all its parts so that "if someone" (l. 23) checks him, he will have no difficulty in determining what he must mainly look for in Scripture and for what purpose (*quem in scopum*,[37] l. 24-25) he must bring back everything that is in there.

The indefinite generalizing of *siquis* in the *siquis recte tenuerit* of line 23 holds attention. One may understand "if someone, some reader," Calvin could clearly have picked up the name of the *candidati* if he had wished. In the French translation of 1560 one reads "that anyone who has well understood the form of teaching that I have followed [. . .]." This description of a reader is in fact more general. That and the fact that the Reformer is repeating what will be the result of his work through the bias of another consecutive proposition, *summam* [. . .] *sic mihi complexus esse videor* [. . .] *ut siquis eam recte tenuerit, ei non si difficile* [. . .], lead one to think that it is a case of a group readers which was larger than the *candidate*. Calvin must judge this "consecutive" repetition to be necessary for this reason.

Then the Reformer takes up conclusively (*itaque*, l. 25) and more heavily the metaphor of access or the way (one can see the need for using *veluti*, l. 25): the "way so to speak, having been paved," if later he publishes explanations of Scripture he will know that it will not be necessary to begin long dogmatic debates nor to run here and there in common places: he will always limit the extent of his explanations thanks to this shortcut (return to the *Institutio* that he is talking about.

In lines 26-28, it was Calvin who had no longer to begin long debates, or to travel in common places. Now, he returns toward the reader by at last calling him with this precise name and that in the singular (*pius lector*, l. 29). And it is not only the "reader" but the "pious reader," which recalls the *pii fere omnes* of the beginning. That seems to confirm the idea that the *ut siquis* proposition began a movement toward an enlarged readership. But this pious reader is the one who will read the explanations or commentaries that Calvin is going to produce. The *studiosi* and the *sacrae Theologiae candidate* would no doubt have been able to bear such discussions, but Calvin wants to spare the reader that thanks to his knowledge of the *Institutio*, as thanks to a necessary work instrument (*modo praesentis operis cognition*

---

37. The use of this rare word in striking. Other words were possible *finis, propositum* (already used) (l. 18).

[. . .] *praemunitis accedat*)."³⁸ The best proof of what he wants to do, is the commentary on the Epistle to the Romans which will provide it.

Almost the last quarter of the text is dedicated to the relationship between the 1539 *Institutio* and the commentary to come. But it enables one to understand that Calvin foresaw the *Institutio* as a general reading guide and also to see that he came back to the idea of pious individuals. He ends the warning by addressing the *amice Lector* (l. 33), a description which is again more general than that of the *studiosi* or of the *candidati*.

This second part of the Latin Warning offers a more precise aim for the great revision of the first edition undertaken by Calvin. In the first part of the Warning, his action was guided by the debt that he felt toward the enthusiastic pious readers of the 1536 text. One suspects nevertheless in this part that he is dealing with more specialist readers or at least those who are more motivated (the *studiosi*). This suspicion is confirmed in the second part by the reference to the *sacrae Theologiae candidate*. But the rapid return to readers of a more general condition—the "if somebody," the individualized "pious reader" of the *institution* and of the commentaries to come and the "reader friend" reveals that he certainly also had them in mind in preparing the new edition.

The French Warning

The commentators often emphasize certain differences between the Latin and French Warnings. However we would like first of all to place the accent on the similarities. In order to do this, one must acknowledge that it was not useful for Calvin to recall the 1536 edition in the French Warning, as the filiation between the first edition and that of 1539 did not exist any more for the French translation of 1541. As almost all the first part of the Latin Warning dealt with the reception granted to the 1536 edition and on that expected for the second, these aspects are generally lacking in the French translation. Nevertheless, from this first part, the distinction made by Calvin between the *pii fere omnes* and the *studiosi* and the welcome given to his efforts and to the *Institution* will be renewed. From the second part of the Latin Warning, the references to the *sacrae Theologie candidati*, to the other readers and to the useful relationship between the *Institution* and the commentaries to come will be developed and spread out differently.

---

38. In 1560, Calvin translates the Latin thus: "By this means the Readers will be consoled with boredom and . . . , when they will be diligent to arm themselves by the instruction of this present Book, in order to have an easy ride in all the rest."

From this point of view, one may say that the second part of the Latin Warning was increased in order to create the two parts which make up the French Warning, but with the use of certain concepts described in the first part of the Latin Warning. In fact, the first half of the second part of the Latin Warning provides an important part of the first half of the French Warning, the second half that of the part remaining in French.

At the beginning of the French text, Calvin says that he is going to show the readers ("In order for the readers," l. 2) the usefulness of the present book, which will allow him to recall the aim toward which they must direct their attention in reading it ("I shall show them the aim," l. 5). The readers are presented in a first time generally, without epithets, so that in one sense their presence in the first sentence replaces the expected title "Letter to the reader." Then, the Reformer first of all makes a remark which is not found in the Latin Warning, a reference to the perfection of the Holy Writings (l. 6–14). But, he says, in spite of this perfection, a person who is inexperienced in this field (= "a person who will not be very exercised") needs help (to properly put in some guide and address in order to know what he must look for") in order to direct his research into Holy Scripture "in order not to stray here and there, but to keep to a certain way in order always to reach the end where the Holy Spirit calls him" (l. 12–14). Calvin comes back here to the metaphor of the way or the access used at the beginning of the second part of the Latin Warning (l. 20, *facilem* [. . .] *aditum*). Moreover, the language ("to always reach in the end," l. 13, and *pergere*, l. 21) reminds one of the objective he had determined in favor of the *sacrae Theologiae candidati*. Before these similarities of language, we must remember that the *candidati* were in the preparatory school that was the Gymnasium and perhaps were not very different from "a person who will not be very well exercised in that." We must also note this "person" is one of the types of readers covered in the French Warning.

Then there is another passage which is missing from the Latin Warning, a reference to those who can act as a guide, those "having received greater light from God than the others." Their work is to "meet the simple ones in this place" (l. 16). One may wonder whether these people having received more light may be held for readers, but the question is posed less for the "simple ones," for it is clear that the *Institution* is intended for them. The relationship between "a person who will not be well exercised" and the "simple ones" is difficult to establish. The group of words "in this place" ties them together. We can say that the "simple ones" represent at least a sub-group of persons who are less "exercised." If one places these groups in relationship with those mentioned in the Latin Warning, they may by their place correspond with the *pii fere omnes* with a remembrance of the manner in which the *candidati* were evoked.

Let us note that up to now in the French Warning these readers do not appear to be "simple ones" because they have not studied Latin. It is a question especially of people who are not *docti*, scholars. What they need quite clearly is help from interpreters so that they may find the "sum of what God has wanted us to teach in his word" (l. 17–18). The term "sum" in Calvin's French naturally recalls the word used in Latin about the more general group of readers (*summam*, l. 21–23 and *ut siquis* of the Latin Warning).

The sentence which follows in the French Warning (l. 18–21) seems to be a gloss of "sum" when it is a question of human commentaries on the divine word; "to deal with the main and consequential matters contained in the Christian philosophy."

The next sentence (l. 21–25) goes back in our opinion to the *ut siquis* (l. 23–24) of the Latin Warning, although in the Latin text there is no reference to the speed of apprenticeship that one may obtain. The "one who is intelligent enough for it" (l. 21–22) may in fact recall the translation of *ut siquis* in the Crespin edition:

> the one who will have properly understood the form of teaching that I have followed.

This person must be counted as a reader, as we have done in the Latin Warning for *ut siquis*. One is reminded of the *schola Christi*, as that may be found in Bernard de Clairvaux, for example.[39] His presence certainly recalls the divine revelation that one must try to seize, but it also expresses an expansion in the matter of understanding, for the "school" is open to all.

Calvin did not return to the *quid potissimum quaerere in Scriptura* (l. 23–24) but uses at lines 23–25 ("insofar as he almost knows where he must bring back a certain sentence, and has own rule to compass everything which is presented to him") the practice of the doublet that one often finds in the French of this era (whether or not it is a question of a translation[40]) to make the words of the Latin Warning *Quem in scopum quicauid in ea [scriptural 24–25]*.[41] That is to say that he translates some of the meanings of

---

39. We have not been in a position to gain from the book by Raymond A. Blacketer, *The School of God: Pedagogy and Rhetoric in Calvin's Interpretation of Deuteronomy* (Dordrecht, the Netherlands: Springer, 2006). During this colloquium, our colleague Christian Grappe has drawn our attention to the interest in this group of words.

40. Cf. Millet, *Calvin et la parole*, 836–37, for usage in translation. We think of Montaigne for the general practice.

41. On the other hand, in the Warning to the French reader of 1560, Alvin translates *quid potissimum quaerere in Scriptura*: "what he must look for in Scripture."

refero: "to go back to something else taken as an end," but also "bring back to something to something else taken as a step in evaluation." Line 25 of the French Warning ("he has his rule to compass everything which is presented to him") is the end of the first part, which, for the most part, takes up the first half of the second part of the Latin Warning.

But it is here that one must have the Latin words that Calvin wrote toward 1538 to 1539 intervene as an erudite sketch (one must think so[42]) of the limiting text of his essay on the French translation of homilies of Saint John Chrysostom, a project which did not see the light of day:

> [. . .] *non minus necesse est scire quid illic [sc. In libris divinis] quaerere oporteat, scopumque aliquem habere ad quem dirigemur. Quod si non fiat contingat profecto nobis multum diuque sine magno fructu uagari [. . .] Superest ergo ut [sc. Plebs Christiana] interpretum opera adjuuetur qui sic in Dei cognition profecerunt, ut alios quoque manuducere ad eam possint, [. . .] nihil aliud mihi propositum fuit quam ad scripturae sacrae lectionem rudibus ac illiteratis uiam sternere* (CO 9, 832–33).

> [. . .] il n'est pas moins nécessaire de savoir ce qu'il convient d'y chercher [dans la Bible] et d'avoir un but auquel se diriger. Faute de quoi, nous serions assurément exposés a errer loin et longtemps sans en tirer grand profit. [. . .] Il reste par conséquent a faire intervener a l'adresse du people l'aide des interprètes-commentateurs qui ont fait des progrès dans la connaissance de Dieu, afin qu'ils puissant guider ver elle egalement les autres. [. . .] Je n'ai eu d'autre projet que d'ouvrir la voie a la lecture de l'Ecriture sainte en favour des gens sans culture ni formation intellectuelle (trad. Millet avec ajout[43]).

Not only does one find echoes of the Latin Warning in there, the word *quaerere* (l. 24) and *scopum* (l. 24) and *uiam sternere* (l. 25), and one may notice also the expression of an aim *mihi propositum fuit* of this Warning (l. 18), but there is also the idea that those who have received more light must help the others, a thought that is present in the French text. That is to say that the

---

42. Millet, *Calvin et la parole*, 173, no. 75, raises the question of why from the Latin preface for the French translation of Chrysostom. He quotes these words in Calvin, *Institution*, for line 40 ("in order to give access to all the children of God to understand Holy Scripture well and properly") of the French Warning (109–10, no. 6). But especially see Millet, *Calvin et la parole*, 170–76, esp. 172.

43. Calvin, *Institution*, Millet, 109–10, n. 6. In the Latin text which is provided, one must correct *scire quod* into *scire quid*, read *in Dei cognition* (and not *in cognition Dei*) and add *ergo* between the two words *Superest ut*.

8. Warnings to the Reader 123

text which was to be a sketch of a preface for Chrysostom's homilies recalls the two Warnings which are of interest to us.

However, there is an important difference in degree to be emphasized between "meeting the simple people" (l. 15–16 of the French Warning) and "paving a way to a reading of Holy Scripture for the uncultured people and those without Latin education" (in order to translate in our turn the Latin of the preface to Chrysostom: *ad scripturae sacrae lectionem rudibus ac illiteratis uiam sternere*). In fact, these *rudes ac illiterate* are described because they are not readers of Latin literature. On the other hand, Calvin has still not referred to readers of the French translation of the *Institution* in this way. Men who could benefit from homilies, the popular sermons of Chrysostom in France could perhaps, in Calvin's mind at that time, well be less instructed or protected than those who were going to read the 1541 *Institution*, in particular the "simple people." The image of the way (*uiam sternere*) recalls the remarks made in the Latin Warning, but there it is a question of a way which was already paved (l. 25 *hac ueluti strata uia*) to the gain of the *siquis eam* [sc. *summam*] *recte tenuerit*, while in the preface to Chrysostom it is the aim which is offered, not that which has been achieved.

Something must have changed in order for Calvin to abandon the plan to translate the popular sermons of Chrysostom and less strongly designates the inexperienced readers. We mean, without seeking to cultivate the paradox, that the "simple" people who must be helped are not necessarily non-Latin-speaking French people. The first part of the French Warning does not make this distinction.

The proof of it is that at the beginning of the second part (l. 26–34 of the l. 26–64), Calvin says that he worked hard to help "in this way those who wish to be taught in the doctrine of salvation" in writing the "present book" (which recalls the title of the Warning "Argument of the present book"). It is only now that he is going to make a distinction of language. He has first of all written the book in Latin, then in French. The Latin text was for "all studying people of whatever nation that they are" (l. 32–32), the French for "our French Nation" (l. 33–34). There were surely "simple people" in both these categories.

We think that there is the same relationship between "those who wish to be taught in the doctrine of salvation" (l. 27–28) and the "people of study" (l. 41) that we have taken up between the *studia*, the *studiosi* and, through usage elsewhere in Latin, the *sacrae Theologie candidate* (l. 9, 11 and 19 of the Latin Warning); that is to say that there is a link of meaning between "wish" in "who wish to be taught" and "study," that being based on the Latin word *studio* and the adjective and the noun *studiosi* which are derived and on their usage at the time. In particular one must notice that the group of words "people of study" is the translation of *studiosi*. One can in fact defend the following proposition, that as a general rule for Calvin the *studiosi* are "people of study" and the *docti* "men of letters."[44] That is to say that what takes precedence in the group of words "all the people of study of whatever nation they are" is the precision "of whatever nation they are." In fact, there are "people of study" everywhere, but for the French "people of study" Calvin was able to use their own language.

It is also in the second part of the French Warning, after his remarks on their languages, that Calvin begins to describe the welcome that will be given to his efforts and to the *Institution*, material that had appeared in the first part of the Latin Warning.

For the first time, the Reformer says that he does not dare "to give too much witness, etc." of his book for fear of holding his work in too high esteem. However, he does not balk at promising that it will be like a key "for giving access to all the children of God to understand Holy Scripture completely and properly." That is to say that he speaks again about the usefulness of the work, as he has done in the Latin Warning from the *ut siquis* the "the one who has knowledge of it." He recalls "all the children of God," whom we must consider as potential readers.

But while one could wait for another development on the *Institution*, a work which would already present a challenge to the "simple people" or to "all the children of God," Calvin takes up (l. 40–46) the passage in the second part of the Latin Warning on his usefulness as shortened by him in writing commentaries.

That said, Calvin comes back to more personal considerations, to say that since all honor for his work must come back to God, all the same he goes on to dare say what he thinks about that. This second use of the word "to dare" here (l. 47, and see above, l. 34) makes one think of the presence of *audio*: (l. 7) in the Latin Warning: *ausus fuissem*. There the author says that he would never have dared to hope for such success, here he does not dare

---

44. In the expression "gens d'estude" [people of study], we understand "study" in the meaning of "zeal for learning." We have not found the group of words "gens d'estude" in Huguet, but he provides the first meaning of "care, zeal, worry," for "estude" (*Dictionnaire de la langue française du XVIe siècle*, vol. 3 [Paris: Didier, 1946], 742). On the other hand, Huguet (vol. 4, 300) picks up the group of words "gens de lettres" [men of letters] in the meaning of "gens lettrés" [men of letters] and that is under Calvin's pen, in particular the "anti-humanist" famous passage in the *Excuse to the Nicodemites* (VI, 600). This Bende is almost all about men of letters. Not that all men of letters are such. "For I would prefer for all human sciences to be exterminated from the earth than that they should be the cause of thus cooling the zeal of Christians [. . .]." See Millet, *Calvin et la parole*, 16. For "men of letters," see also Littre, *Dictionnaire de la langue française*, vol. 2 (Monte-Carlo: Editions de Cap. 1971), 2755.

8. Warnings to the Reader

to pass judgment before that of the readers. Giving praise to God, Calvin describes the usefulness of his enterprise in a more personal way. Everyone should read his book. And one has a better picture of his readership: "I exhort all those who hold the word of the Lord in reverence to read it [...]." It will first of all be a summary of Christian doctrine for them, then an entrance to gain from the Old and the New Testaments. Once the readers have been instructed, they will know that Calvin's teaching was right.

If someone does not understand everything, he must not despair, but continue on his path, hoping to fall upon something that he will understand better and which will help him to understand other passages. Here Calvin pictures less qualified readers: "if someone cannot understand all the content." But above all, those for whom the book is intended must always study in depth what Calvin has written while referring to *Holy Scripture*.

One may note in the French Warning at least ten references to the readers: "Readers" (l. 2) = "A person who will not be well exercized" (l. 9–10), "meet the simple people" (l. 15–16), "the one who will have knowledge of it" (l. 21–22), "those who wish to be instructed in the doctrine of salvation" (l. 27–28), "all people of study, of whatever nation they are" (l. 31–32), "our French Nation" (l. 33–34), "all the children of God" (l. 39), "those who have reverence to the word of God" (l. 51) and "If someone cannot understand all the content" (l. 57).

How far must we establish parallels between the two Warnings? We proposed relationships between the group contained in "a person who will not be well exercised" and the *sacrae Theologiae candidate* (l. 19); between "a person who will not be well exercised" and the "simple people" and the *pii fere omnes* (1.5); between "one who has knowledge of it" and the generalizing *siquis* (l. 23); between "those who wish to be instructed in the doctrine of salvation," "all people of study, from whatever nation they are" and "our French Nation" and the *studia* (l. 0), the *studiosi* (l. 11) and the *sacrae Theologiae candidate*, etc.

We do not wish, in making too many parallels, to take away the nuances from the descriptions used by Calvin. In the same way it is useful to keep the *pii fere omnes*, the *studiosi*, the *candidate* and the generalizing *siquis*, in the same way it is suitable to keep the "simple people," the "people of study," "our French Nation" and "all the children of God" in the French Warning. In fact, in each of the two Warnings the Reformer goes from the general to the more precise in order to come back to the most general.

What is striking in both cases is that the idea of the language used seems to be secondary. Calvin prefers to emphasize the degrees of engagement. The *studiosi*, the *candidate* and the "people of study" are more engaged, enthusiastic, zealous than others, without forgetting that one may count "people of study" among the group of "notre Nation Francoise." On this matter, the place of the French Warning where Calvin mentions the difference of language is significant. His position in the center clearly indicates that the Reformer is first of all interested and above all in "those who wish to be instructed in the doctrine of salvation"; their linguistic competences come later.

We have tried up to now to take up the similarities between the two Warnings. One must not forget the differences. The most important number of references made to the readers in French in relation to the Latin Warning corresponds to the more important length of the French text, which is almost double.

If the French text is longer, there is first of all the general linguistic phenomenon which means that the French cannot be the equal of the conceptual density of the Latin. Calvin gives a great deal of room to the question of the "simple people" and can use expressions which are much more periphrastic to designate readers of all categories. Finally, the Reformer is more loquacious (see the two occurrences of the word "to dare," l. 34 and 47) when it is a question of giving his warning on his writing and his usefulness to "all the children of God" (l. 39) and "all those who revere the word of the Lord" (l. 51). One has noticed that Calvin, in rendering the Latin into French, proved a greater "intellectual insistence" and a "familiar expressivity," as well as an "author's more developed ethos."[45]

In spite of its length, there are at least two aspects of the Latin Warning which are lacking in the French Warning. As we have observed, it almost no question of the first edition of 1536. Then, apart from the similarities of metaphor, one does not as a whole find such a clear reference to the *sacrae Theologiae candidati*.

That led the commentators to see a more technical text in the Latin Warning. Olivier Millet notes that, in the 1539 text, "the popular teaching of 1536 broadened into an apologetic is presented as a theological manual" (he quotes the 1560 French text by adding Latin words of 1539 *sacrae Theologiae candidates et ad divini verbi lectionem*).[46] For this purpose, the same commentator recalls the "doctoral relationship" between the author and his public.[47] However, for Millet this relationship subsists in the 1541

---

45. See Millet, *Calvin et la parole*, 796 and 825–28.

46. Millet, *Calvin et la parole*, 773: "Now my aim was to so prepare and teach those who would wish to devote themselves to the study of Theology (Latin: *sacrae Theologiae candidates*) so that they would have easy access to read Scripture (*ad divini verbi lectionem*), and to gain and advance to understand it, and follow the good and right path without fail."

47. Ibid.

8. Warnings to the Reader

French Warning, "but it no longer has the almost institutional nature [...] suggested by the Latin words of 1539. [...] it is no longer a question of systematically studying Scripture as a theological student can."[48] For this commentator, the French Warning expresses more and better than the Latin Warning Calvin's initial intention in 1536: to provide a catechism for the laity ("even if the simple catechism has become a complex work of which the author is aware, is not easy for the ordinary reader").[49] Our analysis rather shows that the desire to reach out to the *studiosi* is very similar in both Warnings.

Always in respect of the differences between the Warnings, one may recall that the publishers of the *Opera Selecta* provide a response: the French Warning of 1541 would be a vestige of the lost translation of 1536.[50] But one cannot control their words.

Given that the similarities between Chrysostom's preface and the Warnings, it would be tempting to explain the differences in those by saying that the French Warning represents more than the Latin Warning a translation of the preface. Only, examination of the preface ties the two Warnings together more than it separates them.

Another difference between the texts which have been examined is the title that each one bears. As regards the French text, did Calvin think of making an "argument," a summary of the contents, in the first place? Let us point out for our memory that another interesting Calvinian rewrite which was done through the bias of the two languages is announced by a change in the character. In his treatment of the very difficult position of the reformed people who live among the "papists," Calvin passes from the character of the *Epistola* to that of the treatise.[51] But for us the character of the two Warnings is the same.

Our wish to accentuate the similarities between the two Warnings may seem bold. It would be useful to look for a *tertium comparationis* later in the *institutio*.

The commentators agree in saying that the chapter *De vita Christiana*, which appears for the first time as the last chapter of the book in the 1539 Latin edition, must in fact act as a conclusion. Millet writes that it is "completely new in the Latin edition of 1539. It acts as an ending to the whole

---

48. Millet, *Calvin et la parole*, 773–74.
49. Ibid., 774.
50. *OS* 3, XVII.
51. See Millet, *Calvin et la parole*, 815–17 and 827.

of the book, of which it here explains how to put into practice the doctrine which was set out."[52]

In an article dedicated to this chapter, Jacques Pannier lets us know that Calvin wrote it in the spring of 1539, after his return from Frankfurt, when his situation in Strasbourg had become more stable and he had already given the other chapters of the work to be printed.[53] In fact, it was only in May 1539 that he received a salary from the Scolarques in Strasbourg for his lectures in theology and the sermons that he had been preaching for eight months already.[54]

What interests us, apart from the frank and warm tone of this practical chapter on the conduct that the Christian must use, is its beginning. It is possible that it represents Calvin's thought not only on the "ample and diverse" that he must deal with about the nature of popularization that he wanted to do. The Reformer takes note of the verbosity of the "old Doctors" in their moral exhortations where they deal with one virtue in particular. "Now my intention is not to extend the doctrine of life and I want to leave a gap up to there and to declare one virtue especially and to make long exhortations." If one researches that, he says, one could find it in "books by other people and mainly of Homilies by the old Doctors, that is, popular sermons. It will be enough for me to show some order by which the Christian man may be led and guided to a correct aim to arrange his life properly. I shall be happy, I say, to show briefly a general rule by which he may refer all his actions." Now, this last sentence is not found in the Latin text of 1539, but it represents and addition of the 1541 French translation.[55]

The Latin text *ad rectum constituendae uitae scopum deducatur* for this chapter recalls and the lines 24–25 of the Latin Warning and the preface for the French translation of the homilies of Saint Jean Chrysostom through the use of the term of *scopum*. The last phrase added for the French translation of 1541 recalls lines 24–25 of the French Warning: his reader will know "almost where he must recall each sentence." The fact that this text, as the preface to Chrysostom, makes it possible to evoke the two Warnings, Latin and French, pleads, in our view, for an interpretation which sees more similarities than differences between them.

---

52. Calvin, *Institution*, Millet, vol. 2, 1635.

53. Jacques Pannier, "Notes historiques et critiques sur un chapître de l'Institution écrit a Strasbourg," *Revue d'Histoire et de philosophie religieuse* 14 (1934) 219 (206–29).

54. Pannier, "Notes historiques," 218.

55. See Calvin, *Institution*, vol. 2, 1652. For an interesting comparison of two French translations of this chapter, one by Calvin, the other by de La Place, see Millet, *Calvin et la parole*, 829–51, especially pages 833–934 for the beginning of the chapter.

8. Warnings to the Reader

This chapter beginning provides above all an explanation for the way of popularization followed by Calvin. He was looking for a general approach, a fairly broad rule in order to allow it to be used in all situations. John Chrysostom's homilies were too limited in this respect. On the other hand, the rewriting of the 1536 text had to allow a more general approach. The changes and the additions inserted into the 1539 Latin text meant that this time it was worth the trouble of making a translation into the vernacular language.

In order to finish, it is useful to come back to the French Warning of the 1560 edition, which for the first time, is a fairly precise translation of the Latin Warning of the previous editions. We have drawn attention to the change of title that it presents. Literally, it is true that the 1541 French Warning disappears. However, if one accepts the similarities that we picked up between the 1539 Latin Warning and the French Warning of 1541, some of the intentions of the latter were not lost when the first one was translated in a more limited manner.

If the *adeo propensis* [. . .] *studiis ac* [. . .] *sponte inuitantibus respondere* (l. 9–10) of the Latin Warning of 1539, reformulated in a certain manner in 1541 by "those who wish to be instructed in the doctrine of salvation" (l. 27–28), but which becomes in 1560 (to satisfy their wish)," is disappointing, the *studiosi* (l. 11) and the *sacrae Theologiae candidate* (l. 19), doubtless picked up by "a person who will not be very exercised about it" because of similar images (l. 10) and also by "people of study" (l. 31) in 1541, reflect the advantages of the two Warnings when in 1560 one reads, by "coalescence" the periphrasis "those who would like to give themselves to the study of Theology."[56] In the idea of "giving themselves," it is possible to find the strong motivation of the *studiosi* and the *candidati*, and, if one must accept here that, in the group of words "study of theology," the word "study" may include the idea of application of mind in order to learn,"[57] nevertheless the notions of engagement, enthusiasm and zeal which were foremost in the Latin and French Warnings must also come into play.

---

56. For Millet, the fact that the *Institutio* and the *Institution* announce in 1560 the same warning to the reader reflects an important change: "it is no longer a question of popularization, as in 1541, and everything presents itself as if the French readers had become more adult and wise, close in that to the *sacrae theologiae candidati*" (*Calvin et la parole*, 774–75). That is to say that for the commentator the "themes of 1539 [. . .] seem to win, and therefore the 'doctoral' intention of the Latin text" (ibid., 774). We would rather prefer that the ideas of "confluence" (775) and "convergence" (786) recalled by Millet for the 1560 context are already applied to the two warnings of 1539 and 1541 through the interest that Calvin shows for the *studiosi*.

57. Huguet, vol. 3, 742, provides the examples of this meaning "(Masc.) but, apart from a mistake, does not offer any definition. We take these words in Littre, vol. 2, 2286.

9. Patristics

The Patristic Sources in the 1543 Edition of the Institutio Christianae Religionis
John Calvin and the Enarrationes in Psalms of Augustine

Frederic Chapot

IN A LETTER OF 412 to his friend Marcellinus, Augustine acknowledges that his thought on the origin of the soul has developed from his *Treatize on free will*, and he claims a critical permanent look on his work: "I confess that I make an effort to be in the number of those who write as they progress and who progress as they write."[1] He completes this statement by announcing, with fifteen years in advance, his intention to write a critical revision of his works, which will be the subject of the *Retractationes* of the years 426–427.

Calvin, in the 1543 edition of his *Institutio Christianae religionis*, picks up Augustine's quotation in order to end his Warning to the reader, and it will subsist in all the later editions.[2] To tell the truth, Calvin does not grant himself exactly the same meaning as Augustine. The latter wanted to correct an old opinion that he had had and which could make him pass for a Pelagian before the letter; therefore he wished to correct a thought that he considered wrong from then onwards. The Reformer is not in the same state of mind: each new edition of the *institution* is not a *retractatio* in relation to the previous edition, and the changes made are less corrections than developments and extensions, which is not incompatible with Augustine's sentence, however on condition to take it out of its original context. Calvin's work consists essentially in adding, cutting out or moving, without ever

---

1. Augustine, Epistulae, 143 (Ad Marcellinum), 2 (ed. Goldbacher, Vienna, 1904, CSEL 44, 251, 1.11–13): "Ego proinde fateor me ex corum numero esse conari, qui proficiendo scribunt et scribendo proficient." The De libero arbitrio dated 388 for Book I, and from 391–96 for the two following (S. Lancel, Saint Augustine, Paris, 1999, 741).

2. Calvin quotes Augustine in the following form: "Ego ex corum numero me esse profiteer qui scribunt proficiendo, et scribendo proficient" (OS III, 7, l. 8–0).

9. Patristics

suppressing anything, or even to change anything marginal and rare.³ This continuous development from the Latin text of the *Institutio*, from 1536 to 1559, came back to multiply the volume of the initial work by five.⁴

The addition of Augustine's is itself significant of Calvin's work method; the meeting, during the course of his readings, of a beautiful formula, held his attention, and he used it again in his work. Although one may have some certainty, without any witnesses, it is not impossible for Calvin to have set up a collection of quotations, throughout his reading, on the model of the *Florilegium Patristicum* of Martin Bucer: it was a way of working which was widespread in the environment of the Renaissance humanists, also inherited from practices which were witnessed already among the Ancients.⁵ The quotation can be valid for its expressivity, like that in the case of that of the Warning to the reader. It is also at the service and demonstration of the author, most often as witness of authority, other times as the subject of discussion. In all cases, the quotation is strictly subordinate to the Reformer's preoccupations at the time of revision. It can also be an indication of his contemporary readings of the work of reediting. If one allows the use of a collection of quotations, also not certain in Calvin's case, the concomitance between reading the quoted text and its integration into the *Institutio Christianae religionis* is not mechanical: a passage read previously may be picked up again in the work. Nevertheless, a relatively large influx, at the time of revising the text, of quotations extracted from the same work could reasonably interpreted as the indication of contemporary reading of the latter. We have carried out this enquiry, in considering the era of Calvin's time in Strasbourg—from September 1538 and by restricting the body of work to the *Institutio*.

During Calvin's time in Strasbourg—from September 1538 to September 1541—in August 1539, the second Latin edition of the *Institutio* appeared, written during the year 1538, doubtless for the most part before his time in Strasbourg.⁶ In October 1541, it is around the first French edition, created from the 1539 Latin edition, to appear, in Geneva this time. If one

---

3. See J-D. Dubois, "From one edition to the other of the Institution, how Calvin worked," *La Revue réformée* 11 (1960) 39–61, esp. 6–48; J-F. Gilmont, *Jean Calvin et le livre imprimé* (Geneva, 1997), 174–82.

4. According to Gilmont's count, *Jean Calvin et le livre imprimé*, 371–73, the work went up from 85,000 to 450,000.

5. See Fraenkel, *Martini Buceri Opera Latina*, vol. 3, Martin B and Matthew Parker, *Florilegium Patristicum*, édition critique (Leiden, 1988), XII: about the Ancients, T. Doramdi, *Le stylet et la tablette: Dans le secret des auteurs antiques* (Paris, 2000), 27–50.

6. See D-J. Dubois, "D'une édition a l'autre de l'Institution, comment Calvin travaillait," *La Revue réformée* 11 (1960) 39–51, esp. 46–48; J-F. Gilmont, *Jean Calvin et le livre imprimé* (Geneva, 1997), 174–82.

wishes to deal with the contribution of his time in Strasbourg to the writing of the *Institutio*, one must therefore go back to the third Latin edition, which appeared in March 1543 in Strasbourg. In fact, the appearance of this edition was rather late, as we know by a letter that Calvin finished it at the end of January 1543; one learns that upon his return to Geneva he was busy, in the middle of a great many other tasks and at the price of a great effort, with his new edition of the Latin *Institutio*.[7] One may admit that the work had been begun, and the materials gathered, during his time in Strasbourg. In any case, fourteen months passed between the temporary completion of the text and its appearance, either that he needed the time to choose the publisher-printer, or that the latter had too much work, or that the author wanted to revise his text one more time. The authors of the *Biblioteca Calviniana* wonder in fact: "Is there a new revision by Calvin: A publishing plan by Michel Du Bois counteracted by his departure from Geneva?"[8] It is in any case likely, as the publishers of the *Opera selecta*,[9] that Calvin put some profitable time into continuing to work on his text. We believe we found an indication of this in a development in the 1543 edition.

For the additions to this edition, one may take up a development on the practice of music and more particularly of singing.[10] This fact is not negligible, because the *Institutio* only rarely deals with this question. The 1536 edition only contains two very short references, in passing, to the practice of collective singing,[11] to which one must add another reference about personal prayer: whether it be said or sung, it must come from the bottom of the heart. Calvin adds that, far from condemning the word or the singing in the prayer, he recommends them provided that one and the other are sincere: the language, whether sung or spoken, must be dedicated to the sincere praise

---

7. Letter (no. 384) of January 1542 to a friend: "Adde quod Institutionem latinam absoluere aportuit, inqua postquam exierit, uidebis me non leuiter sudasse." *CO* 9, 364; cf. *OS* III, XIX–XX.

8. R. Peter, J-F. Gilmont, *Biblioteca Calviniana: les oeuvres de Jean Calvin publiées au XVIe siècle*, vol. 1., *Ecrits théologiques, littéraires et juridiques, 1532-1554* (Geneva, 1991), 130.

9. *OS* III, XX.

10. On this question, see particularly C. Garsude, "The Origins of Calvin's Theology of Music: 1536–1543," *Transactions of the American Philosophical Society* 69 (1979); B.A. Fommi, *Das weiterwirken der Muskanschauung Augustins im 16. Jahrhundert* (Bern, 1994), 131–39; R. Weeda, *"Eglise des français" de Strasbourg (1538-1563): Rayonnement européen de sa Liturgie et de ses Psautiers* (Baden Baden: Bouxwiller, 2004), 45–49.

11. *OS* V, 409, l. 24: "hic uero aut canerentur psalmi, aut aliquid legeretur [. . .]"; l. 28–29: "postremo [. . .] laudes Deo canerentur" 410, l. 6–8: "sese ad confessionem laudis Deo Canendam bonitatemque eius praedicandam hortarentur."

of God.[12] The statement is less concerned with singing or the community prayer than the individual practice of praying aloud, spoken or sung. It really seems that here Calvin is especially dependent on the teaching of Jesus on prayer, which insists on the discretion and sincerity of Christian prayer, and which was the subject of regular recall among the Fathers.[13]

The 1539 edition does not include any alteration on this point, and the truly important addition on the subject is that of 1543.[14] Here it deals specifically with the question of liturgical singing, even if he acknowledges that here he is not dealing with the subject except in passing.[15] Calvin recalls that it is a very old practice, even apostolic, taught by Paul,[16] however emphasizing that it was not universal. He hangs on Augustine's witness, which relates that it is only under the episcopacy of Amboise that the Milan Church began to sing psalms, at the time of the struggle against Aryanism, before being followed by the other western churches in this usage of oriental origin.[17] Then Calvin quotes an extract from the *Retractiones*, which confirms that the usage only arrived in Africa at the time of Augustine.[18] Then mentioning another passage from the *Confessions*, he emphasizes how much singing encourages ardor in prayer, however on condition that the praying person stays attentive to the spiritual words rather than to the musical modulations.[19] He recalls Augustine's wish to see the usage prescribed by Athanasius, who was careful that the diction should be nearer to reading than to singing. Then Calvin can emphasize the requirement for moderation in singing, in order

12. *OS* IV, 341, l. 5-8, 18-19, 22-27: "Hinc praeterea plusquam clarum est, neque uocem neque cantum (si in oratione intercedanto habere quicquam moment, aut hilum proficere apud Deum, nisi ex alto cordis affect profecta. [. . .] Neque tamen uocem aut cantum hic damnamus, quin potius valde comendamus, modo animi affectum comitentur. Praeterea, quum Dei Gloria in singulus corporis nostril partibus elucere quodammodo debeat, conuenit praesertim linguam huic ministerio addictam esse ac deuotam tum canendo tum loquendo: quae peculiariter ad enarrandam praedicandamque Dei laudem condita est."

13. Cf. Matt 6:5-8. Among the Fathers, cf. for example Tertullien, *De oratione*, 17, 3 (ed. Diercks [Turnhout, 1954], *CCl* 1, 266, l. 8-0) *Deus autem non uocis sed cordis auditor est*, formula taken up by Cyprien, *De dominica oratione*, 4. In Augustine, see M. Vincent, *Saint Augustin, maitre de prière, d'après les Enarrationes in Psalmos* (Paris, 1990), 67-71 and 228-31.

14. *OS* IV, 341, l. 33; 342, l. 34. On this text, see Follmi, *Das Weiterwirken der Musik anschauung Augustins*, 135-37.

15. *OS* IV, 341, l. 3-34; "Canendo uero in Ecclesiis ritum 9ut id quoque obiter dicam).

16. 1 Cor 14:15; Col 3:16.

17. Augustine, *Confessions*, IX, 7, 15.

18. Augustine, *Retractationes*, II, 11.

19. Augustine, *Confessions*, X, 33, 50.

to please God: *Hac ergo adhibita moderation, nihil dubium quin sanctissimm sit ac saluberrimum institutum.*" Through applying this moderation, there is no doubt that this usage is very holy and very beneficial.[20]

This text will remain the main passage of the *Institutio* where Calvin describes liturgical singing in a precise manner. The same preoccupations appear however in another important text on the subject, the Letter to the Reader which precedes his text on "The shape of ecclesiastical prayers and songs." This epistle in French had a first version in 1542. In this, he emphasizes that singing is a help to inflame the heart of man in praising God,[21] but he insists at the same time on the difference between profane music and sacred music, the latter being linked to the text of the psalms and being characterized by its gravity and majesty: "One must always be careful, that singing should not be light and fickle: but it should have weight and majesty, as Saint Augustine says."[22] The attribution of this expression to Augustine presents a difficulty, as the passage could never be identified,[23] and the research that we have carried out from the bank of informatic data has brought no result.[24] For Follmi, Calvin would not rely on any particular passage from Augustine and would only express his intention: even Augustine, a supporter of joyful singing which was agreeable to God, would not have accepted every kind of singing in Church.[25] The fact is not impossible, so much that Calvin, at the end of his letter, in a later addition, takes up expression into account, without referring it to the Bishop of Hippo any more.[26]

This letter was in fact finished by a long addition dated June 1543, and it appeared in this longer form in the 1545 edition.[27] Now, in this addition, the Reformer takes up the idea of moderation which he highlighted in the text of the *Institutio* appearing in March 1543: the music, if it is without moderation, runs the risk of taking on a demoniac quality. Singing must be restricted to

20. *OS* IV, 342, l. 29–31.

21. Cf. Letter to the Reader in the text on "The shape of ecclesiastical prayers and songs" (*OS* II, 11–18, 15, l. 27–30). And in truth, we know by experience, that singing has great power and vigour to move and inflame the heart of men, in order to invoke and praise God with a more vehement and ardent zeal."(See Garside, "The Origins of Calvin's Theology of Music: 1536-1543," 17–18.)

22. *OS* II, 15, l. 30–32.

23. Cf. ibid., and see Garside, "The Origins of Calvin's Theology of Music," 18–19; nor *Epistl* 55, 18, 34, nor *Conf.* X.33 correspond exactly.

24. The Library of Latin Texts (LLT), Turnhout, 2009.

25. 25. Cf. *Enarrationes ad Psalmos*, 32, I, 8 (ed. Dekkers-Fraiport [Turnhout, 1956], CCL 38, 254, l. 20–33) on joyful singing which is agreeable to God. See Follmi, *Das Weiterwirken der Musikanschauung Augustins*, 133–34.

26. *OS* II, 1952, 18, l. 4–8 (see *infra*, n28).

27. See *CO* 6, 170.

Psalms, within the cultural framework, and one must use this gift from God which is music, with moderation.[28] There followed a whole development inspired particularly by Augustine, where Calvin explains that only songs for praising God and inspired by God, otherwise called the Psalms of David, are worthy of being sung. We should note that two quotations borrowed from the *Enarrationes* of Augustine are noticed in this passage.[29]

In comparing these three texts—the epistle of 1542, the *Institutio* of March 1543 and the additions of 10 June 1543 with the epistle—we have certainly the impression of a chronological succession:

> In the epistle of 1542, the reference to Augustine is inexact, and the idea of moderation does not appear in the text;

> In the *institution* of 1543, Calvin relies precisely on Augustine and adopts the principle of moderation in choral practice;

---

28. Letter to the Reader, OS II, 16, l. 15-24: "Now between the other things, which are proper for re-creating man and give him pleasure, Music is, either the first, or one of the main things: and we must consider that it is a gift from God created for this usage. That is why, we must all the more take care that we do not abuse it, for fear of soiling and contaminating it, converting it in our condemnation where it would be dedicated to our benefit and salvation. When there is no consideration other than this one, if it the use of music must move us in *moderation*, to make it serve us in all honesty." And the letter ends with these words: "On melody, the best advice seems to be that it should be *moderate*, so that we have used it to bring weight and majesty to the subject, and even to be suitable for singing in Church as it was said" (p. 18, l. 4-8). See Garside, "The Origins of Calvin's theology of Music," 20-24, which also dealt with Calvin's development, but the subject of which was not concerned with writing the text which appeared in 1543.

29. OS II, 17, l. 12-20: "Now what St Augustine says is true, that nobody can sing songs which are worthy of God, unless he has received from Him: because when we have gone around everywhere to look here and there, we will not find better or more suitable songs for doing so, but the Psalms of David: which the Holy Spirit has told us and made. However, when we sing them, we are sure that God places the words in our mouths, as if he himself was singing in us in order to exalt his glory." Cf. *Enarr. In Ps 34*, l. 1 (ed. Dekkers-Fraipont [Turnhout, 1956], CCL 38, 300, l. 16-21): *Ergo psalmos illi: illi cor nostrum, illi lingua nostra digna cantt; sit amen ipse dignabitur donare quod cantet. Nemo illi cantat digna, nisi qui ab illi acceperit quod cantare posit. Denique hoc quod modo cantamo, Spiritu eius dictum est per prophetam eius, et in eis uerbis ubi nos agnoscimus et ipsum.*" Ex OS II, 17, l. 25-30: "Now the heart needs intelligence. And in that (says Saint Augustine) lies the difference between singing by men and that by birds. For Linnet, a Nightingale, a Popinjay, will sing well, but that will be without understanding. Now the proper gift of man is to sing, knowing what he says." Cf. *Enarr. In Ps 18, II, 1* (Bibliotheque augustinienne, 57/B, dir. M. Dulaey [Paris, 2009], 66): "*Quid hoc sit intellegere debemus, ut humana ratione, non quasi auium uoce cantemus. Nam et meruli et psittaci et corui et picae et huiusmodi uolucres saepe ab hominibus docentur sonare quod nescient. Scienter autem cantare naturae hominis diuina uoluntate concessum est.*"

> In the addition of 10 June 1543, one finds the idea of moderation again, and the reference to Augustine is still exact, since Calvin particularly quotes two passages from the *Enarrationes*.

Everything is therefore presented as if the passage from the *Institutio* had been written between the two versions of the epistle to the reader. That would therefore suppose that Calvin had reworked his text during 1542, beyond January. From that one should conclude that, if Calvin undertook the third revision of the Latin text of his master-work during his time in Strasbourg, he continued this work upon his return to Geneva, between September 1541 and the end of January 1542; later, in front of the delays which occurred to the printing of the work or due to his wish to revise his text again, he continued to enhance it, by means of complementary developments (that on singing would be an example of it) and new quotations. The hypothesis is very plausible in the context of the sixteenth century. The world of printing and bookshop worked in close collaboration with the authors, who did not hesitate to come and supervise the work in the workshops. We have good witness of this for Beatus Rhenanus and his collaboration with the Basel printer Froben.[30] We know as well that Calvin knew this sector of activity very well and was comfortable there.[31] One may well admit that he had delayed in setting down the definitive text, or took back the manuscript in order to finish it. Without going back on the fact that the 1543 edition doubtless best reflects the contribution of the time in Strasbourg to the writing of the *Institutio*,[32] one must accept the hypothesis that this third Latin edition received more reworkings during at least the first year of his second time in Geneva.

This 1543 edition operates reworkings on the 1539 work which are relatively important, connected naturally to the discussions in which he took part and to the disagreements that he had to resolve, especially during

---

30. P. Petitmengin, "How printing was done in Basel at the beginning of the sixteenth century. About 'Tertullien' of Beatus Rhenanus (1521)," *Annuaire des Amis de la Bibliothèque humaniste de Selestat* 30 (1980) 93–106; F. Chapot, "In the office of philologist, Beatus Rhenanus editor of the *Aduersus Hermogenem* of Tertullien (Basel 1521–1528–1539)," in J. Hirstein (ed.), *Beatus Rhenanus (1485–1547), Lecteur et èditeur des texts anciens* (Turnhout, 2000), 277–80 (263–83); L. D. Reynolds, "Beatus Rhenanus and Seneca, *De Beneficiis* and *De Clementia*," in *Beatus Rhenanus (1485–1547): Lecteur et éditeur des texts anciens*, 104 (101–15).

31. See Gilmont, *Jean Calvin et le livre imprimé*, 276–313.

32. There seems to have been a consensus about this matter among Calvin specialists; L. Smits, *Saint Augustin dans l'oeuvre de Calvin. I. Etude de critiaue littéraire* (Assen, 1956), 64; Fraenkel, "*Trois passages de l'Institution* de 1543 and their relationships with the inter-confessional colloquia from 1540–1541," in *Calvinus ecclesiae Genevensis custos* (Frankfurt on Main, 1984), 153 (149–57).

9. Patristics

his time in Strasbourg. The alterations, which are important and which lead to an extension, in volume, of 25 percent, are made up four orders:[33] restructuring, substantial additions, new chapters and the insertion of new quotations.

One may naturally point out obvious continuities from one edition to the other, especially in the sequence of series of chapters: the succession of the first three chapters; the series of chapters 9 to 11 (formerly 5 to 7); the series of chapters 14 to 18 (formerly 8 to 12); the completion of the work on chapter 21 (formerly 17). However, beside these elements of continuity, one may notice restructurization. Thus the chapter on Christian freedom (12) is now situated between that on the relationships between the Old Testament and the New Testament (11) and that where there is a question of human Traditions (13): in the previous arrangement, freedom (13) appeared between the eucharist (12) and ecclesiastical power (14). The old chapter 14, *De potestate ecclesiastica*, has been integrated into a large chapter 8, *De ecclesia*.

Various substantial additions come in to finish the text. In the chapter *De lege* (3), the explanation of the commandment "Thou shalt not commit adultery" includes an excursus on celibacy, which one may explain by the arguments on the same subject held in Worms in November 1540. Chapter 6 (formerly 4) which contains the Explanation of the Symbol, received an addition to his first article on angels and demons, manifestly turned against spiritual people and the Anabaptists, who had drawn the attention of Calvin in Strasbourg. The inter-confessional colloquia of 1540–1541 led him to include developments on the certainty of salvation (chapter 6, formerly 4) and on the eucharist (chapter 18, formerly 12).

Some completely new chapters, chapter 4, *De uotis*, and chapter 13, *De traditionibus humanis*, also reflect problems raised by the inter-confessional colloquia of 1540–1541.

We shall dwell more on the addition of numerous quotations and biblical and patristic references, coming from his reading. By basing ourselves on the edition of the *institution* in volumes 3 to 5 of the *Opera Selecta*, published by Pierre Barth and Guillaume Niesel in Munich, one may try to assess the breadth of the additions in the matter of quotations and patristic references. The following figures were worked out by our efforts and, without claiming absolute exactitude, we can guarantee the orders of size.

---

33. According to Gilmont, *Jean Calvin et le livre imprimé*, 372, the work goes from 200,000 to 250,000 words. On the alterations brought into the 1543 edition, see Fraenkel, "Trois passages . . . 153–54: *OS* III, XXI–XXII.

The 1543 edition brings to the total about 280 additions to that of 1539, of variable importance, of a half-line—in order to facilitate, within the framework of its reworking, a transition—to several totally new pages.

On these 280 passages, about 188 include a quotation or a reference to the Christian literature of Antiquity,[34] which represents about 65 percent of the additions.

The patristic authors used are very varied and depend upon the preoccupations of the time.[35] Annette Zillenbiller for example has shown very well how his ecclesiological preoccupations led Calvin, during those years, to be closely interested in the work of Cyprien of Carthage, of whom it is known that he himself had reflected on the unity of the Church in the middle of persecutions. But it is the work of Augustine which very broadly dominates, as, on these 188 passages, 92 contain a reference or a quotation from Augustine, that is about 50 percent. In other terms, in the 1543 additions, when Calvin invokes Christian authors of Antiquity, in one case out of two one finds Augustine, quoted alone or in the middle of other authors, which makes the Bishop of Hippo the Christian author most used by Calvin.

If one now looks into the works of the Bishop of Hippo that were used, one may notice that about 27 works are at one time or another requested, but that three works are broadly in dominance: the *Letters*, with 13 occurrences; the *Homelies sur Jean*, with 19 occurrences; and the *Enarationes in Psalmos*, with 26 occurrences.

In order to assess the novelty of this attention brought to these three works, we can go back to the charts drawn up by Smits in his these on *Saint Augustin dans l'oeuvre de Jean Calvin*.[36] In order to avoid these ambiguities, we shall here hold onto the quotations, excluding simple references, whose identification is more appropriate to discussion. About the *Letters*, we discover that if their usage is not absent from the 1536 edition, it is rather rare in this first edition, to become more important in the 1539 edition, and even more frequent from 1543. About the *Homelies sur l'Evangile de Jean*, one also

---

34. By the expression: "Christian literature of Antiquity" we include the Acts of the African Councils, but we do not exclude mediaeval literature, especially Bernard de Clairvaux, regularly used by Calvin in these years: cf. A. N. S. Lane, *Jean Calvin, Student of the Church Fathers* (Edinburgh, 1999), 115–50.

35. On the use of patristic literature by Calvin, beyond the works of Smits and Lane, already quoted (See n32 and n34), see R. J. Mooi, *Het kerk—en dogmahistoisch element in de Werken van Johannes Calvijn* (Wagenininingen, 1965); A. Zillenbiller, *Die Einheit der Katholischen Kirche: Calvins Cyprianrezeption in seinen ekklesiologischen Schriften* (Mayence, 1993), and the synthesis of I. Backus, "Kalvin und die Kirchenvater," in H. J. Selderhuis (ed.), *Calvin Handbuch* (Tubingen, 2008), 126–37.

36. See in particular the second volume, *Saint Augustin dans l'oeuvre de Calvin*, II. *Tables de références augustiniennes* (Assen, 1958).

notices that its usage is much rarer in the later editions, but not absent. On the other hand the situation seems to be rather different for the *Enarrationes in psalmos*: they are never quoted explicitly in the 1536 edition; in that of 1539, one can only find a single quotation which is borrowed from them;[37] the 1543 edition keeps a much more important place for the *Enarrationes*, since, staying with the quotations, one may count 20 different *Enarrationes*, for 26 quotations.[38] Naturally, this interest for the *Enarrationes* reminds us of our previous remarks on the reflection that Calvin carried out on music.

The study on these quotations borrowed from the *Enarrationes* enables four series of remarks to be made:

1. In these quotations, generally fairly short, of one to two sentences, Augustine's text is quoted to the letter, naturally by means of some cuts and syntactic adaptations, but with great fidelity; in only three cases the Augustinian text is rewritten (no. 6, 17, 25). Most often, Calvin indicates his source: in 21 cases out of 26, one is given the reference to the work.

2. Sometimes, it is clear that the quotations were chosen for their expressivity. In a general way, these quotations from the *Enarrationes* do not imply any reorientation or inflexion of the line of argument, and most often they are illustrations of the statement.

3. Mainly, one finds three types of addition: sometimes, quoting the *Enarrationes* is part of a larger group of quotations which are borrowed from various authors (no. 12, 17, 19, 22); more often, it belongs to a group of quotations which are all taken from Augustine (no. 1, 4, 5, 7, 8, 9, 10, 13, 20); even more often, in 12 cases out of 26, the quotation is single or accompanied by a second quotation from the *Enarrationes* (no. 2, 3, 6, 11, 14, 16, 18, 21, 23, 24, 25, 26). In these cases, the addition is essentially restricted to the quotation. These different types of addition do not bear witness to the same usage of Augustine's work: in the case of a group of quotations of diverse origin, it is probable that Calvin uses a type of personal repertory or a collection of quotations; on the other hand, every time that he glides along on his own, in a special addition, a quotation from the *Enarrationes*, one may think that it is a question of personal reading, contemporary with revising the *Institutio*.

---

37. *In Ps* 109, 1, OS IV, 278, l. 7–12; cf. *In Ps* 32, 2, 2,2.

38. *See the annexed table. On the usage of the *Enarrationes in Psalmos* in Calvin, see some remarks by Smits, *Saint Augustin dans l'oeuvre de Calvin*, I, 171, and the tables in vol. 2, 230–36.

4. None of these quotations appears in Martin Bucer's *Florilegium patristicum*, which one considers was begun shortly after 1536. In a general way, a quick check has also enabled us to find out that, in total, the 1543 edition does not make an obvious loan from the *Florilegium*.[39]

From these discoveries it is clear that the Reformer used the *Enarrationes* as an illustration charged with authority, and that the addition seems most often to be inspired by personal contemporary reading of Augustine's work. In our eyes, this hypothesis finds an element of consolidation in both quotations from the *Enarrationes* which end the Letter to the Reader introducing the text on "The shape of ecclesiastical prayers and songs," previously described: here there is a convergence which is not the fruit of chance. We can place this fact in relation with Calvin's interest in the psalms in those years.

Naturally, this interest does not date from the 1540 years From his arrival in Strasbourg, he saw the place that the psalms held in the collections of canticles of the town and more generally in those of South Germany. He discovered a practice of singing psalms that was well implanted in the reformed churches: in 1538 the whole psalter was translated into the vernacular and set to music.[40] Also Calvin hastened to offer to the little community of French refugees what had been done in German for the other communities.[41] From 29 December 1538, he announced, in a letter to Farel, that he was preparing a French psalter for his own community, which appeared in 1539 under the title *Aucuns psaulmes et cantiques mys en chant*.[42]

---

39. We confirm on this point most of A. N. S. Lane's *John Calvin, Student of the Church Fathers*, 155, n29. A. Zillenbiller, *Die Einheit der Katholischen Kirche*, 83–86, was however able to establish contacts between the *Florilegium* and Calvin's work, about quotations from Cyprien: she thinks she can state that Bucer's collection is one of Calvin's sources for this author, with the Erasmian edition of the *Opera Cypriani* of 1520 (71–75) and the *Decretum Gratiani* (75–82). Also, as we have said, one cannot exclude that there may have been a second collection from the same Bucer, which would have been lost (Fraenkel, *Martin Bucer et Matthew Parker, Florilegium Patristicum*, XII–XIII).

40. After the 1537 Augsburg edition of the compete German psalter set to music, due to Jacob Dachser, Wolfgang Kopfel (Capito) published one in Strasbourg in 1538: see VEIT, "Le chant, la Réforme et la Bible," in G. Bedouelle and B. Roussel (dir.) *Le temps des Réformes et la Bible*, Paris, 1989, 663–81.)

41. It is known from a letter of J. Zwick to Bullinger, dated 9 November 1538, that the French parishioners already sang psalms in their language: "*Gallis Argentorati ecclesia data est in qua [. . .]psalmos sua lingua canunt*" (*CO* 10/2, 288, no. 151; Pidoux, *Le Psautier Huguenot du XVIe siècle. Mélodies et documents*. 2e vol. Documents et bibliographie, Basel, 1962, 2).

42. Letter to Farel of 29 December 1538, *OC* 10/2, 438, no. 200 (cf. Pidoux, *Le Psautier Huguenot du XVIe siècle*, vol. 2, 20). See Garsude, "The Origins of Calvin's

Later, Calvin's interest in the psalms was never given up, and naturally one thinks of the lessons that he gave about them from 1552 to 1555 and of the *Commentarius* which came out of them, appearing in July 1557.[43] However, if one believes the extract from Smits, the presence of Augustine's *Enarrationes in Psalmos* remains relatively modest in the *Commentarius*: one only picks up thirteen quotations or explicit references. Moreover, in the same way, in the editions of the *Institutio* which are later than 1543 one can only list seven new quotations from the *Enarrationes*.[44] Without wishing to overinterpret an observation like this, it does seem that these figures confirm a particular interest of Calvin's for the *Enarrationes* during the years where he is preparing the 1543 edition of the *Institutio*. Let us add that among the seven new quotations, two came from *Enarrationes* and were already used in the 1543 edition: *Enarr.* 70, 2 (no. 8) and 102 (no. 14) which may suggest that the 1559 additions still depend upon the extract made by Calvin in the years 1541–1543.

One may see in this interest for the *Enarrationes* an influence from Bucer, from which one often recognizes, without ever proving it, the influence on Calvin during his time in Strasbourg. However that is not certain. Certainly Bucer in 1529 published a complete commentary on the psalms, under the pseudonym of Aretius Felinus.[45] Consulting this commentary reveals however that the Strasbourgian Reformer regularly quotes rabbinical commentators, and only selectively quotes the Fathers and the classical writers. Augustine and his *Enarrationes* do not hold a predominant place.

Calvin's source does not therefore seem to be Bucerian, and doubtless one must admit that Calvin undertook systematic and continuous reading of the *Enarrationes*. One understands very well the interest that he could find in this reading, while he had published, with Clement Marot, a French

---

Theology of Music: 1536–1543," 14–15, and the contribution of Ph. François to the present volume, 57 (53–65).

43. Gilmont, *Jean Calvin et le livre imprimé*, On Calvin's hesitations in publishing a commentary on the Psalms, particularly due to that works the Bucer and Musculus had written on them, see his letter which opens in his commentary, *OC* 31, 14–15.

44. We are basing ourselves on the extract from Smits, *Saint Augustin dans l'oeuvre de Calvin*, II, 230–36; in *Ps* 3, 1 in *Inst.* 1559, IV, 17, 21, *OS* V, 372; 33, 1,10, in *Inst.* 1559, IV, 17, 28, *OS* V, 382; 33, 2, 2 in *Inst.* 1559, IV, 18,28, *OS* V, 382; 56, 9 in *Inst.* 1550, 1,8,10, *OS* III, 79; 70, 2, 5, in *Inst.* 1559, III, 25, 10, *OS* IV, 454; 98,9 in *Inst.* 1559, IV, 17, 34, *OS* V, 397; 102,7, in *inst.* 1559, III, 25, 10, *OS* IV, 454.

45. *S. Psalmorum libri quinque ad ebraicam veritatem versi, et familiari explanation elucidati, per Aretium Felinum*, Argentorati, 1529. Bucer explains himself on the usage of this pseudonym in a letter to Zwingli of April 1529, see *Correspondance de Martin Bucer*, vol. 3 (1527–1529), ed. J. Rott and Chr. Krieger (Leiden, 1995), 262.

translation of the psalms. Must one all the more consider that his reading of the *Enarrationes* goes back to his first years in Strasbourg?

If we come back to our earlier observations on his usage of Augustine to define what one calls his "theology of music,"[46] it is not impossible that the continuous reading of the *Enarrationes* is not only later than his time in Strasbourg, but also later than January 1542 and writing the first version of the Letter to the Reader on prayer. We see a compatibility between adding two quotations from the *Enarrationes* in the 1543 rewriting of this Letter to the Reader, which, in a first time, made only one rather vague reference to Augustine, and the place of the *Enarrationes* in the 1543 edition of the *Institutio*. This return to the *Enarrationes*, which Calvin certainly knew beforehand, but which perhaps he had not looked at continuously, can only date from the very last phase of the work on the third Latin edition of the *Institutio*, while awaiting the printing work or even within the framework of a final revision of his text.

These remarks are only hypotheses, and doubtless it would be necessary to explore more systematically the works of the Reformer, and especially his correspondence, in order to confirm them. In any case they show what a precise analysis may bring to reconstituting the history of the different versions of Calvin's *Institutio*. They are also a new witness that the *Institutio*, in Latin and in its French versions, was for Calvin a permanent workshop, that returned to continuously according to his reading. On account of this he was not wrong to write, with Augustine, when he tried his best to do so in the number of those who write as they progress and who progress as they write.

---

46. Cf. Garside's article quoted previously (n10).

10. Images of Calvin

Books by the Reformer Printed or Read in Strasbourg

A Franco-German Story

Olivier Millet

THE IMPORTANCE OF THE time in Strasbourg for the development of the religious works of Calvin is well known; recently, Matthieu Arnold drew up the modern historiography of this episode, in a study which acts both as a synthetic introduction on this biographical and historical theme.[1] Here we want to bring some modest lateral illumination from bibliographical and literary considerations about Calvin's image that one may glean in works of the Reformer which were printed in Strasbourg, or in copies of his works which were kept in this town, insofar as these works reflect a certain manner of presenting himself to the public, for the Reformer, and where, as regards the conserved copies, they hold the indication of a certain perception, by his readers, of his Reformer's work. That will lead us to finish recalling the role of Strasbourg in the modern reception of the *Institution de la religion chrétienne*.

Let us begin with Calvin's Strasbourgian publications. We are not aware of Calvin's publications which appeared anonymously in Strasbourg, and we only hold the particularly meaningful impressions dating *grosso modo* from the time of the author's time in Alsace and the title page of which contains a certain image of the author. Calvin's time in Strasbourg appears from this moment as a turning point in his career.

Before his installation in the city on the Rhine, Calvin had only once shown his editorial activities, as they took place in Geneva, on the title page of *Duae epistolae* which were issued in Basel in 1537;[2] it was then in his

1. Matthieu Arnold, "Le séjour de Jean Calvin (1538–1541), simple parenthèse ou étape capital dans la biographie du Réformateur? Enquête historiographique," *Bulletin de la société de l'histoire du protestantisme français* 155 (2009) 321–33.

2. We refer for the literary history and the bibliographical description of each title to

capacity as Professor in Holy Scripture. The author in fact, on the title page, brings a half-ecclesiastical academic title: *Sacrarum literarum in Ecclesia Genevensi professoris*. It remains on the title page of the 1536 *Institutio* published in Basel[3] and again on that of 1539, published in Strasbourg,[4] the *Johannes Calvinus Noviodunensis*, "coming from Noyon," which already appeared on the title page on the commentary of Seneca's *De clementia* which the young humanist had published in 1532.[5] This common mediaeval and humanist habit, of stating his identity exactly, by showing his little place of origin, adopted in 1532–1539 by the one who then launched into letters with a mixture of audacity and with necessary and prudent modesty will then be abandoned by the Reformer in publications which are directly to his presence or his activity in Geneva. Now, in spite of this repetition in 1539 of mentioning Noyon, it is in fact the theologian who asserts himself from the Strasbourgian period, through the nature of his publications, even if it is not the activities undertaken in Strasbourg that he marks.

Besides, certain initial elements which go along with his Stasbourgian publications enable the young Reformer to be situated in the Protestant Republic of Letters. The dedication to Simon Grynaeus of the 1540 commentary on the Epistle to the Romans[6] is a masterpiece of prudence in his own statement in front of the works of Melanchthon, from Bucer and Bullinger on the same Epistle of Saint Paul. Our author defines his own exegetic program by insisting on the fact that he finishes the methods and results already produced by his colleagues. It goes without saying that the latter are all Protestants, but the French exegetist sees them essentially, in this preface, as members of a Christian Republic of Letters, among which from now on he takes his place. As for the title page of the 1539 *institutio*,[7] printed in Strasbourg, it contains a publicity element, which may have been suggested

---

Roldophe Peter and Jean-Francois Gilmont, *Biblioteca Calviniana: Les oeuvres de Calvin publiées au XVIe siècle*, vol. 1, *Ecrits théologiques, littéraires et juridiques 1532–1554* (Geneva: Droz, 1991); *Ecrits théologiques, littéraires et juridiques 1555–1564* (1994); *Ecrits théologiques, littéraires et juridiques 1565–1600* (2000), abridged for each title by the sign BC followed by that of the publication in question according to the BC system. Here, 3771.

3. BC 36/1.
4. BC 39/4.
5. BC 32/1.
6. BC 40/3. See also *infra* on this matter.
7. BC 39/4. For the other Strasbourgian publications of Calvin that we do not mention here, they are either anonymous, or, with the *épître de Sadolet* and Calvin's reply to this cardinal, the name of Calvin appears only in second position after [. . .] that of the Prelate *Ionnes Cavlini responsio*. We also leave aside the texts which appeared in German, most of them anonymous.

or introduced by the printer, after its subtitle allowing a great many things to the reader: the content of the work, greatly increased, finally corresponding, it is stipulated, to its title: *nunc vere demum suo titulo respondens*. Also what is very significant is the edition, increased again, of 1543,[8] as it contains a Latin eulogy of Calvin, installed however in Geneva from now on, signed by the famous Jean Sturm. This humanist pedagogue and orator praises his old Strasbourg colleague not in an initial piece inside the book, but directly on the title page, and thus gives him, as a writer and as a theologian, an authority which is as much indisputable as commercial. These editorial elements bear witness to a new type of balance between the prudence of the humanist (in 1530) and the theologian from the self-taught beginner that Calvin was and the systematic publicity carried out for his fame, acknowledged from that time onwards. Even if these publicity aspects are due to the printers' initiative rather than to the author, they bear witness to the fact that the name of Calvin does not yet suffice to be imposed by a single mention of his name. In addition, this eulogy was recopied by hand, on the title page of a copy of a 1576 edition of the *Institutio*, an extraordinary edition,[9] especially as it contains a great many other handwritten annotations aiming to place the *Institutio* in a (Nuremburgian) Lutheran and Melanchthonian context, in which Sturm's recommendation could obviously have a certain weight in making the reputation of the reformed Calvin well known. Let us note finally that the French Reformer will allow this Sturmian eulogy to survive in the 1545 French and Genevan edition[10] as well as the Strasbourgian Latin re-edition of the same year,[11] while he had left Strasbourg almost four years before that. In the French version, the text of the eulogy is translated into French in these words:

Jehan Sturmius,

John Calvin, c'est un home d'un jugement qui pénétre jusques au tout, et d'une doctrine admirable, et d'une mémoire singuliere: et lequel en ses Escritz, cest merueilles comment il parle de tout, et abondamment, et purement. Don't son Institution de la Religion Chrétienne, en est un tesmoignage evident. Laquelle une foi la ayant mise en lumière, puis après la enrichit, mais maintenant l'a rendue toute parfaicte. Tellement que je ne sache nully qui ait onc plus parfaictement escrit, ny our demonstrer la vraye Religion, ny pour corriger les meurs, ny pour abatre les abus. Et quiconque

---

8. BC 43/5.
9. See in the catalogue mentioned *infra* n16 no. 20 and the different reproductions.
10. BC 45/6.
11. BC 45/5

> *auront attaint jusques aux poincte des choses qu'il enseigne en ce Livre la, que tells croyent hardiment, qu'ils sont parfaictement éstablis.*[12]

Calvin himself certainly did not translate or correct this version of Sturm's eulogy, for he would not have allowed such complexity of expression, which was alien to his own style; taking up the subject around the presenting turn of phrase "it is" in [. . .] "Calvin, it is [. . .] as well as in "and which [. . .] it is wonderful how he"; a heavy translation of "who penetrates up to the end" to translate *acutissimo*; abandonment of the adjective *varius*, which remains untranslated in spite of the importance of this description (the variety of style) in the ideal literary humanist; a semantic repeat of the antecedent, in a relative proposal, by "of which," then by "in"; "whoever" treated as a plural and therefore followed by the verbal form "they will have," then in its turn repeated by "such ones"; a bad translation, because it is too literal, of *assecutus* par "achieved" (in the meaning of "learned," "understood"); clumsy introduction of "brazenly," and translation of *institutum* by "established," where Calvin himself would probably have put "taught" or "instituted." The translator of this preface not only mis-handles the development of the French language of his time toward the turns of phrase of modern French, but he is not aware of the elegant, economic and efficient nature of the prose of ideas which the author has just invented, as grammatical as stylistic, in the register of the vernacular language. Happily, this clumsy publicity, perhaps due to a collaborator in the printer's workshop, appears on the back of the title page in the French edition;[13] doubtless Calvin did not see it, due to lack of time or interest. The elegant modernity of his own style comes from the sparkling manner of comparing the texts coming from his pen with this poor translation, which also emphasizes the discrepancy which could still be felt between an elegant Latin Strasbourgian printing and a Genevan printing (by Jean Girard) in the vernacular language. However, Calvin's eulogy by Sturm will disappear from the editions of the *Institutio* after 1551. It had become surplus due to the Reformer's fame which from that time was definitively established and due to the authority of his works, but also, doubtless, due to the past years, which had made the memory of his time in Strasbourg fade out. After this Alsatian phase, and with the final installation in Geneva Calvin no longer needed, in any case when he published the works where he completely assumed responsibility, recommendations made by other people.

---

12. Here we introduce the text of the *Calvini opera*, t.3, XXXI.

13. But It continues, in the Latin edition of 1545, to appear on the title page, as in 1543.

10. Images of Calvin

Therefore the Strasbourgian period appears, from the point of view of asserting himself by Calvin as a writer and theologian, as a transition stage; a non-Strasbourgian author, he is but still described sometimes as "from Noyon," who inserts himself into the group of reforming theologians, and who still needs publicity from the famous Sturm. The main thing however is the following fact, well marked by the Reformation historians. With the parallel publication of his *Institutio* of 1539, which is addressed to the theology students, and his 1540 commentary on the Epistle to the Romans, Calvin in Strasbourg defined his methodological singularity, and therefore his authority as a theologian. It consists in the articulation of two types of work: in fact our author foresees that he will keep the study of the theological common places in his *Institutio*, which will allow him to give a brevity and therefore a special clarity to his exegetic commentaries (still to come in 1539). It is correct that in Strasbourg, in 1540, that the *ioannis Calvini Commentarii in epistolam ad Romanos*[14] appeared, which articulated (in the dedication) this complex of ideas. It is also the first work published by Calvin where the name of the author appears thus in the first position on the title page and in first place in the publicity which makes up the title on this page, the first name *Ioannis* being itself printed in capital letters. That is explained by the typographical habits of the printer, Wendelin Rihel, for this type of publication, and by the syntaxical possibilities of the Latin language as an insertion of the author's name in the publicity which acts as a title for a work.[15] Nevertheless, the fact is there: with this first biblical commentary by Calvin, whose preface draws up the program for his exegetic work, our author also confirms, through this accent placed under his name, the role that he plays in this decisive field of the religious reform and the hermeneutic culture of his time.

Let us come now to some aspects of the Strasbourg reception of Calvin's works, as it was read and annotated in the Strasbourgian environment throughout the centuries. The examples that I shall give are inserted into the framework of a search of material bibliography which is currently being undertaken, and which is far from being finished;[16] it is only a question of samples.

---

14. BC 40/3.

15. Cf. for example the title pages of BC 43/5 and BC 43/3, by contrast.

16. On this subject see Olivier M, *Lecteurs de Calvin. Exemplaires annotés au cours des siècles* (Noyon: Musée Calvin, 2009), 86 pages (Catalogue of the exhibition presented in the exhibition room of the Reserve of the BNF in March 2009, then in May-July 2009 in Noyon; this catalogue presents the results of unpublished research, of which we take up certain elements).

Calvin certainly became, at the end of the sixteenth century, a controversial figure in conquered Strasbourg, in spite of the resistance between authors of Jean Sturm, by strict Lutheranism. Therefore it is not amazing that we might meet, in a copy kept (without a list number) at the Protestant Mediatheque of this town, an annotating reader who is a Lutheran adversary of the Calvinist doctrine of predestination.

It is a copy of the *Institutio* printed rightly in Strasbourg, by W. Rihel, in 1543.[17] On the title page it contains owner's marks:

> "*Fui M. Clementis Brecht Argentinensis, 1616, at nunc soit M. Oseae Schadaei Argentinensis.* (I belonged to M. Clemens Brecht of Strasbourg in 1616. But now I belong to M. Oseas Schadaeus of Strasbourg.)" M. Clemens Brecht held at the Academy of Strasbourg a *Disputio apologetica quarta, opposita Johannis Piscatoris* [. . .], *contra absolutum reprobationis decretum*,[18] that is to say a "Fourth apologetic thesis, opposed to [. . .] Johann Piscator (1546–1625)[19] against the absolute decree of disapproval."

He was therefore particularly interested in Calvin's ideas on predestination, since he was against a divine decree of disapproval against the impious (doctrine of double predestination), and from the use of the ideas of Johannes Piscator, a former Professor of the same Academy, sent away because of his reformed positions, and who ended his university career in Herborn. Oseas Schadaeus (1586–1626),[20] who is known as the historian of Strasbourg Cathedral. This copy contains several Strasbourgian annotations, by several different readers. The chapter "De praedestinatione et providential" is the only one which is completely annotated, a proof that his theme was a specific subject of study. In fact, two annotators come in fact with two different inks, one black and one red. The annotator using black ink is against Calvin's ideas, and addresses him on the tone of the controversy, for example page 358:

> *Qua igiiitur, o Calvine, culpa Adam rejiciretur [?] et ad lapsum a Deo praedestinaretur? An quia ex nihilo creates est?* [etc.] [By what fault, oh Calvin, would Adam be rejected and would he

---

17. BC 43/5.

18. Publication under this title, Strasbourg, M. ab Heyden, 1617 (copy of the BNF, record No. D 6676).

19. See on this reformed theologian the rubric of the *Biographisch-bibliographisch Kirchenlexikon*, on line.

20. On this theologian, see the *Allgemeine deutsche Biographie*, vol. 30, Leipzig, 1890, 495. He published a *Summum Argentoratensium Templum: Das ist die auszfrliche Beschreibung dess. Munsters eu Strassburg*, Lazari Zetners Erben, 1617.

be pre-destined by God to the fall? Would it be because he was created ex nihilo?)

By these questions which emphasize an absurdity, the annotator indicates his opposition to the idea of a divine decree of disapproval before the creation of man. This annotator must be M. Clemens Brecht, who was preparing properly, by purchasing and reading this copy of the *institution*, to uphold theses in theology which were against the Calvinist doctrine of predestination and precisely to that of a divine decree of disapproval of impious people. The annotator using red ink is content to indicate the divisions and construction of the text, as well as the continuation and the nature of arguments, also the main "common places" that he marks in the text. It is thus that, on the same page 358, he indicated, in lower case: *Hypothese. II* (Hypothesis no. 2). In rhetoric, "hypothesis" describes an idea or an argument that one can subjugate to a more general idea.

Another copy kept without a reference number in the Protestant Mediatheque bears, among several strata of annotation, some which are much more recent than that of the above copy, but which came out of a Strasbourgian environment. It is a copy of the French *institution*, in the edition brought out in Geneva by Th. Courteau in 1564.[21] In this copy one finds various inscriptions of owners on the front and back of the endpaper, with written essays (letters, complete words, etc.) and, between other inscriptions, this one: *mon dieu je vous aime de tout mon Coeur*. This copy in fact reflects, between other types of reading, that which I shall describe as "spiritual" reading of the Calvinian doctrine. After the annotations and underlinings in red ink, one finds particularly an annotation of another reader, who underlines in black ink and in French, taking out an expression in Calvin's text about predestination, how *la doctrine est douce*. This reader with the vernacular language, a Calvinist himself, is therefore paying attention to the spiritual dimension of the Calvinian doctrine of predestination. The same page also contains a more modern annotation (of the twentieth century), in pencil, *Jesus-Christ*, who therefore insists on the Christocentric nature of this same doctrine. Other modern annotations, in pencil, also insist on the spiritual dimension of the Calvinian doctrine by pointing out the corresponding "common places": for example, page 575 (book III, chapter 23, 5), one reads; *Certitude en X* (= Christ). Besides, underlinings and annotations in red ink, but more modern than the first ones, and dating from the nineteenth century, are found in Book IV, chapter 1, 10 (doctrine of the Church), in Book IV, chapter 14 and chapter 15 *passim* (doctrine of the sacraments) with a bibliographical reference in the bridged French form (I in-

21. BC 64/11.

sist on this point) *RE2 XIII*, page 293,[22] about the mirror image that Calvin uses to explain the nature and role of the sacraments. This reader is also a German speaker, for he notes, in the margin, *Schwarmgeister*, a term which sends a message back to enemies of Luther and the official Reformation that the letter denounced, by this German expression, "enlightened spirits." This annotator who simultaneously uses both languages, French and German is doubtless an Alsatian; perhaps it is Edouard Cunitz, for the writing seems to be very close to his own and the red ink used is the same as that which this scholar uses in another copy that I am going to present now, and which served to prepare the critical edition of the *Institutio* for the monumental edition of the *Corpus Reformatorum*.

This time it is a question of a copy, kept in the Musée Calvin at Noyon, of the *institution christianae religionis*, followed by the *Catechismus*, appearing in Geneva from Robert Estienne in 1553.[23]

This copy contains various ex-libris and indications of origin: *Johan-Georg Greiser et Johan. Stadelmann, 1625; Gryphius, 1709; Andreas Matthias Lozbecki, 1768;* Cunitz (on the back of the cover page).

Edouard Cunitz (1812–1886) is, with Jean Guillaume Baum and Edouard Reuss, one of the three editors of the monumental corpus of the complete works of Calvin in the *Corpus Reformatorum: Ioannis Calvini Opera quae supersunt omnia*, appearing in Brunswick, then in Berlin, from Schwetschke, from 1863 to 1900, in 59 volumes. Cunitz was a professor in the Faculty of Protestant Theology in Strasbourg. Volume 1 of this edition, appearing in 1863, contains the first Latin version of the *Institutio*, that of 1536, then the text of the intermediary versions from 1539 to 1554. Cunitz used this copy[24] in order to prepare this edition of the *Institutio*, and his annotations act to carry out the two following aims: to establish the text philologically, and to show the printer the text to be printed: corrections, size and type of characters, etc. A great many annotations made by Cunitz on this copy in fact indicate textual variants of other versions or editions of the Latin *Institutio*, with their respective dates (1536, etc., up to that of 1559), or even correct the text, or add biblical references, or show exactly in red ink which passages must be printed in italics (*cursiv*) or in smaller characters

---

22. It does not seem that it could be about the second edition (1864–1866) of the *Realenzyklopadie der classichen altertumswissenschaft* of Auguste Pauly, as this encyclopaedia only has 8 volumes in this edition.

23. BC53/6. Reference MC 105.

24. The edition in question, but not the copy, is described in the "Prolegomena" of volume 1 of the *Calvini opera*, p. X–XXXVIII. The editors point out that this edition of the *Institutio* is the "*omnium splendidissima*" and that it is characterized by the typographical elegance as by the textual correction. They were visibly happy to use it.

10. IMAGES OF CALVIN 151

(*petite*). Therefore one finds here the indication, in detail, of the general principles which preceded the establishment and printing of the text of the Latin *Institutio* corresponding to the editions of the so-called intermediary versions, those of 1539–1554, a text which appears with its variants in this volume 1 of this Strasbourgian edition. For Cunitz it was a case of indicating the state of the text of the intermediary versions of Calvin's book, of which the 1553 edition was a part, in order thus to distinguish this state of the 1536 book and that of the last version, that of 1559, but also to point out the transformations that the work had undergone between 1539 and 1554. Cunitz therefore used Roman characters to indicate the 1539 text; the italics acted to point out the additions of the 1550, 1553 and 1554 versions. Cunitz asks for the text printed in capital letters to be removed (to be replaced by lower case), as well as commas. He introduced comma-points, and, in the margin, he points out a variant: "*Hic et in seqq* Editio 1539 pro praecepto mandatum *scribit*" [*Ici et dans les pages suivantes*, the 1539 edition written instead of praecepto mandatum].

On the same page, as often elsewhere, the editor scholar asks by the German word *cursiv*, written in red ink, putting into the italic characters the paragraph concerned, for example, in Calvin's commentary of the 7th commandment of the Decalogue, in chapter 3, 63 and 64. In fact, in the edition of the *Corpus reformatorum*, volume I, columns 410–411, published in 1863, one finds Calvin's commentary on the 7th commandment printed as follows:

> Asserit etiamnum apertius Paulus, dum scribit (1 Cor. 7,7) unmquemque habere proprium donum a Deo: unum sic, alterum autem *sic.65. Quando aperta denuntiatione admonemur, non esse cuiuslibet servare castitatem in caelibatu* [etc.]

In this passage, the italics from 65. *Quando*, etc. correspond with what Cunitz, by means of his marginal annotation, pointed out and required of the printer; the text thus put into italics corresponds to an addition to the 1543 and 1545 editions in relation to the 1539 text. One also finds in this copy other older annotations, of the sixteenth to seventeenth century, often on the same pages as those that Cunitz has annotated; the latter has not erased the previous marks, as if they could not bother the printer, obviously criticized for not taking them into account.

The Strasbourgian editors of the *Corpus Reformatorum* are modern craftsmen with philological reading of which one already finds murmurings in the sixteenth century, under the pen of a Genevan annotator who was already comparing, but only in passing, two editions and two different states of Calvin's text.[25] In the case of the *Corpus Reformatorum*, the establishment of the text is operated directly on old copies and in ink, according to a frequent habit of annotators of old books: annotation in pencil, more respectful of the patrimonial materiality of the old book, would only become common in the eighteenth to nineteenth centuries. Cunitz, one can see, still follows an old habit, that of annotators of the past who personally appropriated a work by writing inside it in ink the marks of their reading and of their dialogue with the studied text. In the case of an edition by Robert Estienne, who today has great bibliographical and commercial value, one may be amazed; but old books did not yet, at that time, have the price that they reach today on the market. It is also probable that old copies of Calvin's books were less sought after by amateurs and institutions than nowadays. Finally, by using red and black ink to prepare his edition, Cunitz did not completely scarify this "copy" for the printer, since the copy, which was kept long after its modern editorial usage, has been conserved for us, contrary to what happened in the sixteenth century, a time when very few prepared manuscripts or annotated printed copies were conserved for printing.

Why is it that in Strasbourg—we have just seen in what material conditions—the first great critical edition of the *Institution* and more generally the first scholarly and philological edition of Calvin's work—was born? Why not in Geneva, which had the bibliographical funds required for the enterprise? Out of respect to the memory of Geneva in the nineteenth century, I shall not answer that last question here. Why not Paris even more? That is because in that capital, the Bibliotheque which is today called Nationale, had not since the sixteenth century, for obvious confessional reasons, entered into a controlled acquisition of the printed works of Calvin, which will only begin in the last decade of the nineteenth century.[26] It is not therefore the French capital which could come into the light. Therefore there remained Strasbourg, with the resources of its libraries, of its Faculty of Protestant Theology and its scholars, as well as linguistic and cultural means connected with the Franco-Germanic character of this city on the Rhine. I shall take the example of the edition of the *Institution de la religion chrétlenne* in its 1541 version in order to illustrate my proposal on this last point.

Until the Strasbourgian edition of the *Calvini opera*, the exact date when the first *Institution* first appeared in its French version. The reasons for this ignorance came, among others, for confusions that go back to the sixteenth century. One may even say that, in the first half of the nineteenth

---

25. See in the reference of n16 *supra*, no. 34 of the catalogue.

26. On this matter see Geneviève Guillemint, "Les éditions de Calvin a la Bibliothèque Nationale de France," *Bulletin de la Société de l'histoire du protestantisme français* 155 (2009) 336–43.

century, the situation on this question of literary history was more confused than ever.[27] The edition of the *Institution* which appeared in 1859 from Meyruis, within the framework of a confessional and unfinished project for publishing the complete works of the French reformer,[28] did not even manage to stand out whether or not the first French edition dates from 1535 and therefore precedes the Latin 1536 version. For the group of French editions, it states: "One cannot exactly determine the number and dates from 1540 [*sic*!] to 1550 [*sic*!]"[29] Francois Guizot himself, in his second biography of Calvin, appearing in 1873, at the end of his career and of his life, wrote again: "It was only in 1540 that the French edition appeared!; therefore he does not enter into "this little problem of bibliographical chronology," and, wondering whether the 1536 edition is the first one, he even states:

> I am inclined to think, like several of the most recent and most scholarly historians of Calvin, that the *Institution* was first of all written in French, published in Basle in 1535, without the author's name [. . .], that the dedication to Francis 1st was written and published first of all in French and 1st August 1535, that is certain: the language and date are positive.[30]

It is therefore in Strasbourg that the light dawned,[31] in 1865, with the enterprise of the *Calvini opera*, whose publishers had a great many copies of Calvin's works and also procured a great many others in order to know exactly the editorial history of works that they wanted to publish according to the canons which were finally worthy of historic and philological knowledge, and therefore also that of the *Institutio* in its different versions. They could thus definitively establish, in the prolegomenes of the volume dedicated to the French version, that the first *institution française* only dates from 1541 and does not precede the version or publication of the Latin edition. But in their admirable enterprise, which is still essential to current research, the publishers of *Calvini opera* in their turn went wrong, not on the chronological and bibliographical data, but in the matter of critical as-

---

27. A specialized work such as *La France protestante* of the Haag brothers, in its article "*Calvin*," does not in fact mark, in 1852, any progress in this respect, when it goes for the first French edition the date of 1535 and for the second that of 1540!

28. It is probable that this project was torpedoed by the Strasbourgian edition concurrent with the *Calvini opera* in the *Corpus Reformatorum*.

29. *Op. cit.*, XIV.

30. Francois Guizot, *Vies de quatre grands chrétiens français* (Paris: Hachette, 1873), 181.

31. Or rather it imposed itself, for the Genevan Senebier had already indicated exact dates in the eighteenth century, without the statements being able to received later, unfortunately.

sessment of the texts that they had before their eyes. In their preface to the French versions of the *Institution*, they claim in fact that the first French version of 1541 is authentic; the French translation of the later versions, including the last, that of 1560, according to them includes also interventions by collaborators of the Reformer, and were not reviewed and corrected by him. Now, in spite of this clear and radical position, which monumentalizes the first French version, that of 1541 as the only authentic one, these Strasbourgian publishers of the *Calvini opera* have however taken the 1560 text as the base for their edition of the *Institution française*, for purely practical reasons. In fact, as that of 1541 is much shorter than the later versions and especially than the last 1560 version, if they had published the 1541 text, the variations which are noted would have been much longer than the text itself. Moreover, their edition would not have pleased the theological historians, who more willingly study the last version of the *Institution*, which is more complete and more technical. Therefore there appeared, with Baum, Cunitz and Reuss, a divergence between the Calvinian and literary quality of the 1541 masterpiece, and the need to provide within the framework of *Calvini opera* all the texts which had appeared definitively under the title of *Institution*, an operation which made it necessary to have recourse to the 1560 text. It is into this breach that Gustave Lanson stepped in 1894, thirty years after the Strasbourgian publication, when in his turn he canonized, but for other reasons, the 1541 version.[32] He showed in fact, with more probing philological arguments than those of the Strasbourg publishers, that the 1560 final version was authentic as well. The paradoxical point of this demonstration rests on the fact that the same scholar however emphasized the unique historical-literary value of the 1541 version, as a first work which systematically deals with moral, philosophical and theological questions in the French language which could from that time onwards seriously compete against Latin in these fields. Also, in 1541 Calvin had had to create a clear, precise and efficient language for a whole work. Inversely, the 1560 final French version, written in a French that was certainly already more flowing than that of 1541, could no longer claim, at the date of 1560, to be in an innovative role.[33] On the foundation of criteria relating from that time for considering the general development of the history of French literature as national literature, the 1541 version was then greeted by Lanson as a masterpiece, and the first monument, at that time, of prose for French ideas.

32. Gustave Lanson, "Calvin's Christian Institution: examination of the authenticity of the French translation," *Revue historique* 54 (1894) 60–76.

33. From Lanson, and with slightly different arguments, but converging, Francis Higman and myself reached the same conclusions.

Duly dated, the text in some way had a value due to its "primitive" nature, and awaiting nothing more than to be reedited for itself.

I would like to end on this Strasbourgian history by emphasizing the Franco-German context of this Rhine enterprise of the *Calvini opera* in the very long Strasbourgian roots. The admirable edition of the last French version of the *Institution*, that of 1560, due to Jean-Daniel Benoit, Professor in the Faculty of theology at Strasbourg, appeared from Vrin from 1957 to 1963, in its turn bears witness moreover to this Strasbourgian root of Calvinian studies, for which one can only congratulate oneself that it is continuing today in this hall. Brought in the first place in 1863 by the Strasbourgians, then in 1894 by Lanson, the 1541 *Institution* still had to be published for the modern public. This has been done three times since then. Now these three editions reflect, each of the in its own way, a Franco-German context. Lanson's intervention gave rise to the publication, appearing in 1911, of the 1541 *Institution* by Abel Lefranc,[34] through a series of conferences, in the Ecole Pratique des Hautes Etudes. After being monumentalized,[35] the text of this version of the *Institution* was presented in a quasi-diplomatic edition, including the imperfections and most of the faults of the original printing. A "primitive," almost unknown, text had to be restored. The cultural context was French and national, particularly with the separation of the Churches and the State. That enabled Calvin to be ranked among the representatives of a Reformation "in the French manner," of a Reformation which was essentially "moral" and religious more than theological, as well as a singular mouthpiece of this French evangelism of which Lefranc, with his works on Marguerite of Navarre and Rabelais, was then exactly one of the best specialists. But there was also a Franco-German context, at the time full of conflicts which were characterized by a sort of emulation. In fact, one must not forget that Lefranc had studied in 1886 in Leipzig and in Berlin, at a time when French people were making an effort to catch up on their relationship with the Germanic world in some fields of philology, and where Strasbourg, incorporated into the new *Reich* with Alsace, could no longer play its role as a bridge between the two countries.

---

34. *Institution de la religion chrétienne*, original 1541 text reprinted under the direction of Abel Lefranc by Henri Chatelain and Jacques Pannier, 2 vols. (Paris: Librairie Honore Champion, 1911).

35. See for example this declaration for the introduction: "From four centuries soon, the unanimous voice of posterity gave the French text of the *Institution* as one of the noblest and most perfect masterpieces of our literature" (*op. cit.* vol. 1, 1). At the same time it was a "unique construction of its kind" and "an essential monument and completely separate from our literature" (ibid).

The second modern edition had a confessional original due to the quality of its only author, Jacques Pannier, but it appeared just before the Second World War, in editions of Belles Lettres,[36] among other masterpieces of classical literature, and Pannier had been one of the collaborators of Lefranc's previous enterprise. Pannier who was a historian of Protestantism could partly take into account modern German critical editions of the Latin *institutio*, which appeared from the 1920s in the series of *Opera selecta*,[37] and its edition distinguishes the two underlying layers of Latin from the French 1541 text, that of the first Latin edition of 1536, and that of the second, of 1539. Pannier thus adopted a method of editing the text that Pierre Villey, who had just distinguished in his edition of Montaigne's *Essais* which appeared in 1922–23 in Paris from Alcan, the successive layers of Montaigne's text. It was a question of indicating the stages of the birth of the "monument," for a "monument" itself has a story, and his edition must rebuild the archaeology of the corresponding "archaeological" strata. But Pannier was not a philologist, and the text that he provided is not safe.

Our edition, which appeared in 2008 in the series of "French literary texts" of the Maison Droz in Geneva, is also in its way a Franco-German story, for which Strasbourg was an obligatory stage, and which filled us with gratitude. It made a particular effort to emphasize some sources, especially with Erasmus and Melanchthon, of a Calvin writer who was certainly French, but who was also an international humanist thinker. More philological than that of Pannier, more critical than that of Lefranc (it relies on the later variations), it however renounces distinguishing the strata of the French text, free to point out the rare additions which were proper to the 1541 French version. In our eyes, what in fact counts most, is to emphasize the effect of the text on the French-speaking readership of 1541. In this direction we have particularly reproduced the references appearing in the margin in the original edition. Our edition therefore takes its place in the rebuilding of the "monument, by making an effort to do justice to it at the same time as a French work and as a book which has fed on a supranational culture. It could not have been done without the previous efforts of Strasbourgian scholars, without their patient work of collection, of comparison and annotation of the copies that the geographical, cultural and religious position of the city on the Rhine enabled them to gather. It is particularly

---

36. *Institution de la religion chrétienne* [1541], 4 vols. Les Belles Lettres, [1936–1939] 1961.

37. Vol. 1, *Scripta Calvini ab anno 1533 usque ad annum 1541* (contains the 1536 *institutio*), ed. Barth (Munich: Kaiser, 1926; reprinted 1963); vol. 3, *Institutio Christianae Religionis* 1559; *Libri I et II*, 1928 (3rd ed., corrected 1968), vol. 5, idem, *Liber IV*, only appeared in 1962.

because Calvin's masterpiece was collected, read and annotated there over several centuries in these wonderful old copies that a new modern edition, closer to the current critical, requirements, saw the light of day.

11. Sadolet

Jacques Sadolet (1477 to 1547) the Enemy of the Strasbourg Years

Annie Noblesse-Rocher[1]

DURING HIS TIME IN Strasbourg, John Calvin was surrounded by friendships: the distinguished company of Martin Bucer,[2] the stimulating student conviviality of this circle set in the house of the Picardian, near Saint Thomas church, the friendship of Sebastian Castellion, who was still a communicant, contributed to make these years a happy time, marked by ecclesiastical and academic respect. It is thus that, on 8 September 1538, the first service in the French language was celebrated by John Calvin in the Chapel of the Repentants (currently Saint Mary Magdalene church) and six months later, on 1 February 1539, the Reformer was appointed Professor of Theology in the Haute Ecole. But for Calvin Strasbourg was also a suffering place, attached to the name of the Cardinal of Carpentras, Jacques Sadolet, the enemy of the Strasbourg years. In fact, it was, during this time in Strasbourg, in 1539, the that famous epistolary exchange between the young Reformer and the cardinal took place, by means of two treatise-letters dated respectively 18 March 1539 (Jacques Sadolet to the Genevans) and September 1539 (Jean Calvin to Jacques Sadolet).[3]

---

1. GRENEP. Faculty of Protestant Theology in the University of Strasbourg.

2. Emile Doumergue, *Jean Calvin, les hommes et les choses de son temps*, vol. 2, *Les premiers essays* (Lausanne: G. Bridel, 1902), 376–526; Philippe Denis, *Les Eglises d'étrangers en pays rhenans, 1538-1564*, Paris, Les Belles Lettres, 1984, 67.

3. *Jacobi Sadoleti . . . Epistola ad Senatum populumque genevensem, qua in obedientiam romani pontificis eos reducere conatur*, Lyon, 1539; *Jacobi Sadoleti . . . Opera quae extant omnia*, vol. 2, Liber XVII, Epistola XXV, *Epistola ad Senatum populumque genevensem . . .* (Verona, 1737), 171–86. *Epître de Jacques Sadolet avec la réponse de Jean Calvin (1540)*, in *"La Vraie piété": Divers traités/de Jean Calvin. Confession de foi de Guillaume Farel*, textes présentés par Irena Backus et Claire Chimelli (Geneva: Labor et Fides, 1986), 65–80; Calvin, *Epître de Sadolet avec la Réponse de Calvin*, in *Oeuvres*, edition drawn up by Francis Higman et Bernard Roussel (Paris: Gallimard, 2009), 43–106.

11. SADOLET

Opponents, John Calvin and James Sadolet however mutually gave themselves to serving to perfect the literary reputation of the enemy and the international dimension, beyond the circle of the theological College or the first circles of the Reformation: the works of James Sadolet,[4] the exchange with Calvin remained the most famous; and the Reformer's Reply to the Cardinal launched the former beyond the circle of refugees.

The parts of the file are well known today. From a historical point of view, in fact, it is not presumptuous to state that, from the publication of Vol. V (1538-1539) of the *Correspondance des Réformateurs dans les pays de langue française* by Aime-Louis Herminjard,[5] in 1878, the file is closed. And the 2009 Jubilee makes the opportunity to definitively separate one of the last points of controversy: the existence, in December 1538, of an ecclesiastical meeting in Lyon, the supposed sponsor of the *Lettre aux Genevois*, through the intermediary of Pierre de la Baume, the bishop of Geneva who was expelled after adopting the Reformation.[6]

Due to this, contemporary historiography has become attached to current theologies, especially ecclesiology and the justification of the believer, presented by the two opponents. But these studies, if one excludes the latest by Bernard Roussel,[7] most frequently neglect the epistolary exchange between Gaspard Contarini, Jean Sturm and Jacques Sadolet, at the time when the *Concilium de emendada ecclesia* (9 March 1537), a preparatory document for holding a reforming council. Now, with a good look, this exchange presents analogies with that of Jacques Sadolet and John Calvin, to the point that one may wonder: has not the exchange between Gaspard Contarini, Jean Sturm and Jacques Sadolet acted for prolegomenes for that which concerns us here, the *Epître aux Genevois avec la Réponse de Jean Calvin*? A synchronic reading of these epistolary exchanges of the years 1538-1539 may allow it to be thought; we propose it in the form of a synopsis, that we give as an annex. Was the enemy of the Strasbourg years, Jacques Sadolet, the servile propagator of the traditional doctrine that one was pleased to depict? Nothing is less sure, if one for a moment leaves the *Epître aux*

---

4. As regards the biography and works of James Sadolet, see R. M. Douglas, *Jacopo Sadoleto 1477-1547, Humanist and Reformer* (Cambridge: Harvard University Press, 1959).

5. *Correspondance des Réformateurs dans les pays de langue français*, collected and published with other letters relating to the Reformation and biographical and historical notes by A-L. Herminjard, vol. 5 (1538-15399, Geneva/Basel/Lyon: H. Georg, 1878) (henceforth: Herminjard, vol. 5).

6. Calvin, *Oeuvres* (see n2) 1021 (notice on *l'Epître de Sadolet avec la Réponse de Calvin*).

7. Calvin, *Oeuvres* (see n2), 43-106 (see also the notice, esp. 1025).

Genevois and if one explores the exegetic works of the cardinal, sometimes less orthodox, hardly four years before his famous initiative. Therefore it is a double reading, synchronic and diachronic, that we use in this study, relying on previous research dedicated to James Sadolet, the exegetist of the Epistle to the Romans.

The Preface to the *Concilium de emendanda ecclesia*

Paul III's pontificate was marked by a large-scale reforming plan dealing for the first time the Roman Curia itself and the renewal of its systems. In August 1535, the Bull *Sublimis Deus* was promulgated, creating a commission to reform customs of the Roman clergy. Some months before that, on 21 May 1535, Paul III had published a new list of cardinals, made up of critical and influential intellectuals, in spite of their small number. This group included a key man: Gasparo Contarini. In summer 1536, Bries were sent to Carafa, to Giberti, Bishop of Verona, in Cortese, to Reginald Pole and to his confessor Tommasio Badia, a Dominican and master of the Sacre-Palais, as well as in Fregoso, the Archbishop of Salerno, and to James Sadolet, Bishop of Carpentras. They all had to meet under the presidency of Contarini, decidedly the man in Paul III's confidence. A first meeting took place at the end of November 1536; its aim was to draw up a conciliating text on the institutional reform of the Church. On 9 March 1537, the commission gave in its report, known by the name of the *Concilium de emendanda ecclesia* .[8] The *Concilium* was very quickly widespread internally. The text circulated in its edition of 9 March 1537 abroad; it was translated into German and reached Luther in this form, in February 1538, thanks to his friend Nicolas Haussmann, who held the original Latin edition. In June 1538, this edition reached the Roman authorities who forbade it from being spread.

The *Concilium* was particularly keen to denounce the most unacceptable situations for the Sovereign Pontiff, resumed under the term of "abuse" (see column 1 of the synopsis). The first denunciation was concerned with

---

8. *Concilium delectorum cardinalium et aliorum Praelatorum de emendanda ecclesia, sdnd, Paulo Tertio ipso iubente conscriptua et exhibitum, Anno MDXXXVIII accessit aequitatis disussio super Concilio Delectorum Cardinalium et ad tollendam per Generale Concilium inter germanos in religion Discordiam*, Anvers, from Ioannem Steelsium, Anno a Christo nato MDXXXIX. The old editions of the *Concilium* are mentioned by Walter Friedenburg, "Das Concilium de emendanda ecclesia, Kardinal Sadolet and Johannes Sturm from Strassburg," *Archiv fur Reformationgeschichte* 3 (1935) 1–69 (esp., 2). On the role of Gaspard Contarini, see Elisabeth Gleason, *Contarini: Venice, Rome and Reform* (Berkeley/Los Angeles: University of California Press, 1993).

the ordination of incompetent clerks, with depraved habits and illegitimate birth, but also dispensations for the marriage of a clerk. The issue was important, due to the claim of the *Lutherani* for the marriage of priests.[9] Other abuses cover the unjustified conjugal dispensation of the laity, but also the surrogate Episcopal benefits and the untimely transformation of ecclesiastical benefits.[10] The negligence of the prelates of the Curia, their absenteeism and their "extra" money were virulently denounced[11] as well as the humanist and philosophical training of the Italian clerks with a reference to the development of Paduan Aristotelism, however well known by Jacques Sadolet.[12] The *Concilium*, one of the sources of which is found to be the *De Potestate Pontificis quod divius sit tradita* of Gaspard Contarini,[13] stating the principles of a Pontificate whose authority is extended into the whole of the priestly body, very quickly was spread internationally.

On 3 April 1538, Jean Sturm replied to the authors of the *Concilium*. The crucial question for Sturm was that of the pontifical authority and of the

9. "*Primus abusus est ordination clericorum, et praesertim presbytorum, in qua nulla adhibetur cura, nulle adhibetur diligentia: quod passim quicunque sint, imperitissimi sint, vilissimo genere arti; sint malis moribus ornate; sint adolescents admittantur ad ordines sacros, et maxime ad presbyteratum* [...] *nec permittat Santitas Vestra ut quispiam ordinetur, nisi ab Episcopo suo, uel cum licentia disputatorum eius* [...] *Abusus alius in dispensation cum constituo in sacris ordinibus, ut posit uxorem ducere, hav dispensation non esset et nulli danda, nisi pro* [...]*causa grauissima: praesertim his temporibus, in quibus urgent Lutherani hanc rem maxime*" (*Concilium delectorum cardinalium* ... , see n7, A4v). For the translation of these extracts into French, see Annie Noblesse-Rocher, "We shall unite our Churches, lay aside offences and shall forget quarrels." The correspondence of Johannes Sturm, Jacopo Sadoleto and Johannes Cochlaeus about the affair of the *Concilium delectorum Cardinalium* (1537-1539)," in Matthieu Arnold (ed.), *Johannes Sturm (1507-1589): Rhetor, Padagage und Diplomat* (Tubingen: Mohr Siebeck), 359-60.

10. "*Abusus alius maximi ponderis est collatio beneficiorum Ecclesiasticorum, maxime curatorum et prae omibus episcopatuum, in quibus usus involuit, ut provideatur personis, quibus conferuntur beneficia, non autem gregi Christi et ecclesiae* [...] *Alius item abusus in permutationibus beneficiorum, quae fiunt com pactionibus, que simoniacae omnes sunt, nulloque respect habito nisi lucre*" (*Concilium delectorum cardinalium* ... see n7, A4v and A5r).

11. "*Abusus etiam est, quod tot Reverendiss. Card. Absint ab hac Curia, nec aliqua in parte faciant quidpiam eius officii, quod spectat ad Cardinal* [...] *Alius abusus magnus et minime tolerandus quo universes populous Christianus scandalizatur est ex impedimentis quae inferentur Episcopis in gubernatione suarum ouium*" (*Concilium delectorum cardinalium* ... see n7, A5v).

12. "*Alius abusus magnus et perniciousus est in gymnasiis publicis, prasertim in italia, in quibus multis philosophiae professores impetiatem docent. Imo in templos fiunt disputations impissimas*" (*Concilium delectorum cardinalium* ... see n7, A5v).

13. Gasparo Contarini, *Gegenreformatische Schriften (1530–1542)*, ed. Friedrich Hunermann (Munster: Aschendorff, 1923), 36–38.

new definition of it sovereignty. It was not, against all waiting, Gaspard Contarini, but Jacques Sadolet who was charged with the reply to Jean Sturm, on 15 July 1538. Doubtless the Curia held him as the most suitable for being understood by the Strasbourgians, after the steps that he had taken in 1537 with Philip Melanchthon; he had tried in vain to circumvent the Reformer, since his initiative remained without a reply.[14]

For the cardinal, a field of understanding was possible for Sturm and himself were humanists; they had been trained in the liberal arts and were proving to be heirs of the beautiful Ciceronian Latin. But Sadolet was rising up against the theological and ecclesiastical innovation which had grown up in the evangelical ranks. His strategy consisted in separating the Strasbourgians from Martin Luther, whom he described as an ignoramus. This strategy expanded during the summer of 1538, when Sadolet wrote a letter-treatise addressed to the German Princes and people, a missive whose address translated the virulence of the subject and the concern for rallying: "The very serious exhortation to the German Princes and people is that they should break with pestilential heresy and pointlessness and should come back into the bosom of the Catholic and apostolic Church of Christ. We had to wish strongly, dear German Princes and people, that all our people should confess the Christian faith and come back to it, the one and only [. . .]. If someone achieves not good works but bad deeds, will he then be justified by faith alone? That could not happen, for faith can only lead to good works.[15]

Despite an attack of malaria which will leave him in precarious health (the lungs and heart were affected) up to the end of his life, in spite of financial worries which he did not cease to complain about during the affair of the *Concilium de emendanda ecclesia*, the Cardinal of Carpentras continued to publicize his worry about the advance of evangelical ideas. In October 1538, he wrote to George, Duke of Saxony, to warn him against the destabilizing doctrine of the Lutherans. But the pressure came above all from the inside and from the Sovereign Pontiff; a letter from Paul III, in November 1538, asked him to act efficiently against the venomous disturbance of the Lutheran heresy in the town of Avignon and the Comtat Venaissin, within his jurisdiction. In fact, from 1535 Sadolet had adopted this offensive attitude.

---

14. *"La vraie piété"* (see n2), 57.

15. "*Ad Principes populosque Germaniae exhortation gravissima, ut desertis et objectis pestilentissimarum haeresium insaniis, in gremium Catholicae et Apostolicae Christi Ecclesiae redeant. Maxime erat optandum, Principes populique Germaniae, ut nos cuncti, qui Christianam fidem profitemur* [. . .] *Si quis opera non bona, sed mala efficiat, is ne fide sola erit justificatus? Non accident hoc, fidem enim ipsam bona opera consequuntur* [. . .]," *Jacopi Sadoleti Opera quae extant omnia . . .*, vol. 2 (Verona, 1738), 331 and 356.

The "Dedication" to Francis I in his *Commentaire sur l'épître aux romains* left little doubt on the intentions of the Cardinal of Carpentras:

> To the very Christian King of France, while in these times every day the religion [. . .] is stirred up by rebellions and by the crowd of those who are fighting violently. I have often thought of writing this work, although I was distracted from it for a great many reasons, I have finished it, in spite of the disturbance of these terrible times [. . .].[16]

The year 1538 ended without an echo from Strasbourg, for Jean Sturm waited for a whole year to reply to James Sadolet; he did so on 18 July 1539.

The Exchange between Jacques Sadolet and John Calvin (1558–1539)

Meanwhile, Jacques Sadolet had written a short letter to the Genevans dated 18 March 1539. Jean Durand, a citizen of Carpentras, presented it to the Little Council of Geneva.

The accompanying letter began thus:

> Famous gentlemen, as my brothers, as it come to my memory that the Fathers who flourished in the primitive church undertook their studies for the greater glory of God and the salvation of Christians, I have written to you, Famous [Gentlemen], this letter as a witness either of my piety to God, or, even better, towards you on his behalf. In this letter, I am acting and thinking that we should together come back to this universal and identical consensus, that of the universal Church. For that reason, I have sent my dear and trustworthy Jean Durand, citizen of Carpentras.[17]

In case the members of the council did not happily and whole-heartedly welcome his composition, Jacques Sadolet warns his emissary to report to him without further delay. This letter of introduction, less well-known than the Epistle, possibly delivers its aim: to make the Genevans come back to the *consensus cordium*, to the doctrinal unity of the faith of the traditional church.

---

16. *Jacobi Sadoleti Cardinalis et Episcopi Carpentoractensis viri disertissimi Opera quae extant omnia. In Pauli eppistolam ad Romanos commentariorum libri tres*, vol. 4 (Verona, 1738), 3.

17. *Jacobi Sadoleti Cardinalis et Episcopi Carpentoractensis viri disertissimi Opera quae extant omnia. In Pauli eppistolam ad Romanos commentariorum libri tres*, vol. 4 (Verona, 1738), 3.

Some months later, in September 1539, Jacques Sadolet was having his composition published in Lyon, by Simon Grypee, reedited from a stylistic, theological and rhetorical point of view. Thus, from 1539 two versions of Sadolet's Epistle: that of Geneva, received by the Little Council, and the re-edited version, published in Lyon.

Two French translations of Calvin's reply are soon going to be placed with the printer. On 4 October 1539, Antoine Pignet (an old student friend of Calvin in Orleans, a pastor not far from Ville-le-Grand near Geneva) wrote to Calvin that he should plan to translate the Epistle. But two weeks later, on 21 October 1539, Guillaume Farel announced to Calvin from Neuchatel that he had appointed a Genevan to translate his reply to Sadolet; he asks Calvin to check this translation. It was in Geneva, on 30 January 1540, with Michel du Bois, that the French translation of the *Epitre de Sadolet avec la reponse de Jean Calvin* was published.

A Synoptic Reading of the Exchanges of the Years 1538–1539

All the protagonists of the affair are humanists; also it is hardly surprising that all their exchanges (see the synopsis below) are inaugurated by an *exordium* including a *captatio benevolentiae*.[18]

The pastors of Geneva showed themselves to be incapable of replying themselves to this letter, and they then applied to the council of Bern.[19] On 23 May 1539, the council of Bern acknowledged receipt of the application and demanded its preachers to reply; in vain, as it is known: on 24 July 1539, Pierre Kuntz suggested that Calvin should be asked to reply to the cardinal. In mid-August 1539, the day after this visit, John Calvin write to Farel:

> "I see that the Genevans are unhappy in a great many ways. Sultzer brought me the letter from Sadolet. I do not wish to reply but our people [Bucer? Jean Sturm?] have asked me to do so.[20]

Calvin announced a *hexameron* of work;[21] he writes very quickly: 65 pages in-octavo, i.e., 11,500 words, in only six days[22] In September 1539, in Strasbourg, Wendelin Rihel published Calvin's Latin reply with Sadolet's Epistle,

---

18. Herminjard, t.5 (see n4), 322.

19. Herminjard, t.5 (see n4), 372.

20. Herminjard, t.5 (see n4) 290.

21. Jean-Francois Gilmont, *Calvin et le livre imprimé*, Geneva, Droz, 1997, 172/

22. H. Lausberg, *Handbuch der literarischen Rhetorik. Eine Grundlegung der literaurwissenschaft*, vol. 1 (Munich, 1960).

according to a Bernian copy of the manuscript version received by the council of Geneva. Meanwhile, the original version, retouched by Sadolet, had appeared in Lyon.

Two French translations of Calvin's reply are soon going to be sent to the publisher. On 4 October 1539, Antoine Pignet (an old student friend of Calvin in Orleans, a pastor not far from Ville-le-Grand near Geneva) wrote to Calvin that he should plan to translate the Epistle. But two weeks later, on 21 October 1549, Guillaume Farel announced to Calvin from Neuchatel that he had given his reply to Sadolet to a Genevan to translate; he asked Calvin to check this translation. It was in Geneva, on 30 January 1540, with Michel du Bois, that the French translation of the *épitre de Sadolet avec la réponse de Jean Calvin* appeared.

A Synoptic Reading of the Exchanges of the Years 1538–1539

All the protagonists in the affair are humanists; also it is hardly surprising that all the exchanges (see the synopsis below) should be begun by an *exordium* including a *captatio benevolentiae*.[23] Although his letter was very short, James Sadolet, on 15 July 1538, introduced it by acknowledging that, like him, Jean Sturm was trained in classical humanism, in the liberal arts and in the Ciceronian language, and that through that they should be able to understand each other.[24] In his *Epistle to the Genevans*, Sadolet confesses also that he likes Geneva for its nobility, its humanism and its citizens.[25] On 18 July 1539, Jean Sturm, breaking with the courtesy of circumstances, goes into a virulent tone; while he had acknowledged in the authors of the *Concilium* a group of scholars,[26] he apostrophizes Jacques Sadolet without taking the trouble of rhetorical flattery: what he holds on to saying to him by this reply was not a pleasant thing to write and will not be so, to read, for the cardinal, as he admits to have been wounded by his commentary on the Romans (it is known that he castigated the libertinism of the followers

---

23. "*Legi librum [tuum] qui quidem liber multa habere mihi visus est quae sint homine libero et erudite digna, nam et elegantia verborum imprimis refertus est et copia sententiarum, apparet in eo persudiosum M. Ciceronis scriptorium esse*" (Walter Friedensburg, "*Das Concilium de emendanda ecclesia . . .*," 51 (n7)).

24. "*La Vraie piété,*" 66, see n2.

25. Walter Friedensburg, "*Das Concilium de emendanda ecclesia,*" 28 (see n7).

26. Walter Friedensburg, "*Das concilium de emendanda ecclesia . . .* (see n) 554. See Bernard Roussel L. "Martin Bucer et Jacques Sadolet: la Concorde possible (autumn 1535)? *Bulletin de la Societe d'Histoire du Protestantisme Francais* 122 (1976) 511.

of justice by faith alone).²⁷ On the other hand, when Calvin replies to the cardinal, in September 1539, the tone of courtesy is upheld: Calvin holds Sadolet in "great admiration and respect," but immediately denounces the fact that the cardinal has used the art of oratory in order to try to maneuver the Genevans.²⁸

For Jacques Sadolet, the subject of discord resides in this *novitas* which came up in the evangelical ranks, in the person of Luther alone. If Martin Bucer, Philippe Melanchthon and himself, Jacques Sadolet, can understand each other on the question of the *duplex justificatio*, on the other hand it must keep away the Wittenberger, the untreatable.²⁹ The tone is no less virulent when Sadolet addresses the Genevans: his *narration* is an act of accusation against the suspects who sow discord and dissent in Geneva.³⁰ But just like 15 July 1538, when he wrote to Sturm, he exhorts to bringing feelings into unity, to consent of the hearts. In reply to Sadolet, Sturm writes a *narratio*, which is also virulent: these accusations of novitas are a crime of false witness, for his own people have never expressed any will for secession, for rejection; the current schism is not due to the evangelists, but to the Roman offenses in respect of them. The *confutation* comes from refuting the accusation of *novitas*. It is with a tone in all similar points that Calvin refutes Sadolet's arguments: the latter is a suspect and a dissembler. The evangelists have more points in common with the old Church than the followers of the Roman Church. This accusation of *novitas* sent by Sadolet to Sturm finds an unexpected echo in Calvin's response to the cardinal.

The *confirmation* develops the argument of the question which was posed in the *narratio*; the letters from Sturm to Sadolet (column 5) and from Calvin to Sadolet show great similarities of content. In the first case, (Sturm to Sadolet), the *confirmation* consists in presenting Jean Sturm's battle; it is a question of the doctrine to be defended, that of a confession of faith, which is expressed in Christ the sole Christian (*solus Christus*), the eradication of ecclesiastical crimes, the rejection of false doctors and sanctification. In similar words, Calvin holds the same discourse with Sadolet, in September 1535; a sure doctrine, a discipline and fair administration of the sacraments, here is the definition of the true Church, a sign of Calvin's battle. This sure doctrine, the confession of evangelical faith, consists in justification by faith,

---

27. "*La vraie piété*," 81n2.

28. "*Is error a vobus tandem indicates et occasum ecclesiae praedicitis verum etiam in pontificbus eam causam constitesse fatemini, qui adulatorum voculas secuti dominus se legume esse putarunt.*" (Walter Friedensburg, "Das *Concilium de emendanda eccleisa* . . . ," 29n7.)

29. Walter Friedensburg, "Das *Concilium de emendanda ecclesia* . . . , 51–52n7.

30. "*La Vraie Piété*," 66n2.

and faith alone, Christ being the only justice. One will note here that the great proximity of formulation on this essential point of the doctrine of faith between these two letters of Sturm and Calvin, addressed in July and September 1539 to the same enemy. The *confirmation* of Sadolet's epistle to the Genevans states not only the need for *caritas* for salvation but its primordial function; Jacques Sadolet departs here from the received doctrine, as explained by Jean Eck in his *Enchiridion*, as we shall see below. John Calvin takes up this theme by denouncing Sadolet's mistaken idea of *caritas*; his denunciation includes penitence and satisfactions, the Eucharistic doctrine, heard confession, the intercession of saints and purgatory, abuses of the ministry, sacrifices, worship of idols, indulgences, which were considered globally as human traditions without a biblical basis.

What is also troubling is the proximity of Sturm's letter to the authors of the *Concilium* and the *Réponse de Calvin* about respectively the authority and tyranny of the pope. Sturm precisely defines the pontifical office: the Sovereign Pontiff must be an administrator of spiritual goods and not a sovereign; only the Roman episcopate is held to define his office. For Calvin, the ecclesiastical power should be restricted to the spiritual life, never to give way to domination nor even appear to do so. A synoptic reading of the exchanges of columns 5 and 6 (from Sturm to Sadolet, 18 July 1539, and Calvin to Sadolet, in September 1539) makes the concomitance of form and themes appear: the *Exordium*, in both cases, denounces Sadolet's attacks, in his commentary on the Epistle to the Romans, or in his attempt to maneuver the Genevans; in both cases, the *narrations* and *confutationes* respond to the accusation of *novitas*, by reaffirming the adherence of the evangelicals to the old Church and in bringing responsibility for schism onto the Roman church; the *confirmationes*, in both cases equally, offer a new definition of faith and the true doctrine, centered on the *solus Christus* and the *justificatio sola fide*, which could only come into contradiction with the ideas of the Cardinal of Carpentras.

In fact, when he wrote to the Genevans, the Cardinal of Carpentras had from 1535 finished his *In Pauli epistolam ad Romanos commentariorum libri tres*: now, about this commentary on the Epistle to the Romans, the cardinal was seen to be accused of heterodoxy due to his idea of justification of man: in fact, in a letter of July 1533 to his friend Erasmus, Sadolet had acknowledged that he planned a half-way charter between Augustine and Pelagio, on the question of grace and merits, an *altera via*. And in fact, when he commented on Romains 1:17 ("The righteous man will live by faith"), Sadolet defends the idea of a natural inner capacity for faith and knowledge, prior to the coming of grace; it is a question of the *initium fidei*: "That is the true beginning of faith (*initium fidei*): when we turn around by our own will towards the greatest and sovereign Good, we find in him a power and a strength in which the freedom of our soul is contained. It is not a question of the effect of good works but a tendency which is suitable for man."[31]

The process of redemption is developed on the basis of a natural capacity for good. Certainly, man is perfected and saved by grace: without it, he cannot have access to God. However, something in man begins the process of regeneration; this *initium fidei* comes from the wish to be saved, and man can by inclining his will contribute to this beginning of grace: in man there is an antecedent to grace, a righteous tendency favoring the welcome of considerate grace. In that, Sadolet imprudently went ahead on a Pelagian route, which was already denounced in the *Somme Théologique* (IIa-IIae, Q, VI, a.1) but suggested (as *actum mais initium fidei*) in this Thomasian work of youth that is the *Scriptum*, a commentary of the Sentences of Pierre Lombard.[32]

Jacques Sadolet was therefore, by conviction, far from acquiescing to the traditional position defended by Jean Eck in the *Enchiridion locorum communium adversus Lutteranos* (1525), for which the *salus fide* must intrinsically include the works of love; love made the *fides informis* of heretics (zealous followers of the salut sola fide) a *fides formata*. It is however this idea that the cardinal defended in his *Epitre aux Genevois*.

We wish, by means of this brief enquiry, to throw a modest light on the Strasbourg environment that surrounded Jean Calvin at the time that he wrote the *Reponse a Sadolet*, but also to recall the ambivalence of Jacques Sadolet's theology, of which John Calvin knew, through Martin Bucer, reader of the commentary on the Romans by the cardinal, the theological setbacks. There is still room to make an enquiry into the possible Bucerian sources of this exchange, especially the writings of the years 1533 to 1534, the *Furbereytung zum Concilio* (1533) but also the *Concilium de pace ecclesiae*, in a note of his *Defensio adversus Axiomata catholicum, hoc est criminationem R.P. Roberti Episcopi abrincensis* (1534).[33]

---

31. *Jacobi Sadoleti . . . In Pauli epistolam ad Romanos commentariorum libri tres . . .* (see n15), 215 B.

32. *S. Thomae Aquinatis Scriptum super libros Sententiarum magistri petri Lombardi*, new edition by R. P. Mandonnet, vol. 2 (Paris: Lethielleux, 1929), 703. On the *initium fidei*, see J. Wawrykow, "On the Purpose of 'Merit' in the Theology of Thomas Aquinas," *Mediaeval Philosophy and Theology* 2 (1992) 97–116.

33. BDS, vol. 5, *Strassburg und Munster im Kampf um den rechten Glauben 1532–1534*, (Gutersloh: R. Stupperich, 1978) (*Furbereytung zum Concilio*, 259–359); BOL, vol. 5, *Defensio adversus Axiomata catholicum, hoc est criminationem R. P. Roberti Episcopi Abrincensis (1534)*, ed. William Ian Hazlett (Lyden: Brill, 2000).

12. Christ Our King

Calvin and the Religious Colloquia of 1539–1541

Volkmar Ortmann[1]

Calvin's Time in Strasbourg and His Participation in Religious Colloquia

ONE MUST UPHOLD CALVIN's time in Strasbourg for as the necessary external condition for his participation in religious colloquia.[2] Certainly, the 1536 *institutio* and especially his reply to Cardinal Sadolet have earned him the reputation of someone who, through the content and the civilized style of his writing, defended the cause of evangelical faith.[3] But it was not his work in Strasbourg that opened to him the possibility of taking part in religious colloquia and to increase his reputation as a theologian there. The starting point of that was his participation in the meeting in Frankfurt in 1539.

---

1. Institut fur Evangelische Theologie, Giessen.

2. Calvin arrived in Strasbourg at the end of the summer of 1538. He was placed in charge of the parish of French-speaking refugees. See Hermann J. Selderhuis, *Johannes Calvin. Mensch swischen Zuversicht und Zweifel* (Gutersloh, 2009), 107. Calvin began to preach on 8 September 1538. See his letter to Guillaume Farel, in Herminjard, vol. 5 (Geneva and Paris, 1874; reprint Nieuwkoop, 1966), no. 143, 111, n10. See also Peter Opitz, *Leben und Werk Johannes Calvins* (Gottingen, 2009), 60–60, esp. 67s.

3. See Selderhuis, 123 (see n1): "Calvin's friends and enemies agreed—and they still do—on the fact that with this letter, he had written a literary masterpiece." See Calvin, *Ad Sadoleti Epistolam*, in *Calvin Studienausgabe*, vol. 1.2, *Reformatorische Anfange* (1533 to 1541), Teilband, ed. Eberhard Busch et alii (Neukirchen-Vluyn, 1994) (henceforth: CSA), 346–429 (here, 337).

The Religious Colloquia

The Frankfurt Meeting

To describe it well, it was a question of a meeting of the Schmalkaldic League; but this meeting is very closely linked to the religious colloquia which took place, at Haguenau, in Worms then in Ratisbon. The proposal to lead negotiations with the Protestants for a union in religious questions had been made nominally by the Prince Elector Joachim II of Brandenburg to the Emperor Charles the Fifth and to his brother, King Ferdinand the First. In fact, the emperor made Johann von Weeze, Bishop of Constance and former Archbishop of Lund, his legate for the Frankfurt discussions with the Protestants. The negotiations began at the end of February 1539, and, after lively debates, the Frankfurt truce was ended on 19 April; the most concrete engagement that was taken there was to set, for the 1st August 1539, a religious colloquium which took place in Nuremberg and which the emperor had to announce that it would be held .[4]

Calvin in Frankfurt

With Jean Sturm and other Strasbourgians, Calvin arrived in Frankfurt on 24 or 25 February, at the time when negotiations with von Weeze, the imperial commissioner were beginning. No doubt Calvin stayed in Frankfurt until toward the middle of March.[5] Therefore he was not present on 19 April, when the Frankfurt truce ended.

His correspondence of the time gives us, beyond the impressions that the negotiations have left of him, the motives of his participation in the Frankfurt meeting. He explains having wanted, through this journey, to

---

4. Upon the opening of the colloquium, see Volkmar Ortmann, *Reformation und Einheit der Kirche, Martin Bucers Einigungsbemuhungen bei de Religiongesprachen in Leipzig, Hagenau, Worms und Regensburg 1539 to 1541* (Mayence, 2001), 78–84. On the letters of instruction from the emperor to his legates, see *Akten der deutschen Reichsreligionsgesprache im 16. Jahrhundert*, ed. Klaus Ganzer and Karl-Heinz zur Muhlen, vol. 1, *Das Hagenauer Religionsgesprach*, teilband 2, (Gottingen, 2000) (abridged: ADRG 1, ii), np. 386, 1057–60; on the Frankfurt truce, see ibid., no. 390, 1072–78.

5. See J. Maarten Stolk, *Johannes Calvijn en de godsdienstgesprekken tusssen roomskatholieken en protestanten in Hagenau. Worms en Regensburg 91540 to 1541)* (Kampen 2004), 117s., according to which "[. . .] het niet duidelijk is hoe lang Calvin in Franfurt is geweest" (ibid., 118); Wilhelm H. Neuser, "Calvins Beitrag zu den Religionsgesprachen von Hagenau, Worms und Regensburg (1540 to 1541)," in Studien zur Geschichte der Reformation, *FS Fur Ernst Bizer*, ed. Luise Abramowski and J. F. Gerhard Goeters (Neukirchen-Vluyn, 1969), 219, calculates that Calvin stayed for a week in Frankfurt. See also Herminjard (see n1), no. 772, 247–60 (*CO* 10/2, no. 162, col. 322–29).

12. Christ Our King

bring some influence onto the negotiations between the members of the League of Schmalkalde; the discussions dealt particularly on sending a delegation to Francis I in order to intercede in favor of French Protestants. Calvin adds that he wanted to become acquainted with Philippe Melanchthon.[6]

As regards the support to the French Protestants, the results of Frankfurt were rather vague: in the propaganda letter addressed to the King of France, he did not talk about it directly, and that is correct if one recalls those indirectly.[7] On the other hand, Calvin's meeting with Melanchthon—and in particular their discussion on Holy Communion—was more important.[8]

As his correspondence shows, Calvin had a deep respect for Melanchthon, whom he defended against all the criticisms about his self-styled "oversweet" attitude.[9] Calvin completely sees the need to allow diplomatic skill to reign in religious affairs also, and to obtain something in the essential questions with the help of concessions in questions of lesser importance. From another side, Calvin expresses criticisms against Bucer; his zeal in propagating the Gospel would compel him to make concessions which also have a theological importance.[10]

Calvin also shows himself as a precise and critical observer of religious negotiations. He weighs up these questions as an independent theologian, positioning himself—in any case in his correspondence—with certainty in relation to Melanchthon and Bucer. But overall, he shows himself to be full of praise for the League of Schmalkalde's engagement in favor of the cause of the Gospel.[11]

---

6. See Herminjard (see n1), no. 772, 247 (*CO* 10/2, col. 322, no. 162): "*Verum cum literas a Bucero recepissem, quibus indicabt se nihildum potuisse de fratrum causa agree, cupido mihi statim incessit eo usque concedendi: partim ne fratrum salus negligenter [. . .] tractaretur: partim ut com Philippo de religion atque Ecclesia ratione commentarer.*" See Stolk, 149 n4.

7. See *CR* 3, col. 695–97k no. 1798.

8. See Stolk (n4), 122s. See Herminjard (see n1), no. 774, 28s (*CO* 10/2, col. 331, no. 164): "*Cum Philippo fuit mihi multis de rebus colloquium: de causa concordiae ad eum prius scripseram, ut bonis viris de ipsorum sentential certo possemus testari. Miseram ergo paucos articulos ipse quidem assentitur [. . .]*" Unfortunately, this letter was not preserved, see Herminjard, No. 751, 146, nn24–25.

9. See Herminjard (see n1): No. 772, 256 (*CO* 10/2, no. 162, col. 328): "*Et sane, ut videor mihi eius [Philippi Melanchthonis] animum perspicere, non minus quam Bucero, dum negotium est cum iis qui sibi indulgeri aliquid volunt.*"

10. See Herminjard (see n1), no. 772, 256 (*CO* 10/2, no. 162, co. 328): "*Tanto enim studio propaganda Evangeli flagrat Bucerus, ut que praecipua sunt contentus impetrasse, interdum sit aequo lenior in iis concedendis quae minutula quidem ipse putat, sed habent tamen suum pondus.*"

11. See Herminjard (see n1), no. 783, 289–95.

Besides, thanks to the Frankfurt meeting, the unity among the Protestants appeared clearer to him, and he felt called to take the position of mediator between the Swiss and the League of Schmalkalde. It is thus, for example, that he emphasized, to Farel, that the League wanted to preserve an alliance with the Swiss and against the emperor and the supporters of the traditional faith.[12]

During his stay in Frankfurt, Calvin could also deepen his knowledge of the politico-religious situation in Germany. And, on the express wish of the League of Schmalkalde, Calvin could take part in the development of this situation: in fact, the report of this Diet states particularly, for future religious colloquia, that the town of Basel must "ask those of Strasbourg, as well as Grynaeus and John Calvin."[13]

The Religious Colloquium of Hagenau (1540)

Context and Development of the Colloquium

The date fixed by the truce of Frankfurt passed. It was only in 1540 that Charles the Fifth invited people to a colloquium in Spire, which was moved to Haguenau due to the plague.

But several factors worked against this meeting. Thus, in the bosom of the supporters of the traditional faith, people were reticent even overtly against having a discussion with the Protestants. Moreover, the Frankfurt truce had certainly shaped the form that the dialogue should take (as at the time of the Empire Diets, the negotiations had to take place in a great committee and in a small committee), but it had not laid down a more precise procedure. The Haguenau colloquium created a block on setting up these rules, but all the same people came to establish the order of the day of a future colloquium which had to be convoked in the autumn of 1540, in Worms.[14]

---

12. See the letter to Farel, Herminjard (see n1), no. 774, 267 (CO 10/2, no. 164, col. 350): "*Volebat [legatus Caesaris] ut se a Sacramentariis nostre subducerent [. . .]. Atque nostril nec Sacramentarios ullos recognoscunt, et conjunctionem sibi esse volunt cum Helveticis Ecclesiis.*" See also Calvin's letter of April 1539, Herminjard, *op. cit.*, no. 784, 293s. (CO 10/2, no. 169, col. 341): "*Foedus Germanicum nihil habet quod debeat pium pectus offendere. Cur enim, quaeso, quas dedit eis Dominus vires non conjungant ad communem Evangelii defensionem? [. . .] Mi Farelle cogita an non faciamus injuriam talibus viris, qui otiose eos criminamur, dum periculo aut terrore quovis dimoveri se a recta linea non sinunt?*"

13. ADRG 1.II (see n3), 1089, 1. 11s.

14. See ADRG 1.11 (see n3), 1975, 1. 2–5: "*Diesselben Stend oder ire Botschafften sollen sich [. . .] eins grossen nd kleinen ausschuss vergleichen und vereynigen [. . .]*"

12. CHRIST OUR KING

Calvin's Participation

In spite of the recommendations of the Frankfurt truce, Calvin was not taking part as an official participant of the colloquium. Doubtless he only stayed a few days in Haguenau, before returning to Strasbourg, doubtless shortly after the official opening of the debates, on 28 June. Also he could hardly take part in the discussions, and particularly in the internal negotiations with the Protestants.[15] Calvin seems to have gained from his presence in Haguenau in order to establish contacts with the main evangelical theologians. Naturally, he took the general climate of the negotiations into account, just as disparities in the bosom of the Catholic States in relation to the reforming doctrine and the religious colloquium. But altogether, as the information that he gave in his letters shows, he had to be content with secondhand news on the proceedings of the religious colloquium of Haguenau.[16]

His assessment of events corresponds completely with that of other Protestant participants, and it gives proof of a moderate optimism.[17] Above all, he finds confirmation of what he had been able to discover in Frankfurt: "Everybody knows that those who came on our behalf are very united together."[18]

The Religious Colloquium of Worms (1540-1541)

At Worms, Calvin counted in the number of official delegates, and the experiences that he had had clearly informed him on what he should expect from this meeting: the enemies of the evangelicals tried everything to work for their loss. Even if one did not know how that would turn out, one thing was certain; they would try it.[19]

See the report of this colloquium, *ADRG* 1 (see n30, teilband 1, no. 37, 146-55). On the proceedings of this colloquium, see Ortmann (see n3), 113-26.

15. See Stolk (see n4), 169. With the exception of the mention pointed out above, the publishing index of the deeds of the Haguenau colloquium does not mention Calvin. (See *ADRG* 1.II—see n3, 1303.)

16. See Stolk (see n4), 173 and n117.

17. See Herminjard, vol. 6 (1539-1540) (Geneva, Basel and Lyon, 1883; reprint Nieuwkoop, 1966), no. 874, 259 (*CO* 11, NO. 228, COL. 65s.): "The intention of our enemies was to increase their league and diminish ours; but we hope that God will turn around this chance. Whatever happens, our people are seeking to multiply the reign of Christ as much as they possibly can, and they have not deliberated" (To Guillaume de Tailly, 28 July 1540).

18. Herminjard (see n160) 260 (*CO* 11, no. 228, col. 66).

19. See Herminjard (see n16) no. 898, (*CO* 11, NO. 243, col. 92s): "*Quid moliantur*

Again, the beginning of the colloquium was difficult. The emperor had called the colloquium for 28 October, but his commissioner, Nicolas Perrenot de Granvelle, only reached Worms on 22 November, so that the official opening of the colloquium only took place on 25 November.

Immediately, questions of procedure again established the order of the day: in the report of Hagenau, there was agreement to negotiate with twice times eleven delegations of two to three people each. Now, they were quarrelling to find out whether each voice would count or whether one party and the other had each to come to a common position.

These formal questions hid a great problem of content; the supporters of the traditional faith were disunited, and the Palatinate, the Principality of Brandenburg and the Duchy of Juliers were inclined to agree with the Protestants.

According to what had been decided among the Protestants, Calvin had to be considered as a theologian from the delegation of Brunswick-Luneburg.[20]

Although the Diet had been called to Ratisbon for 6 January 1541, to general surprise again, on 14 January, a discussion took place between Melanchthon and Eck about original sin, which ended with the formulation of a common article. After this, Granvelle ended the Worms negotiations and adjourned the discussions in the Diet of Ratisbon.

In the correspondence from Worms, Calvin emphasizes this delaying tactic of the Catholic States, that he is against the attitude of the Protestants, who were disposed to promote dialogue while making concessions. But above all, he complains, in his writings to Farel, about the inactivity in which he is restrained.[21]

Nevertheless, one does not feel any resignation in him, it is quite the opposite: for him, the hesitations of the supporters of the traditional faith and

---

adversarii nostril palam est, nempe, ut omnes Imperii ordines in nostrum pernicem arment. Quibus autem artibus nos adoririr instituerint, incertum est. Quidauid tamen habent callidatia in hac postrema action explicabunt" (On the proceedings of this colloquium, see Ortmann, n3, 149–63).

20. On this matter the *Akten der deutschen Reichsreligionsgesprache im 15. Jahrhundert*, vol. 2, *Das Wormser Religiongesprach* (1540/41), teilband 1, ed. Klaus Ganzer and Karl-Heinz Zur Muhlen (Gottingen, 2002), no. 19, l. 22. On the States which should take part in this colloquium, see the report of Haguenau, ADRG 1 (see n3), teilband 1, no. 37, 154, l. 20–26.

21. See Herminjard (see n16) no. 928, 405 (CO 11, no. 268, col. 135): "*Quod rarius tibi scribe inde fit quod nimis sumus ociosi* [. . .]*Nam si vel in speciem aliqua action hic institueretur, mihi scribendi argumentum subministraret. Nunc quid aluid literis complectar, quam quod* [. . .] *mecum piget ac pudet: nos scilicet alterum jam mensem frustra expectando hic desidere.*"

12. CHRIST OUR KING

the disunion in the heart of their camp, and the thoughtful and united attitude of the Protestants, on the other hand, were a sign that Calvin supported the latter. Calvin resumed this conviction in an exercise that was at the same time spiritual and stylistic: a song of praise to Christ, which lends assistance to the evangelicals and offers firmness to them, while their enemies, who can certainly count on violence and power, do nothing but hide their lack of inner assurance: "Is the victory of Christ, our King, not admirable?"[22]

At the time of this religious colloquium, Calvin was working toward his aim, which was to find for the German Protestants their support for their French co-religionists.[23] Martin Bucer also defended, for reasons of political tactics, sending a delegation to the King of France, in order to intercede in favor of the persecuted evangelicals. But the Princes belonging to the League of Schmalkalde did not favorably welcome this idea; thus, Philip of Hesse—no doubt also on account of his bigamy, which placed him at the emperor's mercy—rather placed his confidence in Charles the Fifth.[24]

On the other hand, things presented themselves otherwise for Calvin as a theologian: as his correspondence shows, he does not stop being torn between the wish to leave the colloquium and his wish for those who, especially those like Melanchthon, pressed him to stay.[25] Since their meeting in Frankfurt, relations between Melanchthon and Calvin had deepened. Melanchthon's respect for Calvin, which the latter does not cease to describe, and the fact that he was called a theologian[26] were connected, no doubt, with his participation in the dialogues which in Worms, were held first of all between Protestant theologians.

---

22. Jean Calvin, *Epinicion*, in; CSA 1.2 (see n2), 504–17. Here, 150, 1, 11s.23.25–27; 512, l. 17–2: "*Vox gladius Christo est, et lancea spiritus aris:/ Hostem igitur subita sternere voce potest./*[. . .] *Saepius et variis alternant motibus* [. . .]/ *Compositae interea nobis fiducia mentis./ Et placid constat pectore forma quies./Quis Christus hic neget ad perdendos funditus hostes/Horribles veluti grex oviu ante lupos./ An non mirifica est regis Victoria Christi?/ Nostra quod intrepid corda vigour fovet.*" (On the interpretation of this poem within the framework of religious colloquia, see Erik Alexander De Boer, *Loflied en hekeldicht, De geschiedenis vol Calvin's enige gedicht. Het epinicion Christo cantatum van 1 January 1541* [Haarlem, 1986], 50–57.)

23. Herminjard (see n16) no. 929, 417 (CO 11, no. 267, col. 134): "*Causam fratrum qui crudeliter ab impiis vexantur, qua decet fide ac diligentia suscipimus, Nihil aliud possumus in praesentia polliceri, nisi quod operam dabimus ut sentiatis nostrum stadium ipsorum saluti non defuisse.*"

24. See Oortmann (see n3), 163s.

25. See Herminjard, vol. 7 (1541 to 1542) (Geneva, Basel and Lyons, 1886; reprint Nieuwkoop, 1966), no. 938, 11 (CO 11, NO. 274, Col. 147): "*Ubi ventum est ad Philippum: 'Aliis permitio, inquit: ad temps Calvinum discedere non patiar.*"

26. Doubtless it was Kilian Goldstein who described Calvin in this way. (See Neuser, 234 n4; Stolk, 197n4.

Discussions among Protestants

Before opening the colloquium, the theologians of the Protestant States met from 9 to 18 November, in the place where the delegation from Electoral Saxony was staying, in order to deal with controversial points and to prepare the negotiations to come.

It was within the framework of these preliminary discussions between the Protestants that the *Confessio Augustiana variata* was drawn up; it was sent to the States which defended the traditional faith at the beginning of December 1540, and it caused their opposition, because "in a great many places, and in almost half of them, it was increased, and in some places it was altered on essential points [. . .] Thus, therefore, the confession which would be sent would be something other than that mentioned in the Huguenots' report."[27]

The Protestants' internal discussions began by article IV of the *CA*, the doctrine of justification, in order to pass directly to the points dealt with in Article XX under the title "Abuses: faith and works, mass, monastic vows and celibacy." Finally, the discussions dealt with the pope's primacy. This choice was not the fruit of chance, for in the past, these points always proved to be the main subjects of conflict during religious negotiations. In Worms, the preliminary discussions between Protestants had to act to make them agree with one another, and to prepare their line of argument. In association with these discussions, all the participants had to subscribe to the *Confessio Augustana (variata)*.

At the time of these discussions, Calvin was one of the spokesmen of a delegation. Certainly, he only rarely spoke, but his six interventions constitute, beside those of Melanchthon, the longest contributions. Moreover, they were important resolutions, which, obviously confirmed Melanchthon's positive judgment.

It is thus that Calvin three times expressed himself on justification. He thought it was necessary to clarify what was understood by "faith." In the same way, he thought that the word "justification" needed to be explained. Faith (which justifies), according to Calvin, is the confidence that holds Christ's divine promise, and one must distinguish this from "historical" faith.[28] One must understand "justification" not at all in the meaning of a

---

27. "[. . .] *an viel ortenund nabend uff den halben theil gemert Unnd auch an etlichen rotten in den wesenlichen Puncten geendert.* [. . .] *Und were also ein andere confession, dan der Hagenauisch abschiedt vermocht, ubergeben.*" (See *ADRG* 2.1, see n19. No. 37, 80, l. 8–11.)

28. See the report by Wolfgang Musculus, *ADRG* 2.1 (see n19), no. 183, 475, 1 68: "[. . .] *Defiendam ante omnia esse fidem* [. . .] *quod de fiducia inelligenda sit dictio fidei*

12. Christ Our King

right thing that is "done" by an impious person, but in the meaning that the impious one is declared "right" by Christ's justice.[29]

In the same way, Calvin writes about the praiseworthy nature of works: for him, works take up justification; however, they are subordinate to faith and God accepts them on account of his mercy. Human justice, which is imperfect, could not please God if it is not made perfect by Christ's justice. That is why one should base oneself on the promise which is offered not to those who do good works, but to those who believe. And Calvin exhorts his listeners to call for the Apostle Paul (e.g., Rom 10:5ss.)[30] In works, he thus granted a place inside the process of justification, without putting justification *sola fide* in question. Unity among the Protestants, which Calvin emphasizes also in other circumstances, is shown on this point: in fact, it is astonishing to find how much Calvin argues with the help of formulations of the *CA variata*.

It is also in the meaning of the *CA variata* that Calvin states his positions on the mass: he states that, before everything, it is important to show how far the "enemies" are from the Fathers. In order to correct their mistakes, he refers to Paul and to his mention of the first institution of Holy Communion, which the Protestants have brought into force again.[31] But one difference between Calvin and Bucer comes to light on the matter of the mass, as indicated by the report written by Martin Frecht, delegate from the town of Ulm: "*Sic Bucerus et Calvinus de application disserebant.*"[32] It seems that Bucer thought that one could speak about an "*Applicatio missae*" in

---

[. . .] *et non de historica illa* [. . .]"

29. See *ADRG* 2.1 (see n28), 474, l. 8-10: [. . .] *Justificandi verbum explicandum esse, quo sensu accipi debeat, nempe non de eo, quo significant iustum redddere ex impio, sed iustum reputare eum qui In se nondum sit iustus idque propter alienam iustitiam Christi* [. . .]"

30. See *ADRG* 2.1 (n28), 475, l. 70-0, 14-15, "*Calvinus admonebat considerandum:* [. . .] *An inchoate et imperfect iustita Deo placer posit in se, censebatque non posse, nisi acccedat perfectae Christi iustitiae participation, quae est per fidem* [. . .] *subordinandam enim esse operum iustitiam iustitae fidei* [. . .]" See also *ADRG* II.1 (n26), no. 184, 477, l. 21-23: "*Adeoque nobis non esse respiciendum ad promissiones, quae operantibus, sed quae credentibus paternam pollicentur benevolentiam.*"

31. See *ADRG* 2.1 (see n28), no. 185, 480, l. 25-28: *Ostendum est, quanta intervallo distent adversarii a patribus.* [. . .] *Revocavit eos* [i.e. Corinthios] *ad primam illius institutionem* [. . .]" (See 1 Co 11, 222ss.) See *Melanchthon Werke in auswahl*, ed. Robert Stupperich, vol. 6, *Bekenntnisse nd Lehrschriften* (Gutersloh, 1955), 43, l. 1-18; 44, l. 28-30 (CR 26, col. 380): "*Ex his omnibus satis liquet Missam apud nos convenire cum institutione Christi et ritu primae Ecclesiae.*" On the influence that Calvin has perhaps exerted on the *CA*var, see Neuser (see n4), 220-23.

32. Martin Frecht's report on the negotiations between the Protestants, *ADRG* 2.1 (see n19), no. 224, 568, l. 33.

connection with faith, while Calvin rejected it while thinking that it did not agree with Scripture.[33]

About vows, Calvin stated that nobody could make a vow of something beyond their capabilities, as it was above all obedience which pleased God; that is why, he continued, virginity could not be the subject of a vow, as it is a gift from God. Between these two statements, Calvin lists three reasons for making a vow: gratitude, penitence and education.[34]

Calvin's judgment on the question of the primacy of the pope was characteristic. He is one of the rare Protestant theologians to have expressed himself on this matter, and, after that of Osiander, it is his contribution which is the longest. Here he goes back to the order that Christ wishes for the Church: "*Christus ecclesiam suam ita ordinavit, ut crescat in se.*" For Calvin, the different ministries come from this order: apostles, prophets, doctors, and Calvin even adds an "*etc.*" Peter is depicted himself, says Calvin, with others as a "*sympresbyterum*," and Paul has even claimed more authority than Peter.[35] Altogether, Calvin emphasizes the collegial structure of the Church which is established in the Bible.

The last two stands taken by Calvin have not had any impact on the debates and texts relating to the controversial theological points, but doubtless they had repercussions on Calvin's theology itself.[36]

Ratisbon

During Calvin's time in Worms, news came to him from Geneva, asking him to come back. Calvin would have liked very much to follow up this

---

33. See ADRG 2.1 (see n32) 568, l. 31–33: "[. . .] *Applicatio verbum Dei non habet; ergo reiicienda. Applicatio verbo fit, quod verbum fides arripit. Ut reconciliation verbo credito fir: ita vera in Eucharistia verbo Dei per fidem apprehenso fit.*" See also, about the discussion on mass in Ratisbon, *infra*, n42.

34. See the report by Musculus, ADRG 2.1 (see n190, no. 187, 485, l. 28, p. 486, l. 5: "*Tres causae sunt, quae probari possunt in votis. 1. Ut aliquid Deo gratitudinem testemus.* [. . .] *2. Si volumes Castigare* [. . .] *.3. Est quaedam paedagogia* [. . .]." Later, Calvin deepened this plan again, see *Institution* IV, xiii, 4–5, and Neuser (see n40) 231s.

35. See ADRG 2.1 (see n34), no. 188, 488, l. 14–15, 19–21: "*Christus Ecclesiam suam ita ordinavit, ut crescat in se. Ad hoc instituit Apostolos, prophetas, doctores etc., ubi nulla fit primates mentio.* [. . .] *Nihil huius authoritatis sibi ipsi vendicat. Si intuaeamur epistolas ipsius primates mentio.* [1 P 5, 1], *vocat se sympresbyterum cum aliis. Paulus videtur sibi multo plus authoritatis in Ecclesia Christi usurpasse quam Petrus.*"

36. On this matter see Neuser (see n4), 230–34; Pierre Fraenkel, "Some observations on the 'thou art Peter' in Calvin, at the Colloquium of Worms in 1540 and in the 1543 Institution," *BHR* 27 (1965) 608–28, esp. 607–13 and 620–23; Stolk (see n4), 289–96.

12. CHRIST OUR KING

invitation, but "in spite of my strong resistance," he wrote to Farel, "I am delayed in Ratisbon." Calvin was afraid that the journey could have a bad effect on his health, and he did not want to stay too long in Ratisbon. Also, he felt badly suited for this type of negotiations, doubtless because he thought he could not, in theological questions appear as flexible as Melanchthon, in theological questions, and even less than Bucer.[37] On another side, this judgment seems too modest, considering the acknowledgment that he had found with other theologians in Worms.

On 10 March, Calvin arrived in Ratisbon with the Strasbourgian delegation,[38] and his correspondence testifies his realistic views on the politico-religious situation that he found there: The emperor is inclined to peace: Certainly, the papal legates are trying to work against the religious colloquium, but on behalf of the supporters of the traditional faith, the union is upheld in the religious question. Calvin expresses himself in a less euphoric way than Bucer, but all the same with moderate optimism, while handing the whole project over to God—all the more since he seems to see an assurance in the Protestants that alarms him, even in spite of the "Dysgamie" of Philip of Hesse.[39]

In the first place, Calvin's fear in respect of his long stay in Ratisbon was well founded: sending participants to the diet, which Charles the fifth had explicitly devoted to clarification of the religious question, dragged on; it was only on 5 April that the emperor could officially open the diet.[40] The idea that Charles the Fifth wanted peace was also pertinent: in his opening speech, the emperor clearly emphasized how, in the light of the Turkish threat, it was important, for the Empire and for himself, to settle religious conflicts. The importance that Charles the Fifth gave to this settlement is also shown by the fact that, throughout the religious negotiations, all other affairs of the Diet were suspended.

---

37. See Herminjard (see n24), no. 943, 26 (*CO* 11, no. 277, col. 1560: "*invitissimus enim ratisponam trahor: tum quia ipsam profectionem mihi molestissimam prospicio fore: tum quod* [. . .] *solent saepenumero Comitia ad decimum mensem producer: tum quod minime idonesu mihi ad tales actions videor* [. . .]."

38. See Stolk (see n4) 238s.

39. See Herminjard (see n24), no. 957, 62 (*CO* 11, no. 290, col. 1781): "*Sic, tametsi exigua, nonnulla tamen Wscausam, in qua et ipsius Gloria et Ecclesiae salud continetur, sua moderation gubernet* [. . .] *Unum me terret, quod tantum inter nos video seuritatis* [. . .] *quale est . . . . vel potius . . .* [. . .] *Quidaud accident, numquam se ipsum Dominus abengabit.*"

40. In respect of the following, see Ortmann (see n3), 233–41. On the emperor's opening speech, see *ADRG*, vol. 3, *Das Regensburger Religionsgesprach* (1541), Tielband 1, ed. Klaus Ganzer and Karl-Heinz Zurmuhlen Muhlen (Gottingen, 2007) (*ADRG* 3.1), no. 21, 30–37.

However, the dialogue that began at Worms was not continued. Charles the Fifth soon named three negotiators for each team; Jean Eck, Jean Gropper and Jules Pflug on the catholic side, and Philippe Melanchthon, Martin Bucer and Jean Pistorius on the Protestant side. Under pressure from the Protestants, again, beside Granvelle and in order to preside over the discussions, the Palatine prince Frederick was named, who was well disposed toward the Protestants.

The religious colloquium of Ratisbon began on 27 April 1541. Granvelle gave the participants a surprise in presenting to them the "Book of Worms (*Wormser Buch*)," the fruit of secret negotiations between the Strasbourgian Martin Bucer and Wolfgang Capiton on the one hand, and the counselor of the Principality of Cologne Jean Gropper and the imperial Secretary Gerard Veltwyck on the other hand. In spite of reserves on one hand and the other, quickly and without much difficulty the first four articles of the work were dealt with. But the dialogue threatened to fail on article 5, dealing with the doctrine of justification. On 2 May, after long debates, all the same a common article was presented.

But the joy caused by this agreement was short lived: from article 6, one ran into, after the question of infallibility of the councils, an insurmountable conflict. However, again it was possible to prevent the dialogue from failing to the extent that each party wrote an article on the subject. But the quarrel on the article relating to Holy Communion (art. 14) brought about the final failure of the colloquium: the supporters of the traditional faith were not ready to renounce the idea of "transubstantiation." For this article as for the eight following articles of the "Book of Worms," each time the Protestants wrote an opposing article, and, on 31 May, these documents were sent to the emperor, with the "Book of Ratisbon," Some States attempted a mediation, by offering to renegotiate the disputed articles: on his own side, the emperor made an effort for one and the other side to admit at least the articles on which they had understood each other, and that on one side and the other the articles should be "tolerated." But these efforts failed in the face of the resistance of the papal legates, the electoral principality of Mayence and that of Treves, states which were supporters of the traditional faith and members of the council of elector princes, as well as most of the Curia of princes. Also, at the end of June 1541, Charles the Fifth was constrained in stating that the religious negotiations had failed, and to bring them back to holding a universal council or a national council.

Calvin did not take part in the circle of participants in the discussions, but he naturally followed the negotiations, and was included in the theologians' consultations. He gives his impressions of the Ratisbon colloquium to Farel, and wrote to him about the compromise on justification: "You will be amazed, I think, that [our] enemies have conceded so many thinks, when you read this note.[. . .] In fact, our people have mainly held on to the true doctrine, so that there is nothing [in the agreement] which is not also found in our writing. I know that you will wish for a clearer explanation, and on this point, I agree with you. But truly, if you consider which men we have had to deal with, you will acknowledge that we have reached a great many things.[41]

This letter of 11 May makes one feel, as Calvin did, something of the euphoria coming out of the agreement on the doctrine of justification. Calvin however remains modest, acknowledging how the formula remains limited in relation to the Protestant position: but he is realistic enough to emphasize also that, considering the circumstances, they have reached the maximum of what was possible. Several lines later, however, when Calvin reports the discussions among the Protestants about the article on Holy Communion, it is another tone that is to be understood from him: he emphasizes that the Protestant theologians agree to reject transubstantiation, preservation of the consecrated Hosts and their veneration, then he continues: "I have had to set out in Latin what I thought. Although I had not understood any of the others, I condemned, freely and without any fear of offending [anyone], the local presence [of Christ in the Host]. Believe me, in such negotiations, one must have strong minds, which strengthen others.[42]

While, for the rest, Calvin tries to show humility, this passage echoes the great awareness that he has to uphold and strengthen the participants in the religious colloquium, in difficult negotiations, in defending the evangelical position. In writing these lines, it seems that Calvin is thinking particularly about Melanchthon, who—in contrast to Martin Bucer—was ready to emphasize more the doctrinal differences with the supporters of the traditional faith.[43] One can understand how what Calvin meant when, before the Diet of Ratisbon, he described himself as "not very competent"

---

41. *Johannes Calvins Lebenswerk in seinen Briefen*. Eine Auswahl von Briefen Calvins in deutscher Übersetzung vol Rudolf Schwarz, vol. 1, *Die Briefe bis zum Jahr 1547* (Neukirchen-Vluyn, 219–61), no. 68, 191. Herminjard (see n24), no. 975, 111 (*CO* 11, no. 308, col. 215): "*Miraberis, scio, adversaries tantum concessisse, cm legeris exemplar* [. . .] *Retinuerunt enim nostrie dictinae verae summam: ut nihil illic comprehensum sit, quod non exstet in scriptis nostris. Scio, desiderabis clariorem explicationem, et in ea re me tibi assentientem habebis; verum, si reputes quibuscum hominibus negotium nobis sit, agnosces multum esse effectum.*"

42. Schwarz (see n41), no. 68, 191. Herminjard (see n24), no. 975, 112 (*CO* 11, no. 308, col. 215s.) "*Fuit una omnium vox* [. . .]. *Me quoque exponere Lagine aportuit quid sentirem. Tametsi neminem ex aliis intellexeram, libere tamen sind timore offensionis, illam locale praesentiam damnavi* [. . .] *Crede mihi, in ejusmodi actionibus opus est fortibus animis, qui alios conferment.*"

43. Herminjard (see n24) no. 975, 112 (*CO* 11, no. 308, col. 215): "*Philippus* [. . .] *magis endere, ut rebus exulceratis omnem pacificationis spem praecideret.*"

for religious colloquia: it mattered to him to defend clearly the evangelical doctrine on the outside. And he wrote, that he did not like the process of Melanchthon and Bucer, which consisted in urging, with the help of "ambiguous and crafty formulas" [. . .] about transubstantiation (*formulas de transsubstantiatione* [. . .] *ambiguas et fucosas*)," the supporters of traditional faith toward a compromise, even if, in doing so, they are following a plan.[44]

In Ratisbon, Calvin himself continued to work toward his aim, to win the support of the evangelicals with the French Protestants. He vehemently pleaded for a delegation to be sent to Francis the First; but the German Protestants would only agree to send the King of France a letter, the content of which was extremely displeasing to Calvin. Thus, in contrast with the muddled composition written by Melanchthon, the official letter does not mention the need for a French (national) council, where doctrinal questions would be clarified.[45]

At the end of the religious negotiations, in the month of June, Calvin also did everything to return to Strasbourg. Bucer would have liked to keep him in Ratisbon, just like Melanchthon.[46]

---

44. Herminjard (see n24), no. 976, 115 (*CO* 11, no. 309, col. 217): *Philippus et Bucerus formulas de transsubstantione compsuerunt ambiguas et fucosas, ut tentarent an adversariis possent satisfacere nihil dando. Colsilium hoc mihi non placet, taetsi rtionem habent quam sequuntur.*" Melanchthon and Bucer were aiming to have the adverse part in the word "transubstantiation" renounced, by expressing its meaning in other words. (See Ortmann, see n3, 248–53.)

45. See Herminjard (see n24) no. 1008, 179 (*CO* 11, no. 334, col. 252): "*Quantum ad fraters attinet qui ob Evangelium laborant, non feci quod volui. Causa enim gravem aliquam legationem flagitabat* [. . .] *Literas ergo impetravi.*" On this matter see the letter from Calvin to Farel of 9 June 1541, Herminjard (see n24), no. 997, 151 (*CO* 11, no. 321, col. 236): "*Ac ne in scribendo quidem secuti sunt quod consultueramus ego et Philippus.*" On the letter to Francis I, see ibid., No. 983, 126–32 (*CR* 4, no. 2243, col. 325–28), and Stolk (see n4), 288–94.

46. See Herminjard (see n24) no. 1008, 175 (*CO* 11, no. 334, col. 21): "*Cum nullum aplius in convent usum mei fore suspicarer, magna improbitate missionem extorsi magis quam impetravi: nam et Bucerus me aegerrime a se abire patiebatur, et Philippus,* [. . .] *ragabat ut manerem.*"

13. Consensus and Disagreement

Consensus and Disagreement in the *Little Treatize on Holy Communion* (1541)

Marianne Carbonnier-Burkard[1]

IN HIS BIOGRAPHY OF Calvin, Theodore de Beze made a special place for the *Little Treatize on Holy Communion*, describing it as "a golden little book for the use of its French people."[2] In any case, it is the first work that Calvin wrote under his own name, directly in French. The title given by the Genevan publisher, in 1541, announced a whole program: *Petit traicte de la sainte cène de nostre Seigneur Jesus Christ. Auquel est démonstrée la vraye institution, profit et utilité d'icelle. Ensemble, la cause pourquoy plusieurs des modernes semblent en avoir ècrit diversement*.[3] Calvin developed this pastoral plan, based on disagreements to be resolved, in the introduction of the text. He plans to clarify the subject of Holy Communion, "which for a long time was entangled with several great mistakes," and "developed again from various contentious opinions and disputes," a transparent reference to the Eucharistic conflict between Luther and Zwingli, which was obvious from 1525. "Very useful work" he explained, for these confusions leave a great many faithful people "in doubt and perplexity," while "understanding" of the sacrament is "so badly needed for our salvation." The author therefore proposes to "deal briefly and nevertheless clearly to deduce the majority of what one should know about it." Where, particularly, will a description of a "disagreement" or basic discord be, with the "papists" in distinguishing

---

1. Faculty of Protestant Theology in Paris.

2. "[. . .] *Aureolum denique libellum edidit de Coena Domini in Gallorum suorum usum* [. . .]" (Bèze, "*Vita Calvini,*" in *CO* XXI, 130). Cf. Bèze and Colladon, "Vie de Calvin," 1565 (*CO* XXI, 62).

3. The edition used is that of Peter Barth, *Joannis Calvini opera selecta*, vol. 1 (Munich, 1926) (hereafter, *OS* I), 503–30. See also, in slightly modernized French, the edition of Francis Higman and Bernard Roussel, *Oeuvres* (Paris: Gallimard [Pleiade], 2009) (hereafter, *Oeuvres*, Pleiade), 883–962.

obvious differences, even a "bone of contention" between the Reformers, waiting for a consensus.[4]

Contemporary with the second edition of the *Institution de la religion chrétienne*, translated into French in 1541, the *Petit traité* is like that, typical of a stage of Eucharistic theology of the Reformer, and it is known that it was revised several times from 1536 to 1562.[5] The peculiar interest of the *Petit traité* lies in the specificity of the aim which is announced: a pastoral view, associated with caring to gather the "faithful people" (let us say, the Protestants), by stating, in the language of the people, a common doctrine, a consensus, on holy communion. In this way, is the *Petit traité* evidence of a "Strasbourg moment" of Calvin's, toward 1540? For the fact that with such a subject he wrote in French gives rise to another question: to which French "faithful people," who are still without "reformed" churches, was this common doctrine on Holy Communion addressed? It is from these questions that the analysis of the consensus built by the *Petit traité* will be carried out, in the same way, beforehand, as the enquiry on the context of writing the work.

The Elements of the Context

The context of the *Petit traité* on Holy Communion will be examined from its author's point of view, Calvin in the Strasbourg environment, between 1539 and 1541[6] and from the point of view of the public as seen by the author.

---

4. *OS* 1, 503–4.

5. On the development of Calvin's Eucharistic theology, see Wim Janse, "Calvin's Eucharistic Theology: Three Dogma-Historical Observations," in Herman Selderhuis (ed.), *Calvinus sacrarum literarum interpres* (Gottingen: Vandenhoeck & Ruprecht, 2008), 37–69; Richard Muller, "De Zurich ou Basle a Strasbourg? Etude sur les prémices de la pensée eucharistique de Calvin," in Bernard Cottret and Olivier Millet (ed.), *Jean Calvin et la France* (Paris: SHPF, 2009), 41–53.

6. Both the preface to the Latin edition of the *Petit Traité* by Des Gallars, in 1545, and the *Vie* of Calvin by Bèze and Colladon, in 1565, give a date of writing around 1540. However, a letter from Calvin to Veit Dietrich, 17 March 1546 (*CO* XII, 315–17: no. 781), seems to indicate the date of 1537, corresponding to Calvin's first stay in Geneva (cf. Peter Barth, in *OS* I, 500). It could be that elements of the *Petit traité* were written from 1537, but the final version could only be situated toward 1540 (cf. the word "old" or the length of the polemic between Luther and the Swiss people—"the space of fifteen years").

13. CONSENSUS AND DISAGREEMENT

Calvin in the Strasbourg Environment

It is well known that in Strasbourg, Calvin came close not only to Bucer, but at the same time close to the Lutheran world of the Empire, meeting in the Schmalkaldic League in order to confront the various strategies of Catholic re-conquest of the emperor and of Pope Paul III.[7] This political and military league of German Protestants, united—not without some screeching— by the Confession of Augsburg of 1530, was reinforced from 1536, by the Concord of Wittenberg, which was obtained thanks to the efforts of Bucer and Melanchthon in order to overcome the disagreement about Holy Communion—among others in order to take the Concord of Wittenberg into consideration—this became the common platform for Protestants.

In February 1539, Calvin took part in a meeting of the Smalkaldic League in Frankfurt, and in 1540 and 1541, he took part in colloquia that the emperor organized, successively in Haguenau, Worms and Ratisbon, in order to achieve unity of the Church in the Empire. As a skeptic toward the colloquia, Calvin gained from these occasions for meeting with the politicians and theologians of the Empire: he wins the friendship and respect of Melanchthon, out which he also received kind greetings from Luther, in autumn 1539, and from there, it seems his more clearly favorable appreciation of the German Reformer. As a delegate from the town of Strasbourg at the Worms colloquium, alongside Bucer and Jean Sturm, Calvin with the others signed, in November 1540, the text of the Confession of Augsburg in its new version. In Ratisbon, in May 1541, Calvin intervenes at the meeting of the Protestant delegates on the question of the eucharist, in full agreement against the doctrine of transubstantiation and the adoration of the holy sacrament.[8]

To tell the truth, neither the closeness to Bucer and Melanchthon, nor the interest in the Concord of Wittenberg date for Calvin from his time in Strasbourg. Calvin was very early, at least from 1533, a reader of Bucer and Melanchthon.[9] The doctrine of Holy Communion that he describes in the 1536 *Institutio* brings to various places the mark of the two Reformers, as well as that of Luther and Zwingli.[10] From 1536, just after the end of the

---

7. Cornelis Augustin, "Calvin in Strasbourg," in W. H. Neuser (ed.), *Calvinus sacrae scipturae professor* (Grand Rapids: 1990), 170–72.

8. *Cf. Actes de . . . Ratisbonne, sur les différens qui sont aujourdhuy en la religion*, octobre 1541 (CO V, 568).

9. On the early closeness of Calvin to Bucer and Capiton—therefore at Strasbourg, more than in Wittenberg or in Zurich—and on Melanchthon's influence in the first *Institutio*, see Richard Muller, *art. cit.* (see n4), 41–53.

10. See Richard Muller, *art. Cit.* (see n4). In the *Instruction et confession de foy dont*

Lausanne dispute, Calvin runs to Bern where Bucer and Capiton are negotiating with the Swiss their adhesion to the Concord of Wittenberg which was newly signed with Luther. A year later (September 1537), he was once again in Bern on the same subject, and there he plays the role of mediator between Bucer and the suspicious Swiss, by presenting a confession of faith "*de eucharistia*" which is suitable for signing by Bucer and Capiton.[11] In January 1538, he writes to Bucer without ceremony: doubting the burial of the Concord due to the hostile "obstinacy" of Luther in relation to the Swiss, and even of his own extremists on the presence of Christ's body in the bread, he asks him to intervene on his behalf; and moreover he reproaches him for "handling error at the expense of truth" (a reference to Bucer's participation in the politics of religious agreement as carried out by Guillaume du Bellay on behalf of Francis I).[12] Swept under the carpet at the Zurich synod, from 28 April to 4 May 1538, always with Bucer, the Concord was left in the balance.

In the new edition of Calvin's *Institutio*, which appeared in Strasbourg in August 1539, but already prepared in the summer of 1538 in Basel, a certain reorientation on the matter of Holy Communion can be read: Calvin took away some Zwinglian points and added more Bucerian formulations.[13] However, this is not what struck Veit Dietrich, a pastor in Nuremberg and a friend of Melanchthon: in the autumn of 1539, having read this new edition which had just come out in Strasbourg, he reveals to Bucer his anxieties about Calvin's eucharistic doctrine. Without any delay, Bucer reassures Dietrich. Calvin, he writes to him, approves of the Concord of Wittenberg: he "acknowledges in Holy Communion the true display [the true offer] of Christ's body." He continues his "excesses of language" in the *Institutio* are explained for tactical reasons: Calvin addresses himself to "brothers," especially the French people, who, having been blinded (by Swiss theologians), "go into a rage against us," rejecting all idea of the presence of the body of Christ in the sacrament, for the reason that it would take away "the truth of human nature and to the heavenly glory of Christ." It is toward the aim of pacifying the "dissensions caused by this question," that he uses their lan-

---

on use en l'Eglise de Genève, published in 1537, Calvin resumes the pages of the *Institutio* in a brief article "On the Lord's supper," in *Opera omnia, Scripta ecclesiastica*, vol. 2 (Geneva: Droz, 2002), 98–101.

11. *OS* 1, 433–36.

12. Calvin to Bucer, 12 January 1538 (no 56 A), in *Ioannis Calvini Opera omnia, Epistolae*, vol. 1, 1530 to September 1538 (Geneva: Droz, 2005), 291–304.

13. In 1539, Calvin especially makes use of the word "substance" and explains the formula "substance of the body" which he refused in 1536 (see Richard Muller, *art. cit.*, see n4, 50–51).

guage.¹⁴ Calvin having been warned by Bucer also confirms straight away to Farel and Melanchthon his full membership of the "Agreement between the German churches." He adds that his criticism of the local presence of Christ's body in the bread obviously applies only to "papists," and that he seeks to win over to the Concord of Wittenberg all those who reject it, without properly understanding it.¹⁵

Therefore, to understand Bucer, these Zwinglians who were excited by the dissensions on Holy Communion that Calvin seeks to direct by his 1539 *Institutio* were French people. May one not think that these are the same people to whom Calvin, in the next year, aims his *Petit traité* in French?

Which French Public?

The socio-cultural profile of the French readers of the *Petit traité*, which was already indicated by the choice of the popular language, is confirmed by Nicolas Des Gallars, the translator of the Latin work, in 1545: in his preface, the latter emphasizes that Calvin had in sight a public which was made up of "*illiterati*" and "*imperiti ac rudes*,"¹⁶ otherwise people who do not read Latin, especially referring to women. Calvin says as much in a letter to Veit Dietrich of 17 March 1546, in order to justify the original French language of the *Petit traité*: ordinary people of the country population, not learned.¹⁷ But still?

---

14. Letter from Bucer to Veit Deitrich, 19 November 1539, in Jean Rott, "Documents strasbourgeois concernant Calvin," *Revue d'histoire et de philosophie religieuses* 44 (1964) 325–31.

15. Letter from Calvin to Farel, 20 November 1539 (*CO* Xb, 132, no. 197). Declaration "Antidote" from Calvin, attached to the letter to Farel:

> I saw that a great many people want to be excluded from the *concord* which was drawn up with great benefit between the German churches, because they think that there cannot be substantial eating of Christ's body in Holy Communion, as Luther set it out, with a local and limited presence. I thought it would be useful to refute this vain and frivolous suspicion, and to enlighten them so that they may cease hurting a distinguished apostle of Christ, by whose ministry, in our time, the light of the Gospel has shone; and so that, freed from a misplaced fear, they may heartily accept the *concord*. (*CO* IX, 844.)

Calvin takes up passages from this declaration in *IRC*, 1543, ch. XVIII (cf. *IRC*, IV, 11 and 32).

16. *Libellus de coena Domini*. [Geneva], [Jean Girard]. 1545. Preface of Des Gallars, dated 1 January 1545. f. A2r.

17. "[. . .] *Ratio docendi simplex et popularis indoctique hominibus accommodate . . .*" (*CO* XII, 316, NO. 781.)

The first readers that Calvin must have had in mind as he wrote his *Petit traité* must have been the faithful people who were in his care in Strasbourg from September 1539, these French and Walloon refugees and who had fled France or the Netherlands for "religious reasons," from 1535. To tell the truth, their identity is rather hazy. But in taking care to have his text printed in Geneva (which is better, due to there being no chance for a French text in Strasbourg), Calvin obviously was aiming at a greater public than the hundred and fifty to two hundred homes within his Church. Calvin certainly also had in sight not only his former faithful people in Geneva, especially his refugee compatriots, with whom he had stayed in contact, but also "his French people" (as Bèze states) who have stayed in France.

Through the refugees in Strasbourg and Geneva, through Bucer and Sturm, Calvin was well informed of the situation of the "evangelicals" of the kingdom, who were always tracked, and from 1539 were up against difficulties from a general hardening of the persecution.[18] In this moving environment, all the more as it was necessarily secret, the reformers of French-speaking Switzerland—especially Guillaume Farel—spread into France, from the beginning of the 1530s, new "evangelical" texts inspired by Zwingli, putting forward the "true religion," based on the "pure word of God" in Scripture, and the "inventions" of men. Their argument against the mass broke out publicly in October 1534 with the "affair of the posters": displayed in Paris and in several other towns, a text by Antoine Marcourt, a pastor in Neuchatel, was taken away violently at mass, accused of "idolatry" contrary to the Gospel; this scandal unleashed the wrath of Parliament, launched again in January 1535 by the distribution in Paris of a virulent small book, ascribed to the same Marcourt.[19] For the following years, there were few traces of "evangelicals," small clusters of "brothers," around whom sympathizers gravitated, in contact with one another—dangerous, therefore precarious—with Strasbourg and Geneva, through the intermediary of the network of refugees. It seems that among the "brothers," the ideas of the "Swiss people" ("sacramentary") had progressed[20]—not without dark patches, for from 1536, Farel "calvinized" himself, taking distances with Zwingli

---

18. Cf. the fragment of a letter, no doubt by Calvin, "*Pro afflictis in Gallia*," which can be dated from October 1539 (*CO* Xb, 428, no. 196).

19. *Petit traité très utile, et salutaire de la saincte eucharistie de Nostre Seigneur,* (Neuchâtel: Pierre de Vingles, Nov. 1534; the printer Jean Michel, successor of Pierre de Vingles, will issue a 2nd edition in Geneva in 1542). Perhaps Calvin was inspired by Marcourt's title for his own *petit traité*.... But the subtitle of Calvin's work is original.

20. Some references in Marcel Royannez, "the eucharist among the evangelicals and the first French reformed people (1522 to 1546)," *Bulletin de la Société de l'histoire du protestantisme français* [hereafter *BSHPF*] 125 (1979) 569.

13. CONSENSUS AND DISAGREEMENT

and Oecolampade on Holy Communion.[21] One may note here and there anti-authority gestures on the adoration of the holy sacrament, but no practice of the "reformed" Holy Communion on the Swiss and Strasbourgian model.[22] In the summer of 1538, letters sent by refugees in Geneva to their evangelical friends in Bordeaud give witness of the circulation in France of news coming from Switzerland, such as a premature role of mentor in exile played by Farel and by Calvin.[23]

In one of the letters, Andre Zebedee, ex-regent of the College of Guyenne, a humanist scholar, shows his interest in "a council of German preachers on the Eucharist," where Luther and Melanchthon delegated Bucer (the Zurich synod, 28 April to 4 May 1538).[24] Some months later, in May 1539, Calvin has words with this same Zebedee, who had become pastor of the town of Orbe, a dyed-in-the-wool Zwinglian, opposed to a rallying at the Concord of Wittenberg, and for this reason very critical toward Bucer.[25] With Bullinger and the Zurichians, on the other hand, Calvin stayed on good terms, while reproaching them when necessary for their lack of concern for agreement between Protestant Churches.[26] In another way, it happened that he took on such a pastor for his excessive formulations, which were inappropriate, in the sense of the bodily presence of Christ in Holy Communion.[27] It is a question of Calvin working with theologians of the Swiss space. It is also that of using Swiss and German theologians, "scholars," of which Des Gallars will translate the *Petit traité* into Latin, in 1545.[28] The context of new dissensions between Lutherans and "Swiss people" in 1544[29] is certainly not a stranger to this edition. All the same, it could hap-

21. See Elfriede Jacobs, "Die Abendmahlslehre William Farels," in Pierre Barthel, Remy Scheurer, Richard Stauffer (eds.), *Actes du colloque Guillaume Farel, Neuchatel, 29 Septembre to 1 Octobre 1980* (Geneva-Lausanne-Neuchatel, 1983), vol. 1, 168.

22. It is enough to give credit to Florimond de Raemond, pointing out a Holy Communion service presided over by Calvin near Poitiers in 1534 (*Histoire de la naissance, progrès et décadence de l'hérésie de ce siècle*, 1605, l. VII, 3, 181 b.)

23. See Gabrielle Berthoud, "Lettres de réformés saisies a Lyon en août 1538," in *Etudes et documents inédits sur la Réformation en Suisse romande*. Extract from the *Revue de théologie et de philosophie*, 1933 and 1936 (Lausanne, 1936), 87–111.

24. Letter from A. Zebedee (to Briand, from Geneva, 31 July 1538) in Gabrielle Berthould, *art. cit.* (see n22) 104.

25. 19 May 1539 (*CO* Xb, 344–46, no. 171).

26. See letter from Calvin to Bullinger of 12 March 1540 (*CO* XI, 27–29, no. 213).

27. See Calvin's letter to Richard du Bois, s.d. [1539], (*CO* Xb, 444–46, no. 203).

28. *Libellus de coena Domini, op. cit.* (see R. Peter and J.-F. Gilmont, *op. cit.*, 1, No. 45/7).

29. On the dissensions of 1544, see Heinz Scheibole, "Melanchthon und Bucer," in Christian Krieger, Marc Lienhard (eds.), *Martin Bucer and Sixteenth Century Europe*.

pen that the little book would be very well received by Veit Dietrich, while in 1539 the latter had criticized Calvin's ideas on Holy Communion in the *Institutio*.[30]

Only, in his *Petit traité* in French, Calvin is not addressing his "scholars," but faithful people who are worried about "various opinions and contentious disputes": a great many unstable consciences could not properly decide what they must hold on to, but they are staying doubtful and perplexed, while waiting for [. . .] some agreement "between the servants of God."[31] Therefore who in France was aspiring for a theologians' agreement? In 1530, in order to convince Luther of the interest in a concord on Holy Communion, Bucer had invoked a completely special need for advancing the Gospel in France, discord being a source of trouble among faithful people.[32] Around 1540, in the full politics of the colloquia in the Empire, it is a greater agreement that the Strasbourgians dream of, until a *via media*, aiming at the reform of the Church. At the same time, Marguerite of Navarre and the Du Bellay brothers also dream of a religious agreement to be negotiated between the German Protestant princes and Francis I, in order to relax the repression against the French evangelicals.[33] Calvin himself is only

---

Deeds of the Strasbourg colloquium, 28–31 August 1991 (Leiden, New York, Koln: Brill, 1993), 1:388–90.

30. See his letter to Calvin of 3 February 1546:

> I have read your little essay on Holy Communion and I am in approval that you can use the bread and the wine signs, of such a type that the things which are signified are truly present: if those who do not admit that signs can enable us to be led by you to this idea! (*CO* XII. 266, no. 759)

and Calvin's charming reply, 17 March 1546 (*CO*, XII, 316, no. 781). Several translations into a foreign language have been made from this Latin version. An anonymous English translation thus appeared four times, seemingly at London, in 1548, with a translator's preface and as an appendix, a translation of the Danish liturgy for Holy Communion, baptism and marriage, presented by Miles Coverdale. An Italian language adaptation of the *Petit Traité*, without Calvin's name, appeared in Venice in 1549, due to Tomaso de Moncioli who sweetens the anti-Catholic polemic of the fourth part and adds a final part describing the words of Holy Communion. Unrelated to this text, an Italian translation of Calvin's work was made in Geneva in 1561, by Francois Duron (R. Peter and J.-F. Gilmont, *op. cit.*, t.1, 278–87, vol. 2, 789).

31. *Petit traité* . . . *OS* 1, 503. Cf. 527.

32. See Ian Hazlett, "a pilot study of Martin Bucer's relations with France," in Christian Krieger, Marc Lienhard (eds.), *Martin Bucer* . . . (see n28), 2:516. Already in 1525, Farel and Toussain describe the negative effect of the quarrel between Luther and Zwingli (see Marcel Royannez, *art.cit.*, n19, 555–56).

33. See Maurice Causse, "The *Familière exposition* of Gerard Roussel and the Nicodemian adventure in Guyenne," *BSHPF* 131 (1985) 5–33; idem., "Les dissimulations de Marguerite de Navarre et l'aventure Nicodèmite," *BSHPF* 132 (1986) 347–89; Jonathan

13. Consensus and Disagreement

worried about the intra-Protestant agreement, a Concord of Wittenberg which would be acceptable for the Swiss people.[34] Beyond the *petit traité*, he does not mention the worried French people who would be waiting for such an agreement.

To tell the truth, there was no lack of anxious consciences, "in doubt and perplexity" in the kingdom at that time. Under the pressure of repression, the "evangelicals" had more or less to conform, without subscribing to traditional Catholic practices. On her own land, Marguerite of Navarre protected them, while protecting her chaplain, Gerard Roussel, for whom she had obtained the Bishopric of Oloron from the pope; this old man from the Meaux group, a crypto-evangelical, toward 1534 was the author of an essay on the eucharist with a "sacramentary" inspiration, and initiation of a reformed mass in his diocese.[35] It is toward Roussel, "an old friend who is now a prelate," that Calvin was directing in the second of his two 1537 pamphlets—*Epistolae duae*, castigating the compromises and calling for the break with the Roman Church.[36] In the first pamphlet (substantially republished, in French, in 1543).[37] Calvin was exhorting the faithful people who lived in France not to take part in "the abomination of the mass" completely opposite to Holy Communion, and, considering the extreme risks, he advised them to go into exile outside France. In Strasbourg, in September 1540, Calvin uses the same language of a break and in doing so he contradicts Bucer's writing at the same date: in fact, the latter, who was engaged in the imperial politics of agreement (including a French diplomatic constituency) advocates a conciliatory attitude, at least in a temporary manner.[38]

Reid, *King's Sister-Queen of Dissent* (Leiden: Brill, 2009) 2:497–515.

34. See thus his letter to Zebedeen, 19 May 1539 (*op. cit.*), the "Antidote" of 20 November 1539 (*op. cit.*), his letters to Farel, 27 February 1540 (*CO* XI, 23–24, no. 211) and to Bullinger, 12 March 1540 (*op. cit.*).

35. See Maurice Causse, "La Familière exposition..." (see n132), 30–33; for an analysis of the whole of Roussel's Eucharistic doctrine, see Jonathan Reid, (see n32), 525–50.

36. *Epstolae duae . . . Prior, de fugiendis impiorum illicitis sacris, et puritate christianae religioniis observanda. Altera, de christiani hominis officio in sacerdotiis papalis ecclesiae vel administrandis, vel abiiciendis* (Basel: Oporin, 1537), in Ioannis Calvini Opera omnia, Scripta didactica et polemica, vol. 4 (Geneva: Doz, 2009).

37. *Petit traité montrant que c'est que doit faire un homme fidèle connaissant la vérité de l'évangile, quand il est entre les papists*, [Geneva, jean Girard], Re-ed. 1544, 1545 ... (Calvin, *Oeuvres*, Pleiade, 505–50).

38. See Calvin's Letter dated from "Strasbourg, this 12 September 1540), published after the *Petit traité . . . parmi les papistes*, 1543 (Calvin, *Oeuvres*, Pléiade, 542–50). On Bucer's relations with France, see Ian Hazlett, *art.cit.*, n31, 513–21; and on the *Consilium theologicum* of Bucer (c. end 1540), to which Calvin's letter replies in advance on 12 September 1540, see Francis Higman, "Bucer et les nicodèmites," in Christian Krieger, Marc Lienhard (eds.), *Martin Bucer . . .* (see no. 28), vol. 2, 646–52. On the

Would the "anxious consciences" of the *Petit traité de la sainte cène* not be those of certain "nicodemites" of his friends? Calvin could think of his old co-disciple, who had become a counselor in the Paris parliament, Antoine Fumee: an "evangelical" sympathizer, the latter was at that time in contact with Bucer, among others about a reform of the mass, in the meaning of "spiritual eating" explained to the people, but not in the "profane" meaning of the "sacramentaries."[39] Or of Marguerite of Navarre, with whom Calvin was in correspondence in 1540 to 1541.[40] Or even of Renee de Ferrare, who already in the summer of 1537 he had gratified with a private lesson about the mass.[41] Did the *Petit traité de la sainte cène* act as an additive to the "anti-nicodemist" treatises which were published by Calvin in the same period? In fact, the first four editions of the *Petit traité* are contemporary with these treatizes: from the first one with Michel Du Bois in 1541, to the three others—from 1542, 1544, 1545—with Jean Giraud, who had become the usual printer for the Reformer.[42] Although the hypothesis confronts the presentation that Calvin made of the "contention" among the Reformers as a source of trouble, it must be reexamined from the statement in the *Petit traité*.

In order to address the public of "ordinary people and not scholars," Calvin adapted his writing, as he explains it to Veit Dietrich: expressing himself in French, a less "precise" language than Latin, he tried to be brief, simple and clear, "without obscurity," and as close as possible to his mind ("*fideliter*"). Under this adapted form, Calvin continues, it is about the same

---

contradiction between Bucer's line of thinking and that of Calvin (but was there not between them a sharing of roles?), see Frans Pieter Van Stam, "The Group of Meaux as first target of Farel and Calvin's anti-nicodemism," *Bibliothèque d'humanisme et Renaissance* 68 (2006) 268–75.

39. See the letter edited by Jean Rott, "Miettes historiques strasbourgeoises," in Pierre Barthell, Remy Scheurer, Richard Stauffer (ed.), *Actes du colloquy Guillaume Farel* (see n20), 1:262–67. In this letter dated by J. Rott between summer 1541 (Ratisbon colloquium) and the end of 1544, Fumee appeals to the Strasbourgians to take steps with Francis I to achieve in France a certain freedom of preaching in the evangelical manner. Besides, it is known that Fumee was also in correspondence with Calvin, at least in 1542 to 1543.

40. See Jonathan Reid, *op. cit.* (see n32) 2:556–57.

41. Letter from Calvin to René de Ferrare (Geneva, summer 1537), in Ionnis Calvini, *Epistolae*, 1:225–31.

42. Complete bibliographical description of the editions in Rodolphe Peter and Jean-Francois Gilmont, Biblioteca Calviniana . . . , vol. 1 (Geneva: Droz, 1991), no. 41/4, 42/4, 44/10, 45/8. The work, whose title is sufficient to describe heresy, appears in the first Index of the University of Paris, in 1544 (J.-M. De Buganda, F. Higman, J. K. Farge [eds.], *Index de l'Université de Paris*, Sherbrooke, Centre d'Etudes de la renaissance, 1985, no. 285, and no. 500).

doctrine explained in the *Institutio*, or even, under another form for the people ("*plebs*"), in the *Catechisme de l'Eglise de Genève*.[43]

"A brief summary," "little treatize," the work holds the word, gathered into seventy pages in a small 8.0 format. The material is sensitively more developed in the 1541 *Institution*, where chapter XII, on Holy Communion, takes up forty-five pages in 4.0 format. Even as translated into French, the *Institution* is aimed at a more learned public, being at the same time a manual of "piety" and in a controlled guide for reading Scripture: and from which, for example, the use of scriptural and patristic quotations with marginal references, explanations and discussions on the vocabulary of scholastic theologians. There is no indication in the *Petit traité*, in a rather surprising way, of a formal scriptural reference.

At the end of the introduction to the *Petit traité*, Calvin announces his proposal, in five parts:

1. "For what purpose did the Lord institute this holy sacrament"
2. What result and usefulness do we obtain from it";
3. What is its legitimate use";
4. "What disagreement must the [faithful people] have with the papists";
5. "What was the source of the [apparent] tension between the Reformers" (*OS* 1, 504).

In the 1541 *Institution*, the proposal is not so clear, but one can make out a first part, where one finds again the first and second parts of the *Petit traité* on the meaning of Holy Communion, the opposite of the mass, then a part on the practice of Holy Communion, corresponding to the third and fourth part of the *Petit traité*.[44] In both works, one notes the practical orientation of the teaching on Holy Communion, as of all of Calvin's theology, showing him as a disciple of Melanchthon. However, the fifth part of the original *Petit traité*, and well marked in the title, magnetizes the previous parts, which become elements for a device for the consensus.

---

43. Letter of 17 March 1546 (*CO* XII, 316, no. 781).

44. On Holy Communion, the *Catéchisme de l'Eglise de Genève*, written in autumn 1541, presents a similar proposal through the series of questions (340–73): the meaning (finality of the institution and usefulness for believers, integrating the final agreement of the *Petit traité* then usage (without explicit Anti-Roman debate).

The Device for the Consensus

This device is in three times or three deeds: first of all it lays the foundations (finality and usefulness of Holy Communion, use of Holy Communion), then to determine the "disagreement" with the "papists" and finally to end the "tensions" among the Reformers.

The Foundations

The foundations take up the first three parts of the *Petit traité*: the institution of Holy Communion or its purpose (1st part), its usefulness 2nd part), its usage (3rd part).

The Institution of Holy Communion

Differently from the chapter "On Holy Communion" in the *Institution*, the *Petit traité* does not begin by a definition of Holy Communion, but it explains the institution of Holy Communion as a sign of God's goodwill. On the one hand, the Father gives his children spiritual food or "pasture" or "meat" [i.e., supplies, food]. This food of life is Jesus Christ, who is "given" to us, "distributed by the word" (*OS* I, 504). The Word is "like an instrument through which Jesus Christ with all his graces, [is] given to us. On the one hand, this goodwill is manifested through God's 'condescension' toward men, who are so 'rough and coarse':[45] due to 'our infirmity,' the 'Father of mercy' [. . .] has wished to adjust with his word a visible sign through which he represented the substance of his promises, in order to confirm to us and strengthen us, by delivering us from all doubt and uncertainty" (*OS* I, 505). The definition of the sacrament that Calvin gives from the 1536 *institutio* is found again, quoting Augustine (read again by Luther: an external sign added to the promise of grace in order to confirm it and to uphold the feebleness of our faith.[46]

If the Word and Holy Communion have the same function for Calvin—"to give" communication "(communion)" to Jesus Christ, the symmetry would not be able to mask the inequality of the words: the sacrament

---

45. It is a question of the idea of divine "accommodation," on which Calvin insists more than Luther: cf. *IRC* 1541, ch. IV and X, ed. Olivier Millet, *Institution de la religion chrétienne* (1541) (Geneva: Droz, 2009), vol.1 and 2, 1214.

46. *IRC* 1536, ch. IV (*OS* I, 118–19). Cf. Luther, *Prélude sur la captivité babylonienne de l'Eglise*, by Marc Lienhard, Matthieu Arnold (ed.) *Oeuvres*, I (Paris: Gallimard [Pleiade], 1999), 735, 822.

seems as a second in relation to the Word, in relation to human frailty. Holy Communion was "instituted by the Lord" in order to "help" our faith. It is the main aim of Holy Communion "to sign and seal in our consciences the promises contained in the Gospel," so that "we may imagine true confidence of salvation," "secondly," the sacrament aims to "train us to praise God," "thirdly," to exhort us to all holiness and [. . .] singularly to brotherly love."

Usefulness of Holy Communion

In the triple purpose of Holy Communion in the divine plan—already thus presented in the 1536 *Institutio*[47] there is correspondingly a tripe usefulness for believers, three "fruits"; first of all the confirmation of faith in Jesus Christ, then a public confession, finally an ethical exhortation.

Confirmation of Faith in Jesus Christ

It is on this first fruit of Holy Communion that Calvin extends most, for him, he says, the other two depend, but it is also that the Zwinglians do not give him room.[48] The point of departure of the essay is that of "evangelical" theology, man the sinner before God: none "of us who can find a single grain of justice in ourself." "The wrath of God has appeared to us," "we are therefore already in the jaws of death," without "hope of resurrection." The "heavenly Father" then intervenes, giving us Holy Communion, tending it "like a mirror in which we see our Lord Jesus crucified in order to abolish our faults [. . .] and brought back to life in order to free us from corruption and from death." Holy Communion "guides us and leads to the cross of Jesus Christ and to his resurrection" (*OS* I, 506). It "makes us participants in the death and passion of Jesus Christ," therefore "companions of all [his] goodness and richness." Truly, "this same grace is offered to us through the Gospel," but Holy Communion gives us "greater certainty and full enjoyment" (*OS* I, 507).

Calvin insists on the necessary link between the benefit of salvation in Jesus Christ and participation in Jesus Christ: "because the property of Jesus Christ does not belong to us at all, except that in the first place it was ours, in

---

47. Also in the 1535 edition of the *Loci communes* of Melanchthon (Wittenberg, 1535, f. N9v –O1v), ch. "*De coena Domini*") Cf. Melanchthon's essay, "Du sacrament de la cène," reproduced by Calvin in the *Actes de Ratisbonne* (October 1541) (*CO* 5, 567).

48. See the *Petit traité . . . de la saincte eucharistie* by Marcourt (*op. cit.*): the "spiritual eating" conforms to the true institution of Holy Communion, is only moreover presented with debating points against the mass which form the frame of the treaty.

the first place we *must* be given to us in Holy Communion." For "otherwise there would be nothing solid or sure." The author risks a more technical development: "I am in the habit of saying that the matter and substance of the sacraments is the Lord Jesus,[49] the remedy is the graces and blessings that we have through his means," that is, the confirmation in us of the reconciliation with God and hope of salvation. And to quote Scripture: in the words for instituting Holy Communion, the commandment to eat his body "delivered for us," and to drink his "blood spread for the remission of our sins," marks this link between "participation" with the body and blood of Christ and the "enjoyment" of the fruit of his death and passion (OS I, 507).

On the matter of this "participation," Calvin warns the readers, anticipating the fifth part of the *Petit traité*: We are beginning now to go into this much-debated question both in the past and at the present time; how must these words where bread is called body of Jesus Christ and wine his blood be understood." Not addressing theologians, he resumes his themes in the *institution* of 1539 to 1541. First of all, the "usefulness" of Holy Communion is set out as the criterion of interpretation: "all usefulness that we must seek in Holy Communion is wiped out, except that Jesus Christ is therein given as the substance and foundation of everything," otherwise stating that "true communication of Jesus Christ" is "presented" to us. Besides, the logic of the "satisfaction" of the Son—God made man—imposes on us an understanding of Holy Communion which is not purely spiritual, but charged with "substance": in order to take part in "all the graces that he obtained for us by his death, there is no question that we are participants in his Spirit, but we must also participate in his humanity." Participating in the Spirit and participating in the body and blood, "one [cannot] be done without the other," thus they indicate the words of Jesus Christ himself [John 6]: that "his Spirit is our life" and that "his flesh is truly meat, his blood is truly drink." And again: "in Holy Communion, when we are told that the bread that we take and eat is his body, and that what we drink from the chalice is his blood ... body and blood are spoken about, so that we may learn to seek the substance of our spiritual life" (OS I, 508).

The quotation of the words for instituting Holy Communion asks an insistent question: "if one seeks to find out nevertheless whether the bread is the body of Christ and the wine his blood ...." Calvin replies to this by explaining the idea of "sign," at the heart of the Augustinian definition of

---

49. "Substance and matter," later "substance and foundation": Calvin tries to adjust the word "substance," heavy with a whole complex scholastic tradition. On the use of the word "substance" by Calvin, see the remarks of Francois Wendel, *Calvin, sources et évolution de sa pensée religieuse* (Paris: P.U.F., 1950), 261–62, and Richard Muller, art. cit. (see n4), 45–53.

the sacrament: "if the bread and the wine are visible signs, which represent the body and the blood," a representation carried out by words ("body" and "blood") which are "like instruments" of communication used by the Lord. It is a "manner of speaking" but "very suitable." On the one hand, it is enough to our "capacity," to our limitation, unfit to grasp a "spiritual mystery."[50] On the other hand, if the visible signs show this mystery, "it is not a naked figure,[51] but united with his truth and substance": the bread "not only [. . .] represents [the body] to us, but also presents it to us," it makes it present to us. Whether Holy Communion is at the same time a representation and presence for us of the incarnate Christ, the Lord's words are stamped upon it: God of truth, the opposite of the evil deceiving spirit, "achieves everything that he means." Thus, "if the representation that God makes to us in Holy Communion is true," one must confess "that as the bread is distributed to us by hand, the body of Christ is also communicated to us, so that we should be participants" (*OS* I, 509).

Calvin then resumes this usefulness of Holy Communion: "we can say that Jesus Christ is offered to us, so that we may own him, and have in him full multitude of the graces that we can wish for [. . .]. In that, we have an excellent help for strengthening our consciences in the faith that we should have in him" (*OS* I, 510).

Public Confession

The "second fruit" of Holy Communion is in the encouragement to "confession of praise" due to the Lord for "blessings we have received from him." Holy Communion "wakes us up from laziness," it is the "incentive" which "drives us to do our duty," since the Lord orders us to "describe his death until he comes." Holy Communion is thus a reminder, in order "almost to protest by public confession" to be attached to Christ and thus "to edify ourselves mutually" (*OS* I, 510). For Calvin, this public collective dimension of Holy Communion is secondary.

---

50. In the *Petit traité*, Calvin several times uses the word "mystery," both for describing the "sacrament" (Latin translation for the Greek word *mysterion*), and, as in this case, in order to express what is beyond language (cf. *IRC* 1539 to 1541, ch. XII (1541: ed. Olivier Millet, *op. cit.* II, 1348).

51. "Naked figure": this formula of Luther's criticizing Zwingli's doctrine of Holy Communion became the negative stereotype of the Zwinglian doctrine.

Ethical exhortation

This third fruit, close to the previous one, is also presented s secondary. It is "a vehement exhortation to live in a holy way and especially to keep charity and brotherly love between us" since in Holy Communion "we are made members of Jesus Christ." The ethical exhortation for Holy Communion is accompanied by an "assistant": the Lord "needs to be inside us through his Holy Spirit," as the virtue of the Holy Spirit is united with the sacraments when they are duly received" (*OS* I, 510–11).

On these two useful matters, put forward by Zwinglians,[52] Calvin does not need to insist.

The Use of Holy Communion, or How to Take

For Calvin, the use of Holy Communion is governed by the Paulinian exhortation to "feel properly," before taking Communion, with its corollary, the condemnation of the communion of the "unworthy" [1 Co 11].[53] On condemnation, the commentary is fast: Anyone who approaches this Holy Sacrament with scorn or apathy, not caring very much to follow where the Lord calls him," commits an "intolerable sacrilege" (*OS* I, 511). To take the sacrament, "inconsiderately" without understanding, or hearing the ethical imperative, is breaking the sign, the sacrament.

The "test" required by the apostle before taking communion is much more developed. Calvin takes care to distinguish this "test" from heard confession, through the "sophistic doctors" putting "the poor consciences into a horrible hell." Only "we have to test whether we have a true repentance in ourselves and true faith in our Lord Jesus Christ," the two being linked. Preparation for Holy Communion goes back to the doctrine of justification: "we have to hold in true trust the heart of the Lord Jesus for our only justice, life and salvation." The test before communion, is firstly "anguish" and hunger: "our souls must be driven by hunger [. . .] in order to find their food in Holy Communion" (*CO* I, 512–13).

---

52. See for example the *Petit traicté . . . de la saincte eucharistie* by Marcourt (*op. cit.*): the bread "must be taken in great reverence, in memory of the death and passion of Jesus Christ, representing the fervent love and great charity with which he loved us and his Holy Spirit with which he has made us alive. Meaning also the love which in true charity we must love one another, as members of the same body." (f. C1v).

53. Communion of the "unworthy" (1 Co 11:27): Calvin takes up the translated word from the Vulgate, implicitly in the meaning accepted by Luther at the time of the Concord of Wittenberg (the "unworthy" have a minimum of faith, different from the "unfaithful" without faith).

Calvin goes further. This hunger makes us "aspire for God's justice," and from there it forces us to leave our "iniquity," among other "vices" listed in the Paulinian manner.[54] In order to "claim" to be of the body of Christ, "we must try for "our life to conform to the example of Jesus Christ," especially "to be united among ourselves with an indissoluble friendship," like the "grains" making up bread. "We must not approach [the sacrament] in any way if we carry some hate or bitterness to a living man and mainly to any Christian" member of the Church. It would be "to decry [Jesus Christ] in pieces" (*OS* I, 513).

After laying down these requirements for faith and holiness, Calvin "moderates" them, in order to free scrupulous people. In fact, "on the earth there will not be found a man who has gained so much in faith and holiness of life who has not still a great deal of weakness in one or another way." As a pastor, Calvin reassures the faithful: "When we feel a firm displeasure and hatred of all vices, [. . .] and a wish to live well [. . .], we are capable of taking part in Holy Communion in spite of relics of weakness that we carry in our flesh." As Calvin set it out in the first two parts of the *Petit traité*, Holy Communion is "a remedy that God has given us in order to meet our weakness, strengthen our faith, increase our charity, help us to progress in all holiness of life." Moreover, "if we were weak," Holy Communion "would not do us any good." As Calvin has set it out in the first two parts of the *Petit traité*, Holy Communion is a "remedy that God has given us in order to meet our weakness, strengthen our faith, increase our charity, and help us to grow in all holiness of life." The medical image even acts as an argument a fortiori: "we must all the more make use [of Holy Communion], when we feel that the sickness is pressing us" (*OS* 1, 514–15).

On the question of frequency of Holy Communion, Calvin acknowledges that "we do not have an express order." However, the consideration of the purpose of its institution—a remedy for our weakness, food calming down our hunger—must make a usage to be considered—"which is more frequent than a great many people do." And Calvin in advocating a "habit" which should be "in all well organized Churches, to celebrate Holy Communion often": an indirect criticism of the practice of the Genevan Church, on the model of that of Bern and Zurich.[55]

---

54. The warning of excommunication "of public sinners, in the liturgy of Holy Communion, due to Farel (*Manière et fasson* . . . Neuchâtel, 1533), in use in Geneva before 1542. Similar formula in the liturgy drawn up by Calvin, *La forme des priers* . . . for the Church of Geneva in 1542 (Calvin, *Oeuvres*, Pleiade, 296).

55. Cf. *IRC* 1536, *OS* I, 149–50: and the article on Holy Communion in the *Articles* on the preachers, presented by Farel to the council of Geneva in January 1537.

In any case, "each person in his own place must prepare to receive it every time that it is given out in the congregation," failing "a great impediment which constrains him to abstain from it." There, Calvin takes care to refute three types of false excuses, which are doubtless heard in his pastoral practice, for abstaining from taking communion.

1. The excuse of "unworthiness," this is in contradiction with the purpose and the "usefulness" of Holy Communion. To the surplus "he who wishes to be exempted from receiving Holy Communion, being unworthy, is excluding himself from praying to God (how to pray to God as the Father, "if we are not members of Jesus Christ"?).

2. The refusal to "communicate with the Lord's bread" with "those who call themselves brothers and lead dissolute and wicked lives" is no longer justified: in fact, it is to "the whole Church generally, or even the pastor with the elders," not to an individual, that it pertains to carry out the "discipline," to "judge and discern," in order to allow or to refuse Holy Communion. Certainly, for each person "our duty is to admonish those whom we see living in a wild manner, and if they do not wish to listen to you the pastor should be warned so that he may deal with him by an ecclesiastical authority," by a collegiate judgment of the Church.[56] Calvin refers to the "discipline of excommunication" or "brotherly correction" (according to the rule of Matt 18), the principle of which he had described in January 1537 in the *Articles* for "the preachers" of Geneva. 55 In any case, the judgment of the congregation only affects[57] visible behaviour, but "most often it will happen that the crimes are not so notorious, that one might go as far as excommunication (i.e. exclusion from Holy Communion)." In fact, it is not up to the Church to probe kidneys and hearts; it is limited to preventing counter-witnessing which would constitute participation in Holy Communion by sinners who cause "scandal."

3. The last excuse—the idea that repetition of Holy Communion is superfluous—also contradicts the "usefulness" of Holy Communion:

---

56. From the 1536 *institutio*, (ch. V), Calvin deals with the "discipline of excommunication," based on Matt 18:15-18, belongs to the "Christian community" (*OS* I, 187). The *Articles* for the "preachers" of Geneva, of 1537, arranged that there should be, for carrying out discipline "certain people leading a good life and with good witness among all the faithful people" (*CO* Xa, 8-9). Calvin calls them "elders" here, in Bucer's meaning, as one of the ministers of the Church (cf. the *Ordonnances ecclésiastiques* of Geneva, November 1541). Calvin refers to the "discipline of excommunication" or "brotherly correction" (according to the rule of Matt 18), the principle of which he had explained in January 1537 in the *Articles* for "the preachers" of Geneva.

57. *Articles* ... 16 January 1537 (Ibid). Cf. *IRC* 1536, II, (*OS* I, 91).

"Jesus Christ is never given to us in such a way that our souls are not completely nourished by Him, but he wishes us to be in continuous nourishment" (OS I, 516–17).

All this part on the usage of Holy Communion, replying to concrete questions by the faithful people of Churches which have already been established, is obviously addressed to those of Strasbourg, Geneva, and Switzerland. For French people, the practice of Holy Communion is impossible, since it presupposes an organization of local Churches, with pastors and elders. But is Calvin perhaps seeking also to give the "hunger" for Holy Communion to the brothers scattered in Egyptian captivity,[58] in order to make them dissatisfied with purely spiritual "eating."

The foundations having been laid down, or recalled, about the purpose, usefulness and usage of Holy Communion, Calvin marks the "disagreement" with the "papists" (OS 1, 504).

"The Disagreement"

In naming five major mistakes sown by the "Devil" on the sacrament of Holy Communion, the Reformer takes up the points of the anti-Roman controversy against the mass, well broken in since the posters of 1534.[59]

The Mass as a Sacrifice

From Luther, the rejection of the sacrificial idea of the mass, based on the Epistle to the Hebrews, is the major point in the debate against the mass.[60] Calvin resumes this theme: "this opinion that was held of Holy Communion, that it was a sacrifice to obtain remission of sins" is only "invention" by men, contradicting the certain Word of the one and perfect sacrifice of Christ on the cross (Heb 10). He also provided the reader with explanations for replying to objections by enemies. On the genesis of this error: an ambiguous formula of the "old Fathers" of the Church, reinforced by the "habit" of ceremonies in the Judaistic style. But the impiousness was

58. Cf. *epistolae duae, op. cit.*, 291, 313.

59. Voir les *Articles véritables sur les horrible, grans et importables abus de la messe papale* (the "posters" of October 1534) or the *Petit traicté . . . de la saincte eucharistie de Marcourt* (*op. cit.*), and in addition, certainly, the treatize *De la captivité babylonienne de l'Eglise* by Luther, 1520 (in Luther, Oeuvres, vol. 1 [see n45], 717–54).

60. It is even the 1st point in the *Petit traicté . . . de la sainte eucharistie* by Marcourt (1534). Cf. Guillaume Farel, *Sommaire et brève déclaration . . . , [1534]*, art. 19 on the mass, ed. Arthur-L. Hofer (Neuchâtel: Editions Belle-Rivière, 1980), 124–25.

deepened when "everything had to be transferred to the mass which was proper for the death of Christ, in order to satisfy God for our debts and by this means to reconcile ourselves to him"; from this, "the office of Jesus Christ was attributed [sic] to those who were called priests," is to sacrifice to God and, by sacrificing, intercede in order to obtain for us grace and pardon for our mistakes, "but only an application of a single sacrifice": this is not allowed to be false for the sacrifice was not repeated, "inasmuch as its effect lasts forever" (OS 1, 518–19).

Calvin therefore sweeps away "the opinion of all the people, [. . .] which was approved by all their doctors and prelates, that, hearing or having the mass said, people deserved, by this devotion, grace and justice towards God." As for us, Calvin replies, "we say that in order to feel any benefit from Holy Communion, we do not need to bring anything of our own [. . .], but that we only have to receive in faith, the grace which is presented therein to us, which does not rest in the sacrament, but it sends us back to the cross of Jesus Christ." From this comes the rejection of the Catholic practice of masses without communion of the meeting, the priest "carrying out his role separately" (OS I, 519–20).[61]

Transsubstantiation

Transsubstantiation is another major theme in the debate against the mass.[62] "Invention," and even "lie," Calvin declares: "that after the words spoke with the intention of consecration, the bread is transubsantiated into the body of Christ and the wine into his blood." Here, "no basis in Scripture," no "witness of the old Church," nor coherence with "the word of God," nor even with the nature of the sacrament, which "requires the material bread to remain as a visible sign of the body," for "the signs [. . .] must have some resemblance to the spiritual thing which is depicted there." If the bread after the consecration had no more than the appearance of bread, the substance having become the body of Christ, how could it still be a sign, therefore a sacrament? "If it were only something white without substance, would it not be a mockery to speak in this way?" (OS I, 520–21).[63]

---

61. Cf. *IRC* 1536, ch. IV (*OS* I, 152–50).

62. This point—associated to that of the adoration of the holy sacrament—was agreed among the Protestants at the colloquium of Ratisbon in May 1541.

63. "Transsubstantiation" (formulated as a dogma of the Catholic "Church at the 4th Council of Latran, 1215) is only described in the *IRC* 1536m by a mocking word (= *prodigiosa transsubstantiatio*," *OS* I, 140–52). But in the *Institutio* of 1539–1541, the criticism occupies more than two whole pages.

In the Zwinglian debate against the mass, this criticism of the doctrine of transubstantiation is often associated with the "local presence" of the body of Christ, a subject which is more touchy for the Lutherans.

The Local Presence of the Body of Christ

From the "fantasy" of transsubstantiation "after several other follies," and even "gross abominations" came out. Thus, "one does not know what local presence was imagined." This is the opinion "received by great and small people in the Papal Church" and today cruelly upheld by fire and sword, that Jesus Christ is contained under these signs and that is where one must seek Him." It requires people to acknowledge "either that the body of Christ is immeasurable, or that he can be in various places, and in saying that one comes at least to the point that he is no different at all from a fantasy." Worse: "he wanted to set up such a presence, through which body of Christ was enclosed within the sign, or it is united locally, it is [. . .] a damnable error": it is at the same time to destroy the "glory of Christ" who has gone up to Heaven and his humanity. For Calvin, again taking up the Zwinglian argument brought in from Augustine, since the Ascension Christ is "exalted to heaven," "but not by changing his human nature," according to Scripture. That is why, "we must always lift our minds on high, in order to seek our Redeemer" (OS I, 521).[64]

Moreover, the "perverse opinion" of the local presence of the body of Christ "has generated a great many superstitions, especially the adoration of the holy sacrament. It is only "pure idolatry" contrary to the Word: we have no order to adore, but to take and eat" (OS I, 522).

On the "local presence" of the body of Christ, Calvin has measured his words[65] If he once more uses Zwingli's arguments against the Lutheran doctrine, he connects his criticism of the "local presence" to the doctrine of transubstantiation and to the practice of adoring the holy sacrament. Thus the arrows do not reach Luther: they are even faithful to the Concord of Wittenberg.[66]

64. "Lift our minds on high . . . ," "lift our hearts on high": these paraphrases of *Col* 3, 1–2 (cf. the "Sursum corda" of the mass), already in *IRC* 1536 (OS 1, 144), make up a part of the Zwinglian essays on Holy Communion (see Marcourt, *Petit traité . . . de la saincte eucharistie*, op. cit., f. D1r).

65. To be compared with the *Petit traité . . . de la sainct eucharistie* by Marcourt (1534) where the subject takes up 28 of the 72 pages: the only designated target is the Catholic practice.

66. "They do not believe in any transsubstantiation, nor the local inclusion of the body and blood in the bread, nor the permanent union with that outside the enjoyment

Communion in a Single Kind for the People

Deprived of the sacrament of blood, "the poor faithful people are maliciously defrauded from the grace [of the] Lord." It is also a question of an tyrannical invention, by the Papacy. The latter goes against, with specious arguments the express command of Christ: "that they all may drink of it," in order to give the priests "some privilege beyond the people," Calvin again sharpens the "democratic" claim which was launched by Luther in 1520 (OS I, 522–23).[67]

The Ceremonies of the Mass

As for "the manner of celebrating Holy Communion," the "Devil" has cut it off from the "doctrine" and reduced it to ceremonies. This point had particularly excited Marcourt's eloquence and that of Calvin is not at peace, describing the mass as "pure antics and trickery."

"Antics" in other words a mime without a sensible word."[68] For Calvin, Scripture and Augustine show that

> the sacraments take their virtue from the word, when it is preached intelligibly.

Now,

> in the mass, [. . .] one may consider that the whole mystery is blessed, unless from everything is done and said in hiding, so that one can hear nothing.

The consecration is even

> a type of witchcraft, considering that like sorcerers, by murmuring and making a great many signs, [the priests] think they can prevent Jesus Christ from coming down into their hands (OS I, 524).

---

of the sacrament" ("Formula Concordiae Lutheri et Buceri" [in German] in *Reformierte Bekenntnisschriften*, ed. Heiner Faulenbach and Eberhard Busch, vol. ½, *1535–1549*, [Neukirchen-Vluyn, Neukirchener Verlag, 2006], 86–87).

67. Cf. IRC 1536, ch. IV (OS I, 150–52). Luther, *De la captivité babylonienne* (see n45), 717–26.

68. Cf. *Articles véritables sur . . . la messe papale* (op. cit. art. 4): "the time is taken up in antics, howlings, singing, ceremonies, lights, incense-burning, disguises and such types of antics."

An "acrobatics" otherwise called a "farce," made up of "jumble and expressions": Calvin attacks the multitude of ceremonies of the mass, which only act for "amusing the people." The "messengers" allege the example of the Old Testament, but "since Jesus Christ was manifested in the flesh, then, the doctrine was clarified even more, the figures have been diminished." Thus, "going back over ceremonies which were abolished, is to rebuild the veil of the Temple, which Jesus Christ broke by his death" (*OS* I, 524–25).

Calvin therefore disqualifies the mass as Jewish and pagan at the same time, in both cases, a religion of gestures, gesticulation.

Having reviewed the various points of the "papal mass," Calvin takes care to make a summary of it by punching: "abominable sacrilege" that the mass understood as a sacrifice, errors and sources of idolatry and superstitions such as transubstantiation and local presence, violation of the Lord's command and depriving the people of the chalice, "superfluity," which was as useless and dangerous as the ceremonies of the mass, contrary to the "simplicity" of Holy Communion (*OS* I, 525–26). The "evangelicals" in France are warned: far from being a successor of Holy Communion, the mass is the opposite: to go to mass is therefore not an anodyne action, a theme that Calvin will take up again in his "anti-nicodemite" treatises.[69] As for the faithful people, in the Empire or in Switzerland, Lutherans or reformed people, they are making a common front against the mass: a good basis in the perspective of an agreement.

The Luther-Zwingli Contentions or How to Solve Them

This last part, which is fairly short, responds to Calvin's project which was announced in the title and in the preface: to deal with the "contention" "so bitterly fought in our time" about Holy Communion. On this "unfortunate" discord between the Reformers, Calvin preferred "that the memory of it should be completely wiped out." If he thinks that it would be useful to return to it "briefly," it is in order to help "a great many good troubled consciences." Now the description of the origin of the conflict is the necessary preface to its solution (*OS* I, 526–27).

---

69. The different points of opposition between te mass and Holy Communion are also described, but briefly, in the *Petit traité ... entre les papistes*, 1543 (Calvin, *Oeuvres*, Pléiade, 517–19).

History of the Bone of Contention

First of all, the author asks of the faithful people (his readers), not to be too scandalized that such a great argument has taken place among those who should be like captains to place the truth in the light." One must consider "in what an abyss of shadows the world was," when those men have begun to bring the truth of the Gospel into the light. The description of this conflict will also, according to Calvin, enable the drama of the event to be played down (*OS* I, 527).

The main actors are presented, with the summary of their respective positions.

Luther first of all. While condemning transubstantiation, Luther seemed to keep the traditional doctrine: "on the corporal presence of Christ"; he said the bread was the body of Christ, inasmuch as it was united with it. Moreover, he adjusted the similarities, which were rather hard and rough." Calvin minimizes this: "he did it as though he were constrained, so that he could not otherwise explain his intention, for it is difficult to make anyone understand such an elevated thing, without using some impropriety" (*OS* I, 527).

Zwingli and Oecolampade, in their turn. Considering the diabolical mistake of the "carnal presence of Christ," which was taught for "more than six hundred years," the source of "dreadful idolatry," they "applied all their understanding to shout against it." Bow-based on the doctrine of Christ's humanity raised to heaven since the ascension, they "forgot to show which presence of Jesus Christ one must believe is in Holy Communion and which communication from his body and from his blood one receives from it."

Luther therefore thought "that they did not wish [wished] to allow anything other than the bare signs, without their spiritual substance" and "began to resist them under the nose, until they were denounced as heretics." From there (toward 1525), the debate between Luther and the Swiss people "was always inflamed with time," "by the space of about fifteen years" the attempt at agreement (in Marbourg in 1529), having failed (*OS* I, 528).

After having explained and excused the sharp edge of the positions, Calvin places himself in the role of mediator and goes shoulder to shoulder with the enemies.[70] Luther has not explained his difference with the "Papists" enough on the matter of the "local presence" of Christ; he used "hyperbolic methods of speaking," which were "very difficult" to understand. As for the "others," they have made more of an effort to ruin the evil than to build for goodness." Thus, "one party and the other went wrong, in not

---

70. The same posture is already in his letter to Bucer, of 12 January 1538 (*op. cit.*, 296–97).

having the patience to listen to one another, in order to follow truth without complaint where it would be found" (*OS* I, 529), Calvin treats the conflict through analyzing the psychological mechanisms and the relativization of forms of language.[71]

A Proposal for a Formal of Agreement

Calvin makes the point of the situation: today, "this unhappy disceptation" [dispute] has almost calmed down, although it does not yet have a formula for public "agreement."[72] While waiting until a synod which could deal with this formulation could assemble, "it must be enough for us that there is fraternity and communion among the Churches and that everyone agrees as much as necessary to gather together." And Calvin proposes the terms of an agreement between all the Churches of the Reformation which might include the Swiss Churches, who were uneasy with the Concord of Wittenberg "We confess therefore with one voice that in receiving the sacrament in faith, according to the Lord's command, we are truly made participants in the proper substance of the body and blood of Jesus Christ." It is a question of a summary of the teaching of the second part of the *Petit traité*. In relation to the formula of the Concord of Wittenberg,[73] we note the deciding place of faith and the introduction of the word "participation" (in the substance of the body and blood of Christ), which expresses, more clearly than the word "*exhibit*" in Melanchthon and Bucer, a dynamic between the believing subject and Christ, by taking away the idea of a substance "in itself."[74]

[71]. Calvin shares Bucer's conviction that in essence the reforming theologians are in agreement among themselves, the conflict on the sacraments coming from misunderstandings (see Martin Greschat, *Martin Bucer (1491–1551): Un réformateur et son temps*, translated from German by Matthieu Arnold [Paris: P.U.F., 2002], 144).

[72]. The Concord of Wittenberg, signed by the theologians of Wittenberg and Strasbourg, had to be officially ratified by the evangelical Churches of the Empire, and while awaiting a general consensus, had not been published.

[73]. Concord or Wittenberg (*op. cit.*) "with the bread and the wine, the body and blood of Christ are truly and substantially present, presented and received." Further: in Holy Communion, "the grace and benefit of Christ are given each time to those who truly repent and who allow themselves to be consoled *by faith* in Christ."

[74]. The words "communication" (= communion) or "participation" translate more or less "*exhibere*" used by Melanchthon in the *Apologie de la Confession d'Augsburg* (1531), then in the Confession of Augsburg called "*variata*" (see Richard Muller, *art. cit.,* see n4, 46–50). Note that the two words "*communicatio*" and "*exhibere*" are associated in the presentation of Holy Communion in the *Loci communes* of 1535 (*op. cit.*, f. O2r.). See also art. XXII of the *Confessio Helvetica prior* of 1536, written by Bullinter, Myconius and Grynaeus, with the advice of Bucer and Capiton, in the perspective of an agreement with Luther (but art. XX restricts the communication of the body of Christ

The formula for the summary is complemented by a precise question which divided the Reformers: "how is that done?" Calvin's reply is intended to have a resemblance to Luther and Zwingli, by holding two polarities together: "on the one hand we must, in order to exclude any carnal fantasies, lift up our hearts on high to heaven [. . .],[75] on the other hand in order not to lessen the effectiveness of the sacrament, we must think that this is done through the secret and miraculous virtue of God and that God's Spirit is the link of this participation, for which reason, it is called spiritual" (OS I, 529–30).[76] In order to prevent two dangers—the "carnal" imagination and the flattening of the sacrament—Calvin makes a double gesture: one of the believer, "lifting our hearts on high" to the heaven of the Ascension, the other of God, or more precisely of the Spirit, a stirring force, which makes the "link of this participation." The theologian places an important precision there in relation to the essay in the first two parts of the *Petit traité*, where he finished explaining this "communication" (spiritual mystery) better. The introduction of this word for the Spirit in the formula of Calvinian agreement softened the formula of the Concord of Wittenberg in Bucer's meaning,[77] and somewhat breaks the balance attached by Calvin between Luther's and Zwingli's positions (so much so that the last word in the *Petit traité* is to describe the "participation" in the substance of Christ as "spiritual."[78]

Did this new "formula for agreement" associating the words of the theologians of Wittenberg and Zurich, while proposing others, respond to the expectations of French "evangelicals"? In any case, it is not easy to see who the numerous French faithful people who were disturbed by the Luthero-Zwinglian contention which Calvin said he could see ("I see a great

---

to that of the "fruits" of the sacrament: salvation and remission of sins).

75. Repeat of a theme which was already described in the fourth part of the *Petit traité*, about the local presence.

76. The same words in the Geneva *Catéchisme* (1542), 53rd Sunday, no. 354 and 3555.

77. According to Francois Wendel, Calvin read in a sermon attributed by Erasmus to Chrystostome (1530) the idea of the Spirit as a link of our union with the Christ (*op. cit.*, see n48, 268). He was also able to read in Bucer (thus in *Enarrationes in Epistulam ad Romanos* (March 1536): "For sacraments administered to adults to be carried out and be what they mean effectively, God must act in them and breathe through his Spirit on the souls of those who receive them. In this way, the latter receive from certain faith what they understand the sacraments to mean" (quoted by Rene Bornert, *La Réforme protestante du culte a Strasbourg* . . . [Leiden: Brill, 1981], 320). Calvin has already used this idea in the text of confession *De eucharistia* (Sept. 15370), submitted to Bucer, in the *Instruction*-catechism of 1537, and even during the Dispute of Lausanne, Oct. 1536 (see Wim Janse, *art. cit.* [see n4] 43–44, 50, and Richard Muller, *art. cit.* [see n4] 51–52).

78. For Richard Muller, the spiritualist turning of Calvin is marked from the *IRC* of 1539 (*art. cit.* [see n4], 51 and 53).

many troubled good consciences."). In fact, is this declaration not an illusion intended for the theologians of Wittenberg? These disoriented French faithful people could well be an alibi. For the Strasbourgian theologian that Calvin was at that time, a formula for agreement modifying the terms of agreement between Melanchthon and Bucer had to be justified, in a "spiritualist" manner, in order to enable a rallying of Swiss people.[79] When read again in this perspective, the plan for the *Petit traité* is not as simple as Calvin let it be understood.

With the *Petit traicté de la saincte cène*, Calvin was offering to the French-speaking public of 1541, in a clear language "very familiar," a solid doctrine which was "substantial" on Holy Communion, at the same time soundly argued and "spiritual." None of the small books which were published up to then on this matter—by Farel, Marcourt, or Roussel—could rival this book on all these planes at once. Neither could any book accumulate so many messages toward several potential publics. With the French "evangelists," the *Petit traité* in pocket form, easy to hide, could reassure those who were clashing in purely negative "sacramentary" positions, on traditional Eucharistic piety. In the same time, not yielding anything on mass, rejected altogether, it was against Rousselian attempts for moderate reform of the mass, and through that took part in the anti-Nicodemite battle.

Among the faithful refugees in Strasbourg, and those of the Church of Geneva, the *Petit Traité* could be read as a superior catechism and a manual of the Protestant consensus on Holy Communion, while awaiting the formalization of a Luthero-Reformed "agreement." In the end, the *Petit traité* (maybe even better than the *Institution* in French) allowed Calvin to claim to be the reformer of the French-speaking world, at the same time as being a theologian and pastor. As a pastor, Calvin was responsible not only for the refugees in Strasbourg and, at a distance, the faithful people of Geneva, but also the French "evangelicals," at the bosom of a great field of mission, which was high-risk and promising. Being strong in this responsibility, he could offer to his theological colleagues in the Schmalkaldic League a new and wider agreement on Holy Communion, moving the lines fixed by the Concord of Wittenberg, above the heads of all the great "captains" of the Reformation.

This aim of extending the Protestant agreement met little echo. The attempt of the *Petit traité* to make the words of disagreeing theologians agree could not open onto an official agreement, in good and due form, among the Lutheran, Swiss and Genevan Churches. The Latin version, which could

---

79. For Richard Muller, the "spiritualist [turning point] of Calvin is marked from the *IRC* of 1539" (*art. cit.* [see n4], 51 and 53).

have enabled him to obtain support in the Empire, failed badly, shortly before the war of Schmalkald, followed by the Interim of Augsburg. In the new context of 1548, which seemed to announce the end of the Protestant Churches in the Empire, Calvin and Bullinger came close to each other, in order to draw up in 1549 a separate agreement on the sacraments, the "Consensus Tigurinus," with words other than those of the consensus of the *Petit traité*. Having become the witness of a stage which was bypassed by the Consensus with Zurich, the *Petit traité* was not republished at all in Geneva after 1549.[80] In France, however, in the new reformed Churches which saw the light toward 1560, it was again able to find a precarious use, by threading its way between the stitches of censorship, before disappearing with the wars of religion.[81]

If Bèze in 1565, and again in 1575, describing the life of Calvin, praised the *Petit traité* so much, it was for its pacifying virtues: "the miserable dispute started up on account of Holy Communion [which] had lit a fire for putting division between the Churches," Calvin had succeeded in putting it out by a "clear description of the subject," leading to a "resolution followed later by all people of good judgment."[82] However, Bèze in Geneva was well placed to find out that since 1534 the fire had spread, more violently than ever, between Lutherans and "reformed people," with this time Calvin—and his successors—in the position of soldiers. But for him it was a question of showing that Calvin had been the man for consensus on Holy Communion, a broader consensus than the single *Consensus Tigurinus*, unjustly attacked by the Lutheran Westphal. Therefore, do keep the memory of the "golden little book."[83]

---

80. However, some republications for scholarly use, in the collections of Calvin's works: in the *Opuscula omnia*... published by Des Gallars (Geneva: Jean Girard, 1552) and, after the Reformer's death, in the *Recueil des opuscules* (Geneva: Jean-Baptiste Pinereul, 1566; Geneva, Jacob Stoer, 1611) nd in the *Tractatus theologici omnes* (Geneva, Pierre de Saint-André, 1475, 1597; Stoer, 1611, 1612; Vignon et Chouet, 1617).

81. Two editions are noted, without any alteration of the initial text, in 1561 and in 1562, without the place or name of the printer. The 1561 edition, bearing the title *Traité de la sainte cene*... by M. Jean Calvin, was no doubt produced in France, perhaps at the time of the Poissy colloquium. That of 1562 is followed by "the manner of interrogating children whom one wants to be given Holy Communion, a sign of a catechetic usage of the *Petit traité*" (J.-F. Gilmont, *op. cit.* II, no. 61/25 and no. 62/15).

82. [Bèze and] Collandon, *Vie de Calvin*, 1565 (*op. cit.*, see n1, 62).

83. Bèze, "*Vita Calvini*," 1575 (*op. cit.*, see n1, 130).

14. Conclusions

The Objectivization of History, between Linguistics and Socio-Psychology

Gilbert Vincent[1]

THAT THE DELICATE TASK of concluding was given to me is certainly a sign of respect and confidence to my place, on behalf of the organizers, by Matthieu Arnold in particular. I am certainly very honored by it, but I am afraid of disappointing everyone here, both my own old reading of Calvin, which brings out a type of archaeology and hermeneutics, at the risk of appearing too far removed from the constraints of simple erudition, such as the present contributions have on the contrary remarkably assumed. I therefore would ask everyone, and first of all the organizers of the colloquium, to kindly excuse me for the "lightness" of my present essay. Moreover, I would ask those present at the conference not to treat me harshly for not succeeding in doing justice to each person's contribution: in spite of certain general common features—the only ones that I shall risk saying something about—the various approaches are so specific, even original, that putting their secret dissertations in evidence seems to me like something beyond my knowledge and my know-how. Therefore one may not expect more from these few "conclusive" remarks than a very free commentary, either on points which often came up during this colloquium (even if it is only in a more or less allusive manner), either on questions which are to be brought into consideration for my own curiosity and about whom there is no proof that they are very pertinent. That is to say that my essay could not earn the old name of "conclusion," of which the author of the *Dictionnaire de la langue francaise* Alain Rey, tells us that it meant, up to the sixteenth century, "to enclose within an argument." At the most, if one dares to give it an ennobling status, could one say that, at least for its first part, it takes up the "criticism," in the philosophical meaning of the word, that is in the meaning

[1]. Faculty of Protestant Theology, University of Strasbourg.

of considerations relating to the conditions of possibility of the venture of thought to which we were associated at the time of this colloquium.

1. Conflicting Constitution of the Matter Being Studied

And Conditions of Distancing Oneself

PHILOSOPHY, BEING UNABLE TO claim any legitimacy other than itself, in our time often remaining challenging, which consists in occupying the margins or, according to some people, parasiting essays by other people, the specialists—the legitimacy, at the best, of the general practitioner—I shall make an effort to "make a virtue of necessity" and, for example, to change my ignorance in such a type of naivety whose only eventual virtue is to inspire the courage to come back to some evidence, to emphasize presupposed ideas which may be prejudged and to open the tracks of which however nothing guarantees that they would not be a smokescreen or impasses. But, overall, is not every researcher, he too, often led to make a virtue of necessity? By stating that the body of researchers who were gathered together on the occasion of this colloquium found itself in this type of situation, that if destitution forced them to prove inventiveness, I can prevail upon myself with some notations borrowed from the recent study by our colleague Matthieu Arnold, entitled: "John Calvin's time in Strasbourg, Historiographical survey."[2] As he states there, as the first person, since Doumergue that "the biographies have not even brought any new factual information" on this famous time, how can one doubt the pertinence of this global assessment? However, how not to add now, in the light of various and subtle contributions to this colloquium, that the absence of new facts is not an unacceptable mistake? It is known that scholarly history also advances on two feet: that of the invention of facts (that invention which is always more than a simple collection!) and that of interpretation of the latter (for without interpretation, one has no more to do, either with "facts," so called, but with simple brute facts). Moreover, it is known that interpretation depends upon the diversity of the disciplinary procedures which is liable to take the questioning applied to the available facts, each procedure corresponding to placing into a more or less original perspective of the latter. Finally, it is well known that, in interpretation, various noteworthy inflexions and enrichments may lead to reformulation, without the transformation of available historiographical

---

2. The complete title is: "Le séjour de Jean Calvin a Strasbourg (1538–1541); simple parenthèse ou étape capital dans la biographie du Réformateur? Enquête historiographique," *Bulletin de l'Histoire du Protestantisme Français* 155 (2009) 321–33.

14. Conclusions

questions within a community of researchers, always characterized by some practices of thinking and due to the fact that research develops according to some privileged directions which will appear, retrospectively, as much as axes of displaying a style, even that of a particular historiographical school.

Thus, a good example of a way in which one may "make a virtue out of necessity," *l'histoire de la réception* of a work or of a complex phenomenon—such as "Calvin in Strasbourg"—corresponds itself to an interval which is sensitive in relation to the usual questionings and represents an occasion which is favorable to the appearance of new questions. Where it occurs, the interval corresponds to a form of objectivization or procedures which were implemented in previous works, therefore there is a precious possibility of distancing oneself from them. The reader of Calvin could only see a useless sophistication in this and, even worse, a type of epistemological substitute for speculative ambition which the theologian never makes the mistake of denouncing, wishing to emphasize his type of precept, which was previously Aristotelian, more phenomenological recently returning to the "matters themselves." Now, any gain in reflexivity—for such is the issue of the interval that we have just mentioned—does not imply that one loses the view of reality. The matter from which one thus finds oneself distance, is in fact, illusion, which is more empirical than realistic, with a perfect coincidence between—historical-"facts" and—historiographical-"facts." To sum up, the gain in reflexivity goes along with a new display of the interpretative space, with a freedom which has grown, for the researcher, in the choice of interpretative hypotheses which are slightly deviant and innovative in relation to current questions of protocol within his own disciplinary field. But how can one claim that the increase of freedom does not conceal an increase in arbitrary writing? This type of suspicion, without ever being possible to be definitively suppressed, may however be temporarily laid aside from the time when one sees that the interpretative freedom of the researcher does not allow one to be guided—therefore regulated, if not controlled—by questions, perspectives or explanatory procedures whose epistemic relevance, even if it seems threatened within its disciplinary field, may be better ... in neighboring disciplinary fields (but, it is true, even the idea of a "neighborhood" between disciplines remains problematical, as Michel Foucault had begun to show in his famous *Les Mots et les choses!*).

At the time of this colloquium, it is certainly with the linguistics that the neighborhood has been narrowest and, shall I dare to say, the most fertile. Without new data in relation to Calvin's biography, the Calvinian corpus was submitted to a tight examination, not only of its internal characteristics and its potential for variation, but even in its linguistic, pragmatic and sociolinguistic conditions, of possibility. Thus care was taken not to fall into the old problem of "the man and the work," the latter generally assimilated into its manifest content—on the surface, as one says in semiology—that is, its "doctrinal" content, the latter has assimilated into a genius, a sort of demi-urge owing nothing, either positively or even negatively to other people or to its time. Thus the temptation for hagiography was removed; but one could expect at least, in a university colloquium having achieved what Jean Grelsch called "the hermeneutical age of reason.[3] However one must not forget that the said temptation keeps its power for intellectual habits so alive that if the latter seem obsolete to us today, it has ended up by imposing the famous "linguistic turn" into most human sciences, the major effect of which was the desacralization of every corpus and the de-heroization of every author. Such has been the price to pay for one and the other to reveal in themselves the features of common humanity, of a common and profound ending. Thus the theme, which is dear to Richard Stauffer, of "Calvin's humanity," found again an undeniable actuality, by means of reducing the most psychologizing of the perspective which was formerly defended by our master of Calvinian studies. I cannot detail her all the loans made to most of the members of the conference to the linguistic, and more globally, literary analysis: sometimes it is the philology which has come first, sometimes the semantics and pragmatics; sometimes the question of the plurality of literary genres, sometimes the sociolinguistic approach. The most noteworthy, as it seems to me, is therefore the form that most of the subjects of study have taken under the eyes of one and the other, that is to say a discursive or inter-discursive form (correspondence, colloquia, controversy . . .), even the paralinguistic, expressive and aesthetic form (hymnological, liturgical, etc.)

The course of action which was taken thus bore witness to the price given to demand, apparently negative, for a renewal of the interpretation pointed out by Matthieu Arnold in the above study: moving away from the center. In this respect, the comparison, we know, is a necessary but not adequate condition, an individual or collective person, a historic moment, etc.—in relation to thanks to other similar ones; inadequate, however, to achieve efficiently a blockage to praiseworthy or disparaging prejudgments: how often, in fact, does the "horizontal" contrast between the words not transform itself into a vertical difference in attitude which accuses a hierarchical inequality? The problem which one meets is heavy with "ideological" implications when, being a question of an era of profoundly divergent reforms, the objects of study are as much crystallizations of intentional comparisons, in the spirit of the first protagonists, to move their cause forward. Out of this difficult problem comes: how, in our turn having recourse to

---

3. Jean Grelsch, *L'âge herméneutique de la raison* (Paris: Cerf, 1985).

14. Conclusions

other points of view of actors who do not even hesitate to use the comparison for purposes which cannot be interested any more, actors who would never be so violently opposed if their bone of contention had not been the question of knowing who deserved to be attributed with the insignia of Truth, and who had no grounds for citing it, under pain of a mortal lie—in a similar historical context, it is known, any divergence of opinion is designed as the expression, not of some mistake, but of the lie (that is one of the rare points of agreement of the enemy brothers) of its author, the devil: the latter would like above all to lead faithful people astray, to turn them away from a Truth that one then judges to be inconceivable, that it is monstrous and therefore diabolical to think that its normal state could be that of spreading, sharing or of plurality.

At the time of this colloquium, each person seemed to have been very particularly attentive, in marking out a field of comparison, not to use the unit of measurement surreptitiously—Truth or doctrine, but also moral exemplarity—in use by one protagonist or the other, even in both main camps, Catholic and Protestant. It is thus that, at various times, a hypothesis of the existence of a "field" of humanism was formulated. The transformation of the landscape and, going forward, the movement of the topics that were held was sensitive from that time, especially the change of orientation as already described, of a doctrinal perspective toward a more firmly discursive perspective, in the attention of the researcher who from that time onwards was used to practicing the phenomenological *epoche*, placing obvious contents between parentheses as required, or "doxemes" (to take up an expression which was dear to Jean-Pierre Deconchy)[4] of the corpus in question.

In my turn, I shall put forward the idea that the notion of the "field" is in fact liable to give substantial services, especially epistemological, for the time when it is a question of explaining how, in an oversaturated symbolic environment, can crystallize systems—of thought but also of action and organization (ecclesiological, for example)—which are varied and soon concurrent. As Jean-Claude Pariente has demonstrated,[5] the idea of a field is complementary to that of individuation, which can be applied to collective bodies and, previously, to processes which, in order to return to our field of study, will give birth to that which little by little will become "Protestantism," that is to say at the same time doctrinal (or at least a constellation of doctrinal topics which are considered to be mutually compatible, not because one magisterial instance of this would have thus been decided, but during the

---

4. Jean-Pierre Deconchy, *L'orchodoxie religieuse: Essai de logique psycho-sociale* (Paris: Les Editions ouvrières, 1971).

5. Jean-Claude Pariente, *Le langage et l'individuel* (Paris: Armand Colin, 1973).

establishment of relations for recognition which in some way were lateral) and, as has just been suggested, an ecclesiological—confederal—style of exercise. The sociologists have also recourse to the idea of a field. If, under their pen, the idea of a conflict of contrary forces, sometimes even violently drawn up one against the other, is predominant, it is that, except when they are dealing with "social movements," except when they notice the emergence of new actors, who are more or less autonomous, the sociologists, and especially those who adopt a model of bourdiensien analysis, deal with current relations which the trained social actors maintain. Now, in physics or in crystallography—if one holds onto the philosophical analysis by Gilbert Simondon of research conducted in crystallography[6]—the concept of a field is aimed to take into account phenomena which are more inchoate, genetic phenomena, therefore of potentialization and actualization. The concept of a field makes it possible to lift the substantialist mortgage with its diverse elements or variants—of which the pre-formist mortgage, which makes this situational fundamental condition a bargain, the contingency, which the professional historian knows how to acknowledge, while the apologist—who sometimes disguises himself under the features of the historian—is unaware of it or hides it as much as possible. After all, the idea of a field of gravity provides, also, a fairly good approximation of which happens in a hyper dense relational field, when each person looks for allies and, in order to increase his chances of finding it, he tries to convince them, while they are still only potential allies, that they are like him facing the common threat, which cannot be more real or present, of adversaries and soon enemies who are determined to eliminate all opposition or would it not be any trace of affirmation and position which do not comply with the idea that they are supposed to act in their interests.

The major epistemological difficulty, in any colloquium like ours, is probably the following: how thanks to which analytical models, to avoid "understanding" the individuation from the individual, which would come back to reduce the potential to the present time, to forget that the first one flows into the second and that, certain such resurgencies, it can mingle into the present in the form of more or less insistent possibilities or suggestions. "The field of humanism" is no doubt a happy expression, for this one places the emphasis not on one or several clearly defined bodies, not on authorities which have already been set up, but on multi-directional *réseaux d'échange*, where the desire for cooperation holds the wish for competition in respect, where aiming for the affirmation of his convictions, the proclaimer does not

---

6. Gilbert Simondon, *L'individui et sa genèse physic-biologique* (Paris: Presses Universitaires de France, 1964); idem., *L'individuation psychique et collective* (Paris: Aubier, 1989).

14. Conclusions

forget that any affirmation must logically, if not dialogically, lead to negation—according to the proverb: *omnis determination negation*—a condition of possibility of any differentiation of points of view. In a truly relational network—a model other than that of a field, but not at all incompatible with it—the one which whom one is in dispute is not an enemy but an "objector," an indispensible auxiliary in the coproduction of an argument whose author acknowledges his sources; of whom, in acknowledging the declarant, he thereby acknowledges the polyphonic texture of "his" voice, conveyed by a co-enunciation of a dialogical structure. If it is so, in principle, how does one explain the more or less rapid mutation of the field of humanism—where evangelism takes the part of a component—to the polemical field of a dogma engaged in the bitterest controversies, where cooperation ceases to be the highest possibility in order to become an almost obligatory tactical conduit for who knows or more exactly who believes it is engaged in an inescapable competition? In fact the question does not stop one from asking to find out how one passes—slow process but where, as in crystallography, one sometimes has to deal with sudden mutations—of a state of the field where the Erasmian position is possible, where therefore, in spite of Luther's injunction to join up with shilly-shallying his field again, a humanist defends the legitimacy of a third position, in a new state where what remains of a position of this type, in which irenism is presented not as a fault but as a higher form of clairvoyance if not courage, is finally subordinated to aiming for bribery: where, as Bishop Sadolet witnesses, one aims, not to seek with the adversary a field of understanding, but to thus disarm and weaken the field in which he is a part!

A great many theses could serve to reinforce the feeling that a number of studies presented at this colloquium have contributed to deconstruct—which does not mean "destroy"—"traditional" images which are intended to celebrate Calvin's merits. It is that, as an indirect consequence of a situation of marked research, one has recalled, through a certain indigence, the scrupulous researcher, in front of parsimonious documentary data, cannot reasonably sacrifice aspiration to intelligibility to the requirements of legend. In fact, however hard one tries, it is not possible, for the moment, to completely take the Calvin of Strasbourg out of the shadow cast by the high statures of Bucer or the Sturms. There is something rather strange, in Calvin's career: like a new time of latency, after his frantic arrival in Geneva, before his almost triumphal return in this same city. But, everything considered, is the thing so surprising, after the bitter failure which the Reformer suffered in Geneva? Could one not advance the hypothesis that Strasbourg allowed him to learn a lesson from his failure, at least to develop better, having left so imperiously, although something pushed by Farel's pressing invitation, to rebuild the Church in Geneva?

The other reason that could explain that several members of the conference contributed to the discreet deconstruction of the reformed "golden legend," is, we have already pointed it out but one should insist more on this point, that the core of the Calvinian corpus, the Institution de la religion chrétienne, is a sedimentary text, of an almost alluvial type; its configuration changes, and with it its thematic priorities change. It is clear that the questions asked of a work of this type and, through them, the objectivation of the work depend very broadly on the patient editorial work which was carried out by the pioneer enterprise of Jean-Daniel Benoit, work which enables the contemporary reader to find redactional stages of a lecture whose tormented course presents a great many new directions or confluences, a number of whirlwinds, parades, falls etc. One could multiply the analogies between the multiple sorts of accidents which are typical of a watercourse and the various events which have left their mark in Calvinian writing. It is always the case that, suddenly, the *Institution* has nothing of a finished product: it is a work of which the "last" edition is only such by accident, if one may say so; it is why nothing is opposed to the idea that there is, in this lecture, movement to go further, either there where Calvin—finality obliging—was forced to stop. An amazing conjunction of the constancy of the intention of system and the role of circumstances, or more precisely reflection on the sense of circumstances! An amazing conjunction between firmness of the discursive project, on the one hand, twists and variations of an enunciation as though it were needled by recalled quotations, on the other hand, whose study—several members of the conference have shown this—is of great interest to pull together the Calvinian discursive dynamic! Is it to grant the demon of hagiography to state that, in the 1541 edition, whose preparation corresponds to the time spent in Strasbourg and that, if the tone is that of conviction, this does not completely flow, far from it, in the form of polemics?

2. Borrowings and Tradition: From Cooperation to Competition

The question that one could not avoid at the beginning was to know who, in the 1541 edition, can reasonably be considered as a witness of Bucer's influence or actors meeting in Strasbourg or in the colloquia in which Calvin took part, such as that in Ratisbon. But what is the measurement of reasonability, in the matter? And what does one mean by speaking of "influence?

14. Conclusions

Using this term is often a discreet manner of emphasizing that the object or subject that is influenced owe what they are to a game of extrinsic determinations. That is why, inversely, in denying the role of such and such an influence on a subject, a work or an action, one allows it to be understood that the entity in question is only due to itself, to its own power of self-determination, to be what it is. The alternative seems to be implacable, the Kantian paradox of affirmation of determinism and that of freedom. But does the conclusion—which would wish for the alternative to have no loophole, impose itself? Good sense or at least the memory of certain linguistic usages—should encourage us to remember that there exists, over and above the categorical couple of the influencer and the easily influenced person, a third category: the easily influenced person. The term, it Is true, is ordinarily used for purposes of depreciation: an easily influenced subject would be a weak person, too weak to strongly and efficiently resist bad influences! Let us therefore firmly reject any contamination of the semantics by a summary moralism, and let us rather pay attention to the pragmatic complex structure of the loan.

This type of phenomenon, too often one tends to forget it today, has recently given rise, from a Leroi-Gourhan,[7] to precious analyses of which I give the essentials here. According to our author, who is very particularly interested in the problem of transfers of techniques, the borrower is rarely passive. If he were, or if he was only that, the object would not really be *borrowed*, but more simply *moved* from one society to another, from one group to another. In order for there to be a loan, *strictu sensu*, it is necessary for the "moved" object to make sense for the borrower, that the latter uses it according to the rules of use prescribed by its form our its "normal" mode of operation. In other words, the one who handles the object is competent as regards the regular usage of the said object; or, if he does not have this competence at all, he must have some competence for learning and, thus, to become a competent user. Let us therefore say that the borrower is almost competent, and that the object often represents a challenge for him: to discover the rules of usage, which, when followed, will enable the user to overcome the type of strangeness of the object, which will make its meaning—which corresponds to the discovery of the congruence of the function that it incarnates and of the end of which he receives the promise—will be so well "understood" that it will take place in the heart of the new cultural environment of the borrower. The borrower is certainly not the inventor. But his role could not be minimized, for he must become capable of transforming an unusual object at first glance into an object of more or less

---

7. Andre Leroi-Gourhan, *Milieu et techniques* (Paris: Albin Michel, 1945).

current use, and, in order to do this, expanding and sometimes transforming his repertoire of expertize. Thus to redefine, the borrowing situation, however ordinary it may be, clarifies the rarer situation of invention. The weight of old prejudices relating to the genius or, much more prosaically, the need—not at all "natural"—to connect the right of ownership to the right of first occupant or of the first user lead us in fact too often to conceive the invention independently of the environment which makes it possible, independently of traditions—contained but also and especially usages and rules of usage—which make up the cultural repertoire common to several groups and societies, sometimes far away in space or in time: the invention exists, but it exists inasmuch as the rush of dispersed possibilities in the heart of a common cultural repertoire; which explains that the phenomenon of simultaneous invention is not at all exceptional!

Thus we tie up again with our reflections on relational fields and networks. These make the spread of a common culture possible; habitual, in the case of cooperative networks, but which does not disappear at all when competition wins over cooperation: in order to win against the adversary, is it not necessary, in counter-arguing, to take a little seriously the argumentation that he uses against you or, short of this, the reasons for his hesitations and refusals? Others have already noted this, and especially Rene Girard: the relationship is very narrow, between mimicry and conflict. But while this author above all places the emphasis on the conflictual and often tragic outcome of a mimicking relationship, one must not forget that the opposite is not at all rare: a relationship of conflict and lead to and accelerate the process of reciprocal imitation. This is what Paul Veyne cleverly observed in *Les Grecs ont-ils cru a leurs mythes?*[8] where, before quoting Bourdieu and referring expressly to his idea of "symbolic field," specific and autonomous but "shared among centers of power," he notes that one of the effects of controversy (for example between Bossuet and Jurieu, but the remark is equally valid for the century of crystallization of reforms), is to oblige each of the controversialists to become more cautious in the use that he makes of quotations if he does not want, at the time that he imagines that he is increasing his authority thanks to that, reputedly, of quoted authors, to serve his cause. From Paul Veyne again, one could hold the idea of "programme of truth" and point out after him that if conflicts may often weaken such a program, they may sometimes strengthen it; so much, if not more than cooperative relationships.

Thanks to such sketches of modelization, justice could be given to the others, including adversaries. For, contrary to a modern representation

---

8. Paul Veyne, *Les Grecs ont-ils cru à leurs mythes?* (Paris: Seuil, 1983).

14. CONCLUSIONS

accredited by practices and theories of communication which substantiate the idea of a profound asymmetry between sender and addressee, the feature of a "dialogic" relationship that one should take it on its cooperative side, is to bring forward the construction of a state of thought which tends to become common to the protagonists: in order to convince others, may one not seek to use arguments which are liable to meet his assent? Now, to have recourse to arguments to which he may subscribe, is to accept to be linked, at least temporarily, by criteria of the plausible and of the implausible which are his own. In the same way, if one wishes to respond to him in a pertinent manner, one must enlarge if not modify his own criteria in relation to what makes a discourse either sensible or not. As regards our field of study, one of the main merits of research conducted by Francis Jacques[9] on dialogism is to lead us to put aside recurrent questions of priority, almost indiscernible questions, it has already been suggested, of those of ownership. The latter have become important, today, insofar as intellectual property goes hand in hand with important economic advantages. Now, at the time of reforms, the questions of ownership are clearly less decisive, so that it seems to us as if the casualness in borrowing is, most often, only a manifestation of the intensity of exchanges, including altercation. In the perspective of dialogism, the question of ownership appears to be without a real object: how in fact, in an authentically dialogic co-enunciation, to unravel what is mine and what is thine? Quite simply, there would have been no dialogue, therefore no dialogic productiveness, if each of the speakers was taking care to defend jealously the stock of utterances of which he claims to be the exclusive owner: each of them, in such a case, must communicate nothing to the other, for fear that the latter did not take hold in one way or another of these same "utterances"; no-one would even formulate objections, precious turning-point utterances which enable two distinct universes of thought to be connected and offer the possibility of reaching "in common" a thinkable unpublished work, which up to then was inaccessible to one and the other of the protagonists.

It is useless to dwell more on this point: a pragmatic approach moves and therefore renews so many ancient topics, dated insofar as they come from an available state of knowledge in which linguistics or its hermeneutic renewal—philosophic—did not count at all. Deprived of categorical resources of linguistics and socio-linguistics, may one do otherwise than concentrate one's attention on a corpus of utterances, each of which was taken according to its immediate semantic—or surface—value, and, for fear

9. Francis Jacques, *Dialogiques. Recherches logiques sur le dialogue* (Paris: Presses Universitaires de France, 1979).

of being dragged into an indefinite movement of paraphrases, can one do better than to draw up, in front of a considered corpus, all of the "causes" which are capable of explaining its existence? With the *commentary*, the commentator is installed into a relationship of too great a proximity with the corpus commented on. With the causal explanation, the analyst tries to take away any risk of connivance by drawing up between himself and the corpus a game of relationships of causality which are supposed to relieve the primacy of exteriority. The interest of more pragmatic approaches, following the example of some of the studies presented at the time of our colloquium, is, as the question of borrowing has shown us, to free us from a sort of obsessional quest about the priority to be granted, either to the internal approach, or the external approach. The main fault of this type of alternative, falsely adorned by explanatory titles, for one, and of comprehension, for the other, is that in one and the other case one fails to take plausibly into account the *genesis* of a work in an environment which contributes to modeling the author of the work in question, an author who moreover would fail to create the work if he was not engaged in a field characterized by his lines of power, resistance and rupture. It is not a question of recommending a ? compromise between internal reading and external reading, but to draw up a model of complex interactions, and above all to imagine a system which is sensitive to different phenomena of retroaction, a system in which the actors are at the same time capable of reflexivity and engaged in multiple relationships of interdependence, positive in cooperative, negative in concurrence—these values having nothing fixed, all things considered, as has been recalled after Paul Veyne.

The epistemological services of a dialogic model have just been sufficiently emphasized. However, may I be allowed to add that a model of this type enables one to play the part of historicity of an utterance which, being historical, precisely, could achieve nothing and therefore would be nothing outside a dense and broadly unforeseeable space of co-enunciation. The share of historicity, is that of *contingence*; especially meetings and modalities of these same meetings. Pragmatics comes here to meet scholarly history, while biography moves away from models which are too well marked by a summary psychology which often repeats a simplistic characterology. One could specify this point by emphasizing the possible double contribution of a hermeneutics designed in the manner of Paul Ricoeur, who on the one hand places the accent on the narrative identity of a personage and on the other hand de-psychologizes the notion of author by referring it to a space of more or less heterogeneous expressibility, on the internal (types of lecture) and external (controls and censures) frontiers which are more or less porous. Certainly, "great authors" exist, and Calvin certainly deserves to count among them: those are "great" who impose their mark—their style—on certain possible discursives, on usages which have the effect of modifying the rules of expressivity in force, and thereby to modify the course of tradition, inasmuch as memory not only of things said but even possibilities of saying otherwise.

Therefore innovation is possible—and this possibility is illustrated by the great authors, "great" because their works are great. Now, this is not possible independently of any tradition. A work may modify the tradition; but only locally, not globally. That is to say that the most innovative lecture is not free from any *répétition*, the repetition or revival being the price to be paid if one wishes to benefit from a more or less common regime of intercomprehension. In terms of theory of communication, one would say that a minimal redundancy—but how to determine the minimum? Is a constraint for any message, also it may be unforeseeable (unforeseeability being a formal property of the message). Therefore autonomy is only relative, just as unforeseeability. Remembering this point, is, again, a way of deconstructing the figure of the genius as well as that of a work whose author would not have contracted any debt to anyone, known or unknown.

In short, however innovative a work may be, it cannot "borrow" multiple sources of expressivity ("traditional" authorities), if one may risk this pleonasm, contemporary authorities, without forgetting anonymous, impersonal, common language authority). It is a matter of constitution: without borrowing, without belonging to this tradition, the work would be too innovative to be audible; so that in believing to honor it in placing it aside, one would condemn it author to total solitude; worse, to retreat into a world which, failing sufficient numerous intersections with the worlds of others, would be non-world, and the subject a sort of autistic person. However, and thus I begin the series of my more specific questions, does not the dominant acceptance of the concept of tradition, in a Catholic environment, represent a serious categorical obstacle, at the time when it is important to acknowledge dialectic, constituting the intention of reform and reliance on traditional sources? Inversely, does it often prevent Protestant historiography—supposing that something like that still exists!—to greet the resources of innovation which are available to the Catholic tradition, including when this is intensely opposed to the Reformers' projects? There again, the alternatives are ruinous. That of continuity and rupture is not an exception. Like the others, it makes us forget that in wishing at any price to find in reality the trace of distinctions of reason—which moreover are only terminological distinctions—one betrays the complexity of reality, which is better expressed in terms of continuum among the *polarities* than in terms of exclusives.

3. Affective Charge of Theological and Ecclesiological Engagements

The few more circumscribed questions that I shall allow myself to deal with now were suggested to me for the most part by my reading of a colloquium similar to our own, which was held in 1964 in Strasbourg to commemorate the 400th anniversary of Calvin's death. The works were published under the title: *Regards contemporains sur Jean Calvin*.[10] These questions obviously bear witness to my own curiosity—a fault which was sharply rejected by Calvin as by a great many spokespersons of the Christian "tradition," as Hans Blumenberg recalled a short time ago in his work: *La légitimité des Temps modernes*! It remains to be discovered whether these questions are pertinent or if the fact that they were not tackled means that they have lost a great part of their interest for historiographic research!

My first question—outside that of tradition, recalled instantly—concerns the Calvin-Bucer relationship and their definition of the "office of doctors." In the 1964 colloquium, Willem Dankbaar pointed out some hesitation, already with Bucer, about differentiation of ministries. With Calvin himself, the office of doctor is sometimes distinct from that of pastor, but sometimes also almost confused with it. What weight could one grant to the hypothesis according to that very experience of Calvin in Strasbourg could have been decisive in this matter? Let us ask the exact question: if there is something good floating in the theory, would this feature not be placed in a close relationship with the very style of the Calvinian lectures, in which the care for doctrinal elaboration generally goes along with a deep concern for pastoral construction which is manifested elsewhere than in the sermons alone, not only at the time of application of a biblical text to the life of the believer, but already, prior to that, in the exegesis of the intention of the author of the text?

If this mixed style is that of the later editions of the *Institution*, would it not be, *a fortiori*, that of the 1541 edition? One will succinctly recall what is in there of this style, by saying that even when it gives itself away—that one wishes to excuse this expeditious appreciation!—in the defense of double predestination, in which he himself prettily called a "labyrinth"—moreover, this is more speculative than conceptual. Calvin did not cease to have recourse to the pastoral, almost therapeutic, argument of the so-called "sweetness" of the effects of doctrine, which was capable of giving faithful people the "peace of the soul" to which they aspired. Whatever one thinks, could

---

10. *Regards contemporains sur Jean Calvin: Actes du colloque Calvin Strasbourg 1964* (Paris: Presses Universitaires de France, 1965).

it be that the pastoral round of Calvin's theological utterances should be accentuated during his time in Strasbourg, on the one hand under Bucer's influence, on the other hand because he was directly in charge of a parish, which furthermore is a *parish of refugees*?

Another merit of this style deserves to be recalled, that in no way invalidates—on the contrary!—the previous remark on the importance of the pastoral intention in Calvin: what may be called his Aristotelian style, which could, rather curiously, evoke this sense of prudence that our Reformer reproaches in Bucer. Even more curiously, is it not amazing to discover this feature in Calvin's lectures, that is called systematic and is judged even systematic to excess? This feature is concerned with the sense and care for "measurement," of "moderation." Now, as in Aristotle, the "correct environment" corresponding to the sense of measurement is placed, according to the circumstances and situations taken into account, sometimes closer to an extreme, sometimes nearer the other: sometimes it would be important to calm troubled consciences, by instilling fear into them! Upon meeting the reputation which is often given to him, that of a lover of the system or of an intemperate person, one discovers thus another face of Calvin, a face which is dear to Richard Stauffer, and especially a form of theology which probably thereby complies with the spirit of biblical texts, which are themselves also written in terms of particular situations, broadly contingent and therefore not always repeatable, as Calvin is attached to showing it in his own biblical commentaries.

Would the feature on which we have just placed an emphasis not naturally be to encourage assertion, even strengthening, in an idea like that of Calvin, for concern for unity? In 194, J. Courvoisier tackled this type of question, whose ecclesiological stake is obvious. Hypothesis: would his time in Strasbourg not have made Calvin sensitive, more so than if he had stayed in Geneva, to a certain legitimate variability in the ways and customs, even in the matter of ecclesiology or biblical authority which was legalized? In fact, Calvin never abandoned the idea—the question is posed, obviously, of finding out whether his practice always corresponded to this idea—that different practices can be justified regarding local usages or circumstances. In other words, the sense if not the requirement for unity in him, does not go against attention to diversity. There again, one would have to deal with polarity in him, with a concrete dialectic which is capable of giving place to multiform compromises.

The opportunity arose, at the time of this colloquium, to tackle the question of Calvin's relations with *anabaptism*. Now, examining things closely, one is surprised to find out that Calvin's extreme severity in relation to the Anabaptists is the counterpart of his concern for unity, in spite of or through a certain diversity. Diversity, in fact, does not only correspond in his case with different contexts; it is concerned with different spiritual constellations, disparate psycho-spiritual situations. From this Calvin's insistence, again completely pastoral, on *sanctification* and on the danger that there is in confusing sanctification—a process—and holiness—a state. If it is so, the Church is and remains in his eyes a composite entity, basically heterogeneous. In more theological language: it is not made up of perfect people, but of Christians who were often sharing if not torn apart by various allegiances: Christians who were certainly engaged, in principle, in a process of conversion and regeneration, but who are not miraculously preserved from risk of relapse. It is worth borrowing this quotation from Marc Lienhard, delivered at this colloquium: "one must tolerate something of human stupidity"; but it is no doubt right to correct this in the sense that seems to me to comply with Calvin's pastoral intention: certainly, one must count with human stupidity, but one must not forget human *fragility*, what is truly something else, and which directs tolerance in a really new direction: that of a certain form of concern.

It cannot be prevented: in spite of his pastoral preoccupations, Calvin does not hesitate to demand the excommunication of the Anabaptists. How to interpret this extreme rigour? Before even trying to interpret it—for example by invoking the strength of "programmes of truth" which were dominant at this time—one must not forget, not in order to excuse it but in order better to take the measure of it, to compare this rigour with the practice recommended by one of the fathers of the modern idea of tolerance. John Locke, who thought that it would be insane, in a society that one seeks to make more and more civil, to tolerate the intolerant. Would John Locke therefore be intolerant? And if one hesitates to judge him so, must one not hesitate to judge Calvin in the same way? As for that, would the ecclesiological formula defended by Bucer be more favorable to a practice of tolerance? Regarding a regime of multitudism, the Anabaptists certainly should be able to be tolerated, as the magistrate often wished it; but regarding the circle of "professants" who were dear to Bucer, does not the Anabaptist group appear in the twin grouping?

It is not doubtful that Calvin learned a great deal from Bucer, but also with the civil authorities, in the matter of excommunication. It remains to be determined what his personal ecclesiological experience—since he was a pastor of the refugee community—could have brought him. Within the framework of a psycho-sociological approach, one could say that a church of refugees, that is to say the faithful people who paid dearly for affirming the possibility of continuing to profess their faith, is an *"active minority."* Now, is such a minority often not tempted by hyperconformism, that is to

14. Conclusions

say by over-accentuation of the features which, in a given situation, define excellence, including the religious type? Hyperconformism, one knows, gets on well with a hyper-normative attitude, therefore with a great distrust of everything which seems to resemble relaxation, which are themselves compared to lax practices? In front of this hyper-puritanical temptation, the magistrate—that was often reported at the time of the colloquium—seemed to adopt an attitude of conciliation, more realistic. In a society where tolerance very quickly comes up against limits of tolerance, there remains to the magistrate only one solution: to reserve the use of excommunication; therefore to take back from the religious power what is like a decisive weapon. Was it inevitable that Calvin kept the memory from his time in Strasbourg of an unbearable iron arm between the magistrate and ecclesiastical authorities? Was it completely impossible for his conflict with the Anabaptists and his own theology of sanctification should lead to self-limiting the usage of excommunication, whatever the holder of this sad power? Over that, is it not natural to abstain from judging from the course of history from its terminus? One must probably, always again, remember that these are many undecidable things in history in the course of happening, and that the Liebnizian theory of an endogenous development has a part connected with a very doubtful monadology, not with dialogism

In 1964, Richard Stauffer presented a good study on "lectures on myself in Calvin's sermons." Now, one knows how much, in his commentaries on the Psalms—often evoked within the framework of our own colloquium—Calvin willingly identifies himself with David, God's elected exposed to the mockeries and hostilities of his adversaries, identifying the latter with the enemies of God himself. It is also known that this argumentation (my enemies are God's enemies) is mobilized against the "blasphemers," accused of denying the doctrine of double predestination or, at least, to seek to tone down the force of the doctrine in order to protect oneself better from it. If one cannot deny the pregnancy of this climate of persecution in the formation of the Calvinian "I" and in what appears to us as the interiorization of a type of reversibility between the figure of the persecuted and the function of persecutor, could one give way to the hypothesis that something in the experience of exile that Calvin knew in Strasbourg, leaves its mark in the conscience of his own identity? Especially, would there be room, in Calvin's mind, for an "I" which would remember being an exile and having been welcomed? Is it possible that in Geneva nothing would have later irritated him as much as the arrogance of the "bourgeoisie," who were proud of belonging to the City by right and who were so ungenerous in the grant of the right of citizenship, a privilege reserved by them to an elected few? Let us freely continue on the launch of this type of remark while extending it to a more extensive context: *L'Europe moderne*—this question has been asked several times here—is certainly, first of all chronologically but also on principles, a Europe of exiles. If it is so, is one not justified in seeing in the shared experience of exile the melting pot of an aspiration to the universal which is certainly constitutive of the Lights, but which would be announced clearly in the field of humanism, sometimes reinforced, sometimes covered over by dogmatic disputes on election?

In his great book on Bucer, Gottfried Hammann draws up a direct connection, in this theologian, between the refusal to Satanize the adversary and the absence of marked sensitivity to *millenarianism*. What would the outcome of this observation be, if one undertook to compare Bucer and Calvin on this point? With the latter, few millenarist effects, apparently; but it is what gives all his sense of appeal to sanctification, the latter presupposing a relatively long time of possible progress, never completely irreversible all the same. The most likely hypothesis, is that the Satanization of the other could be the counterpart of the enlarged feeling of being elected, less with others—in a virtually exponential number—who against the others, or it would only be their immense majority. One must certainly count with what Stauffer writes about the figure and strategy of the preacher, who acknowledge that he is the first to have to be taught, who firmly refuses to loosen the ties with all the faithful people. All things considered, one thus withdraws from observing Calvin's attitude of deep ambivalence, from which one may wonder if it is always emphasized as much as it should be. Ambivalence, due to an intimate conflict between two postures; one, of *authority*, which is expressed through everything that Calvin can say or implement in the matter of collegiality and even of sharing ecclesiastical responsibilities with the ordinary faithful people; the other, of *autoritarisme*, pointed out a great many times by the biographies and, already, by Theodore de Beze. Now, in this perspective, how not to consider as amazing the fact that, in Strasbourg, and in spite of the form of "active minority" which must be that of the French parish, Calvin was not drawn into the major conflicts, nor with enemies, nor with colleagues, nor with the magistrate? It is however true that, as has been recalled, the Anabaptists are a major target of Calvinian attacks. Does it follow that an irascible temperament may in some manner "need" a target? Similarly, how to play the part, as a theologian, between what would bring affective motives into relief and what would bring truly theological motives into relief? It could be, after all, that, as one believed to have to speak about a "situation theology," so it may be necessary to speak about an *affective* burden of theological enunciation, a heavier burden than the question of salvation comes to be confounded with that of election and, more particularly, with that of election of the enunciator?

14. CONCLUSIONS

Finally, an access to the affective source of a theology whose systematicity is often exaggerated or the rationality could be given to us by some of the developments in Calvin's argumentation in chapters dealing with *predestination*. One discovers there that, contrary to semantic rules that he generally tends to respect, Calvin uses lexical distinctions as guides for indisputable analysis. This is manifest when it is a question of justifying double predestination, to assert that salvation of some cannot fail to work in the damnation of the others. When, in fact, Calvin puts forward the ledical or nominal distinction of love and hate; at the point of forgetting, in his argumentation this other and more fundamental distinction between statements of "*de re*" and statements "*de dictum*": it goes without saying, in his eyes, that there is no "real" love which only implies a "hatred" which is just as real and present. But In thus despising the *complexity* of the real, would Calvin not seek to protect himself against his own *ambivalence*?

That leads me, to finish, to remember the engagement of a man beside Calvin, in Strasbourg: Castellion. One knows the dramatic consequences of what, in Strasbourg, was then like a relationship of deep esteem and maybe even of close friendship. How to explain that Calvin's friendship for Castellion could have changed into hate? The affective sources of this sudden change largely escape us. There remains what we know from the criticism, by Castellion, of any continuity, of any unconditional allegiance. Castellion, it seems to us, knew that one must say "no!" even and especially to a friend, when the latter asks one to keep the voice of his conscience quiet, in particular when one witnesses an abuse of authority. In forcing Castellion to be exiled in order to escape his prosecution, would Calvin not have abused the authority with the most terrible and probably the most disputable of biblical statements—and liable to cover the worst excesses in the matter of confusion and lability of affective and relational registers—when, in his developments on double predestination for example, he goes back on his own account, the threat of exclusion hovering over all heads, the too famous: "who is not with me is against me"? But who therefore is the "me"? Is it Calvin, or would it be only an image of him who swells up in the struggle and who ends up haunting it? Is it one of the "me's" of Calvin only, or would this me be en route to becoming tentacular and stifling? The question of either the "me's" will be passionately debated with Montaigne. But does it not announce itself already through the intensely conflictual of Calvin and Castellion?

Index of the Works of Jean Calvin

(titles quoted, when this takes place, according to *BC*
and put together according to its chronology)

SENECA, *Libri duo de clementia*, commentated by John Calvin (1532): 176.

Christianae religionis institutio (1536): 59, 124, 125, 126, 130, 131, 136, 137, 142, 147, 148, 154, 155, 156, 160, 161, 167, 168, 176, 183, 184, 186, 189, 205, 225, 234, 239, 241, 242.

- CH. IV: 234, 241, 243.
- CH. V: 239.

Epistolae duae de rebus hoc seculo cognitu necessariis (1537): 176, 231, 240.

Epistola to Duchemin (1536): 140.

Instruction and confession of faith as used in the Church of Geneva (1537): 137, 225.

Articles . . . of the "preachers of Geneva" (1537): 239.

Institutio christianae religionis

(1539): 11, 12, 80, 111, 123–34, 135–57, 160, 162, 165, 167, 168, 176, 179, 184, 185, 189, 227, 235, 241.

- CH. I: 125, 126.
- CH. II: 125, 127.
- CH. III: 125, 128.
- CH. IV: 125, 127.
- CH. V: 125.
- CH. VI: 125.
- CH. VII: 125.

- CH. VII: 125.
- CH. IX: 125.
- CH. X: 125.
- CH. XI: 125.
- CH. XII: 125, 130, 236.
- CH. XIII: 125.
- CH. XV: 125.
- CH. XVII: 11, 132.

Jacopo Sadolet and John Calvin, *Epistola ad Senatum Populumque Genevensem. J. Calvini responsio* (1539): 12, 124, 191, 192, 197, 199, 200-202, 204, 205. French version: *Epistre au Sénat et Peuple de Genève, avec la response* (1540): 197.

Aucuns pseaulmes et cantiques mys en chant (1539): 10, 53, 54, 61, 67, 69, 74, 169.

- Psalm 25: 57, 60-65, 68, 69, 70.
- Psalm 46: 57, 68, 69, 70.

Commentarii in epistolam Pauli ad Romanos (1540): 11, 21, 80, 93-122, 124, 129, 141, 176, 179.

- French translation of 1550: 94.
- 1551 edition: 93.
- French translation of 1550: 94.

The deeds of the imperial conference held in the city of Reguespourg (1541): 219, 225, 234.

Institution de la religion chrétienne (1541): 11, 12, 78, 135-57, 160, 186-90, 224, 233, 241, 258, 264.

- CH. IV: 234.
- CH. X: 234.
- CH. XII: 232, 236.

Little Treatize on Holy Communion (1541): 13, 124, 223-49.

Form of ecclesiastical prayers and songs (1542): 75, 76, 163, 164.

Catechism of the Church of Geneva (1542): 232, 233, 238, 246.

Explanation on the Epistle to the Romans (1543): 94.

Institutio christianae religionis (1543): 11, 12, 125, 159–73, 177, 178, 280, 185.

- CH. III: 166.
- CH. IV: 166.
- CH. VI: 166
- CH. VIII: 166.
- CH. IX–XI: 166.
- CH. XI: 166.
- CH. XII: 166.
- CH. XIII: 166.
- CH. XIV–XVIII: 166.
- CH. XVIII: 166, 227.
- CH. XXI: 166.

Little Treatize, showing what a man of faith should do among the papists (1543): 140, 231, 244.

Epinicion Christo cantatum (1544): 211.

Institutio christianae religionis (1545): 125, 178, 185.

Institution de la religion chrestienne (1545): 177.

De scandalis (1550): 140.

Institutio totius christianae religionis (1553): 137, 183, 184.

Institutio christianae religionis (1553): 137, 183, 184.

Institutio christianae religionis (1554): 125, 184.

In librum Psalmorum commentaries (1557): 58, 170.

Institutio christianae religionis (1559): 52, 137, 139, 160, 183, 184, 226.

- I, ix.1: 126.
- I, ix.3: 128.
- II, viii.26: 128.

- III, iii, 14: 127.
- III, x: 132.
- III, x, 2: 132.
- IV, I, 1: 127.
- IV, I, 14: 128.
- IV, i, 29: 128.
- IV, ii, 1: 127.
- IV, xvii, 5: 130, 131.
- IV, xvii, 8: 130, 131.
- IV, xvii, 14: 130, 131.
- IV, xvii, 14: 130, 131.
- IV, xvii, 20s: 130.

Institution de la religion chrestienne (1560): 139, 145, 146, 154, 157, 187, 188. – IV, xvii, 11: 227.

- IV, xvii, 32: 227.

Institution de la religion chrestienne (1564): 181.

- III, xviii, 5: 182.
- IV, I, 10: 182.
- IV, xiv and xv: 182.

Correspondence
- To Renée de Ferrare [summer 1537]: 232.
- Letter on the Eucharist [September 1537]: 247.
- To Martin Bucer, 12 January 1538: 39, 40, 226, 245.
- To Viret and Coraud, 14 June 1538: 41.
- To Louis du Tillet, 10 July 1538: 41.
- To Guillaume Farel, end July 1538: 42.
- To Guillaume Farel, toward end September 1538: 44, 205.
- To Antoine Pignet, 1 October 1538: 124.
- In Geneva, 1 October 1538: 45.
- To Guillaume Farel, 1st half October 1538: 44, 45.

Index of the Works of Jean Calvin

- To Guillaume Farel, 29 December 1538: 57, 67, 169.
- To Antoine Pignet, 5 January 1539: 45, 46.
- To Guillaume Farel, 16 March 1539: 48, 50.
- To Andre Zebedee, 19 May 1539: 229, 230; 47.
- To Guillaume Farel, 2nd half of August 1539: 47.
- To those who are afflicted in France, October 1539: 228.
- To Guillaume Farel, 20 November 1539: 227.
- To Richard du Bois [1539]: 229.
- To Guillaume Farel, 27 February 1540: 230.
- To Heinrich Bullinger, 12 March 1540: 229, 230.
- To Pierre Viret, 19 May 1540: 50.
- To Guillaume Farel, 27 July 1540: 209.
- To Guillaume du Tailly, 28 July 1540: 209.
- To Guillaume Farel, 9 June 1541: 218.
- To the magistrate of Geneva, 7 September 141: 51.
- To Guillaume Farel, 10 September 1541: 52.
- To Guillaume Farel, 16 September 1541: 52.
- To Conrad Hubert, 24 September 1541: 52.
- To Conrad Hubert, 24 January 1546: 43.
- To Veit Dietrich, 17 March 1546: 224, 227, 229, 232.
- To Conrad Hubert, 19 May 1557: 59.

Biblical Index

Column 1, page 1

Psalms—line 1

Matthew—line 11

John—line 14

Romans—line 21

Column 1, page 2

1 Corinthians—line 1

Colossians—line 5

Hebrews—line 8

1 Peter—line 10

Annex

Table of Quotations from Enarrationes

In the patristic sources in the 1543 edition of the Institutio christianae religionis.

Table of quotations from the Enarrationes in Psalmos d'Augustin introduites dans l'edition de 1543 de l'Institutio Christianae religionis.

When the Augustinian reference is not given by Calvin, it is indicated in italics in the table.

1. Abbreviations: A. Augustin. Works of Augustine: In Ps. Enarrationes in psalmos. C; C. ep.
2. Parm:.*Contra epistulam Parmeniani*;
3. De sp. Et litt.: *De spiritu et littera*;
4. Epis: *Epistulae*;
5. Tr. In Ioh.: *Tractatus in Iohannis euangelium*.

No	In Ps.	Ref. OS	State of	Mode of insertion
1	31,2,7	3,299	Textual quotation With a cut in middle	Addition of a Series of three Quotations from A: 2 *in Ps.* + *Epist.* 155
2	31,2,9	4,119	Textual quotation With cut in middle	Addition of this Single quotation From A.
3	45,13	3,254	Textual quotation With a cut in Middle and some Slight changes	Following a Series of Quotations from A, addition of a New series of two Quotations from *In Ps.*

No	In Ps.	Ref. OS	State of	Mode of insertion
4	61.4	4,136	Textual quotation	Addition of two Long quotations From A: *In Ps.* + *Tr. In Ioh.*
5	68,1,5	3,133	Textual quotation	Addition of Three quotations From A, which come to add Themselves to Others
6	70,1,2	3,254	Précis of thought Of A.	Following a series of quotations from A, addition Of a new series of Two quotations from *In Ps.*
7	70,I,19	3,335	Textual quotation	Following a series of quotations from A., addition of a new series of three references: 2 in *Ps.* + 1 *De sp. Et litt.*
8	70,II,5	3,299	Textual quotation	Addition of a new Series of three quotations from A: 2 *in Ps.* + *Ps.* + *Epist.155*
9	77,2	5,284	Textual quotation	In the middle of an addition of quotations from A.
10	77,2	5,272	Textual quotation With some cuts	In the middle of an addition of quotations from A.
11	84,9	4,240	Textual quotation, with modification of syntactic structure	After quotations From Aug, addition of 2 quotations from *In Ps.*
12	88,I,5	4,218	Textual quotation; Only *sanctis* is replaced by *seruis*	The quotation From A. is complemented by another from Bernard de Clairvaux
13	94,6	4,325	Textual quotation	Addition of a long quotation from the C. *ep.*+ *In Ps.94*
14	102,20	4,124	Textual quotation	Addition from John Chrysostom two quotations extracted from *In Ps.*

Annex

No	In Ps.	Ref. OS	State of	Mode of insertion
15	109,13	3,133	Textual quotation, syntactic adjustment	Addition of three Quotations from A., which come to be added to others
16	113,II,3,4	3,98	Modified quotation	Addition of the quotation from A.
17	113,Ii,5	5,157	Precis of development of A.	In middle of several patristic quotations
18	113,II	3,99	Textual quotation	Addition of quotation from A.
19	113,II,5,6	3,102	The first part is a textual quotation, the second is abridged	In a long addition, among other quotations, especially from A.
20	118, XXVII,3	3,335	Textual quotation with some cuts	Following a series of quotations from A., addition of a new series of three references: 2 *In Ps* + 1 *De sp. Et litt.*
21	129,3	4,120	Textual quotation	Addition of this single quotation, after a first one from Paul
22	137,18	4,238	Textual quotation	Quotes the Ps. And the *In Ps.*, then gives a commentary on it
23	137,15	4,124	Textual quotation	Addition to John Chrysostom, two quotations taken from *In Ps*.
24	139,18	4,240	Textual quotation	After quotations from A., addition of two quotations from *In Ps*.
25	144,6	3,53	Slightly rewritten Text	Addition of this single quotation
26	144,11	4,246	Textual quotation, with adaptation in syntactic context	Addition of this single quotation in a passage which already relied on A.

Index of Modern Authors

Abramowski I., 11
Abray L.J., 13, 14, 20
Adam J., 13, 21
Arnold M., iii, vii xi, 1, 7, 38, 45, 54, 62, 96, 97, 143, 207
Backus I., 138, 158
Barth P., 183, 184, 189
Battles F., 97
Baum G., 150, 154
Baumgart P., 63, 71, 72
Becker W., 63
Bedouelle G., 16, 140
Benoit J-D., 76, 84
Berthoud G., 189
Bizer E., 77, 78, 170
Blacketer R.A., 83, 121
Blumenberg H., 224
Bopp M.J., 15
Bornert R., 1, 15, 18, 19, 208
Bouwsma W. J., 99
Brady Th., 1, 3, 4, 5, 12, 13
Buckwalter S., vi, viii, xiii, 51, 96, 106
Buganda, de J.M., 192
Bunz E., 71
Busser F., 99
Burger C., v, viii, xii, 23, 26, 27
Busch E., 2, 169, 204

Cadier J., 69
Carbonnier-Burkard, vi, viii, xv, 97, 183
Carl H., 73, 78
Castan J., 67
Causse M., 190, 191
Chapot F., vi, xiii, xiv, 58, 75, 86, 110, 130, 136
Chatelain, 188

Chimelli C., 158
Classen, C.J., 78, 92
Collonges J., 7, 62
Cottin J., 59
Cottret B., vii, 184
Courvoisier J., 96, 106, 225
Cramer U., 3
Cunitz E., 23, 150, 151 152

Dankbaar W., 224
De Boer E.A., 175
Deconchy J.-P., 215
Defaux G., 40, 41, 42, 44, 45, 48
Delectra D., 39
Denis P., 56, 158
Detmers A., 104
Deppermann K., 13
Dollinger P., 2, 3
Douglas R.M., 159
Doumergue E., vii, 131
Du Cange C., 117
Dulaey M., 135

Ehrenspreger K., 79
Elsmann T., 67
Engel C., 68
Farge J.K., 192
Faulenbach H., 204
Foucault M., 213
Fournier M., 68
Fraenkel P., 131, 136, 173, 140, 178
François P., 82, 107, 108
Friedensburg, 165, 166
Friedrich R., 17, 103, 161
Fuchs J., 2
Fumaroli M., 91

Index of Modern Authors

Ganoczy A., 81, 97
Ganzer K., 170
Garber K., 170
Garside C., 134, 135, 142
Gérold T., 51
Gilmont J., xvii, 107, 108,109, 131, 132, 136, 137, 141, 144, 164,189, 190, 192, 210
Girard J.-L., 146, 187, 191, 210
Girard R., 220
Girardin B., 76, 84, 85, 86, 89, 90, 93
Gleason E., 160
Goeters J.F.G., 170
Grappe C., v, vii, xiii, 75, 78, 121
Greschat M., 1, 5, 11, 13, 67, 100, 102, 207
Guizot F., 153

Haag [brothers], 153
Halkin L.E., 2
Hammam G., 17, 104, 153, 228
Hammerstein N., 63, 64, 65, 71
Hasper H., 39
Hatt J., 19
Haub R., 5
Hazlett I., 101, 102, 168, 190, 191
Heim F., 108
Herminjard A.-L., xii, xvii, 23, 24, 25, 27, 28, 29, 30, 31, 32, 33, 34, 35, 36, 37, 43, 50, 97, 159, 169, 170, 171, 172, 173, 174, 179, 181, 182
Higman F., 154, 158, 183, 191, 192
Hobbs G., 16, 85
Hofer A.-L., 201
Holder R.W., 79
Hollander A. Den, 201
Holtz S., 63
Holzhauer H., 67
Hotson H., 73
Hunermann F., 161
Huguet E., 110, 124

Im Hof U., 62

Jacobs E., 189
Jacques E., 261
Janse W,, 184, 208
Jeannin M., 87
Joachimsen P., 65

Joby C.R., 52, 54, 58, 59
Jundt A., 7

Kaufmann T., 62, 104
Keute H., 62
Kittelson J.M., 62
Kloker M., 62
Kok J.E., 82
Krebs M., 101
Krieger C., xvii, 1, 16, 100, 106, 141, 189, 199, 191
Kroon M., 102, 106
Kruger E., 102
Krumenacker Y., 58
Kuhlmann W., 69
Kurucz, 69

Lane A., 138, 140
Lang A., 106, 155
Lanson G., 154, 155
Laurand H., vii, 1
Lausberg H., 164
Lehmann Y., 52
Lenger F., 73
Leroi-Gourhan A., 219
Lienhard M., vii, xi, 1,5, 11, 12, 13, 16, 20, 61, 82, 100, 104, 106, 189, 190, 191, 194
Littré E., 124, 129
Livet G., 2, 6, 12

Maarten J., 11, 35, 170
McKee E., 27
Mahrle W., 67
Massen T., 71
Meerhoff K., 71, 77, 82, 83, 84
Menk G., 67
Mertens D., 63
Meyer C., 52
Millet O., 11, 40, 41, 46, 54, 58, 59, 75, 82, 83, 91, 107, 108, 109, 111, 112, 113, 114, 121, 122, 124, 126, 127, 128, 129, 143, 194, 197
Moeller B., 61
Mooi R.J., 138
Morerod J.-D., 51
M uhlack U., 64
Muller R., 82, 83, 184, 185, 186, 196, 207, 208, 209

Index of Modern Authors

Neuser W., 101, 117, 170, 175, 177, 178, 185
Nijenhuis W., 64
Noblesse-Rocher A., xiv, 75, 78, 158, 161, 61

Oberle R., 1,
Oberman H.A., 81
Opitz P., 27, 79, 165
Ortmann V., vi, viii, xiv, 11, 169, 170, 173, 174, 15, 1779, 182
Oswald J., 69
Oyer J.S., 100

Pannier J., 96, 106, 128, 155, 156
Pariente J.-C., 215
Parker D.C., 54, 75, 76, 87, 91, 93, 94, 95
Parker T.H.L., 54, 75, 76, 87, 91, 93, 94, 95
Peter R., xvii, 132, 144, 189, 192
Pidoux P., 39, 75, 140
Pietrzyzuk Z., 66
Pollet J.-V. , 1

Raphael E., 1
Rapp E., 2, 12
Reid J., 191, 192
Reinhard W. , 12, 71
Reuss E., 23, 150, 154
Rey A., 211
Reynolds L.D., 136
Ricoeur P., 222
Rohm T., 69
Rosenberg B., 9
Rott J., 3, 11, 20, 21, 28, 29, 66, 101, 141, 187, 192
Roussel B., xv, xvi, 16, 41, 80, 85, 140, 158
Royannez M., 99, 190
Rudersdorf M., 71
Runciman M., 39

Saebo M., 16
Sallmann M., 16
Schafer R., 77, 79
Schang P., 6
Schindling A., vii, xvii, xviii, 6, 7, 61, 63, 65, 68, 69, 71, 73, 117

Schmidt C., 7
Schwarz R., 16, 181
Selderhuis H., 27, 51, 96, 97, 138, 169, 184
Simondon G., 216
Smits L., 136
Soares N.C., 83
Spicq C., 87
Spiker van't W., 13, 51, 101, 102, 106
Stam van F.P., 85, 92, 98
Stauffer R., 189, 192, 214, 225, 227
Steinmetz D., 81
Stern S. , 122, 123
Steinmetz D., 122, 123
Stickelberger H., 27
Stolt M., 35, 36, 170, 171, 173, 175, 178, 179, 182
Strohl H., 20
Strohm C., 96, 99
Stupperich R., 168, 177
Sydow J., 63

Thompson J.L., 82
Toellner R., 67
Topper T., 71

Veit P., 140
Veyne P., 184
Vincent G. , 211
Vincent M., vi, xv
Virck J., 6

Walker W., 44, 45, 46
Walt van der B.J., 82
Weber E., 18, 39
Weeda R., v, xii, 38, 50, 51, 52, 55, 57, 58, 59, 132
Wenzel E., 69
Weyl R., 9
Willer J., 52
Wolff C., vii
Wright D.F., 106

Zigler W., 14, 61
Zillenbiller A., 138, 140
Zuber R., 61
Zub Muhlen K.-H., 138, 140

Subject Index

Part 1—Works of John Calvin

Seneca—Libri duo de clementia (1532), 136n30
Christianae religionis institutio (1536), 231
Epistolae duae de rebus (1537), 231
Instruction et confession de foy (1537), 185n10
Jacopo Sadolet (1540), 232
Aucuns psaulmes et cantiques (1539), 47
Commentarii . . . Pauli ad Romanos (1540), 77n11
Les Actes . . . Reguespourg (1541), 232
Petit traité, (1541), xv
Forme des prieres, (1542), 56n31
Exposition sur . . . Romains (1543), 76
Institutio christianae religionis (1543), 98
Petit traicté . . . papistes (1543), 112n21
Epinicion Christo , (1544), 175n22
Institutio christianae (1545), 231
De Scandalis (1550), 233
Institutio . . . religionis (1550), 62
In librum Psalmorum . . . (1557), 233
Correspondence from 1537 to 1557

www.ingramcontent.com/pod-product-compliance
Lightning Source LLC
Chambersburg PA
CBHW050437240426
43661CB00055B/2422